D1085165

Rethinking the Rhetorical Tradition

JAMES L. KASTELY

Rethinking the
Rhetorical Tradition
From Plato to Postmodernism

Yale University Press
New Haven and London

For Amy,

whose generous criticism has helped me think better, whose
quiet integrity has reminded me of the costs of acting justly,
and whose friendship and love have been the best of gifts

Copyright © 1997 by Yale University.

Set in Sabon type by Keystone Typesetting, Inc.
Printed in the United States of America.

Library of Congress Cataloging-in-Publication Data

Kastely, James L., 1947–
    Rethinking the rhetorical tradition : from Plato to postmodernism
/ James L. Kastely.
        p. cm.
    Includes bibliographical references and index.
    ISBN 0-300-06838-7 (cloth : alk. paper).

    1. Philosophy — Authorship.   2. Rhetoric — Philosophy.   3. Plato.
4. Postmodernism.   I. Title.
    B52.7K37   1996
    190 — dc20   96-26861

A catalogue record for this book is available from the British Library.

10 9 8 7 6 5 4 3 2 1

Contents

Acknowledgments

I began work on this book while I was at the University of Hawaiʻi at Manoa, and I owe a special debt to my students and colleagues there who encouraged my explorations and patiently listened to my ramblings as I began to work through the ideas that were occupying me. Two of my largest debts are to Professors Dennis Ellsworth and Robert Ball, who kindly allowed me into their courses as I belatedly began to learn Greek and Latin. For their support I thank Professors Robert McHenry, Beth Tobin, Gay Sibley, Daniel Stempel, Reinhard Friederich, Glenn Man, Valerie Wayne, Miriam Fuchs, Craig Howes, John Rieder, Cristina Bachilega, and Nell Altizer. Special thanks to Professor Karma Lochrie of Loyola University of Chicago. Linda Middleton and Brien Hallet were two graduate students who were especially important in helping me to develop my ideas in ways that I had not anticipated. For her special support, I thank Dean Barbara Aldave of St. Mary's University School of Law. At the University of Houston, Professors Harmon Boertein, John MacNamara, Ann Christensen, Lois Zamora, and Maria Gonzales welcomed me and encouraged my work, and Lee Smith has been invaluable in her ongoing effort to educate me in the ways of the Lower Division Studies program. At the University of Chicago, Professor Wayne C. Booth taught me what it meant to read critically and to attempt to do justice to authors and their works, and Professor Charles Wegener first taught me rhetoric in a course so fertile that I continue to learn from it and steal from it. Through his friendship and by his example, Professor Robert Martin taught me the power of scholarship to contribute to an understanding of the drama of human life. Judith Calvert, at Yale University Press, took over this project at a key moment, and it was her energy and faith that directly led to its publication. Dan Heaton was an excellent manuscript editor whose careful attention to the text improved the clarity of my prose and whose good humor and common sense made it a pleasure to work on the various details of the project. Two anonymous readers for Yale University Press exemplified careful and fair-minded criticism. As someone who values refutation, I thank them for the way that their refutations led me to strengthen my arguments. My largest debt is to my wife, Amy. Her intellectual companionship has fostered so many of the ideas that are central to this book. Her abiding interest in promoting a just society has helped me understand the ways in which injustice undermines dignity. This book would not have been possible without her. I would also like to thank my son, Joe, and my daughter, Christina, for their numerous refutations of me, which have taught me to listen more carefully and have helped me learn that I still have much to learn.

Earlier versions of several chapters of this book were published previously. Chapters 2 and 5 were originally published in slightly different versions in *PMLA*, Chapter 2 as "In Defense of Plato's *Gorgias*" (106 [1991]: 96–109) and Chapter 5 as "Violence and Rhetoric in Euripides's *Hecuba*" (108 [1993]: 1036–49). Both essays are reprinted by permission of the copyright holder, the Modern Language Association of America. The first and quite different version of Chapter 7 was published as "Complicating Sartre's Rhetoric of Generosity" in *Philosophy and Rhetoric* 22, no. 1: 1–27. Copyright 1989 by the Pennsylvania State University; reproduced by permission of the Pennsylvania State University Press. Chapter 6 is an expanded version of "*Persuasion:* Jane Austen's Philosophical Rhetoric," which was published in *Philosophy and Literature* 15 (1991): 74–88 and is reprinted by permission of its copyright holder, the Johns Hopkins University Press.

Refutation
Rhetoric as a Philosophical Problem

Rhetoric has returned; this has become a truism among theorists of discourse in the late twentieth century. But postmodern rhetoric, according to John Bender and David E. Wellbery, is a very different intellectual practice from that of the classical tradition:

> The contemporary return of rhetoric presupposes, through its very structure as return, an end of rhetoric, a discontinuity within tradition, and an alteration that renders the second version of rhetoric, its modernist-postmodernist redaction, a new form of cultural practice and mode of analysis. To understand the significance of rhetoric today is to understand why and in what ways it is discontinuous with its past. ("Rhetoricality," 4)

What is left of classical rhetoric survives "in strangely contracted form as a subject taught in universities" (6). Bender and Wellbery argue that other disciplines, from sociology to linguistics to public relations and literary criticism, have arisen and appropriated much of what was studied in classical rhetoric. The new rhetoric is decidedly post-Nietzschean, no longer attempting to develop a practical discourse for civic life but rather marking what it means to be a creature born into language.

It is easy to discern behind this definition the impulse to a new formalism, and it is worth noting how this definition and impulse are challenged by some recent political approaches that are also appropriating rhetoric as the paradigm for discourse. But what is more to point is to understand the significance of the claim to discontinuity. On the one hand, such a claim is a straightforward recognition of historical change — of the fact that the assumptions, methods, and contexts of intellectual practices change over time. On the other hand, the claim raises questions as to what, if any, role classical rhetoric can play in current inquiries into the status and consequences of discourse. Given the fact that contemporary historical circumstances differ from those in which rhetoric arose and first flourished, is there a way to read the texts of the classical tradition that is not merely an attempt to resuscitate a dead practice, that is not merely an antiquarian appreciation for what is no more, that is not finally an anachronistic attempt to bring forward an intellectual discipline whose purpose and practice are tied to historical circumstances quite disparate from the present? Put simply, is there a way in which the past can speak meaningfully to the present?

To raise these questions is to ask what use is there in the study of the classical rhetorical tradition. But the problem of the utility of the study of classical rhetoric is not new. Some recourse to utility is a standard feature in the classical defenses of rhetoric. Further, the concern with use arises not only as a response to the claims of a postmodern study of rhetoric but also as an issue for more traditional scholarship. Richard McKeon raised a similar problem of the purpose of histories of rhetoric by charging those histories that failed to be relevant to present rhetorical practice with pedantry: "Histories of rhetoric, which throw little light on the principles or purposes by which present methods and uses of rhetoric might be evaluated or changed, tend to be pedantic explorations of traditions of rhetoric as an art of persuasion and belief, of deception and proof, of image-making and communication, which follow through the consequences of pejorative or positive judgments posited as premises" ("The Uses of Rhetoric," 1). McKeon sought historical studies that would clarify the present situation, and his demand was that scholarship on rhetoric have a point, for he wished the study of the classical rhetorical tradition to become an investigation of the ways in which elements of that tradition could speak forcefully to the present. Such a study would allow the present to recover as well as it could a sense of its own historicity, of its own contingency.

The demand for a historically relevant study of classical rhetoric assumes that along with the discontinuity of the two versions of rhetoric that Bender and Wellbery put forward, there must also be some shared concerns that would allow past and present to engage in a meaningful dialectic. But in eschewing the traditional concern with utility and civic discourse for a focus on our linguistic predicament, Bender and Wellbery seem to have made impossible such significant sharing. Fortunately, classical rhetoric is more diverse than its standard histories have allowed, and concerns that seem to be peculiarly modern or postmodern have significant antecedents in the past. Indeed, one strand of classical rhetoric anticipates contemporary rhetorical concerns and provides resources for formulating the issues that may be more productive than the contemporary approaches. The abiding linguistic skepticism and concern with justice that feed the two major contemporary theoretical appropriations were concerns for early rhetorical thinkers. But to understand the ways in which classical rhetoric can speak to a postmodern rhetorical theory, we need to turn not to the positive theorists within the classical rhetorical tradition but to Plato and the Greek tragedians, for, in their skepticism, they saw more clearly both the need for and the difficulties encountered by rhetoric.[1] And it is their posing rhetoric as a philosophical problem that provides an opening for a productive dialogue between past and present.

Appearing in fifth-century BCE Athens, during a period in which a variety of new discursive forms were coming into prominence, rhetoric both drew on and contributed to these forms. Its relation to philosophy and tragedy was particularly rich. As the role of discourse became increasingly important in civic life, it naturally became a topic for a tragic drama actively engaged in promoting and questioning a democratic ideology and for Plato's philosophic inquiries that worried over the unreflective organization of personal and political life.[2] To reread Plato and the tragedians as neither opponents nor disciples of rhetoric but as thinkers worried about the role of public discourse is to discover a serious skeptical interrogation of rhetoric that differs from the way in which the rhetorical tradition has conceived of this criticism.

Seen from this perspective, Plato and Sophocles appear more sympathetic to rhetoric than has often been acknowledged, and Euripides seems far from being an uncritical disciple.[3] The issues engaging these three thinkers were not the problems of the corruption or incompetence of individual rhetors but the more endemic problems of the way injustice is rooted in the very nature of language and of the way past and present operations of power effectively preclude a genuine public discussion that might advance the cause of justice. The point of these challenges was not to discredit rhetoric or to create a hierarchy of discursive forms but to deal with deep problems of injustice that did not respond to normal practical discourse. What Plato and the tragedians did was to articulate the difficulties encountered by rhetoric as the philosophical problem of the impossibility of a just community and then propose ways of acting in a world in which injustice as a theoretical concern was insolvable and as a practical exigency was irremediable.

To look to Plato, Sophocles, and Euripides as rhetorical theoreticians is also to open classical rhetoric in a new way that can make it a resource for clarifying and deepening issues that occupy a modern and postmodern rhetoric. For as Michel Meyer has pointed out, the repeated articulation of the death of the subject has not led to a new approach to thinking but only to an iteration of what he labels as "propositional logic" — a mode of reasoning in which a genuine questioning has been excluded preemptively:

> Closure [of a reasoning process sufficient to itself] may then be perceived as unmasked on the individual (psychoanalysis) as well as on the collective (Marxism) level. But in thus doing, these new "rhetorics" reveal themselves immediately for what they are: guarantors of the closure of propositional *logos*. These guarantors are themselves closed rhetorically which is something Popper denounced with regard to psychoanalysis and the ideological analysis of ideology, that is Marxism as well. The function of the rhetorization of *logos* is to preserve the resolute automatism of the latter. This in turn maintains the sophistic role of rhetoric which allows it to reduce any question to an "already there" answer. The fracture caused by the radical problematization of the last century is thus swallowed up in a purely rhetorical non-identity. It is perhaps to this phenomenon that we owe the survival of propositional *logos*. ("Toward an Anthropology of Rhetoric," 133)

The significance of what I will call the skeptical thread of classical rhetoric is that it offers a direction away from a "propositional" logos because its primary concern is justice and not knowledge. The critiques offered by Plato, Sophocles, and Euripides put rhetoric into question. By seeing both the necessity for and the difficulty of rhetoric, these thinkers developed a productive skepticism that makes rhetoric a problem of action. In Meyer's language, they developed answers to the question of rhetoric that were not already provided for by the definition of rhetoric as persuasion; rather, their questions concerning rhetoric could provoke answers that were, in turn, new questions. Consequently, for Plato and the tragedians closure was not the issue. Instead, they made rhetoric an issue of dealing with injustice in such a way that injustice became the responsibility of their audiences and demanded that the audiences act on this responsibility. Their writings became intellectual and political interrogations, and it is these modes of questioning that the skeptical thread of classical rhetoric offers to modern and postmodern rhetorics as a way of moving beyond the death of the subject to a new mode of theorizing discourse that reconceives of the world as place for action.

Plato's particular opening of rhetoric as a question was developed through his explorations of the Socratic elenchus (refutation). The purpose and reach of the elenchus has become a point of controversy recently for analytic philosophy.[4] At issue is whether Socratic refutation can lead to positive conclusions or whether its force is solely negative. But as Meyer would surely claim, many of the analytic philosophers miss the serious point of the elenchus by focusing on it as a process of syllogistically uncovering propositions rather than understanding that it is an inherently rhetorical strategy.[5] However, if Socrates is read not as an inept or naive metaphysician but as a moralist — which even his severest critics acknowledge as his philosophical role — then the importance of refutation for him can be appreciated more fully. The question that needs to be asked is why does Socrates engage in refutation. What does he hope to achieve by undermining the purported wisdom of others, and why does such a skeptical inquiry need to be conducted publicly? The most immediate answer is that he is obeying the oracle as he understands it, but such an answer does not explain why he understands the oracle in a particular way. It is reasonable to ask why refutation should be the central and indeed the only political action that Socrates undertakes in response to the oracle. What is there in the nature of political life that requires a vigilant skepticism that not only endangers the skeptic but appears to erode the normal values that necessarily underlie a community? This is to take Socrates' political activity with the seriousness that both he and the Athenian public did.

The question of the need for a political skepticism becomes particularly pressing if it is also recognized that the elenchus does not lead to knowledge. Indeed, Richard Rorty denies that Socratic conversation need have any goal other than the engagement and fulfillment of the conversations themselves: "The pragmatists tell us that the conversation which it is our moral duty to continue is *merely* our project, the European intellectual's form of life. It has no metaphysical nor epistemological guarantee of success. Further, and this the crucial point, *we do not know what 'success' would mean except simply 'continuance.'* We are not conversing because we have a goal, but because Socratic conversation is an activity which is its *own* end" ("Pragmatism, Relativism, and Irrationalism," 734). But Socrates would never accept such a characterization of his conversations and their purposes. To do so would be to transform a life that is inherently political (that is, a life possible only in a *polis*, as Aristotle was to say later) into an aesthetic diversion. It would be to make the modernist move of translating the concerns of public life into the concerns of private life. Further, it would be to deny that the Delphic oracle was the origin of Socrates' own form of this political life. But to say all this does not answer the pressing question: what could be the point of a questioning that cannot escape its own situatedness and achieve a stable closure? Answering this question will lead us to the recognition of the relation of language to politics and will allow us to reunite the rhetorical concerns that seem to be separated by postmoderns who emphasize either language as a formal system or politics as a historical and material concern. The Socratic practice of refutation argues that it is the nature of language as a formal system to implicate creatures who participate in symbolic action in political concerns, and most immediately to entangle them with problems of injustice and inadvertent injury.

The Platonic insight into the injustice and inadvertent injury that inhere within the use of language puts the rhetoric that his dialogues develop very much in line with what Meyer argues is the interrogative rhetoric that was lost at the very beginning of the rhetorical tradition, when Aristotle codified inference as syllogistic structure and hence determined that the primary function of language was to assert propositions (*Rhetoric, Language, and Reason,* 63).[6] Socratic refutation does not assert; it questions. And in its questioning it allows rhetoric a way of conceiving language, politics, and individuals that does not require recourse to the Cartesian notion of the autonomous subject. What Socrates' refutations open up are the constructedness of any individual or state and the web of entangled commitments that any individual or society inherits and acts upon and must accept responsibility for. When Socrates queries an individual as to who he is, he is not seeking knowledge of an individual's identity so much as attempting to locate responsibility for the way that individual acts in the world. What he is seeking to recover is the way that power is diffused and distributed in a polis, and his refutations disclose an understanding of power close to that of Foucault.[7] The major difference is that Socratic refutation can suggest both a reason and direction for action in a way that Foucault's analyses cannot.[8] This need for skepticism and the argument for skepticism as political action become Plato's sophisticated justification of rhetoric, and his presentation of rhetoric as a problem of action for his readers.

Sophocles and Euripides locate the problem of rhetoric differently from Plato.[9] Their abiding concern is not with inadvertent injury but with the preclusion of speech. It is helpful to read them anachronistically as offering a skeptical rejoinder to Jurgen Habermas's theory of communicative action.[10] By focusing on the inescapable historicity of the situations of both speakers and audiences, the tragedians dramatize the ways in which audiences are unavailable and in which speakers fail through no fault of their own. In effect, they challenge any theoretical paradigm that requires a disinterested or neutral stance toward a communicative situation, arguing that humans can never occupy such a place precisely because of the way discourse is entangled in history. If the *Oresteia* can be read, at least in part, as a tragic celebration in which a discursive agon replaces the violence of a blood feud, then Sophocles' *Philoctetes* and Euripides' *Hecuba* can be read as tragic critiques of the earlier celebration of hope that rhetoric could supplant violence as the mode of political mediation.

Sophocles and Euripides begin with injured characters who no longer have a reason to listen to political discourse or who are denied access to public speech. In a stunning anticipation of the contemporary problem of addressing the homeless and the politically disenfranchised, Sophocles explores what, if any, resources are available to return to society those marginalized by society. In the *Philoctetes* he explores not the problem of recognizing the need to speak to the marginalized but the more difficult problem of how to speak to the marginalized since their marginalization induces in them rightly a skepticism as to the possibility of a political discourse that is just. He shows that the problem of acknowledging the pain of the disenfranchised and of not seeking merely the appropriate covering strategy to manipulate them again is not a problem of the speaker's individual integrity or resolve but the harder problem of trying to find a genuine opening when past rhetorical practices have severely undermined the credibility of any public discourse. Neoptolemos fails as a rhetor because his society has abused the social trust in the past. His desire and skill are insufficient to overcome history.

Euripides, in an equally stunning anticipation of problems of political critique, asks in *Hecuba* how a rhetor manages to get those in power to take her discourse seriously, especially since it is the nature of power to render reason immaterial. The consequence of these tragedies is to interrogate rhetoric, to make it into a question, and that is to recover it as a live problem for the audience. The depth of Sophocles' and Euripides' criticism is apparent when we contrast them to a contemporary discourse theoretician like Habermas, who in his model of a universal pragmatics makes the tight distinction between a freely developed understanding and the forcing of a viewpoint on another.[11] The tragedians would see his effort to make rationality a ground to support this distinction as naive because Habermas must abstract from the elements of the discursive situation and privilege them in their formal abstraction as conditions of understanding and discount the elements in that situation that become the crucial problems for political speech. Habermas's theory of discourse depends upon denying the very insights that give Greek tragedy a political content and that make its plots possible.

Habermas is not alone in his denial of the skeptical insights of Greek tragedy. The classical rhetorical tradition did not itself take up the challenge issued by Plato and the tragedians, although its chief defenders certainly thought that they were responding to the challenges to rhetoric, and particularly to Plato's critique. But the ways in which they understood Plato's skeptical interrogations of rhetoric translated the potentially radical openings of his critique into tamer criticisms that quieted the serious disruptions that Plato attempted. Reading Plato from the viewpoint of thinkers invested in a theory that the proposition was the central element for understanding meaning, the defenders of rhetoric saw Plato as raising difficulties only about the adequate control of syllogistic reasoning. They saw him either as putting forward unrealistic standards for practical discourse or as indicting a practice because of the particular abuses of individuals. The tragedians' concerns with rhetoric were by and large ignored rather than answered. In this turn from Plato and ancient tragedy with its reformulation of the skeptical criticism into issues of personal competence and corruption, the defenders of rhetoric inaugurated the tradition of defining rhetoric as the pragmatic study of persuasive speech and as the necessary training for public life. This was the understanding that was then inherited in the refinements and reiterations that comprise the classical rhetorical tradition.

The central figure in the standard accounts of classical rhetoric is Aristotle, and the central text is his *On Rhetoric*. As George A. Kennedy remarks: "Most teachers of composition, communication, and speech regard it as seminal work that organizes its subject into essential parts, provides insight into the bases of speech acts, creates categories and terminology for discussing discourse, and illustrates and applies its teachings so that they can be used in society" (translator's introduction to *On Rhetoric*, ix). Kennedy also notes that it was Aristotle who advanced the discussion of rhetoric by demonstrating that it was a neutral art of communication. And although questions of rhetoric's moral status would continue to haunt discussions of its role in civic life, Aristotle determined the strategy for answering such questions and laid the philosophical groundwork for the serious technical discussion of rhetoric as an art. His text presents a sophisticated justification for rhetoric as a practice that is essential for civic life. His account of the need for an art of persuasion and his delineation of the resources of such an art provide strong support for the standard defenses and histories of rhetoric. Rather than being a prosaic encoding of existing practice, his treatise is itself a radical project that is founded on and explicitly addresses the problem of indeterminacy. It is easy to see how its intellectual reach could have supported the understanding of rhetoric as the art of persuasion that has dominated the history of rhetoric until very recently.[12] What Aristotle offers is a nuanced account of the possibility of action in a world of radical indeterminacy.

Aristotle conceives of his *On Rhetoric* as a reformation of the existing rhetorical theories and practices. His objection to the practice of rhetoric in his time is that speakers had limited their efforts to trying to move an audience by engaging and manipulating its emotions. These prior writers on rhetoric had restricted the art to appeals to *pathos* (emotion), which is only one of the sources of persuasion, and a less important source at that. Aristotle does not formulate this failure as an ethical corruption but as an artistic infelicity. The problem of appealing either primarily or exclusively to the emotions and prejudices of the audience is that the decision that is finally rendered is not an accurate one because the audience who makes the decision has had its judgment distorted. What an exclusive appeal to pathos prevents is appropriate invention. Aristotle compares an audience determined simply by an emotional appeal to a warped carpenter's measure: the ability to measure accurately has been destroyed in both and as a consequence neither functions as a reliable guide that can discriminate between true and false appearances.

What is needed to reform rhetoric is to delineate an art whereby one can go from the way the world appears to what those appearances most likely entail. This means establishing a conduct of rhetoric that distorts appearances as little as possible. Since the material of rhetoric is necessarily appearances and opinions (that is, things that can be other than they are [1357a12]), the art of rhetoric needs to provide a way or method of moving from the currently available appearances and opinions to new perspectives and understandings of the world. This means that the central concern for rhetoric is logos, and an art of rhetoric should first set forth the discipline of probabilistic reasoning. Accordingly, Aristotle will begin his reformed rhetoric by claiming that the enthymeme is the body of the persuasives (1354a3). The larger structure of Aristotle's text bears out this reform. His first book will deal with the most crucial concern, invention; his second book will worry about how to communicate this invention effectively to a particular audience; and his third book will deal somewhat grudgingly with presentation and delivery.

However, before Aristotle launches his reform, he feels the need to answer a series of charges that have been brought against rhetoric. He will do so by justifying its utility and its ethical neutrality as a *technē*. Aristotle's first point is a remarkable claim: truth and justice are naturally stronger than falsehood and injustice, and rhetoric is helpful in aiding the judgment to follow its natural inclination toward truth and justice. This is a crucial assumption, for if it is true, then Aristotle need not take seriously the skeptical insight that injustice is the natural state. The force of his point becomes clearer in the context of Martha C. Nussbaum's account of Aristotle's philosophical interest in appearance:

> But if it is a universal human desire to grasp the world and make it comprehensible to reason, then it seems clear that oversimplification and reduction will be deep and ever-present dangers. In seeking to be at home, we may easily become strangers to our home as we experience it. . . . Aristotle (like the Heraclitus of our epigraph) believes that most of us have, to one degree or another, through the grip of hedonism, materialism, mechanism, or some

other simple picture, become strangers to some aspect of the life we live, the language we use. (*Fragility,* 260)

One chief task of rhetoric, then, would be to overcome our self-induced alienation and to help us see the world as it genuinely appears. Rather than contributing to the distortion of our perception of the world, a genuine rhetoric would promote a clearer and more stable vision. Further, it seems to follow that if we currently do not see the world truly, then this is not a problem in nature or even a problem inextricably embedded in our cultural inheritance or in our limitations as creatures who meet the world through the mediation of symbols, but it is a problem that admits of correction or at least improvement. The problems that beset rhetoric are not philosophical but technical. If we are estranged from the world, then rhetoric may provide one means of overcoming or coping with such estrangement.

Aristotle is not as naively optimistic as his first point might lead one to believe, for he immediately follows this point with the recognition that it is not easy to persuade people, even when a speaker has knowledge. Presumably a strong justification for the study of rhetoric is that such a study would increase the likelihood of success. But even in the best situations persuasion is a tricky and complicated business.

Aristotle's third point addresses directly the old charge that the sophists and rhetors taught their students to argue both sides of the case. The charge implied that rhetoric had no integrity but was merely an opportunistic relativism, ready to put its efforts forward on behalf of anyone who would pay. Aristotle meets this charge by showing that the activity of arguing both sides of an issue has been misconceived as an issue of ethical smarminess rather than properly understood as a key technical strategy that is an integral part of invention. The importance of being able to argue both sides is to ensure invention of a determination that is sufficiently complex and powerful to survive in a world in which it will be contested. In a world of contending opinions and unstable and varying appearances, there needs to be an intellectual device that can deal with these materials and incorporate them into the opinions and appearances that are to eventuate from the act of invention. The technique of arguing both sides of a case, then, is a method of discovery and not an admission of a lack of integrity.

Aristotle follows this justification by arguing the need for and legitimacy of self-defense. This point looks as if it is in direct response to the exchange between Socrates and Callicles in the *Gorgias* in which Callicles was continually berating Socrates for philosophy's inability to equip its adherents to defend themselves in the larger political arena. I will leave aside whether

Aristotle is, in fact, responding to Plato, and instead I will suggest that the force of this point can be understood as directed to a world in which the natural tendency of truth and justice to prevail has been thwarted by past acts of bad rhetoric and that people can anticipate having to use speech to defend themselves against both misunderstanding and aggression. In such a world, the competent practice of rhetoric is essential if justice is to have a chance at being the principle and practice that orders a particular community. It is out of the rhetorical agons that justice will be secured.

Aristotle's final point is that rhetoric is a power, and like every power, except virtue itself, it is subject to both proper and improper use. When rhetoric is practiced corruptly, it is not the fault of the art but of the individual practitioner. This is the important theoretical move that establishes rhetoric as an ethically and politically neutral technical art. While admitting the possibility of corruption, Aristotle denies that such corruption inheres in the practice of rhetoric. He thus challenges a main contention of the skeptical attack on rhetoric by arguing that the skeptical charge has mistaken accidental and occasional error for a systemic deficiency. This point is thus tied to his first one, in which Aristotle argued for the natural superiority of truth and justice. His response to skepticism is that, in principle, the truth and justice should prevail. If they do not, then the problem lies with individual misdeeds. Any corruption or incompetence in the practice of rhetoric is accidental and not endemic. The response to such difficulties encountered in a practice so defined is to propose reform, and hence Aristotle will now put forward an account of rhetoric as a technē that will aid in restoring the natural order of truth and justice. Again, he is not saying that this is an easy task; just that it is one that, in principle, is possible.

Part of the perspicacity of Aristotle's reformulation of rhetoric can be seen in his definition of the art. He does not define rhetoric as an art of persuasion but as the art capable of discerning the available means of persuasion in any given case (1355a14). Presumably there will be situations in which even the most skillful rhetor will be unable to move an intransigent audience. Equally, such cases can be presumed to be exceptions and not the norm. They establish the limit of rhetoric's efficacy, but they do not call into question the possibility of persuasion. The point also highlights the importance of the audience for Aristotle. What is indeterminate for rhetoric and hence under the governance of the art is the judgment of the audience. The object of rhetorical invention is a decision that best accommodates the audience's interest in a particular situation. Neither the audience's interest nor the configuration of the particular situation is given in advance of the act of invention. The initial and crucial skill for a rhetor is the ability to locate where this interest should lie and how such an interest can best play, given the possibilities and limitations afforded by that particular situation. This is a problem of having an inferential procedure that can move from the complex and indeterminate world of appearances to a grounded judgment as to the best action or decision for a particular audience. By rendering the situation determinate, a rhetor also renders an audience temporarily determinate. Consequently, the first task of any rhetor will be to understand the audience, for it is the audience that will determine how rhetors deploy their art.

Aristotle's starting from the need for a rhetor to invent the determination that best suits the audience is the key move in his reform of rhetoric from manipulation to discipline. Logically, if the purpose of rhetoric is defined as locating the decision that is best for the audience, then invention becomes the foremost concern for the rhetor, who will be guided by the need to discover these interests and then communicate a determinate judgment of how the audience should act. The art of rhetoric will reside in the invention and communication to the audience of how it should understand a particular situation so that its interests are best served. It will be the audience that finally renders any given situation determinate by making a particular judgment. The audience as judge also affords another check to the possible corruption of rhetoric. An active audience, one that is involved in a decision in which it has a stake, is more likely to be a watchful audience and to challenge understandings that run counter to its interests. Thus Aristotle will shift the paradigm from forensic to deliberative rhetoric to build in the situation of an audience deciding a course of action in a situation in which it is affected by the outcome of the action. Aristotle's interested audience ceases to be a means to the rhetor's private ends and instead becomes the end that governs the art and ensures theoretically the art's integrity.

What rhetoric renders determinate is the audience's understanding of itself in history. The three types of decisions that affect an audience and the three corresponding branches of rhetoric concern time past (forensic), time present (epideictic), and time future (deliberative). The objects of the three branches, respectively, are the just, the noble, and the good/useful. In effect, rhetoric negotiates our ongoing understanding of who we are. The role of political discourse is to mediate a community's self-invention, as it engages in the continuous process of trying to understand both what its identity is and how, given that identity, it can best act. Hence, Aristotle's rhetoric builds from its founding assumption of the indeterminacy of praxis and sees political identity as subject for a necessarily ongoing political contest. Rhetoric thus aligns itself with freedom and power as the instrumentality that offers a community the power to freely determine its identity in history. Persuasion is the mark of a community committed to freedom, and political discourse becomes the essential activity within that community. A reformed rhetoric is ultimately justified as central to the necessary human task of self-invention. Such a rhetoric is not a mere technical skill that aids in political administration but is a way of proceeding that is at the heart of communal life.

Further, since the rhetorical act rarely occurs in isolation but instead is almost always contested (hence the need for book 2), the larger activity of rhetorical life becomes self-correcting, provided that all have worked hard to master the art. In the give-and-take of communal exchange, the corrupt and incompetent should eventually stand out as they are challenged to defend their determinations and are unable to do so under the scrutiny of an open and public observation. If all points of views are allowed to speak as forcefully as they can, then logically the strongest point of view should finally prove victorious. Truth and justice should prevail naturally. The problem of corruption can be translated into the problem of competence, and the challenge to rhetoric is met by rhetoric's becoming more fully itself. If there is any problem, it is not that there is an excess of rhetoric but rather that there is not enough. Rhetoric is the answer to the problem of corrupt rhetoric.

Even if this answer misses the deeper point of Socrates' skeptical interrogations of rhetoric, it is nonetheless a powerful and attractive answer, not the least because it holds out the possibility of human beings' having a serious say in their destiny. It offers the world as a place of action, as a setting in which human concerns can be addressed effectively. Having recognized a radical indeterminacy, it offers the comfort of an earned and relatively stable closure. It brings potential opposition to silence by requiring that opposition to speak forcefully and then answering the opposition with a more powerful reason. In Aristotle's rhetoric refutation becomes simply one move in the larger project of persuasion; its concern is not with an endemic injustice but with the strategic problem of countering another rhetor's arguments. The role of refutation is limited to bolstering the persuasiveness of one's speech by showing that the rhetor is aware of objections, has taken them under consideration, and can accommodate any challenge they offer.

In the rhetorical agons producing persuasion, order and freedom are reconciled. The occasional failure of rhetoric through either incompetence or corruption ceases to be a troubling problem, for theoretically such failures can be corrected communally by subsequent rhetorical acts. Standing between logic and politics, rhetoric makes for an ethical politics by deploying a syllogistic reasoning that allows one to move from existing appearances and opinions to an inferential discovery of a community's true interests and of its most beneficial actions and understandings.

Crucial to this understanding of rhetoric is the audience's ability to become present to itself through discourse. This reformed rhetoric assumes that a rigorous public contest and consequent reflection on the discoveries produced by that contest can allow a community to recognize its identity. But it is just such recognition that the skeptical thread of classical rhetoric challenges. Plato's concern with refutation follows from his belief that one can never become present to oneself, that all self-understanding is partial and deceptive — a mere play of shadows. Refutation becomes a continual political necessity precisely because well-intentioned individuals and communities repeatedly fall into the trap of believing that they understand who they are and who the Other is. Refutation undermines this understanding and the comfort that follows upon it, and it continually demands that individuals and communities take responsibility for a world oblivious to the suffering of others. The abiding problem for rhetoric arises not because people are evil or incompetent but because all vision is inescapably partial. It is this insight that explains how Socrates' questioning of others can be regarded as a political act. In a Platonic universe, the true and good do not triumph, even theoretically; rather, the irremediable fact of his universe is that injustice is ineradicable. The philosophic problem is how to live responsibly in such a world; Socrates' answer is that one must use rhetoric to indict one's own loved ones.

Refutation does not stand in simple opposition to persuasion. They are far more entangled. In the standard accounts of rhetoric that follow Aristotle, refutation always formed part of a persuasion to which it was subordinated. Its task was both to acknowledge and, as well as it could, to silence the other voices in a rhetorical agon. If it sought the Other, it sought to dominate and contain any potentially dangerous claims or implications raised by the Other's voice. When refutation's mission was not such obliteration, it was assumed to be a resource that would permit competing rhetors mutually to discover new possibilities through the rigors of give-and-take. In such conceptions of rhetoric, refutation would then disappear, not because it had succeeded in dominating the Other but because there ceased to be an Other and instead there was only a new and homogeneous community. In either its malign or benign forms, refutation at the service of persuasion sought to make the Other disappear.

But when the relationship is inverted and refutation employs persuasion, the point is not to bring the Other to silence but to provoke the Other to speech. The assumption behind a refutative rhetoric is that through persuasion we have made ourselves blind and deaf to Others, that we have successfully persuaded ourselves and sometimes them, that we understand them and that we can occupy their position and see the world through their eyes. As Kenneth Burke argues in his *Grammar of Motives*, there is an imperialistic motive within language itself. The skeptical tradition, which begins with Socrates, argues that this motive cannot be reformed, although we can be persuaded that we have, in fact, reformed ourselves and that injustice is a problem that is now in the past. It is this temptation that refutation seeks always to resist, and one way of resisting this temptation is to point out continually that it is not personal intentions for good or evil that have produced this injustice and blinded us to it; rather, the inescapable partiality of language and the recognition of our own good intentions have made us unavailable to deal with an injustice to which we, simply by virtue of being born into and living in a language, have contributed. Refutation seeks to make us assume a responsibility for this world while recognizing that we can never be fully present to ourselves.

Sophocles and Euripides directed their questioning not at the audience's capacity to achieve a self-presence through discourse but at the availability of a public space in which an Other can speak or has reason to participate in a dialectical communal invention. If the self-correction of rhetoric depends upon an Other genuinely participating in a public contest, Euripides deals with the way such Others are in fact precluded from speaking by the distribution of power: reason cannot operate because violence is built into the very fabric of community life and determines in advance who can speak. As Hecuba will claim, people are not masters of their own destinies but slaves to a system of power relations and understanding that can contain any genuine challenge to the status quo. Sophocles questions whether the Other to a political contest should even attempt to participate. He argues that the lessons of history make impossible any faith in the efficacy of reason or persuasion. The difficulty resides not in any flaw in either reason or persuasion but in the limits imposed by the audience. An unscrupulous rhetor, one who views speech only strategically, can never be available for the kind of public contest that Aristotle deems necessary for the self-correction of rhetoric. In the *Philoctetes* Odysseus is protean in his ability to translate all discussion into strategic manipulation, and his obsession with strategies disables him from seeing where his true interests lie. But Odysseus's undermining of rhetoric is not limited simply to those situations that involve him directly. His strategic deployment of rhetoric helps shape the historical background from which other rhetors, and in particular Neoptolemos, must speak. Since no rhetor enters an innocent universe free from strategic manipulation, past acts of manipulation undermine the credibility of even an honest rhetor, for that rhetor cannot ensure that his or her very honesty cannot be taken over strategically and used by a corrupt rhetor. Further, an audience that recognizes how those in power in a community have deployed rhetoric strategically in the past learns from history to suspect all public discourse. In this earned cynicism an audience can become so disillusioned that a rhetor, even an honest one, will be able to say nothing to that audience. In the two cases imagined by tragedy, the silence of the Other is the consequence not of a political contest but of the impossibility of such a contest. What tragedy puts in question for rhetoric is the availability of the audience. It challenges not only persuasion but also refutation, demonstrating the necessity of refutation and showing the conditions that hinder refutation. Like Plato, they offer refutation as an answer that becomes a question.

Audiences fail to become participants in a rhetorical exchange because their power renders them indifferent to others, or because their trust has been so violated in the past that they can conceive of any speech only as a cynical attempt at manipulation, or because they remain ignorant of who they are and how they have been formed by history. Neither Plato nor the two tragedians offers a stable solution to the problem of the unavailable audience. What they do offer is a sense of the urgency of the problem. The dialogues and the tragedies leave as a question for their readers and spectators the problem of reaching an audience either to make it aware of its participation in injustice or to bring it back within a community. Consequently, the dialogues and dramas become ways of engendering and situating political responsibility by requiring their audiences to reflect upon their own implication in injustice.

Because the issues raised by Plato, Sophocles, and Euripides do not admit of stable answers, they become philosophical problems. Michel Meyer makes such openness the mark of philosophic discourse: "Philosophy differs from daily discourse because of this simple fact. In the case of daily discourse, questions are resolved and are made to disappear. This solution does not amount to reflecting on them. In the case of philosophy, on the contrary, questions are kept alive through discourse, because to philosophize is nothing other than to surrender oneself to a radical problematization and to reflect that same problematization through the answers it suggests" (*Rhetoric, Language, and Reason,* 74). The abiding issue that makes rhetoric a philosophical problem is injustice. The urgency of this question resides in the fact that it locates rhetoric as a problem of action and not as primarily one of knowledge. If a world of injustice is intolerable and if to be a creature of language is to be implicated in the ongoing injustice of that world, then action is demanded. In particular, since injustice is partly a problem of language, then some form of speech is necessary. In a world of injustice, rhetoric is essential for a viable political existence.

But if the very linguistic and historical conditions that make rhetoric necessary also fate it to be ineffective, then rhetoric becomes both a political and philosophical question. What is at issue is not how we can know but whether any action of ours can be an effective rejoinder to a pervasive injustice. What Plato, Sophocles, and Euripides do is to make rhetoric a question for their audiences, and it is the ongoing formulation and reformulation that opens responsibility for rhetoric as a philosophical and political opportunity. It is not the failure but the success of persuasion, or at least of some past persuasions, that creates the difficulties that occupy classical skepticism. For persuasion to succeed, the Other must be silenced or disappear. This silence or disappearance takes the form of preclusion. And it is the occurrence of preclusion that demands refutation, as refutation attempts to open an audience closed by a past persuasion that was too successful. The skeptical interrogation of persuasion seeks to pose rhetoric as a question in order to recover the world as a place for possible action. This interrogation offers itself as a productive doubt that generates political responsibility by showing how the fact of injustice sets an audience the task of trying to appreciate their involvement in past and ongoing injury to others.

This skepticism of Plato and the tragedians differs from the skepticism that has been the focus of modern philosophy. Stanley Cavell characterizes such skepticism as arising from a failure to know: "I do not, that is, confine the term [skeptic] to philosophers who wind up denying that we can ever know; I apply it to any view which takes the existence of the world to be a problem of knowledge. A crucial step for me, in calling an argument skeptical, is that it contain a passage running roughly, 'So we don't know (on the basis of the senses (or behavior) alone); then (how) do we know?'" (*Claim*, 46). Cavell sees such skepticism directed at either knowledge of the world or knowledge of other minds, but Socratic and tragic skepticism is not concerned primarily with either of these issues. Even the standard accounts of rhetoric freely admit that the situations with which it deals do not admit of knowledge and do not permit certainty. The lack of knowledge is one of the conditions for rhetoric to be. Rhetoric seeks to provide guidance in situations in which the relevant knowledge cannot by itself lead to a conclusion that could serve as an adequate basis for action or understanding. What classical skepticism puts into doubt is the possibility of finding a way of acting that is adequate to deal with the injustice that the rhetor encounters. So the conditions of action and not the conditions of knowledge are called into question. The conditions that threaten to undermine rhetoric are both formal and material, but both conditions raise questions about the availability of the audience. Hence Socratic refutation is always directed at a particular individual in an attempt to move that character to become an audience that is willing to risk its self-understanding to take appropriate responsibility for its position in the world.

Kierkegaard argued that it was the direction of the questioning at a person that distinguished Socratic negation from Hegelean negation, in which negation was an inherent part of thought:

> In this sense, Socratic questioning is clearly, even though remotely, analogous to the negative in Hegel, except that the negative, according to Hegel, is a necessary element in thought itself, is a determinant *ad intra* [inwardly]; in Plato, the negative is made graphic and placed outside the object in the inquiring individual. In Hegel, thought does not need to be questioned from the outside, for it asks and answers itself within itself; in Plato, thought answers only insofar as it is questioned, but whether or not it is questioned is accidental, and how it is questioned is not less accidental. (*The Concept of Irony*, 35)

Because refutation is not an inherent element within thought for Plato but an accident of human relations, it becomes an ethical and political activity. It originates in a choice made by Socrates to act responsibly in the world as it is constituted. Further, in Plato refutation does not offer the sort of negation, as in Hegel, that then moves as part of a process to a new synthesis. This positive movement is absent. Instead, the dialogues record a series of failures, enacting the problems of the available audience that is one of the key insights of a Socratic skepticism. If Plato offers refutation as a way of acting in a world in which injustice is an abiding problem, he is careful to emphasize that the success of such action is remote but that nonetheless the obligation to so act remains.

It is the audience as problem that ties the skeptical thread of classical rhetoric to the modern and postmodern rhetorics. If these more recent rhetorics speak little of refutation, they are fully aware of the problem of the unavailable audience. Indeed such a problem was fated to emerge as soon as the stable order of feudalism gave way to a Brownian movement of individuals with the rise of industrialism and a capitalist economy. The problem of the possibility of public discourse becomes entangled with redefinition of public life as a function of private interests. Romain Laufer puts the new problem for rhetoric this way: "This very notion of political economy constitutes a Copernican revolution with respect to the Aristotelean notion of domestic economy (oikos homos). For Aristotle, domestic economy is dependent on politics. Liberalism realizes the marvel whereby at the very moment that economy becomes the place of politics par excellence, it escapes political rhetoric: it escapes rhetoric because it is the object of a science (political economy) and it escapes politics in the classical sense because this science deals with private behavior" ("Rhetoric and Politics," 188). Again, public speech is precluded not because of personal corruption or incompetence but because of transpersonal circumstances that constitute the conditions under which political speech is possible or impossible at that historical moment. The rhetorical crisis of a liberal society is, then, a variation of the old skeptical themes of preclusion and of the need for refutation.

Again, this skepticism is not a preoccupation of the standard tradition. As Thomas C. Conley notes, standard eighteenth and nineteenth century rhetorical theory tended to consolidate the teaching of rhetoric into a fairly perfunctory activity with an increasing belletristic emphasis (*Rhetoric*, 224, 253). The interesting theoretical work was done elsewhere. The newly emerged literary form—the novel—assumed the place of ancient tragedy and provided the most revolutionary critiques of speech. M. M. Bakhtin has written insightfully on the essential link between speech and the novel. The social interplay of positioned speech defines the novel for him:

> The novel can be defined as a diversity of social speech types (sometimes even diversity of languages) and a diversity of individual voices, artistically organized. The internal stratification of any single national language into social dialects, characteristic group behavior, professional jargons, generic languages, languages of generations and age groups, tendentious languages, languages of the authorities, of various circles and of passing fashions, languages that serve the specific sociopolitical purposes of the day, even of the hour (each day has its own slogan, its own vocabulary, its own emphases)—this internal stratification present in every language at any given moment of its historical existence is the indispensable prerequisite for the novel as a genre. ("Discourse in the Novel," 262–63)

It was precisely the consequences of the historical fluctuations within social speech that permitted novelists to investigate the social implicatedness of their characters. If the move within an increasingly liberally organized society set the conditions for social revolution by redefining the public in terms of the private, the novel was medium through which the rhetorical ramifications of such a shift were explored.

As we might expect, one of the most interesting early skeptical interrogations of the possibilities of speech in a liberal society was produced by a conservative critic of that social change. At the beginning of the nineteenth century Jane Austen took up the problem of speech and silence: her economically dislocated heroines needed to speak for themselves as the economic and social certainties of the past century disappeared. The old rules of life, for example that "it is a truth universally acknowledged, that a single man in possession of a good fortune, must be in want of a wife," now had to be read ironically (*Pride and Prejudice*, 1). If women were to survive economically, it became imperative that they speak, but this imperative was frustrated by social circumstances in which direct speech was forbidden to women. The indirection forced on women made them rhetorical. Since the Habermasean meetings of an unpositioned universal self committed to seeing the viewpoint of the Other were denied them, their speech needed to become figurative and their judgment ironic.

The younger Jane Austen heroines needed to become good Aristoteleans, learn prudence, and practice persuasion. Hence the need for heroines such as Elizabeth Bennet and Emma Woodhouse to undergo educations at the hands of Darcy and Knightley and to curb their tongues and become discursively more prudential. Such restraint became the mark of a maturing, as the heroines became more skillful in the discourse of men. Social acceptance required the diminution of the female voice.

But an older Jane Austen turned her ironic and skeptical eye on such prudence — seeing it as life-denying. Women needed a new rhetoric, one that was not simply dictated by economic concerns, and in *Persuasion* Austen surveyed the discursive prospects of women and argued for a new rhetoric of generosity that might be able to free them from the self-interested and devitalizing constraints of prudential discourse. A silenced Anne Elliot, in her confrontation with nihilism, allows Austen to arrive at insights similar to those of the skeptical thread of the classical tradition and to reinstitute rhetoric as the philosophical problem of the precluded opening. What *Persuasion* confronts is the lost public space of discourse; what it offers is rhetoric as a problem; what it recommends is taking risks.

Little over a century later Sartre was to argue that the absence of an audience and the consequent need for writers to risk themselves defined the problem of writing for modernity. Again, the problem was nihilism (understood by Sartre not as the problem of discursive preclusion but as the problem of inessential connection to the universe), and the proposed response was generosity. Like Austen, Sartre understood the theoretical incoherence of the autonomous self, and he realized that writers can only exist as writers if they can find readers who will read them. This is the problem of the public. What gives this problem its particular modernist edge is the technological and economic revolutions in which the process of writing has been transplanted from its role in a particular and localizable polis into a potential consumer item in a new global capitalist communication network. The question becomes: how can one write when the historical continuity between writer and reader that gave political content to the acts of reading and writing has been breached by what Laufer would call the liberal organization of society, in which an effective concept of the public has been eviscerated by the emergence of a new authority vested in interests that are private?

But if Sartre is perceptive in his locating the problem of the public in a post-Enlightenment world, his solution to the problem, the appeal to individual free will, reinstates the Enlightenment understanding that provoked the discursive crisis of modernism. While Sartre's critique would push him to recover rhetoric, his solution is to eschew rhetoric for a potentially universalizable political discourse that was the aspiration of the Enlightenment. Sartre's difficulties are developed into a full-blown philosophical system by Habermas in his attempt to use the Enlightenment to correct the Enlightenment. But each posits a universal or potentially universalizable human reason, and consequently both require the potential actors in a discursive encounter to assume positions that can never be available to them. This finally is their antirhetoric. It is a position committed to an ideal concept of communication in which there can be a meeting of two selves fully present to each other, although ironically, these selves must be empty if they are to meet. It is ultimately the dream of recovering an Edenic existence that would then do away with language.

In Sartre's enunciation of the problem of writing, the impossibility of modernity's supplying an answer to itself as an intellectual and political crisis becomes evident. Unable to shake fully free of its Enlightenment foundations, modernism cannot appreciate the new opening to rhetoric that occurs when the possibility of a modernist discourse itself becomes a problem. In his trailing Kantianism, Sartre will inadvertently displace the opening to rhetoric with the implicit closure of a universalizable, position-free discourse. Having analyzed the problem of writing as the need to break free of the preclusions that peremptorily foreclose discourse, Sartre's turn toward an authenticity is a return to the subject, to the Kantian good will that loses the very historicity that his analysis of rhetorical preclusion opened. The Sartrean impasse leads either to the stressing of the formal dimensions of language and thus to the skeptical debunking of deconstruction or to the need for political action and thus to Marxist critiques of discourse. Hence postmodernism arrives as a schism between knowledge and action, between form and power, and it is without resources to negotiate this division.

The deconstructive criticism of Paul de Man represents one of the two paths taken from a modernism that equivocated on the rhetoricity that its analyses were driving it to discover. His work is particularly interesting for an inquiry arguing for refutation as the philosophical problem for rhetoric because the ironic readings that de Man offers present an alternative form of negation — one that argues that the endemic problem of discourse is not the fated occurrence of injustice but the impossibility of knowledge. De Man's epistemological skepticism is a negation rooted in a formalist appreciation of language. He understands the world as an iterated textuality that in its infinite turning cannot close, despite the efforts of those readers who see texts as forms of communication, but must provoke an ongoing series of misreadings. Like Socratic refutation, de Manian deconstruction leads to aporias, but these aporias are not part of a necessary attempt to take responsibility for injustice but rather momentary exaltations of joy or flashes of despair.

De Man represents the most formidable challenge to the standard understanding of rhetoric since the classical interrogation of the possibility of discursive action in a world in which injustice is inescapable. His formalist account of rhetoric subordinates persuasion to figure and undermines the possibility of pragmatic discourse achieving its purported goal of generating relatively stable new understandings. Further, de Man's deconstruction claims to be impervious to refutation, for its skepticism can undermine the foundation of any criticism directed at it. Thus de Manian deconstruction offers a central challenge not only to standard histories of rhetoric but to my own revisionary project, which argues for refutation as the philosophical problem that gives rhetoric a point. The authority of refutation to speak to postmoderns needs to be established through an agon with de Manian deconstruction. If Socratic refutation cannot lead a de Manian deconstruction into a Socratic aporia that locates a political incoherence within de Man, then it must be silent.

Deconstruction, however, does not represent the only area of postmodern rhetoric that has responded to the failure of discursive coherence in the modernist attempt to write in a world in which audiences are problematic. Those political and discourse theorists who have focused on the role of ideology in the maintenance of power systems have also been led back to rhetoric. Their concern has not been with formal instability but with the way in which power inscribes itself into subjects. In the recognition that force is not necessary to legitimate a ruling order, these theorists have explored the way in which language facilitates power, and in recovering the connection between discourse and power, they have recovered the relation between language and injustice.

Political critics have shown an appreciation for the skeptical critique of rhetoric, and Terry Eagleton, for one, reads Plato's account of rhetoric with an acuity that is lacking in many traditional students of rhetoric: "As far as rhetoric is concerned, then, a Marxist must be in a certain sense a Platonist. Rhetorical effects are calculated in the light of a theory of the polis as a whole, not merely in light of the pragmatic conjuncture fetishized by post-Marxism. Rhetoric and dialectic, agitation and propaganda are closely articulated; what unites them for Plato is justice, a moral concept itself only calculable on the basis of social knowledge, as opposed to *doxa* or ideological opinion" (*Walter Benjamin*, 113). But if a Marxist theory of rhetoric shares Plato's concern with injustice, it does not go far enough with Plato to recognize the heterogeneous origins of injustice. In particular, it needs to develop a Socratic appreciation for the way language itself leads to the developing and maintaining of injustice.

If deconstruction understands formal instabilities, it fails to appreciate power; if Marxism understands power, it slights the inherent force of form. At this juncture within postmodernism, the work of Kenneth Burke, with his deep appreciation of both formalism and Marxism, becomes illuminating. Very much a modern or postmodern Socrates, Burke returns to a celebration of the negative and of the ongoing need for a linguistic skepticism if there is to be a politics adequate to deal with the inherent tendency to hierarchy within language. With Burke, the relevance of the skeptical tradition and, in particular, of the Socratic elenchus is recovered. And with Burke, the concerns of form and power, knowledge and action, are reunited by his offering of rhetoric as a philosophic problem.

In his comic jibes and fertile play, Burke takes on the role of Socrates, accentuating the negative, being shameless, and just causing trouble. His way of talking about the inherent injustice with which we are fated to deal is to claim that we are "rotten with perfection." In its irony this characterization of human purpose is worthy of Socrates. In teaching us the tricks that we can play on ourselves, he is revitalizing the Socratic rhetorical practice of attacking the ones we love. And like Socrates, he can present us with a potentially corrosive understanding that does not undermine the possibility of action but that sets justice as our problem. In this ironic appreciation of language and action, Burke's work argues for the relevance of rhetoric to the postmodern world, and it recovers the philosophical problem of rhetoric that is embodied in the ongoing need for refutation.

Burke's work in rhetoric returns us to the problem that began this chapter: what utility is there in the study of the rhetoric of antiquity? My answer is that such a study justifies itself as a refutation of postmodernism. This refutation takes the form of recovering positions that have been taken inadvertently and that have been assumed to be not choices of the particular discourse theorists but discoveries about language or power. What postmodernism has forgotten, for all of its theoretical sophistication, is that it is itself a rhetorical and hence historical product. This may seem an odd claim, for postmodern thought is often marked by a recognition of contingency or by an awareness of its historicity. The one thing that seems true for postmodern thought is an unwillingness to make universal claims. Derrida's writing under-erasure, for example, registers postmodernism's recognition that it cannot escape from the errors that it is analyzing.

Andrzej Warminski has made a strong case for de Man, someone often perceived as a formalist critic, to be, in fact, a writer practicing a more sound version of historical materialism. And Richard Rorty's embrace of a liberal irony is an unambiguous commitment to contingency:

> The ironist, by contrast, is a nominalist and a historicist. She thinks nothing has an intrinsic nature, a real essence. So she thinks that the occurrence of a term like "just" or "scientific" or "rational" in the final vocabulary of the day is no reason to think that Socratic inquiry into the essence of justice or science or rationality will take one much beyond the language games of one's time. The ironist spends her time worrying that she has been initiated into the wrong tribe, taught to play the wrong language game. She worries that the process of socialization which turned her into a human being by giving her a language may have given her the wrong language, and so turned her into the wrong kind of human being. (*Contingency, Irony, and Solidarity,* 75)

There is much in such a statement that a rhetoric of refutation could endorse. But where a refutative rhetoric and a Rortyean postmodernism part is over what is entailed by ironic or refutative inquiries. As Rorty readily admits, his ironist "cannot give a criterion for wrongness" (75). What this means, for Rorty, is that nothing follows from her inquiries — they are inherently private. So for Rorty, the public-private split, which is itself a historical product of liberalism, ceases to have an openness for historical change because his ironist is placed beyond any public claim on her. If she engages in politics, it will be because of what is, in the final analysis, an aesthetic decision. No oracle has set her a task of being politically responsible — no political obligations press on her. She finds the pain of others unpleasant, so she seeks social organizations that reduce such pain. One can easily imagine an ironist not so sensitive.

But for Socrates, to be born into a language is to be born into ways of not seeing; it is to be born into ways of denying the Other and of not knowing oneself. One's social and political implication is a consequence of birth, so the choice to be only a private individual is never available. The very activity of attempting to understand oneself and take responsibility for that self is necessarily social and historical because one begins as implicated in the perpetuation of injustice, in the exclusion of others. To engage in refutation is not to become sensitive to others' pain but to take responsibility for it. Socrates' politics are not metaphysical, in Rorty's sense of providing an ultimate grounding, nor are these a product of aesthetics or edification. Rather they follow from a recognition of one's embeddedness in language as an embeddedness in both a formal and historical dynamic. The publicness of language does not allow one to entertain the private intellectual diversions that occupy the Rortyean ironist. A return to a classical rhetorical skepticism with its very different sense of public and private, then, allows one to understand that Rortyean irony is a particular type of practice available because of liberal choices to redefine life as inherently private and only derivatively and arbitrarily public.

Rorty's ironist investment in the primacy of the private, like de Man's deconstructionist contention of the necessary instaniation of error in any reading, is an attempt to move beyond history, rendering the postmodern intellectual impervious to serious revision. Theirs is world, in effect, without surprise, for all of the moves are known in advance. But a Socratic refutation would ask what are the commitments and omissions that such understandings conceal. This placing of postmodernism within rhetorical history is not yet another discovery of the politics of theory but a much more particular discovery of the inherent relation of language and injustice as an abiding problem for any rhetorical study. The importance of this insight is that it provides a reason not simply for the continued study of ancient rhetoric but also for the study of postmodernist discourse. The point of all such study is the ongoing need to assume responsibility for our own involvement in and contribution to injustice. Injustice is not only what someone else has perpetrated; rather, it is a problem of taking appropriate responsibility for the way the world is. This makes one of our most important tasks that of self-indictment, of not exonerating ourselves from responsibility by citing our good intentions and actions but rather diligently looking for what we have not been able to see. This makes the rewriting of history an ongoing task for us, as we seek to understand injustice in ways that past histories have not allowed.

A study of the skeptical thread of ancient rhetoric and its relation to postmodernism has the potential for allowing more members of the present intellectual community to understand the political and philosophical force of academic movements in multiculturalism or antiracist and feminist studies. These movements are too often conceived as pursuing some particular agenda and are not understood as engaging in a practice that is similar to Socratic refutation. Hence, either their criticisms are dismissed or ignored as the griping of malcontents, or their investigations of the rootedness of injustice are taken as personal attacks directed against the good intentions of the established academic community. But if such critiques are read as refutation, then it is clear that their work is essential for contemporary universities, for they recover the way culture, race, and gender have functioned as elements in the production of specific forms of injustice. Seeing critique as refutation would allow us to understand political commitment not as merely a choice by an individual scholar (although on some level, it is surely that) but as the register of responsibility that sees the role of reason in political life not simply as instrumentalist to the powers that be but as justified to the extent that it challenges those powers.

To challenge accepted accounts is to act on the heritage of Plato, Sophocles, and Euripides. And to be open to such challenges, and indeed to seek such challenges, is the responsibility of all who have been educated by the skepticism of ancient rhetoric. The persuasive force of the critiques of postmodernism and their appreciation for the rhetoricity at the heart of language have opened new areas for rhetorical study, but these advances themselves stand in need of criticism. What is not needed is a reactive opposition that belligerently defends the standard histories of rhetoric by insisting on rhetoric's utility, or a recuperation of a modernist notion of subjectivity as a step to recovering agency; rather, what is needed is an appreciation of the advances of postmodernism that recovers the political point of such work. This is not to impose an exterior criterion of relevance but to understand the way an intellectual project is always already political and is necessarily contributing to the maintenance of injustice. There is no escape from that situation, for, as the ancients have taught, the philosophical problem of injustice follows not from the activities of the evil but as an unintended complication of the activities of the good. The best any of us can do is to refute and to seek refutation. The ancient rhetorical skeptics understood this, and they have bequeathed this understanding to the present. The task of the present is to act on this insight.

PART I

Socratic and Tragic Skepticism

2

In Defense of Plato's Gorgias

Although rhetoric emerged as a force in Greek life at the beginning of the fifth century BCE (Barilli, *Rhetoric,* 3), the history of rhetoric can be read as a series of responses to Plato (Hunt, "Plato," 3–7). Plato's use of eloquence in *Gorgias* to interrogate the practice of eloquence initiated the argument over the integrity of rhetoric and the status of writing (Barilli, *Rhetoric,* 6–9; Kennedy, *The Art of Persuasion,* 14-1e; Vickers, *Defence,* 1–213). For the standard histories of rhetoric *Gorgias* is an attack that condemns the practice as a knack by which rhetors use deceit and manipulation for their private advantage.[1] These accounts often see Plato as led ineluctably to a distorted view of rhetoric by his class affiliations and idealistic metaphysics. And he is regarded as either unable or unwilling to comprehend the exigencies and merits of a pragmatic discourse rooted in historical circumstances, committed to flexibility, and seeking workable solutions to actual problems (Havelock, *Liberal Temper,* 240–54; Popper, *The Spell of Plato,* 15–28). He is charged further with trading unfairly on the excesses of a few practitioners to indict a beneficial practice. George Kennedy voices a common complaint when he laments that, for political reasons, Plato could not see the utility of rhetoric; rather, embittered by Socrates' death, "he is so prejudiced he appears to weight the scales in turn against rhetoric" (*The Art of Persuasion,* 15). Brian Vickers agrees and argues that *Gorgias* is best read by placing it initially in its historical context and by understanding Plato's fierce opposition to democracy (*Defence*, 88). The Plato who results from this reading is irresponsibly biased, contemptuous of the common people, and deeply angered over the democratic organization of Athenian society. As Vickers reads it, *Gorgias* is not so much a philosophical investigation as a polemic deceitfully presenting itself in the guise of a fair-minded and rational inquiry (90).

Thus in the standard account in the histories of rhetoric *Gorgias* either exemplifies bad philosophy or, at best, makes the trivial point that the practice of rhetoric can be abused. But such a reading is possible only if the complexity and elusiveness of Plato's dialogue form are ignored. The conventional reading of *Gorgias* depends on disembodying arguments from their integral roles in the dialogue and addressing them as if they were simply a series of objections that happened to exist in dialogue form. Those who object to the dialogue take their dissatisfaction with it at face value and do not consider that part of *Gorgias*'s rhetorical strategy might be to provoke dissatisfaction and, further, that this provocation might be essential to Plato's understanding of the philosophical importance of rhetoric. What a majority of rhetors interpreting the dialogue have failed to understand is that Plato does not believe that the philosophical significance of rhetoric can be developed and contained in a series of detachable arguments and conclusions. If, however, we take the dialogue's rhetoric seriously, not only does Plato emerge as the most sophisticated and profound rhetorical theorist, but the dialogue also suggests an alternative way to write the history of rhetoric, a way that values rhetoric for its role in refutation and not for its utility in pragmatic discourse.

The misreading of Plato on rhetoric is particularly unfortunate at a time when the epistemological adequacy and pedagogical relevance of ancient rhetoric is being questioned (Knoblauch and Brannon, *Rhetorical Traditions*, 22–50). One legacy of the standard history of rhetoric is that it allows Plato to be appropriated for an attack on rhetoric (Knoblauch and Brannon, *Rhetorical Traditions*, 45–46). But he, more than anyone else, understood what is at stake in a defense of rhetoric, and *Gorgias* develops a philosophically sophisticated rhetoric and argues its centrality for education. Indeed, the education that *Gorgias* makes possible is neither dogmatic nor technical; rather, it is refutative. And because it offers an education in and through refutation, it seeks to create rhetors who are civilly responsible. And it aims at expanding rather than contracting the ranks of who can speak.

If Plato, however, is judged by the standards of fairness, the dialogue appears to fail miserably. For example, how can Socrates possibly use the citizens' treatment of a rhetor as a measure of the rhetor's genuine excellence? Every reader of the dialogue knows that the citizens of Athens condemned

Socrates to death. Does the dialogue want us to treat this fact as evidence of Socrates' worthlessness as a teacher? If not, how are we to reconcile the apparent contradiction in Socrates' position? Or consider Socrates' attack on Gorgias when Gorgias is trying to argue for a just use of rhetoric. Gorgias is honest enough to acknowledge that rhetoric is abused, and Socrates uses this admission, in what appears to be a radical simplification of its meaning, to show that Gorgias has contradicted himself and to suggest that teachers, at least those who teach rhetoric, are responsible for the actions of their students — a thought that must prompt a cry of "unfair" from any teacher reading the dialogue.

Equally, any reader of *Gorgias* must be struck by the weakness of some of its arguments. Discussions of its logical difficulties are common in the articles and commentaries on this dialogue (Adkins, *Merit,* 280; Dodds, *Gorgias,* 30; Irwin, *Plato's Moral Theory,* 311). More than one reader has worried about the slipperiness of Socrates' position and the ambiguity of his motives. Charles H. Kahn is certainly right when he suggests that we feel that Polus has been not defeated but merely outwitted ("Drama and Dialectic," 93). But the readers are not alone in their unease. The dialogue itself constantly points out its unsatisfactoriness. Polus defends Gorgias after becoming convinced that Socrates tricked him into an admission that does not represent his true position on rhetoric. Callicles, in turn, takes up the argument because he believes that Polus has been shamed into a confused silence by Socrates' deliberate muddling of nature and convention.

What is remarkable, though, is that *Gorgias* repeatedly anticipates the criticisms that friendly and hostile readers might bring against it. For example, Eric A. Havelock supports his reading of the dialogues by arguing that Plato lacks sympathy for and understanding of a pragmatic reasoning that seeks to deal with the historical world as human beings encounter it (*Liberal Temper,* 249). But, of course, a perception of the same lack in Socrates and in others who adopt philosophy as a way of life is what antagonizes Callicles (484c–86b).[2] This thematization by the dialogue of possible objections to it should cause us to pause and to consider, at least momentarily, that the dialogue may be trying as part of its philosophical and rhetorical method to provoke dissatisfaction in its readers (White, *When Words,* 94–95). Such an understanding is given credence by Socrates' refusal to claim that his position is true and by his maintaining only that he has not yet been refuted.

Polus's responses to Socrates provide a good indication that Plato is conscious of the bizarreness of some of Socrates' arguments. Polus at times appears almost dumbfounded at the absurdity of Socrates' claims (473a). They so obviously run counter to what just about anyone, if questioned, would say.

Plato had to be aware that Socrates' claims that it is better to suffer an injustice than to do one and better to submit to punishment than to avoid it would invite protest. He certainly was aware that Socrates' view of what is noble opposed the *ēthos* of Athens's aristocracy. We can read Plato's awareness of the outlandishness of Socrates' arguments in the refusal of Polus to accept them even though they quiet his objections. The force of their logic is insufficient to overcome their radical rearrangement of commonly held beliefs. As Callicles says later, if Socrates is right, the world will be turned upside down (481c). Socrates also silences Callicles but does not persuade him. Nor can Socrates' inability to convince any of the rhetors simply be accepted with regret at the inadequacy of those with whom he talks. Rather, his ineffectiveness signals a major failure in the dialogue. He ends the exchange, not victorious but isolated — no one will talk with him. This is not how a character who values dialectic wants to end up.

This deliberate contravening of expectations should suggest that any reading hoping to elucidate the dialogue's sophisticated arguments cannot begin by translating them into syllogisms that are disembodied from the context; the arguments must be viewed in the particularity of the situation that they are trying to close (Adkins, *Merit*, 267–68; Kahn, "Drama and Dialectic," 75–76; Plochmann and Robinson, *A Friendly Companion*, xxxiv). That is, to understand its philosophical import, the dialogue must be read rhetorically. The characters cannot be viewed uncritically as mouthpieces for certain positions. Nor can the rhetorical and philosophical choice to present the contest of philosophy and rhetoric in a dialogue form be seen as irrelevant or inessential to what the dialogue has to say about either of them (White, *When Words*, 94). Nor should we assume that the dialogue's understanding of the terms philosophy, rhetoric, and politics is simple or straightforward.

The form of the discourse — its narrative structure — is essential to figuring its content (Kahn, "Drama and Dialectic," 76), and seeing this opens up a new set of questions. Chief among these is, Why does Socrates desire to talk with Gorgias and the others? Does the dialogue suggest why such a conversation might be essential if Plato's account of rhetoric is to have a philosophical point and not merely be a polemic rehearsing the corruption of rhetoric by individual rhetors? Early in the dialogue, Socrates addresses this point by explaining that he will continue to ask questions and pursue a dialectical form of discourse even though he has a good idea of what Gorgias's answers might be (454c). Socrates is not being disingenuous; instead, he is emphasizing that if dialectic is to move the two of them forward together, they must proceed in a certain way. The point can be pushed further: if the rhetors are set up only so they can be knocked down and if they do not put forward the best defense available for rhetoric, what purpose do they serve? Why does Socrates need them? What is it about dialectic, as it is represented in this dialogue, that requires its form to be communal? And what does the communal nature of dialectic do to the ostensible distinction between philosophy and politics as separate ways of life?

Seeing the rhetors as essential to the dialectic opens up more new questions. Why are there three rhetors, and only three? Why does Gorgias (the most admirable of them) recede into the background after the first third of the dialogue and allow his corrupt and less talented students to make absurd defenses for rhetoric — defenses that ignore his concern with justice? There is, of course, the fairly obvious point that Socrates' confronting several rhetors allows the dialogue to highlight its commitment to rhetoric. Socrates treats each of the three quite differently: he is respectful, even deferential, to Gorgias; he is deliberately provocative with Polus; and he is aggressive with Callicles. Thus Socrates indicates his grasp of the rhetorical insight that knowing the ēthos and pathos of the audience is crucial for anyone who is seriously trying to persuade.

More important, through his narrative development Plato can emphasize the tensions and equivocations that mark a defense of rhetoric. The dialogue's rhetors offer two distinct lines of defense. Gorgias seeks to justify rhetoric by its communal utility, while Polus and Callicles admire it for its ability to confer power on the individual agent. These defenses are not coordinate, but they represent varying understandings of rhetoric and power. Plato will build on these differences to raise two difficulties for rhetoric: intentional abuse and inadvertent injury.

The dialogue's narrative structuring of the two defenses is revealing. *Gorgias* begins with a displacement that should caution any reader seeking a straightforward contest between rhetoric and philosophy. Socrates has come to question Gorgias, and a reader might anticipate a magnificent interchange between two of Greece's greatest teachers, but the contest does not come off. Instead, Chaerephon speaks for Socrates and Polus for Gorgias, and the dialogue encounters a problem with this substitution: Socrates' student does not know which question is appropriate until Socrates, in a remedial crash course in dialectic, shows him, and Gorgias's student answers the question with a collection of true but vacuous points that do not lead to his conclusion (Friedlander, *The Dialogues*, 245–46). The students of the dialectician and the rhetor are both inept, and the failure of education (which will emerge as a political problem for the dialogue) has dramatically become a theme.

When Socrates and Gorgias take over the discussion, progress is made toward defining rhetoric, and the dialogue proceeds to the point at which a communal refutation might be possible. Socrates' questions to Gorgias have made clear Gorgias's commitment to justice and belief that rhetoric, to empower its practitioners, must be used in a community. Rhetoric and community are essentially related; consequently justice is a constitutive concern for rhetoric. The dialogue has opened rhetoric to dialectical investigation only to have Polus intervene and focus the discussion on rhetoric as pure agency. The middle of the dialogue then develops as a dialectical purification of the commitments that are entailed when rhetoric is equated with private effectiveness. The role of the community, equivocally maintained in Polus's account of rhetoric as private agency, is taken to its logical conclusion when Callicles argues that the community is simply an available means to the rhetor's private ends (Dodds, *Gorgias,* 15; Kahn, "Drama and Dialectic," 98). The inherent contradiction of Callicles' position, which finally makes action impossible, leads the dialogue back to community and, in particular, to the historical community of Athens. The debate has, however, shifted from being an inquiry into a theoretical justification for rhetoric to being an empirical investigation that seeks a noncorrupt rhetor.

If the dialogue has circled back to the relation of rhetoric and community, the return becomes problematic not simply because of the substitution of an empirical for a theoretical inquiry but because of the narrative action. By this point Socrates has alienated the three rhetors, so there is no potential community between him and them, and the exchange closes with its dialectical protagonist speaking only with himself. Finally, the dialogue concludes in what appears to be a most contradictory manner when Socrates puts forward a myth whose intent is clearly rhetorical. Having failed as a dialectician to sustain a productive and potentially communal conversation, Socrates unapologetically takes on the role of rhetor, telling a myth designed to appeal to the imagination and trying thereby to induce the audience to adopt the ēthos of a dialectician. The dialogue ends with the participants seemingly unaware that its original problem was lost in the discursive shuffle and that its concluding action undermines its apparent attempt to discredit rhetoric. The participants make no claim to have investigated sufficiently the relation of rhetoric to justice. Gorgias's understanding of rhetoric is left half developed, and readers who hoped that the dialogue would advance their understanding of the relation of philosophy and rhetoric must be disappointed as soon as they can free themselves from the rhythms of the narrative.

To explain why the dialogue ends so unsatisfactorily, we must return to the first major redirection of the narrative, for guiding this redirection is an important equivocation on power. The slippage in the narrative that occurs when Polus displaces the refutation of Gorgias by interjecting himself into the discussion picks up and thematizes the slide from Gorgias's belief that power is grounded in the community to Polus's acknowledgment of power only in the needs and wants of private individuals. The corollary of Polus's understanding is that all public relationships are merely masks for private interests. His collapse of public into private causes him to misinterpret refutation in its communal character and to read it merely as a disguised form of aggression. Plato thus anticipates the redefinition of the public by the private that Romain Laufer argues is one of the distinctive features of the modern liberal state ("Rhetoric and Politics," 188). The public/private confusion is a consequence of a failure to understand the inherent publicness of rhetoric. Polus assumes that the real purpose of dialectic is to assert the self at the expense of another. Since his sole criterion is victory, for him the interaction between two people in a discourse can only be competitive and can only close with the triumph of one and the defeat of the other. In his understanding there can be no place for either cooperation or public interest.

But Gorgias's defense of rhetoric requires both of these, and it is precisely the problem of rhetoric's essential commitment to cooperation and public interest that opens the possibility of exploring why rhetoric might be a crucial art for a community. Gorgias's role is not simply to be the foil who makes errors that Socrates can then point out; rather, it is to be a dedicated rhetor whose conversation reveals his social commitments. The dialogue begins with Gorgias because he is a decent character who seeks public good and whose principles are worth exploring. Not surprisingly, Gorgias intervenes on several occasions to keep the interchange going when it is in danger of closing prematurely because of either Polus's ineptness or Callicles' intolerance. Unlike Polus and Callicles, Gorgias does not defend rhetoric as a means to increase personal power; he sees it as an art existing for the benefit of the community. For him, rhetoric is a guide that helps the public decide the best course of action. In Gorgias's example, a rhetor can be valuable in helping a doctor persuade a reluctant patient to take a painful medicine. By extension, the public office of rhetoric is to serve the community by persuading it to undertake advantageous actions when through ignorance or fear it is unwilling to do so. Rhetoric can make available to the community technical understandings (in the broadest sense — namely, the various intellectual expertises), so they can be integrated into communal life. Given Socrates' failure to make dialectic compelling to either Polus or Callicles and his consequent isolation at the dialogue's end, Gorgias's earlier defense of rhetoric acquires serious force.

The dialogue itself calls attention to its argumentative slippage. Socrates is careful, when giving Polus his unfavorable account of rhetoric, to point out that the account might not coincide with Gorgias's view and that he himself does not yet know what Gorgias means by rhetoric: "I'm afraid it may be a bit ill-bred to say what's true. For I shrink from saying it, because of Gorgias, for fear he may think I'm ridiculing his own practice. But anyhow, whether the rhetoric Gorgias practices is like this, I don't know — for in fact nothing was made clear for us in our recent discussion about just what he thinks — but anyhow what *I* call rhetoric is nothing at all fine" (462e–63a). In giving no further account of Gorgias's understanding of rhetoric, the dialogue leaves a major portion of its central project incomplete. Dodds argues that Gorgias, despite good intentions, has an understanding of rhetoric that is finally shallow (*Gorgias,* 8). Gorgias's lack of substance creates a difficulty for Plato that he solves by entangling the reader in sorting out the serious arguments against rhetoric. As I shall argue, Plato uses Socrates' apparently unjust attack on Pericles to present the reader with the project of defining the office of a philosophical rhetoric.

Neither Polus nor Callicles possesses an understanding of rhetoric sufficiently sophisticated to nurture philosophical inquiry. Each conceives of rhetoric only in impoverished terms. It is in his initial response to Polus that Socrates lays out his infamous charge that rhetoric is mere flattery, and not an art but an *empeiria* (a knack). This charge has often been taken simply as Socrates' (unfair and unsympathetic) characterization of rhetoric. But if one looks at this charge within the context of the dialogue, it is not Socrates' final word on rhetoric but rather his opening of rhetoric for discussion. It is, then, the charge against rhetoric that he must answer if rhetoric is to be defended as a worthy practice. Not surprisingly, Polus misses the point of the charge, and in his eagerness to show that rhetoric is good and profitable he shifts the defense of rhetoric from being the justification of a public practice to being the advocacy of power as an instrument to effect a private will. For him, there is never a question of whether rhetoric represents a form of human excellence; rather, he values rhetoric as an unfettered agency that allows him to pursue his desires unchecked through manipulation of a community (466b–68e). Polus's admiration of rhetoric as unlimited agency, however, is not merely an intellectually shallow position adopted by an immature and ambitious young man. The philosophical interest in the Polus section arises because his unreflective endorsement of an ēthos of exclusively external goods gives freedom a market definition: it is the absence of constraint on desire. The world that Polus wants to argue for closely resembles the modern world as characterized by Alasdair MacIntyre (*After Virtue,* 34). And, as MacIntyre points out, in such a world public and private interests are irrevocably severed, or, rather, public interest becomes merely an instrumental extension of private interests. In such a world public concerns must always be unstable, and arguments about power will inevitably be expressed in the language of private interest.

Still, Socrates' arguments with Polus are not allegorized propositions; they are specific responses designed to be effective with a particular audience (Adkins, *Merit*, 267–68; Kahn, "Drama and Dialectic," 75–76). To gain purchase on Polus's unreflective valuing of personal agency, Socrates uses two argumentative strategies: he appeals to Polus's understanding of power, and he exploits Polus's unresolved and confused attitude toward public opinion. First, Socrates shows that agency acquires force only in the presence of a purpose and that agency is useless to someone who is incapable of reflecting on purposes. Second, Socrates tries to show Polus that the community does not really believe that if doing wrong brings reward and goes unpunished, the deed is good.

This second argument has seemed unsuccessful, if not perverse, to many commentators (Adkins, *Merit,* 267–68; Irwin, *Gorgias,* 156–58). But it is central to the redefinition attempted by Plato's rhetoric. Again, Plato is fully aware of how radical the argument is, for he has a dumbfounded Polus blurt out that what Socrates is claiming is monstrous—not simply absurd, but a distortion of normal human values. It seems self-evident to Polus, and to many readers of the dialogue, that a person confronted by the choice of either doing or suffering injustice would choose to do it. Put in its simplest terms, pain is bad, and it is preferable that someone other than me have to endure this evil. Initially, Socrates says that he would prefer neither to do nor to suffer wrong and that the happy person is one who avoids both evils, but the argument reverts to seeing the issue as a binary opposition between doing and suffering wrong. Since most persons presumably would agree with Socrates that it is best to avoid both, it is reasonable to ask whether this binary opposition represents the only choices. The dialogue suggests that it does. After raising the possibility of an alternative, the dialogue pointedly returns to its binary opposition, and Polus's and Socrates' exclusive concern with the dilemma argues that doing and suffering injustice are irreducible features of human life. I take Plato's insight to be that we cannot avoid these features. It is not a question of deciding to be good or evil; rather, since some consequences of action always escape prediction or control, anyone who acts will occasionally cause suffering. Equally, since no one can create a totally secure environment in which all relevant aspects are under control, everyone is fated to suffer at some time. Although it is prudent and praiseworthy to try to minimize either the causing or the undergoing of suffering, the problem for philosophy is how to live responsibly in a world in which even our best efforts fall short. Clearly, any consideration of that problem is beyond Polus, but it will occupy Callicles and Socrates and will anchor any reading of the dialogue that tries to do justice to Plato's philosophical rhetoric.

Callicles is a considerably more substantive opponent for Socrates. Callicles' understanding of the relation among power, agency, and community is not weakened by the equivocations that make Polus's position vulnerable. Callicles unabashedly argues for the value of personal power, for if one is to be invulnerable to suffering it will be through acquiring sufficient power to control the relevant aspects of the natural and political environments. He is not really attempting to defend tyranny; rather, he wants to make the case for a life of complete, full, and rich expression. The argument between Callicles and Socrates is about what constitutes the best way to live. Callicles champions the appetites and passions as forces that attach us to life and that give being alive a point. What he advocates is an ēthos of self-cultivation; what he wants is a life that is grand and magnificent. His is an ethics of the sublime life as opposed to an ethics of the ordered or limited life. Callicles' argument is best appreciated when read as a Nietzschean conviction that a truly creative life is deeply impious toward conventions that impose unnatural limits on the projective force of desire. An artist's creativity or will to power must continually break old forms as it reorders its surroundings, making a world that corresponds to the artist's passions. Such creation is not motivated by a concern for the community; rather, it flows from the joy of imposing one's own order on that which is other (Nietzsche, *On the Genealogy of Morals,* 86–88; essay 2, sec. 17–18). If read in this way, Callicles' position is not a self-evidently bankrupt ethics of cynical manipulation for personal advantage but instead a defiant transvaluation of democratic values (Dodds, *Gorgias,* 15).

It is important to emphasize that Callicles is not offering a renegade position but representing a warrior ēthos. He does not aspire to be an aristocrat; he is one. What he seeks to do is to defend this way of life against the small-minded or small-souled. When Socrates attacks Callicles' understanding of ethics, he is questioning some of the basic ethical terms in classical Greek culture (Adkins, *Merit,* 239, 259; White, *When Words,* 95–98). His project of radical political reform, if successful, would invert Callicles' world by redefining what a noble life is.

Because the nature of the noble life is being contested, the virtue of courage takes on special importance. It is an essential virtue for both the political and the philosophical lives. Its role in political life is obvious, but Socrates wants to stress its role in a philosophical life. To practice philosophy as Socrates understands it requires the courage to reject conventional understanding. One has to be willing to accept isolation as the price of thinking for oneself. This Callicles is willing to do. But as admirable as this kind of courage may be, it is easier to exercise than the courage that is more immediately involved in the philosophical life. One can exploit dialectic only if one is willing to open oneself to refutation. This Callicles is not willing to do. The terror that always lurks in a dialectical inquiry is caused by the almost certain prospect of finding out that one is not who one thinks one is. This openness requires enormous courage because in such an inquiry one risks discovering commitments that were acquired inadvertently and, even more likely, wrongs that were done unintentionally but for which the inquirer must accept responsibility.

This responsibility is the source of Plato's interest in rhetoric. Behind Socrates' commitment to dialectic is his understanding that because we are creatures born into languages and engaging in practices that are expressions of cultural or political commitments, we stand in an ethical relation to ourselves and others that has the force of feeling natural, of reflecting the order of the universe, but may, in fact, keep us apart from others and ignorant of ourselves. As a modern critical language that is self-consciously rhetorical might phrase the idea, it is our blindnesses that constitute our vision. Socrates understands that we are not in control of our lives and not in the position to give vent to natural appetites or to attach to the world by the force of our native passions, because we are cultural and not natural creatures. The dichotomy between nature and convention is false, for we can never arrive at a natural self. This impossibility, as deconstruction argues, is both logical and ontological.

It is indicative of the sophistication of *Gorgias* that it does not stop its inquiry at this point. Indeed, its final sections are particularly relevant to a critical community such as today's professoriat, which is wrestling with problems of political commitment that deconstructionist thinking seems to vitiate. Socrates' and Callicles' search for an Athenian who was a true politician is an attempt to reconstitute politics by grounding an understanding in political practice rather than in political theory. And this attempt can be read as an effort to ground their argument materially. For this reason, it becomes crucial to ask whether the dialogue has presented an inaccurate and misleading representation of Athenian political leaders. As Vickers's attack on Plato makes clear, if we take Socrates' assessment of the four Athenian leaders uncritically, we are guilty of misreading important democratic accomplishments and of failing to understand the genuine achievements of persons who used rhetoric to aid and not to flatter the polis:

> If Plato has not actually distorted the facts [in his account of the four leaders], he has "selected his details in such a way as to put the conduct of the Athenians in the worst possible light" (D[odds, *Gorgias*] 359). The walls that Socrates refers to so dismissively are "the defensively vital 'Long Walls' connecting Athens and its harbour at Peiraeus," while the dockyards at Peiraeus "were important in Athenian defence and sea power," both being "examples of shrewd and far-sighted strategic projects undertaken on the advice of popular leaders by a democratic assembly" (I[rwin, *Gorgias*] 119). (It is due to them both, one might add, that Athens enjoyed the stability that made Plato's

career at all possible!) Socrates later subsumes Themistocles' ship-building proposal under the charges of gratifying the people's desires, but he "omits to mention" that it had to compete against a "proposal to distribute the necessary money among the people," so that "it is a gross over-simplification — typical of Socrates' political comments — to suggest" that Themistocles was "just humouring political whims," and not showing statesmanly foresight in persuading the people to accept a long-term asset for national defense (I[rwin, *Gorgias*] 237). As Irwin judges, "Socrates' version of these incidents conceals the serious questions of policy sometimes at stake and the solid grounds for measures taken against these politicians. His story is a perversion of the historical conditions, as far as we know them" (I[rwin, *Gorgias*] 235). Popper's comment that "Plato's description of democracy is a vivid but intensely hostile and unjust parody of the political life of Athens" does not, perhaps, seem far out. (*Defence,* 89–90)

I quote Vickers at length because he responsibly makes important charges against Plato. No defense of Plato should slight these charges, not simply because the account of Athenian political life that Plato produces is apparently questionable but, more importantly, because this historical account is essential to his philosophical inquiry into rhetoric as a practice capable of having integrity.[3] Plato stands in need of defense.

It is hard to imagine that Plato did not intend Socrates' charges against the Athenian leaders to be challenged. Surely, Plato could not have been ignorant of the practical importance of ensuring the defense of Athens, nor could he have been blind to the political obstacles that stood in the way of any attempt to get the funds necessary for the public projects. And he could not have expected the audience of the dialogue in his day to be ignorant of these conditions. As Callicles' unsuppressible and mounting anger demonstrates, Socrates is being intentionally provocative.

Again, the dialogue anticipates the criticisms that it provokes. Socrates concedes: "My friend, I am not reproaching [Pericles and the others] any more than you are, as servants of the city. No; I think they've proved to be better servants than the present, and more capable of supplying the city with what it had an appetite for" (517b–c). There is no reason to assume that this recognition, although intended as faint praise, is meant ironically. It is an acknowledgment on Socrates' part of what these leaders accomplished. In fact, if the four Athenian leaders were not examples of civic-minded individuals, they would be inappropriate candidates for Socrates' opening of political practice to philosophical refutation.

The dialogue warns that Socrates' criticism of these leaders is not what a reader might take it to be. Socrates feels the need to reach out to Callicles at this point in their dispute to suggest that they are not in disagreement but rather that they have misunderstood each other: "Well, now we're doing a ridiculous thing, you and I in our discussion. All the time we're having a dialogue we never stop coming round to the same place all the time, with each not knowing what the other is saying" (517c). Socrates then proceeds with a crucial clarification of his position. His clarification involves a return to the analogy of rhetoric and cookery that he had made earlier, in his discussion with Polus. In that discussion Socrates had focused on cookery as a knack that lacks a logos and that accomplishes its purposes by offering an ignorant person pleasure in place of a good. He used the analogy to suggest how a practice might be perverted so that its social purpose was replaced by the individual practitioner's benefit. The example thus came to demonstrate how an unscrupulous character can corrupt a practice for personal gain. What Polus sought in rhetoric was a means to personal power that was not restricted by purposes integral to and hence limiting for a practice. Socrates, at that point, was trying to establish grounds to show that it is impossible to have a practice that is not limited by a purpose and that the mistaken pursuit of pleasure as the good produces unintentional self-injury. In effect, Socrates introduced a notion of practice that is very close to MacIntyre's idea of an internal good (*After Virtue*, 186–89). An object cannot be internally good unless it is pursued as the goal of a practice in which an appreciation of human excellence inheres.

But when Socrates returns, in his discussion of the Athenian leaders, to the analogy of cookery and rhetoric, he puts the comparison to quite a different use. He is no longer concerned with the problem that rhetoric can be corrupted to promote private ends. One can regret such abuse, but it finally does not constitute a philosophical difficulty.[4] Socrates now explores abuse that does raise such a difficulty. In his revised account of the social practices that provide the material goods necessary for human existence, the practitioners are the wholesalers, retailers, and manufacturers who in good faith produce and distribute these goods. Socrates charges them not with corruption but with ignorance: "If a vendor or a merchant or a producer of one of these things, a baker, cook, weaver, shoemaker, tanner, supplies these fulfillments of bodily appetites, it is not surprising that when he is like this, he and other people suppose that he takes care of the body. Everyone supposes this who doesn't know that there is another craft, gymnastics and medicine, besides all of these, which is really care of the body and which fittingly rules over all crafts and uses their works—for it knows what food and drink is worthy and base for the excellence (*aretē*) of the body, while all others are ignorant of it" (517e–18a).

To appreciate the shift in Socrates' argument, we need to see the force of this restatement. Socrates is no longer charging bakers, for instance, with putting themselves forward falsely as experts on bodily care. Rather, they are practicing the art of baking in good faith, and they believe that they provide a socially useful product. In defense of bakers it is reasonable to say that their practice originated as a natural response to a fundamental need: we must have food to live. Consequently our ancestors developed ways of transforming our natural environment into objects that nurture us. Baking is a conventional practice. As we are born into a world in which such practices exist and as such practices can point to a history that has confirmed their worth empirically, we will naturally and reasonably accept them as worthwhile activities. We may modify and transform them, but we have no reason to doubt their utility. At least we do not until a baker, practicing the art in good faith, produces a bread that turns out to cause some injury — just as many of our attempts to preserve food or to make it more easily available have led manufacturers in good faith to introduce preservatives into their products, and we then discover that these preservatives are carcinogenic. Often the carcinogenic effects have not immediately shown up. The damage has thus been masked, and the manufacturers, together with a society that required modernization of the food supply, have unintentionally produced serious bodily harm. It has then taken medical or nutritional researchers to point out the injury and to suggest new constraints for the production of food.

If one applies this analogy to rhetoric and political practice and, in particular, to the four leaders whom Socrates singles out for criticism, it becomes clear that he is not indicting them for intentional corruption; rather, he is suggesting that they engaged in political activity in good faith. Their purposes are what separates them from the politicians contemporary with Callicles and Socrates. Indeed, these four leaders become philosophically relevant precisely because they allow Socrates to raise a serious problem that cannot be discounted merely as a product of human corruption or incompetence. What Socrates claims is that the way the four leaders met the perceived and immediate needs of Athens caused the people an injury that is not apparent. Underlying Plato's charge is the insight that injury to others is not (at least for those who seek good) a problem of will or even finally of knowledge; rather, doing injury is an inescapable aspect of a being who is born into a world that is shaped by a language and by conventional practices that embody a particular set of values.

As far as I know, Plochmann and Robinson are the only other readers of the dialogue to grasp Plato's criticism of Pericles: "Pericles could have had the interests of the citizens at heart but he misread their real needs, giving them a supposed benefit that in the end corrupted them" (*A Friendly Companion*, 384, note 20). But this point needs to be put more forcefully if the thrust of

Plato's criticism is to be understood. If Pericles had the best interests of the citizens at heart (and he must have had for Plato's example to have a purpose), why was he unable to see their needs? Why did he injure Athens when he intended to benefit it? Plato's answer (the point of this section's discussion) is that Pericles did so because he was a bad rhetor and that his rhetorical failure was not a consequence of personal corruption. Rather, Pericles, like the bakers, pursued in good faith a set of inherited practices. His apparent successes then confirmed him in these practices. He excelled in the pragmatic discourse of parliamentary decision making that Havelock views as the basis of liberal government (*Liberal Temper,* 248–49). Such discourse moves from the citizens' beliefs and values to the discovery of a political policy. The utility of this discourse is one of the central tenets of the standard defenses of rhetoric. But what such discourse cannot do is refute the leaders and citizens, for it is directed toward finding the most efficient means and is unable to explore the polis's commitments and responsibilities. It is discourse that excludes the Other. For pragmatic discourse, the polis is given and, in its obviousness, is not subject to examination. The citizens would have no motive to examine their commitments and responsibilities to and for the polis. The goodness of their intentions is evident to them. But in Socrates' view an identity is never given prior to a discussion but is, instead, a consequence of dialectical engagement. The task of a philosophical rhetoric is to provoke such engagement by challenging the parties through conversation. This rhetoric seeks not to persuade or guide the citizens but to refute them, so that the commitments inhering in their languages, institutions, and practices will be available for them to reflect on and to reconstitute.

Underlying a pragmatic discourse's inability to lead citizens to examine commitments and responsibilities is the problem of criticizing a practice from the inside. As Nietzsche shows, this criticism requires a transvaluation of value. What liberal critics such as Popper and Havelock fear is that such criticism finally involves an appeal to an absolute standard, outside history. Their fear of the political consequences of this appeal is one source of their objection to essentialism. But Plato in his redefinition of rhetoric offers an alternative transvaluation that is radically open.[5]

What Socrates opens is the problem that he and Polus discussed about our inadvertently and inescapably injuring others, but it is no longer a simple problem that can be remedied by an individual agent consciously trying to do good. Rather, it has become generic to any action. We are born into worlds that are meaningful before we arrive, and it is part of our natural development to take them over. And although they are inescapably conventional and hence embody understandings of what reality is and what is of value, these worlds appear to us to be natural arrangements of human practices. That is, we do not feel them as distinct from us; rather, they constitute the natural forms in which we understand ourselves and others. Such historically encoded understandings make up the languages into which we are born. We act, then, in good faith in the world. But what if a language that we inherit embodies a misunderstanding of ourselves or of others? The Pericles section of the Gorgias argues that languages not only can but must embody such misunderstandings. A language's corruption is not accidental, and we cannot escape from the ethical consequences of that corruption by resolving to do good, for it is the nature of language to be inadequate to a complete representation of ourselves and others. This is, in part, because language is different from what it represents and, in part, because our natures are not fixed; or, if they are, we can nevertheless have no understanding of them in essence.

The problem of causing inadvertent suffering is of special concern to those who seek to live proper lives and to use their actions to aid the common weal. The problems for rhetoric that are philosophically troubling are not those that involve the intentional exclusion of others from the community. However upsetting is the conscious use of race, gender, class, or creed to deny a person a voice, the more disturbing insight is that we undoubtedly exclude others from the community not because we wish to do them injury or because we possess despicable motives but because we are trapped in our languages. There is no political stance that can ensure that we act justly toward others. This predicament explains *Gorgias*'s philosophical commitment to rhetorical openness. The dialogue's justification for rhetoric is that it is the one intellectual practice that allows us to live responsibly in a world in which we are inadvertent origins of others' suffering.

As creatures who have bodies, who are bodies, we are necessarily bound to act on and in a material environment and to engage in political relationships with other such actors. We do not have a choice to pursue or not to pursue the political life. The choice is whether to pursue it critically or uncritically. The confusion in which Socrates and Callicles place themselves begins by their false assumption that the political and philosophical lives can be isolated from each other. The choice that the dialogue must explore is whether one should lead a philosophically criticized political existence. Once the question is put this way, it is easy to see that there is no choice for anyone who wishes to act responsibly.

The need for a philosophical education of politics then arises not when individual actors intentionally pursue private goods at the expense of the public but when they try in good conscience to aid the polis. To the extent that political agents are acting in good faith, they will resist this education, for by the languages in which they were raised and in which they frame the values guiding their actions, they are doing a good job. To suggest otherwise is to appear either deliberately subversive or mad. The irritation and frustration felt by Callicles during the dialogue become more understandable if he is seen as speaking for a traditional view of the aristocratic life. Because Callicles has been well brought up, he can rest confident that he is pursuing a life of excellence. Socrates suggests the force of such an understanding when he sees himself and Callicles as similarly in the thrall of two loves, the will of each man captured by a person and by a practice. One's involvement with whom or what one loves does not easily lend itself to criticism, and it is natural to mistake criticism of a loved object as an attack on it, as Polus interprets Socrates' attempted refutation of Gorgias. This fact of human nature poses a serious problem, for what attaches us most deeply to life is also what we are least willing to engage critically. When in noble service of what we love, we are least able to see how we may inadvertently cause suffering.

We are not merely dispassionate beings who pursue reason; we are also passionate and historical beings inescapably entangled with and in material and social environments. If we are to be available for philosophical education, then we need an art sufficiently powerful that it can induce us to risk losing our beloved persons and practices and understandings as we seek to know them and ourselves better through a dialectical refutation. As the dialogue amply demonstrates, human beings resist education. Socrates fails to refute Polus, for example, through an inability to get Polus to open himself up to a serious inquiry into rhetoric. In one way it does not matter whether Socrates' arguments with Polus are faulty, for they are ineffective. If they succeed in silencing Polus, there is no indication that his silence is other than temporary or that Socrates has made any serious impression on him. Nor does Socrates succeed any better with Callicles, who certainly does not become convinced of the value of philosophy. Instead, Callicles learns the wrong lesson: that it is best not to talk with Socrates.

As Sophocles and Euripides will show, the power of dialectic is severely limited by the ēthos of the potential audience. If humanity had a philosophical ēthos, dialectic could proceed, but, with rare exceptions, the world agrees with Callicles that philosophical reflection is irrelevant to practical affairs. If dialectic is to help ongoing efforts at constituting communities and selves that are committed to justice, engaged in pursuing a humane excellence, and open to claims that they inadvertently exclude or injure others, then it, in turn, must seek help. Philosophy needs rhetoric. Gorgias argues that rhetoric's social utility can be understood as its ability to make technical expertise available to the community. But we need to expand this understanding so that rhetoric can make more than technical expertise available. Rhetoric needs to undertake the more difficult task of making us available for dialectical refutation. Rhetoric needs to make those who are unwilling to undergo suffering do so voluntarily. It needs to remind us that evil is not simply a problem of bad motives but that our languages inevitably limit whom we can see as human. And rhetoric needs to provoke all of us so that we do not rest content in the satisfaction of our good intentions. A philosophical rhetoric will continually seek to refute our understandings of ourselves and of others so that these understandings do not become fixed and thereby close us to the voices of others. If we cannot prevent ourselves from causing inadvertent injury, we can through a philosophical rhetoric open ourselves to claims that we have treated others unjustly.

Socrates' assertion that rhetoric is justified because it allows us to attack ourselves and the persons we love has often been dismissed as a sarcastic reduction of rhetoric (Vickers, *Defence,* 101). But for Socrates rhetoric is essential precisely because it allows us to indict ourselves and our loved ones (508b–c; 527a–c). Again, his claim is apparently outrageous and can easily be read as a mocking of rhetoric's inutility: "Then for someone's defense for his own injustice, or when his parents or his friends or his children or his native state do injustice, rhetoric is no use at all to us, Polus, unless someone supposes it is useful for the opposite purpose — that he should denounce most of all himself, then his relatives, and whatever other friend does injustice; and should not conceal the unjust action, but bring it into the open, to pay justice and become healthy; . . . he should himself be the first denouncer of himself and of the rest of his relatives, and use his rhetoric for this, to have his unjust actions exposed and get rid of the greatest evil, injustice" (480b–d). If such a claim can seem like simple mockery when taken by itself, it acquires a totally different force when read with the realizations that causing inadvertent suffering is inherent in symbolic and other forms of action and that we most resist dialectical refutation in those areas in which we are most passionately committed. The irony is that the intensity of our concern with good is what prevents us from seeking the good appropriately. For this reason, self-contradiction is not some anomaly that can be corrected simply by making sure that one's personal motives are good, but rather it is the fate of those who do not become consciously rhetorical.

The loss is not simply political. As Socrates mentions, the subject of the dialogue is what is most important for a person to know (472c–d). Unless philosophers are skillful rhetors, they will not be able to provoke the community to refute them. If refutation requires another person to proceed, philosophy itself is not possible without rhetoric. The dialogue's action demonstrates this problem. If Socrates remains in the isolation that befalls him at the end of the dialogue, he cannot practice philosophy, because there exists no one to refute him. Activities peculiar to social animals require communities and cannot be done in isolation. Although the tone of the dialogue is anything but tragic, Socrates' isolation at the end is a denouement equivalent to that of many ancient tragedies. Unless Socrates can be refuted, the *Gorgias* threatens to become the tragedy of rhetoric.

It is reasonable to believe that Plato wrote the dialogue to offer us Socrates to refute. This offering is prompted by love. The dialogue hopes to engage its readers by giving an incomplete account of rhetoric. The Pericles section, in particular, demands that we confront its own apparent injustice and try to attach appropriate responsibility to Socrates for his seemingly outrageous claims. When we respond to this demand, we become entangled with Socrates' rhetoric, and as we attempt to reconcile his character with his apparently irresponsible attacks on Pericles, we find that we are forced to question Socrates, Plato, and ourselves. As we engage Socrates' arguments and accede to, resist, or play with his reasoning and with Plato's way of presenting the dialogue, we bring ourselves into a dialectic with *Gorgias,* and we make possible a relation among Socrates, Plato, and ourselves that can take us closer to carrying out the political action that our world requires.

Further, once we get caught up in a refutation with the dialogue, our terms lose their fixed meanings. This is true for the terms *philosophy, rhetoric,* and *politics,* and it is also true for *teacher.* The dialogue's farcical opening suggests that education is going to become controversial in the dialogue, and the topic certainly does when Socrates suggests that teachers are responsible for the actions of their students. How are we to read this claim? If we read it in what I take to be its most ordinary and obvious way, the claim is outrageous. But if we put education in the context of refutation, the claim registers our responsibility in a refutative conversation. Once a refutation begins, the positions and the languages of the participants cease to be fixed. Being a teacher can no longer be read as a professional role that one assumes; rather, it marks one of two positions in the dialectic. To teach is to question, as to educate is to punish and to discipline is to heal. To fulfill one's position as a teacher is to practice philosophy as rhetoric — to understand the particularity of the other member of the refutation (that is, to recognize the historical, passionate, and rational elements of the other person as they have been brought together to constitute an individuality), to be sensitive to the language and the commitments informing that particularity, and to induce reflection on the language lived with and by the other individual. It thus is the duty of anyone who would be a citizen to become at times a teacher and in that way to promote the continual reassessment of political commitments that is needed if a community is to be just, self-controlled, courageous, open, and vital. Socrates' claim to be the only true practitioner of politics is a consequence of his willingness to assume the responsibility for being a teacher (521d). Such citizenship is what Plato offers to any reader of the dialogue.

As James Boyd White argues, the myth with which *Gorgias* closes is not an account of a life hereafter but rather an allegorical statement of the relation in which a just person stands to an Other (*When Words*, 101). Judge and the one judged stand naked before each other. The issue is whether one has the courage to present oneself for the most telling of examinations, in which motives, purposes, and commitments will not be clothed or cosmetically enhanced, and equally whether one has the courage to conduct such an examination. This understanding of courage as a political virtue makes possible the genuine sharing necessary for a community.

Such courage must also inform the act of reading the dialogue. As contemporary criticism has accommodated itself to the insight that there are no innocent critical stances, that we are "always already" in some language, we must not collapse the ideal of standing naked before a text with the impossibility of an innocent reading. The rhetorical inquiry that Plato offers does not involve a recovery of an original intention or of a presence. It seeks, instead, to open us and the texts that we read. In this respect, *Gorgias* prefigures its subsequent commentaries. It argues that reading the dialogues is an attempt not to return to some original meaning of Plato's but to engage his and the reader's own language critically. Who Plato is and what he means will be continually reinvented as readers try to be adequate to the questions raised by reading the dialogue.

It cannot be accidental that the dialogue ends self-consciously with a narrative fiction. For its end is an opening. On the most obvious level, the ending's rhetoric calls out for a reader to reconcile the form of *Gorgias* with the dialogue's apparent hostility to the content that the form embodies. Is Plato inconsistent in his ending, or is he asking us to effect a synthesis where we may see only an opposition? In our answer to this question, we will either enter into conversation with the dialogue or cast the problem off as yet another inconsistency in a polemic out of control. Either reading will entangle us in issues of justice. If the conventional histories of rhetoric have chosen what I believe is the wrong way to read the dialogue and to defend rhetoric, they have done so out of their love for both rhetoric and democracy and their deep commitment to a just discourse. I believe that the dialogue shares a love for rhetoric, promotes the genuine meetings of persons that are essential for a democracy, and tries to do justice to the complexity that it sees. Further, the dialogue tries to provoke readings like those embodied in the histories of rhetoric, for it seeks to make us speak or write on those issues about which we care most passionately. It will, following its own logic, attack those it loves so that they cannot rest content in an unreconstructed understanding of who they are but will take a risk and find out what they can become.

3

Persuasion and Refutation
Meno's Challenge

Plato's *Seventh Letter* testifies to his literary and philosophical self-consciousness.[1] Its recognition of the inadequacy of language for communicating an accurate or stable understanding of thought is as thoroughgoing a critique of representation as that of any poststructuralist. Like the poststructuralists, Plato argues against reading a text solemnly, as if its understanding can best be uncovered through an exegetical fidelity to authorial purpose. But, as most who comment on this letter immediately remark, Plato wrote. This then leads to the inevitable question: what did Plato seek to accomplish in and by his writing, if he thought that language was incapable of capturing and communicating thought? Why would anyone who believed in the futility of communicating thought write? It is not enough to recognize that an answer to this question begins by exploring the philosophical consequences of writing dialogues and by acknowledging the inherent rhetoricity of such philosophizing. Nor is it finally sufficient to show that Plato's writing contradicts itself by requiring what it seems to deny in order to act as writing.[2] Plato is fully aware of the apparent contradiction of putting a distrust of writing in writing. To turn to rhetoric as the key to Plato's writing assumes that we know what rhetoric is and that we can obviate the paradox of Plato's writing by asserting the figurative or tropological nature of communication. But as the more rigorous deconstructionists have shown, this understanding of figurative discourse is itself not stable and to pursue it thoroughly is to encounter an aporia.[3] However, unlike deconstruction, the aporia in Plato's writing is not a limit that frustrates inquiry but a necessary moment propaedeutic to inquiry. And it turns out that such inquiry is not merely edifying but practical.[4]

Plato's style itself raises issues about instruction and persuasion. Unlike the rhetors and sophists who were his contemporaries or Aristotle who came later, Plato does not offer either a set of rules or procedures to be memorized or an art of rhetoric; rather, he embodies rhetorical practice both within his dialogues and as an essential feature structuring his differing dialogues. He places his readers in aporetic situations that parallel or follow upon those of Socrates' interlocutors within the dialogue. It is precisely the reader's experience — the aporia generated by the text — that makes rhetoric a philosophical issue. Stanley Fish labels such a text as dialectical: "A dialectical presentation, on the other hand, is disturbing, for it requires of its readers a searching and rigorous scrutiny of everything they believe in and live by. It is didactic in a special sense; it does not preach the truth, but asks that its readers discover the truth for themselves, and this discovery is often made at the expense not only of a reader's opinions and values, but of his self-esteem" (*Self-Consuming Artifacts,* 1–2). The dialectical structure of the dialogue induces a kind of reading that becomes part of an alternative education designed to make citizens who are gentle and also capable of meeting their audiences in the radical particularity that must be assumed if a rhetor is to act justly toward an audience and not simply manipulate it.[5] The situations in the dialogues repeatedly demand that the readers assess not only the arguments or myths set forth but also the motives and, by extension, the characters. These demands lead ineluctably to the reader's making judgments that prove to be wrong, obtuse, hasty, partial, or fail in a variety of other ways. Through this process of taking positions that must be rethought the reader becomes implicated in the issues of the dialogue and his or her understanding is then put in play. To read Plato is to engage the issue of being an adequate reader, and this, in turn, raises the issue of being an adequate — that is, a just — citizen.

As the early dialogues frequently dramatize, the failure of characters to make philosophic progress is due as much to their ethical and political limitations as to their intellectual limits. The dialogues become an extended instruction in political tolerance and continual exploration of the practical possibilities of freedom and justice. Inevitably, the dialogues pose the questions "what is persuasion?" and "how does persuasion function as a fundamental element in the practical and intellectual lives of any polis that is a product not merely of accident or force?" All of which is to say that for Plato rhetoric is not a technē to be learned but something like a more complicated practice (a bios) that is both deeply self-reflective and constantly creative, diagnosing the particular ēthos of a particular audience and tailoring a discourse that can lead that audience to reconstitute itself as a political body no longer enslaved by the received understandings that pass for wisdom but desirous of avoiding self-deception and of forming itself through an ongoing public discourse that discovers where justice lies. In his rhetoric Plato seeks not the utopia of an ideal state but critical, though generous, inquiries into those topics out of which citizens acting in concert can construct a viable human community guided by a respect for justice.

Socrates' practice in the dialogues is refutation.[6] To understand Plato's writing and to be able to speak about his rhetoricity requires first understanding philosophical rhetoric as a necessary consequence of a desire for justice by creatures born into language. To frame the Socratic elenchus in this way is to challenge analytic philosophy's understanding of the nature of argument in Plato. The most recent and powerful analytic account of Plato's elenchus has been developed by Gregory Vlastos in his attempt to articulate the operation of a Socratic philosophy in the early dialogues.[7] Vlastos's account of the elenchus is important for two reasons. First, he analyzes the elenchus as a particular type of syllogism, and second, he then argues that the premises required to make this syllogism work are deeply flawed and that Plato's recognition of this led him to abandon the elenchus as an unsatisfactory philosophical method. I shall challenge both of Vlastos's claims by arguing that refutation in Plato should be read as flexible rhetorical practice and not a logical form. Further, I shall argue that only by understanding the need for refutation that arises because we are rhetorical creatures can we understand how Plato's dialogues work as both philosophy and writing. This will lead us to understand how reading Plato's dialogues entangles us in a lifelong search for justice in which we can never achieve our goal but which nonetheless engenders not a futile life but rather the fullest life that one can lead.

For Vlastos, the problem of the elenchus arises because of a logical gap: "How is it that Socrates claims to have proved a thesis false when, in point of logic, all he has proved in any given argument is that the thesis is inconsistent with the conjunction of agreed-upon premises for which no reason has been given in that argument?" ("Socratic Elenchus," 49). What troubles Vlastos about Socrates' exchanges with his various antagonists in the early dialogues is Socrates' apparent blindness to the logical difficulties that inhere within the form of argument that he employs. He believes that Socrates' claims to seek and, at times, to have discovered truth are possible only if Socrates had operated under certain assumptions that he has never made explicit. Working backward from the form of the argument, Vlastos uncovers these assumptions. Then, having made the assumptions explicit, he shows how untenable they are. This demonstration, in turn, provides a crucial moment in Vlastos's history of Plato's movement from Socratic moralist to metaphysician. The logical conundrums of the elenchus provoke a behind-the-scenes philosophical crisis for Plato that, according to Vlastos, can be resolved only by developing a metaphysics that guarantees both the reach and the stability of Socrates' argument.

Behind Vlastos's criticism of the Socratic elenchus lies a questionable assumption. While acknowledging that the Socrates of the early dialogues displays no interest in justifying his methods of arguing, Vlastos assumes that Socrates must believe that the force of his arguments derives from their capacity to entail logically the conclusions they discover. Thus Vlastos is led to postulate a standard elenchus and to claim that it is equivalent to a logical form of argument that Aristotle calls "peirastic," in which "a thesis is refuted when, and only when its negation is derived 'from the answerer's own beliefs,' [*Sophistic Refutations* 165b3–5]" (*Socrates,* 111). Vlastos makes this claim because he believes that the only force sufficient to change or secure belief is logical validity: "How do you 'compel' your adversary to affirm what he denies? In an argument your only means of compulsion are logical. *So to compel Polus to 'witness' for not-p Socrates would have to give Polus a logically compelling proof that p is false*" ("Socratic Elenchus," 48, emphasis Vlastos's). This claim immediately raises two questions: (1) is it true that the *only* means of compulsion in an argument are logical? And (2) whether this claim is true or not, is there any evidence that Socrates or Plato subscribes to such a view? My answer to both of these questions is no.

Richard McKim has argued that Socrates' method in *Gorgias* is "psychological, not logical" ("Shame and Truth," 36–37). Socrates' arguments are founded on the efficacy of invoking shame in his interlocutors. McKim argues that Socrates sees shame as a natural sign that reveals what one actually believes and that therefore it can be a very effective authority in making one come to understand what he or she really believes (39). Shame thus offers an alternative means of compulsion to logic. Its force is seen in *Republic* 1 when Thrasymachus blushes (350d).

The dialogues seem to be deeply skeptical about the efficacy of logic or of logic alone to compel belief. Socrates rarely convinces his interlocutors in his early dialogues. Even when he has logically confounded them, they grant little authority to such logic. As Adimantus remarks:

> No one, Socrates, would be able to controvert these statements of yours. But, all the same, those who occasionally hear you argue thus feel in this way. They

> think that owing to their inexperience in the game of question and answer they are at every question led astray a little bit by argument, and when these bits are accumulated at the conclusion of the discussion mighty is their fall, and the apparent contradiction of what they at first said, and that just as by expert draughts players the unskillful are finally shut in and cannot make a move, so they are finally blocked and have their mouths stopped by this other game of draughts played not with counters but with words: yet the truth is not affected by that outcome. (*Republic*, 487b–c)

Adimantus is merely one of many characters who point out to Socrates the ineffectiveness of his contradictions. So both the dramatic structures of the early dialogues and the explicit comments in the dialogues suggest strongly that Plato did not assume that logic, in fact, compelled audiences. Indeed, if it did, there would be no need for a dialogue form, and instead arguments could be put forth in the pristine form of unembellished syllogisms. But precisely because he knows that people would rather ignore logic than be compelled to renounce a belief they hold dear, Plato needs to go beyond logic to rhetoric and to worry about the conditions of persuasion. This does not mean that persuasion is accomplished either easily or frequently but rather that the issue of changing a belief or compelling a change of belief is a rhetorical and not a logical problem for Plato.

But the need for an airtight syllogism with its ability to compel agreement leads Vlastos to first postulate a logical difficulty and then find the solution to this difficulty in *Gorgias*. As Vlastos sees it, Socrates' refutation in its apparent claim to discover truth needs a certain premise that will allow Socrates to proceed confidently in his questioning of others. This assumed premise is: "Anyone who ever has a false moral belief will always have at the same time true beliefs entailing the negation of that false belief" ("Socratic Elenchus," 52; see also *Socrates*, 113–14). Vlastos admits that Socrates never says this and also that if he were to make this assumption, he could not defend it — at least, he could not defend it independent of the metaphysics that Plato was to develop in the middle dialogues. Still, if Socrates believes that refutation can move from the discovery of inconsistency to the claim that this discovery shows a belief to be false, then he needs some premise that allows him to go from inconsistency, which is a problem of formal validity, to falsehood, which is a problem of the relation of a particular claim to a larger, external whole. But such a premise invites challenge: what reasonable assurance is there that one possesses even one true belief if all that the elenchus can discover is that at this point in time two beliefs held by the interlocutor are merely inconsistent. Why cannot both beliefs be false? Vlastos believes that it was the pressure of such epistemological questions that led Plato to his doctrine of recollection to render coherent Socrates' ongoing search for truth. Metaphysics comes to the rescue of morality.

But it turns out that Socrates' logical difficulties are not merely formal problems. Like many commentators, Vlastos recognizes that the Socratic elenchus is intended to have existential consequences. Formal problems suggest both flaws in the instrument and the possible inadequacy of the instrument to achieve its purpose. Socrates pursues refutations not for their own sake but to help him discover the noblest way to live. The discovery of truth is justified by the contribution that knowledge of truth will play in the direction of a noble life. Again, working backward, Vlastos can ask what confidence Socrates has that his negative elenchic discoveries will aid in the positive search for truth. Underlying the analysis of Socrates' formal problems is Vlastos's psychological hypothesis that for Socrates the potentially corrosive effects of the elenchus are offset by another belief of Socrates. According to Vlastos, Socrates could relentlessly pursue his undermining of contemporary beliefs because this negative pursuit was authorized by a belief in the positive consequence to be achieved through a series of negative arguments. What sustained Socrates was his conviction that the elenchus discovered truth, that it not only disclosed the confusion inhering in an unreflective stance toward a received ethical tradition but also established conclusions that were true.

Vlastos's textual support for this reading occurs in *Gorgias,* 479e, when Socrates in concluding his elenchus with Polus claims that it has now been proved true that one who does injustice and escapes punishment is more wretched than one who is punished for wrongdoing. But can this one sentence bear the weight that Vlastos wants it to? Is Socrates giving a considered judgment that is the conclusion of an inquiry into the epistemological status of the elenchus? How seriously is Socrates affirming the truth of the particular conclusion to which he has dragged Polus screaming and kicking? The dialogue itself cautions a reader against reading any statement as a literal avowal of either an implicit or explicit position. Later in the dialogue, Socrates is quite explicit when he states that he does not possess the truth. Having silenced Gorgias, Polus, and Callicles, Socrates says first: "So, then, I shall continue the discussion as seems best to me; but if anyone of you thinks that any statement of mine is contrary to the truth, he should take issue with me and refute it. For it is by no means from any real knowledge that I make my statements: It is, rather, a search in common with the rest of you, so that if my opponent's objection has any force, I shall be the first to admit it" (506a). A short time later, he asserts again the provisional nature of his understanding: "Remember that my position has always been the same: though I have no real knowledge of the truth of these matters, yet just as on the present occasion, I have never encountered anyone who was able to maintain a different position in such a discussion and not come off covered with ridicule" (509a). These later claims contradict the earlier claim if we take the earlier claim to truth literally. However, if we take it as shorthand for the claim that the elenchus, as it has been conducted, has led to this conclusion and that this conclusion makes a claim on us to either accept it or to challenge it again, then there is no conflict between Socrates' earlier and later claims. Further, if we read Socrates' claim to truth to be less absolute, it fits better the continual reoccurrence of the aporias in the dialogues.

To see a more epistemologically cautious Socrates is to challenge Vlastos's account of Socrates' psychology. Vlastos seems to feel that without some sort of belief in the final efficacy of his questioning, then Socrates would lack reasons for continuing his search. But again both Vlastos's view of Socrates and his account of a psychology necessary to persevere in a climate of recurring and pervasive doubt are questionable. Richard Kraut sees a Socrates who is more subject to doubt and who rests uncomfortably with his own conclusions, and Kraut believes that "when he [Socrates] contrasts the small, human wisdom that he possesses — a wisdom that cannot teach virtue — with the greater wisdom of the gods, he is seriously entertaining the possibility that the full science of virtue may be beyond a human being's capacity to acquire and teach" ("Comments," 69). Socrates' use of the elenchus supports Kraut's picture of a less secure Socrates.

It is worth asking why Socrates seeks self-knowledge by questioning others, especially when he continually fails to make progress toward his own enlightenment even as he exposes the confusion of others. If we assume that Socrates is engaged seriously in attempting to fulfill the commands of the Delphic oracle and that he is not simply engaging in an altruistic educational enterprise, then it is reasonable to assume that he does not feel that he has achieved truth, but that he is entitled to some confidence in his understanding because it is empirically confirmed by its withstanding attempted refutations. Also, if one takes seriously Socrates' concerns with action and their connection with courage and justice, then there is no need to analyze his psychology, as Vlastos does, and require some postulate that would reassure Socrates as to the truth of his project. Rather, if Socrates feels powerfully the problem of doing injustice to another, then such a concern could motivate a continual desire to be just in a world in which he recognized that one's relations with others are not mediated by knowledge but that the just person must always be prepared to stand naked in front of the other.

Thomas C. Brickhouse and Nicholas D. Smith develop a fuller account of the elenchus by arguing that Socrates sees it as more than a pursuit of logical contradiction.[8] They emphasize that "Socrates sees himself, not merely as engaging in an important intellectual enterprise, but as 'fighting for what is just' (32A 1–3)" ("Socrates' Elenchic Mission," 131). Further, they recognize the protrepic aspect of the elenchus: "But given the goals of his mission which Socrates articulates in the *Apology*, the point of interrogating all who think they know is not merely to shame them, but rather to encourage them to seek the best sort of life" (153). As they lay out the multiple purposes of Socrates' use of his elenchus, they are led to recognize its inherent rhetoricity: "It follows that the elenchus is a tool for normative persuasion intended to make a real difference in the actions people undertake" (156). The larger purposes of the elenchus suggest that it might be profitable to seek a solution to what has been considered to be a logical difficulty (the move from consistency to truth) by looking at the elenchus as a rhetorical practice.

Hugh H. Benson's analysis of the elenchus as a dialectical method supports such an inquiry. In arguing in support of the nonconstructionist position, Benson sets forth three methods of argumentation: the sophistical, the demonstrative, and the dialectical.[9] The sophistical is clearly rhetorical, for it aims to persuade someone about a proposition; the demonstrative qualifies as logical, for its concern is with validity; the dialectical borrows from each of these two methods and attempts to persuade a particular person through a sound argument ("Problem of the Elenchus," 71). Like Brickhouse and Smith, Benson emphasizes the need of the elenchus to address the audience in its particularity and to make the important distinction between validity and persuasion. In effect, he is arguing that an audience need not be compelled by a syllogism merely because its form is sound. The logic of the argument does not necessarily translate into practical consequences.

But in laying out his three argumentative methods, Benson also displays philosophy's suspicion of persuasion. Persuasion initially enters his categories in his account of the sophistical method. The criterion that governs persuasion is the success or failure of a speaker in changing an audience's conviction. Benson argues that there are no constraints on this method; anything that works counts. The role of a demonstrative method is to provide the constraint that lends respectability to a dialectical argument. It is worth asking whether such an understanding of persuasion is sufficient or whether persuasion does, in fact, bring certain constraints with it if the change of conviction is to count as persuasion and not as some other type of change. For example, we ordinarily do not treat changes of conviction wrought through deception as persuasion. Also, persuasion seems to suggest a stability to the change of belief. This does not mean the change of belief needs to be permanent, but it must remain for a certain time or else we say that one was not really persuaded. So persuasion itself may provide Socrates with an authority for his elenchus that is different in kind than the authority of logical validity and cannot be reduced to mere unconstrained efficacy with an audience.

It helps to understand the force and authority of persuasion by returning to the claim by Brickhouse and Smith that Socrates tests not only propositions but more importantly lives. This suggests that the elenchus imagines and requires a broader context than is possible when it is considered only as a logical operation. If the consistency at issue is not merely that of a particular syllogism but that of a structure of beliefs as it is informed by the experience, history, taste, and self-images of a particular person, then it needs to address both the individual's multiple and special authorities. James Boyd White's analysis of Socrates' strategy of attacking Callicles through a series of shameful images provides a good example of the larger issue of consistency at work in an elenchus.

But the context in which refutation is to work needs to be broadened still further, so that its focus is not merely individuals in their full historical particularity but the life of a polis as a polis. Most analyses of the elenchus proceed atomistically, investigating Socrates' success or failure with a particular individual and ignoring the larger social dimension of Socrates' practice. Socrates' individual refutations are part of an ongoing process that transcends the individual and acquires a civic purpose as he makes clear in his famous image of the gadfly: "It is literally true, even if it sounds rather comical, that God has specially appointed me to this city, as though it were a large thorough-bred horse which because of its great size is inclined to be lazy and needs the stimulation of some stinging fly. It seems to me that God attached me to this city to perform the office of such a fly, and all day long I never cease to settle here, there, and everywhere, rousing, persuading, and reproving every one of you" (30e). Through his individual refutations Socrates pursues his divinely ordained civic mission. Refutation then is not merely a form of argument but a form of life, a bios. And like any other form of life, it is not to be judged atomistically but as a process. This makes the key issue not the success or failure of a particular argument but rather Socrates' ability and commitment to a life of continual openness and challenge.

Socrates' most important interlocutor is the city itself. The city in its multiplicity of perspectives, beliefs, and bioi provides both the challenge and the resource for Socrates' mission. For Socrates a premature and self-deceiving belief that one has discovered the truth is a continual and serious danger for a philosophic life. One challenge that the city provides is the continual difference in perspectives that arises from the many differences among its citizens. Such differences can be a resource for an ongoing inquiry that is continually challenged to establish the authority of its conclusions when asked new and different questions by citizens whose interests arise from their different positions within the polis. Also, the common or shared identity of a city, if stable, is never fixed or final. Like an individual's self-understanding, a city's understanding of its values and commitments is continually undergoing revision, since it is necessarily located within both the determination and contingency of history and nature. Brickhouse and Smith are right to suggest that the "process [of self-knowledge through refutation] may never be complete," but the point has to be made even more strongly ("Socrates' Elenchic Mission," 147). The process can never be completed as long as the city is alive because the city grows and changes, and hence what it is is in flux. Within such flux, there is, of course, more or less stability, as with any individual life. And while Socrates may be entitled to some confidence concerning the soundness of the elenchus from an induction based on his past successes, the nature of his enterprise precludes his reaching knowledge. Indeed, any intellectual process is finally valued to the degree that it contributes to Socrates' ongoing inquiries into justice.

The problem of the elenchus, then, is answered not by logically securing propositions but by embedding philosophical discourse in a society. This is a rhetorical problem — one whose magnitude is as great as any logical difficulties that Socrates may have been thought to encounter. His rhetorical task is to constitute Athens as his audience. What he needs to do as gadfly is to sting Athens into a kind of action. He needs to make the citizens willing to assume the role of judge, and this is to make them take a responsibility for their individual lives and the lives of the city. If the citizens can become judges and learn to function critically, then discourse can become a resource for the city to constitute and reconstitute itself. Rhetoric would cease to be some instrumentality and instead become the resource through which the city could pursue justice. Socrates' initial challenge is to make the city desire to be rhetorical; the rhetorical task of refutation is to induce a political eros. Such desire cannot be brought about through teaching, but refutation may be able to engender or provoke or awaken such desire. It may very well be that virtue cannot be taught, but it is still not futile to discuss virtue because it may be possible to persuade someone to seek virtue. Rhetoric would then become both the means by which someone is initiated into the philosophic life and the way in which such a life was conducted. For such a philosophy to be, it would have to be public. In an important way, understanding would cease to be the possession of individuals and would, instead, be a collectively held bios open to all in the city who would open themselves. Civic life would then become a continual public discussion of justice.

In pursuit of such discussions, Socrates began by examining those with a reputation for being most knowledgeable. He examined politicians, poets, and skilled craftsmen — all who have a claim to know something. But his practice of the elenchus extends finally to everyone in the city, as he makes clear in the *Apology* when he rejects the possibility of being let off the charges if he no longer engages in refutation: "Well, supposing, as I said, that you should offer to acquit me on these terms [that I cease refuting people], I should reply, Gentlemen, I am your very grateful and devoted servant, but I owe a greater obedience to God than to you, and so long as I draw breath and have my faculties, I shall never stop practicing philosophy and exhorting you and elucidating the truth for everyone that I meet" (*Apology,* 29d). And as the *Meno* shows, Socrates is willing to extend his examinations even to slaves. The only restriction on an interlocutor is that the person must speak Greek. In theory, the elenchus should work on anyone in the polis.

In practice, it seems to have only limited success, and in this it seems to contrast poorly with the techniques of the rhetors that apparently can be mastered with little difficulty by most. This contrast is brought out explicitly in the issue of the nature and efficacy of persuasion that pervades Socrates' engagements with Gorgianic rhetoric. In *Gorgias* Socrates and Gorgias agree that persuasion is distinct from teaching, and they further agree to limit rhetoric to persuasion alone, since it achieves conviction without possessing knowledge. In *Meno*, Socrates and Gorgias seem to be in agreement that virtue cannot be taught, but an important division between them emerges over how one should proceed if virtue cannot be taught. According to Meno, Gorgias believes that people should be taught to speak (95c). Does this then mean that Gorgias believes that rhetoric, or at least his version of rhetoric, can be an acceptable substitute for virtue? Does Gorgias's recommendation to learn to speak well argue that discussions of virtue are irrelevant and that one's concern should not be to be virtuous but to be effective? Rhetoric would then become an alternative to virtue and philosophy. A Gorgianic rhetoric would allow one to make his or her way in the world and would hence be a sort of course in survival skills. If so, then Gorgias's understanding of rhetoric challenges a Socratic rhetoric and its philosophical and political projects, for in Meno, Socrates meets a character who has been shaped, in part, by another mode of rhetoric. In the *Protagoras,* Socrates claimed that it was safe to converse with the sophists if one had an antidote to counteract their teaching. Has Gorgias given such an antidote to Meno so that he can resist a refutation by Socrates? At the very least, Meno presents Socrates with the problem of being effective with an audience whose own training provides a stance with which to resist refutation. *Meno* thus becomes a dialogue of particular importance to the viability of a

Socratic rhetoric, and Meno, a student of Gorgias, presents an occasion for Plato to explore both the necessity and limit of a Socratic rhetoric.

In the *Meno*, Meno is portrayed as a student of Gorgias. He not only touts Gorgias's understanding of virtue but has been formed by a Gorgianic education in rhetoric. He confidently displays his skills to Socrates. And Socrates attributes the current state of affairs in Larissa to Gorgias's teaching. What was a materially prospering city has now also become one that conceives of itself as philosophically well endowed, as it has fallen in love with Gorgias's wisdom.[10] Socrates contrasts the philosophic self-assurance of Larissa with the pervasive self-doubt of Athens. Meno, like his city, is taken with himself and views the world as a relatively straightforward place for action. Everything appears to be easy. This is the self-comfort that Socrates must perplex.

As Sternfeld and Zyskind note, the dialogue opens abruptly with a question that lacks a context (*Plato's Meno*, 20). Meno simply asks: "Can you tell me, Socrates, whether virtue is acquired by teaching or practice; or if neither by teaching nor practice, then whether it comes to man by nature, or in what other way?" (70a). The design of this opening raises the problem of what motivates Meno's question. Is it a genuine question asked by a character seeking to be informed about virtue, or is it a question from someone who does not really believe that there are serious difficulties raised by the question? Put another way: is it a philosophical question? A reading of the dialogue will depend upon how this question is taken, for to decide whether the question is serious, the reader must take a position on the character of Meno. Is he a candidate for a philosophical education and hence someone capable of undergoing refutation, or is he someone who would prefer to evade the rigors of the elenchus?

The Meno who emerges in the dialogue turns out to be anything but philosophical. He is clearly an attractive character and one accustomed to getting his own way. Socrates calls his self-indulgence tyrannical and suggests that there is a connection between Meno's penchant for taking the easy way and the political values nurtured in a city that has been educated by Gorgias: "But as you think only of controlling me who am your slave, and never of controlling yourself—such being your notion of freedom—I must yield to you who are irresistible" (86e). Meno understands freedom simply as getting what he wants, as being in a situation in which there are no obstacles that resist his will. And it is precisely his nurtured fondness for self-indulgence and his predilection for things that come easy that create the rhetorical challenge for Socrates. Although apparently talented, Meno resists the rigor of a philosophical life for the same reason that many privileged young people resist serious education: their allegiance is to a life of comfort. Meno is willing to dabble in philosophy, but he is not willing to work at it. In its affirmation that rhetoric provides an easy way for dealing with problems, a Gorgianic education has given Meno not a position that challenges the Socratic enterprise but a self-contentment that resists the operation of refutation. Confident in his own attractiveness and in his natural abilities, Meno simply does not take the issues that he discusses seriously; rather, discussion for him is more recreational — offering either diversion or an opportunity for personal display.

The reason for the lack of context for Meno's opening question becomes clear: there is no particular motive behind the question; it does not arise from any abiding problem that Meno faces. It is not even certain that the question is, in fact, even a casual request for enlightenment, for, as soon becomes apparent, Meno believes that he knows what virtue is. So when he asks Socrates about the way in which virtue is acquired, he may very well be angling for an opening to show Socrates what he has learned from Gorgias. Socrates certainly is not convinced that Meno is serious. The heavily ironic tone of Socrates' response — his excessive praise of Larissa — suggests that he considers Meno and his fellow citizens to have inflated self-images, as they now all ape the grand and bold style of Gorgias, a style that allows him to answer all questions on any topic.

Socrates' response to Meno and, in particular, his claim to know nothing about virtue catches Meno by surprise. So much so that Meno has to ask if Socrates is in earnest. Meno is taken aback by a discursive style that is plain and constrained. Meno's response suggests that he is momentarily confused as to how to read Socrates. Braggadocio is supposed to be met by braggadocio, not by an admission of ignorance. But in meeting Meno in this unanticipated way Socrates manages to pique his interest. This is an important preliminary move if Socrates is to transform a question that has no recoverable motive into an occasion for serious inquiry. In his unorthodox response, Socrates has become interesting to Meno; this interest may blossom into a motive for asking the kinds of questions that Meno seems to merely play with.

If Meno is not fully certain about how to read Socrates, he is nonetheless supremely confident in his understanding of what virtue is. His pride in his Gorgianic education quickly surfaces as he boasts of Gorgias's knowledge and admits that he shares Gorgias's views. It turns out that for Meno nothing could be easier than saying what virtue is, as he immediately launches into what appears to be a definition, in all likelihood one that was learned from Gorgias.

Meno's first definition of virtue is a straightforward enumeration of the duties that are appropriate to the different ages and genders. Socrates will quickly put this definition into question, but the dramatic play of the dialogue will also raise questions about this answer. First, if the knowledge of virtue is so unproblematic, why did Meno raise any question about the acquisition of virtue? Second, how does such a straightforward account of what virtue is square with Meno's later claim that Gorgias laughs at those who try to teach virtue? For as Meno has presented virtue, the teaching of it ought to be a simple matter. That he does not see the incoherence in his and Gorgias's position suggests how unexamined that position really is. His has not been an education of questioning but one of accepting, and what he has apparently accepted are formulaic accounts of how things are that have the particularly attractive feature of making the world unproblematic, of being a place in which one who holds the simple formulas can answer all questions.

Socrates begins gently to undermine the thrall of Gorgias that has overtaken Meno, for Meno is not an entrenched cynic given over to some opportunistic method of exploitation, but a young man caught up in the excitement of entering a world of intellectual discussion. His headiness is that of a young person who has felt the attractiveness and power of a sophisticated mind. Further, his progress under Gorgias and the ease with which it occurred have flamed his infatuation with his ability to speak well. What Socrates needs to do is to use the energy of Meno's infatuation and redirect it to philosophy. He must change both the object and the force of that desire.

To pick up a theme central to the dialogue, Socrates cannot teach Meno to desire to engage in the philosophic life nor can he teach him philosophy, but he can attempt to persuade him of the desirability of such a pursuit by displaying the attractiveness and power of the philosophic life. If, as the dialogue will provisionally conclude, virtue is not knowledge and hence cannot be taught, then persuasion becomes an especially important potential alternative to instruction, for its task becomes the inculcation of desire, and rhetoric assumes a contributory role in the production of virtuous citizens. The difficulties in creating such desires and in tying down emerging understandings of political virtue become the philosophical center of the dialogue, as its dramatic development lays out the importance of rhetoric and raises serious questions as to its efficacy.

Under Socrates' prompting Meno offers a series of definitions of virtue, all of which fail by producing multiplicity where Socrates sought unity. But, as is always the case in Plato, the failures are instructive, and in Meno's repeated attempts some progress is made. Meno, however, is quickly frustrated and questions the value of the kind of answers that Socrates gives as a model of how to define a term. This prompts Socrates to explain to Meno how a refutation proceeds: "I should have told him the truth [when I said that figure is the only thing that always follows color]. And if he were a philosopher of the eristic and antagonistic sort, I should say to him: you have my answer, and if I am wrong, your business is to take up the argument and refute me. But if we were friends, and we were talking as you and I are now, I should reply in a milder strain and more in the dialectician's vein; that is to say, I should not only speak the truth, but I should make use of the premises which the person interrogated would be willing to admit. And this is the way in which I shall endeavor to approach you" (75c–d). Socrates' account of refutation is intended, in part, to allay Meno's increasing frustration and to make explicit the friendship and genuine concern that prompts such refutation. The distinction between eristic and dialectical refutation involves the stance of the two parties.[11] Eristic refutation assumes the form of an intellectual combat; dialectical refutation takes the form of a shared exploration. One does not seek to triumph over the other member of the refutation but to use the process of questioning to lead that person to understand what he or she really believes. Meno is a prime candidate for such questioning because his youth precludes his having the inflexible character that could be challenged only by combat, while his incoherent views on virtue stand in need of the rigorous rehearsal and revision that an elenchus can provide.

However, it is not clear that Meno really wants the benefits that refutation appears to offer, and it becomes increasingly clear that he is unwilling to submit to the frustration and discomfort that are necessary parts of the growth that occurs during a refutation. And, like many other characters who become discombobulated during the refutation, he begins to blame Socrates for his feeling inadequate rather than seeing this feeling as a motive for improvement:

> O Socrates, I used to be told, before I knew you, that you were always doubting yourself and making others doubt; and now you are casting your spells over me, and I am simply getting bewitched and enchanted, and am at my wits' end. And if I may venture to make a jest on you, you seem to me both in your appearance and in your power over others to be very like the flat torpedo fish, who torpifies those who come near him and touch him, as you have now torpified me, I think. For my soul and tongue are really torpid, and I do not know how to answer you; and though I have been delivered of an infinite variety of speeches about virtue before now, and to many persons — and very good ones they were, as I thought — at this moment I cannot even say what virtue is. And I think that you are very wise in not voyaging and going away from home, for if you did in other places as you do in Athens, you would be cast into prison as a magician. (79e–80b)

Meno's complaint introduces two important topics: (1) when one is refuted by Socrates, both tongue and soul become torpid — one's normal way of speaking ceases to work, and one's way of making sense of the world is thrown into confusion, and (2) because Socrates engages in such refutations, he is at considerable political risk. Refutative torpidity is a key moment for rhetoric. If prior to the elenchus the interlocutor could rest comfortably in the unexamined and comforting belief that his or her understanding was in fine shape, no such comfort is possible once the refutation begins its corrosive examination. If a refutation is working, one is uncomfortable with how one understands oneself because the self-image that had formerly been a sense of pride and self-satisfaction is no longer possible. This creates the possibility for a new openness. But it requires the interlocutor not to hide from his shame but to resolve to reform himself so that there will be no future reason to have shame. The interlocutor is offered the chance of becoming a judge in a new way. In the *Republic* Socrates explains refutation to Thrasymachus as allowing one to assume a new position: "But if, as in the preceding discussion, we come to terms with one another as to what we admit in the inquiry, we shall be ourselves both judges and pleaders" (348b). To become a judge of one's own discourse and ultimately of one's own life is to adopt a critical posture toward oneself, to make oneself the subject of an inquiry. In the move from unreflective self-contentment to a reflective self-doubt, one's relationship to the world changes, for one assumes a new responsibility for both tongue and soul. Indeed, in this exploration of their language, the parties in a refutation can uncover ways in which their souls have been formed. That is why both tongue and soul become torpid, for it is not simply that a language has encountered some difficulties that could be met theoretically by a strategic revision in the way things are put, but rather that things can no longer be put.

But as *Republic* 1 shows, and as Socrates mentions elsewhere, there are ethical and political consequences that follow on experiencing such a state. If one can tolerate the discomfort, an internal reform begins and a character like Thrasymachus can become gentler. This gentleness is bred out of a new humility and leads to a new tolerance. It is a disposition that is essential if there is to be public discussion of justice. So the first order of business for a Socratic rhetoric is to reform its current audiences so that they can assume this new posture that is both critical and tolerant. What Socrates is asking his audiences to give up is the security of a fixed understanding that usually works to congratulate the audience for being who it is, for such an understanding can only be defensive and constantly engaged in protecting a complimentary self-image.

Given the preliminary rhetorical task of the Socratic elenchus, a philosophical inquiry is necessarily political. So it should not be surprising that Meno would move easily from his personal discomfort to the political danger that Socrates incurs when he examines someone else's language. In his critiques of ideology — of the unexamined languages that have sway over the characters —

Socrates engages and challenges political life not on the surface level of particular policies but on the deep level of the inherent justice or injustice of the city. When he calls the individual interlocutors to account for their words, he is also calling them to account for their city. The elenchus not only engenders intellectual doubt but more importantly demands political accountability. The deep defensiveness that so often arises in someone undergoing refutation is not merely a register of intellectual discomfort but a display of that person's wrestling with and attempting to suppress shame. The incoherence revealed by the elenchus is as much ethical and political as it is intellectual. If such rhetoric can succeed, it is a very powerful political resource in the pursuit of justice.

Meno's attempt to deny the possibility of serious inquiry can be read as a response to the threat to his self-image posed by a Socratic refutation. When his characterization of Socrates as a torpedo fish fails to dissuade Socrates from going on with the refutation, Meno then argues for the futility of an inquiry that starts from the ignorance of both participants. Socrates' reply has been considered by Vlastos and some others as marking a serious departure in the Platonic corpus, as Plato moves into theorizing about the nature of knowledge. His theory of recollection and its demonstration in his exchange with the slave boy are supposed to mark the shift to metaphysics.

The problem with this reading is that it ignores the rhetorical purpose that guides Socrates' response. A look at the design of the response helps make clear the rhetorical nature of the elenchus.[12] Socrates could take Meno's objection as a serious announcement of an epistemological skepticism, and he could then attempt to develop arguments that would demonstrate the possibility of knowledge and hence the purposiveness of inquiry. Instead, Socrates takes Meno to be challenging the desirability of practicing inquiry more than the possibility of practicing it. He sees the epistemological skepticism as a cover for an ethical indolence. Meno's objection is entangled with problems of how virtue is acquired, and it anticipates the subsequent discussion that seeks to displace a discussion of virtue from ethical and political contexts into epistemological contexts. The thrust of Socrates' refutation is evident in the comment that he makes to Meno after he has completed the demonstration: "Some things I have said of which I am not altogether confident. But that we shall be better and less helpless if we think we ought to inquire than we should have been if we indulged in the idle fancy that there is no use in seeking to know what we do not know — that is a theme upon which I am ready to fight, in word and deed, to the utmost of my power" (86b–c).

This comment is also important in revealing the tentativeness with which Socrates puts forth his account of recollection. This should be a reminder that this account of knowledge as recollection is not a straightforward enunciation of a theory but rather a figured representation that calls attention to its own distant and possibly fanciful origins.

To answer Meno's objection Socrates does not challenge his claims or undermine his terms but instead tells a story. The refutation will be narrative rather than syllogistic; its intent will be to make a motive available in the light of a skeptical attack. It will not challenge the skepticism directly by showing how it might entangle itself in a contradiction; rather, it will attempt to create a desire sufficiently powerful that the motive force of the skepticism will be vanquished. Recollection will be offered as a myth and not as a theory. Its original authority is not some act of mind but divine and poetic inspiration. Hence it is not subject to syllogistic proof but instead operates as a powerful image that ought to engage a soul capable of virtue. To treat recollection and the immortality of the soul as the presentation of a metaphysical doctrine is to distort Socrates' attempted refutation by refusing to recognize the strategy that necessitates the particular rhetorical solution.

The myth says that the soul is immortal and since it has existed eternally, it has come to know all things. What is called learning then is really recollection. Further, the myth claims that "there is no difficulty in [the soul's] eliciting, or as men say 'learning' out of a single recollection, all the rest, if a man is strenuous and does not faint" (81d). This last claim is as amazing as the claim about the soul's immortality and its possession of all knowledge. It immediately raises the question of how it would be possible from a single recollection to recover all knowledge. Unfortunately, the myth is silent on this point. It gives no explicit account of how this might be done, as one might have expected if this were an attempt to reground an epistemology by a new metaphysics. Rather, the myth recommends hard work and promises only an extended and arduous effort. The point of the myth is not to offer a method but to recommend making the effort. Socrates underlines this point by making the moral of the myth explicit: "And therefore we ought not to listen to this sophistical argument about the impossibility of inquiry; for it will make us idle, and is sweet only to the sluggard; the other saying will make us active and inquisitive" (81d). Nowhere does Socrates claim to have shown that the skeptic's argument is unsound; instead, he claims that it is ethically destructive because idleness is the consequence of its narrative. It is this narrative that he challenges by attempting to give an imaginatively more compelling account of learning. Socrates reads Meno not as intellectually troubled but as prone to intellectual indolence, and it is this problem that the myth of recollection seeks to address.

Indeed, as a later section of the dialogue will show, it is wise to downplay the metaphysical implications of the myth and to highlight the activity that it recommends. Socrates' mode of demonstration supports this. Rather than arguing for any metaphysical presuppositions, he, in effect, performs a drama —that is, he translates or transfigures the myth from one literary form to another. In this transfiguration, with its multiple presentations of the same insight, Socrates models the very activity that he will later recommend as the way to achieve recollection.

The point of the enacted demonstration is to show the benefits conferred by refutations (which was what Meno was really questioning all along) and to show how a progress might be possible. This second point has to be put that tentatively. Socrates does not want to mislead Meno as to the difficulty and frustration that attend serious philosophic effort, nor does he want to suggest falsely that understanding is a product of mere syllogistic or geometric reasoning. He ends his demonstration by emphasizing the preliminary state of the slave boy's understanding and pointing out again the need for additional work: "At present these notions have just been stirred up in him, as in a dream; but if he were frequently asked the same questions, in different forms, he would know as well as anyone at last?" (85d).

This concluding question makes explicit the role of refiguration. One needs to be asked repeatedly the same questions in different forms. The suasive force of this approach is grounded in experience. It is almost as if this approach seeks to give one familiarity with the thing to be learned. How we come to know a person may be a more appropriate paradigm for this understanding than how we come to know the solution to a problem in geometry.

Only at the end of this myth and its brief discussion by Socrates and Meno does the true difficulty of persuading Meno become apparent. Meno appears moved by the myth and ready to begin anew a joint inquiry with Socrates. But just as the new inquiry begins, Meno slides away from a more focused refutation by blithely agreeing to continue the inquiry and then reverting to his original question. It is as if Meno is coated by an intellectual Teflon. It is hard to get a point to stick. But this predilection for intellectual slipperiness is tied to an ethical and political stance.

Socrates charges Meno with being incapable of self-control. For Meno, freedom lies not in the disciplined pursuit of a purpose but in his ability to manipulate an Other to do his will. His lack of intellectual discipline is a product of Gorgianic education, in which the ability to speak means the ability to get others to do what you wish. But such a rhetoric makes any intellectual exchange impossible and eviscerates any political discourse, because all uses of language are understood to be inherently manipulative. The tyranny that Socrates had earlier charged to Meno arises from his education in a Gorgianic rhetoric. For in a world of manipulation there are only masters and slaves, and those who control discourse become the masters. Thus when Socrates jokingly says that Meno has no interest in self-control but thinks only of exercising his mastery over his slave, Socrates, the joke is very serious.

The rhetorical problem that Meno poses is: how can one persuade those who believe that virtue is merely a mask for self-interest and that all discourse is finally a sophisticated battle of competing attempts at manipulation? This is a problem that Sophocles also takes up in the *Philoctetes*. Meno is a particularly frustrating case because he holds his views amiably and unreflectively. If he were Callicles or Thrasymachus, then Socrates could locate a set of philosophical commitments that would allow him to engage Meno's language and show its incoherence. But Meno seems to lack this type of commitment. He is not driven by the dream of power, as are Callicles and Thrasymachus; instead, he is mired in an indulgence bred apparently from an easy life whose lessons have been reenforced by a Gorgianic education. Socrates' problem is how to get a comfortably situated person to be aware of and take responsibility for a set of intellectual and political commitments. His problem is not making the horse drink but leading it to water in the first place.

Since Socrates cannot get Meno to participate in the search for a definition, he will meet him on his terms. He will now adopt the method of the geometricians, not as a superior form of argument but as a lesser alternative for dealing with someone who lacks the character to enter a refutation. Indeed, the dialogue's presentation of the hypothetical method raises important questions about its adequacy for pursuing ethical and political questions. Simply following its own suppositions, it proves that if virtue is knowledge, then it can be taught. The argument is internally consistent, but Plato has Socrates challenge the argument first by testing it against reality and second by suggesting that the initial survey of potential propositions was defective in a way in which the geometric method itself was impotent to uncover. After concluding that on the supposition that virtue is knowledge, it should be teachable, Socrates tests this conclusion by an empirical investigation: he looks for actual teachers. This test alone suggests a lack of parallelism between geometric and ethical and political arguments, for no one would seek to confirm geometric conclusions by empirically examining, say, existing circles or triangles. And the empirical test raises difficulties because neither Socrates nor Meno knows of a single teacher of virtue. In their search for a teacher, they turn to Anytus, a character who makes clear the political import of this dialogue.

But even as Socrates consults Anytus, he changes slightly the nature of the question that they are pursuing. Rather than asking who are the teachers of virtue, Socrates reframes the inquiry as if it were a search for a teacher for Meno, as if Meno were actually looking to become virtuous: "Very good. And now you [Anytus] are in a position to advise with me about my friend Meno. He has been telling me, Anytus, that he desires to attain that kind of wisdom and virtue by which men order the state or house, and honor their parents, and know when to receive and when to send away citizens and strangers, as a good man should" (90e–91a). Meno has never suggested that his interest in the question of how virtue is acquired arises from a desire on his part to be virtuous. If anything, he has tended to treat the matter of acquiring virtue almost as an academic question whose attempted solution will occupy or divert him but will never entail consequences for his life. The empirical search for teachers has been transformed by Socrates into a search for a teacher for Meno. Implied in this reformulated search is the project of replacing Gorgias and his instruction in rhetoric with a teacher who could teach virtue. Such instruction could undo or at least reorganize a Gorgianic education.

Also, in shifting from the general search for teachers of virtue to the particular search for a teacher for Meno, Socrates is extending the logic of a larger shift that moved from the formal proofs of the geometric method to the empirical tests that must be the final proof of any ethical or political discussion. The nature of virtue as a topic requires this movement from the intellectual to the practical. As Aristotle was to remark later, no one studies ethical questions for purely theoretical reasons; rather, all ethical inquiry is intended to enable one to act better.

Anytus seems, on the surface, a good candidate to aid Socrates and Meno in their search for a teacher of rhetoric: he is the son of a wealthy but modest Athenian who made rather than inherited his fortune; he has received a good education; and the Athenian people have already recognized his worth, for they have chosen him to fill some of their highest offices. If anyone in Athens would know who the teachers of virtue are, it should be Anytus. Further, Anytus appears to have the commitment to living and participating in a civic life. Unlike Meno, Anytus has particular values that he holds deeply.

But it quickly becomes evident that Anytus's commitment and his fixed understanding lead him to a blind self-assurance that issues in an increasingly violent intolerance. Socrates' suggestion, which surely could not have been innocent, that possibly the sophists are the teachers of virtue draws outraged denial from Anytus. Socrates is so impressed by the anger of Anytus at the suggestion of the sophists' being teachers of virtue that he asks Anytus whether any sophist has injured him. Anytus's reply begins to reveal his inadequacy as a guide in educational matters, for it turns out that he has no firsthand acquaintance with the sophists. Nonetheless, he is convinced that they are pernicious. Socrates cannot resist getting a little dig in at such an astounding confidence in the rightness of his opinion, given Anytus's lack of acquaintance with the sophists.

Indeed, the force of Anytus's character appears to reside in his uncritical allegiance to the current understandings that circulate among Athens's upper class. Plato first displays Anytus's allegiance in his suggestion that any Athenian gentleman would be able to instruct Meno in virtue, and Plato then uses this suggestion to raise questions about the coherence and the soundness of his beliefs. The irony surrounding this claim is that Anytus's proposed source of education is, in fact, very close to what Protagoras recommends when he argues that the citizens of a polis possess a common political understanding in which they instruct the young and that the method and matter of a civic education does not parallel that of a technical education.

Socrates lets the irony pass and focuses instead on whether it is true that the citizens can instruct the young in virtue. For what Anytus has given Socrates is a best-case scenario: if teachers of virtue do exist, one is most likely to find them among the citizens who are renowned for their virtue. And if one looks to their success or failure in teaching their sons virtue, such a search ought to determine whether virtue can be taught, for these citizens would possess both virtue and the desire to pass such virtue on to their sons. But as Socrates surveys the prominent citizens, he finds that they have all failed to pass on such knowledge to their sons, even though they have looked carefully after their training in lesser matters. Socrates then draws the reasonable conclusion that their failure as teachers of virtue suggests that virtue cannot be taught.

Anytus, however, is not so dispassionate at the end of the survey. He has lost an understanding of the point of the inquiry and assumes that Socrates' discovery of the failure of Athens's preeminent citizens is an attempt to slur these men. He ignores Socrates' acclamation of these men's virtue and focuses only on Socrates' repeated discovery of their failure as teachers of virtue. Anytus's blindness is revealing. His deeply entrenched but uncritical loyalty to Athens does not permit him to discuss rationally aspects of the city's political existence. An attempt to examine the city that does not lead to praise he takes as being not only critical of the city but intentionally slanderous.

And in his outrage at what he takes to be Socrates' intentional insult to the city, Anytus issues a thinly veiled threat: "Socrates, I think that you are too ready to speak evil of men; and, if you will take my advice, I would recommend you to be careful. Perhaps there is no city in which it is easier to do men harm than to do them good, and this is certainly the case at Athens, as I believe that you know" (95a). Since Anytus will be one of Socrates' three accusers at his trial, Plato's having him make such a threat becomes thematically significant. The dialogue confirms the thematic importance of the threat by having Socrates say prophetically that some day Anytus will understand the true meaning of defamation.

Anytus's quick slide into anger and the threat of violence suggests the precariousness of Socrates' situation, and it sets a challenge and shows the limits of a Socratic rhetoric in a related but different way to the challenge posed by Meno. For if Meno is difficult to refute because he appears to bring no abiding commitment to his conversation with Socrates, Anytus proves equally recalcitrant because of his tenacious and defensive commitment to Athens. Meno and Anytus represent the limits within which an elenchus can work. For his rhetoric to have a chance at being effective, Socrates needs an audience that is staked in the subject under discussion but sufficiently open to challenge so that an inquiry can go where it must go and not be required to confirm a preexisting conclusion. Anytus's threat points out the real dangers for one pursuing a Socratic rhetoric. Further, it makes clear the importance of a Socratic rhetoric of refutation to a polis. For if there is to be a viable political existence in which topics like justice can be genuinely explored in public, then characters like Anytus need to be made gentle, and this is one of the goals and consequences of a Socratic refutation. This need for gentleness almost involves the activity of refutation in a vicious circle, for it raises the question of how one induces the very quality that is a prerequisite for the activity that is to be undertaken. The answer is that it depends upon other qualities and values that an audience might possess. For example, if a belligerent character did value courage, then Socrates might be able to show how that character's actions were not consistent with courage, and this demonstration might, as in the case of Thrasymachus, cause shame. This shame could be a prelude to a developing gentleness. But as both Callicles and Anytus show, Socratic refutation is more apt to produce belligerence or surliness than gentleness. However, without gentleness, there can be only unreflective agreement and confirmation of current understanding or rancorous exchanges that create a violent anger and distrust that must eventuate in acts of injustice. Anytus, even more than Meno, serves to demonstrate that the question of the acquisition of virtue is not a theoretical but a crucial practical question whose solution has profound repercussions for the city.

After Anytus has departed in a huff, Socrates and Meno continue briefly their search for teachers, only to find that they cannot discover any. This leads Socrates to deal with the second difficulty for the geometric method. What Socrates now does is suggest that his and Meno's initial survey of options was too hasty. With its focus on entailment and validity, the geometric method is incapable of locating this kind of error, for all it can tell one is whether the conclusion follows validly from the premises. But since the point of an ethical inquiry is not just to guarantee the validity of its conclusion but to discover a truth about the world, or at least to provide good reasons for acting in a certain way, the geometric method by itself will always be insufficient to the complexity of ethical inquiry.

Socrates now proposes that true opinion can be as good a guide as knowledge. The example with which he illustrates this point is revealing. Picking up on the theme of guidance, he asks: "And a person who had a right opinion about the way [to Larissa], but had never been and did not know, might be a good guide also, might he not?" (97a). The example suggests that the understanding relevant for virtue is an ability to discern a way. The test of virtue is its efficacy as a guide to action and not its epistemological warrant.

The difference between true opinion and knowledge has to do not with the truth of the guidance but with the stability of the person's understanding. Knowledge abides; true opinion need not. Socrates makes this point through his analogy of true opinion to Daedalus's statues, which are beautiful but, if left alone, tend to wander off. To be a valuable possession, they need to be tied down. With respect to true opinion, such a tying down is called recollection (97d–98a). This new aspect of recollection helps clarify Socrates' early account. The notion of recalling previously existing ideas is downplayed while the notion of fastening is played up. The question is: how does one fasten down an opinion?

The answer is with hard and strenuous work. In particular, what one must do is make repeated inquiries from a variety of perspectives. These multiple inquiries will begin to confirm or challenge or modify the conclusions of each other. They will also deepen the inquirer's understanding, and the quality of the inquirer's grasp will change. The grasp will be more secure and fitted to its subject, and it will be capable of extending the understanding of the subject in new ways; that is, it will be able to apply its understanding creatively. This will allow it to be a guide, to find ways, and especially to find ways in new situations in which there cannot yet possibly be knowledge. The second half of the dialogue dramatistically renders the multiplicity of related inquiries that make a recollection.

Following the conclusions of Socrates' search for teachers of virtue, it is now reasonable to conclude that no one yet has attained knowledge. For if that person did, presumably he or she would have been discovered as a teacher of virtue. Human wisdom seems to be limited to true opinion. The tentativeness of Socrates' own conclusion confirms this, for he claims not to know the truth of what he said but only to conjecture it. The only thing that he claims to be certain about is the difference between knowledge and true opinion, a difference that seems to parallel the difference between divine and human wisdom.

Socrates is led to the tentative conclusion, then, that virtue is acquired neither by nature nor by instruction, but is, rather, a gift of the gods. Political wisdom is analogous to divine and poetic inspiration, its authority residing in the beauty and efficacy of its product and not in some intellectual pedigree. This tentative conclusion is followed by a call to action. And the dialogue ends with a focus on rhetoric and its importance to the civic life.

If teaching virtue is not possible, then a Socratic refutation emerges as an alternative to teaching and to a Gorgianic education, which is itself based on a kind of persuasion. The dialogue that has denied the possibility of teaching virtue ends by affirming the possibility of persuasion through refutation. This is not a theoretical confirmation but a practical discovery that demands being acted upon. Meno is now to seek out Anytus and attempt to persuade him and to conciliate him, and if Meno can accomplish this persuasion, he will "have done good service to the Athenian people" (100c). So an act of rhetoric calls forth another act of rhetoric, and he who has been refuted assumes the role of refuter. In this way a new fabric of city life would be woven by a continually developing rhetorical web of public discourse.

Such a view of Socratic rhetoric is utopian, and it is challenged by the very dialogue that suggests it. For we as readers know that Meno did not succeed and that Anytus was not conciliated. We are ignorant of whether Meno actually attempted such a reconciliation or whether Anytus belligerently resisted refutation; all that is certain is that he persisted in seeing Socrates as a danger to the city that needed to be met not by words but by violence. The dialogue's reversion to Anytus at its end emphasizes the serious political reality in which a Socratic rhetoric must function and, by raising the issue of its particular failure, offers this rhetoric as both an obligation and a problem for its readers. The thrust of the ending is not theoretical but practical.

The dialogue's entanglement of the elenchus in practical politics also suggests a different way of looking at what has been called the problem of the elenchus — the apparently unjustified move from consistency to truth. Vlastos sought the authority for such a move in a set of propositions that would allow Socrates to claim that the test of consistency was the assurance that a truth had been discovered. The theory of recollection then became the metaphysical move that could ground this epistemological claim. But if recollection is taken at first as a myth to inspire effort and then as an activity of tying down, and if knowledge does not seem possible for humans, then *Meno* opens up a new way to understand the authority of the elenchus.

If stable true opinion is the best that can be hoped for and possibly achieved by the best of people, and if such opinion is achieved only through an arduous and extended process of tying the opinions down by investigating them through a multiplicity of perspectives, then the authority of the elenchus must be finally and necessarily social and not logical. This is not to argue that the elenchus is illogical or indifferent to logic but that logic is only one necessary contributing element, which by itself is insufficient to authorize a legitimate confidence in its own discoveries. The drama of the dialogue suggests that there is a centrifugal force to an elenchus, as the initial two parties seek the opinions of others as part of their ongoing search. This is part of the tying down, and an intolerant and recalcitrant perspective such as Anytus's is an important part of the political reality that must be taken into account if the opinion tested is to be adequate to the demands that it will encounter. Any political guide will need to deal with Anytus, for he will surely stand in the way of an unfettered investigation of justice, which if it follows the dramatic logic of *Meno* will become an investigation of Athens's justice. Further, the fullest range of perspectives cannot belong to an individual citizen or even a small group of citizens. The demand of recollection that an opinion be tied down from a variety of perspectives makes a full public discussion, in which all the various perspectives within the city are interrogated, the goal of an elenchus if it is to secure most firmly the opinion under investigation.

But even such an extended inquiry would not be a guarantee of knowledge. The tentativeness of the dialogue's conclusion and its rejection of teaching as a mode of transmitting or engendering virtue suggest the provisional nature of any political understanding. The turn to refutation, to Socratic rhetoric, is a turn to an ongoing process that is defined by its critical stance toward its own discoveries. The danger of the slip from holding an understanding as true opinion to conceiving it as knowledge is dramatized in the certainty with which Anytus holds received current opinion in Athens. The other danger is represented by a Meno educated only by Gorgias, for such a character having given up on the possibility of acquiring virtue from education has turned to speaking well as an alternative. Implicit in such a turn is a cynicism about the ethical or political productiveness of discourse, as the practical consequences of discourse are downplayed and rhetoric becomes mere exercises in intellectual display and diversion or extended tyrannical exercises of a will to control. Meno's education has deprived him of a political content, as his world can only be one of private interests since, given his belief in manipulation, no public existence is possible. If, for Plato, an ideal philosopher is both spirited and gentle, then Anytus and Meno in their respective intolerance and indifference represent debased forms of these dispositions that are essential for a citizen in a polis that would be ordered by justice. To counter these current debased political options, Socrates needs to reconstitute the contemporary audience into a rhetorical audience. The citizens need to become both gentle and critical, tolerant and responsible. Such ethical and political transformation is the objective of Socratic rhetoric.

Socratic rhetoric thus confronts the tyrannies of intolerance and manipulation, and it offers new understandings of courage, justice, and freedom. In his most famous figure, that of the prisoners in the cave, Plato argues that the original human condition is one of imprisonment. Humans did not start out free and then fall, as Rousseau was to argue later; rather, they are imprisoned and ignorant of their situation. The task of rhetoric, of argument and figure that seeks to refute, is to effect the prolonged political movement from an unrecognized imprisonment to a more dazzling, if less comfortable, freedom. This definitive and original imprisonment establishes the abiding problem that a Platonic rhetoric needs to address: how does one move a person from an ideology that works precisely because of the comfort that its representations offer? Its images have the force of reality and the suasions of self-evidence. A Platonic rhetoric faces a particularly difficult task, since it would take away both the clarity and comfort and have no immediately satisfying representations to put in place of the shadows. Rather, one who is persuaded by such rhetoric would live with doubt and dissatisfaction, and that person's speech would frequently stumble as he or she searched for a language that was adequate or usable to suggest a vision which itself was unstable and difficult to communicate in the everyday world of physical reality and practical politics.

Such a rhetoric would have much in common with some current critical discourses. It would see problems of justice and freedom as fundamental, and it would see such problems as rooted in an inherited understanding that had acquired the force of self-evidence. The initial and always abiding task of such a rhetoric is the negative one of undermining self-evidence and puncturing the self-assurance that supports intolerance. This negative task would be accompanied by the equally important task of making the audience gentle and of making it sufficiently courageous to continue its search for justice even when the completion of such a project is inherently beyond human capability.[13] The elenchus embodies this rhetorical project, and it offers students of rhetoric an alternative way to conceive of their activity.

To return to an insight of the *Meno:* virtue is not knowledge, so it cannot be taught. Consequently, the important and definitive philosophical activity is not teaching but refutation. Put in a slightly different way: philosophy is not about the validation of abstract reasoning, nor is it an explicit, literal enunciation of some doctrine. Rather, it is figurative and allusive, and in its presentations it enacts and hopes to provoke an ongoing attempt to find ways to be responsible to the ideal of justice in a world in which all find themselves imprisoned both by particular inherited languages and by being creatures who approach the world through language and are thus both enabled and limited by language.[14] When written in this way, this philosophical rhetoric is inexorably fluid—changing and reshaping its suasions as it meets its readers in their radical particularity. Its guiding insight is that for such creatures perspective is inescapable, and the twin temptations available to creatures embedded in historically determined languages, customs, and practices are to despair of the possibility of responsible discriminations between perspectives or to assert the superiority of one's own perspective, as if it were not a perspective but in fact a representation of an atemporal logos that ordered the cosmos. Through its dramatic representation of the Socratic elenchus, *Meno* argues that the issues surrounding the acquisition of virtue are not epistemological or logical conundrums but abiding political realities that give justice a philosophical point.

Socrates' myth of recollection, a myth whose origin is not recoverable by reason, is a narrative response to Meno's deconstructive insight into the impossibility of either opening or closing systematic inquiry. In having Socrates respond to this insight by a construction that is clearly announced as literary or imaginative, Plato is showing that he understands the force of the skepticism directed at inquiry. And in having Meno voice the skepticism, Plato is also showing proleptically an understanding of a difficulty that has haunted deconstruction: if the skeptical insight is granted, how is it possible to defend a political position or commitment? This is the political equivalent to what Vlastos takes to be the logical problem of the elenchus. The political problem is not, however, to move from consistency to truth but to move from a skeptical and critical play to a stable political commitment. Plato's solution, as it is embodied in the drama of *Meno,* is that such a difficulty can be lived with only if the primary function of rhetoric is conceived of as refutative. Such an understanding of rhetoric makes it a practice of infinite revision, of constant resecuring of positions, of recollection. This practice is social and entails a commitment to the pursuit of justice, for only in a world that is fully just could such refutation approach its ideal power for disclosing the realities in which people live. And because such a world is finally not possible, part of the task of philosophical rhetoric is to supply ethical and political narratives that promote and sustain both the gentleness and courage necessary for the continual pursuit of refutation.

The revolutionary thrust of the elenchus is to offer a new understanding of political responsibility in which the significant issue is not conscious intent but unconscious imprisonment. A philosophical rhetoric is the continuous inquiry into this unconscious imprisonment and the consequent disclosure of responsibility. This kind of rhetoric then offers the world as a place of action. It provides a guidance in the absence of an absolute standard, or at least in the absence of an absolute standard that can be known. It transforms its audiences into judges, into people who actively criticize and take responsibility for current injustice. In this way it offers the possibility of meaningful citizenship, as political life becomes a creative revision of human possibility in a public inquiry to realize a just social organization.

Such is the legacy of Plato's understanding of rhetoric. He offers not a method of persuasion but rather induction into a life constituted through refutations that entangle one in a pursuit of justice. One cannot be taught how to live such a life, how to acquire the virtues that are necessary to sustain it, but one may be persuaded that only in such a life will a measure of freedom be possible and that only in such a life can one begin to fulfill one's obligation to be just. The difficulties faced by such rhetoric should never be underestimated, but Plato's figurative presentation of the philosophical life in his character, Socrates, is a rich resource that can guide those who seek to live in this way. Still, those who wish to learn from Socrates must seek both to refute him and to be refuted by him, and this requires them to read the dialogues not as a rhetoric that seeks to teach particular doctrines but as a rhetoric that through its refutations makes its audiences feel their own entanglement in issues of justice in such a way that to face themselves they must embark on a continual inquiry into justice and must seek to transform the possibilities of action by engaging in and standing for refutation.

4

Sophocles' Philoctetes *and the Crisis of Rhetoric*

The issue raised by Plato in the *Meno* of the intractable audience and the threat that it poses to rhetoric is given an even darker turn by Sophocles in the *Philoctetes*. Both Meno and Anytus begin from privileged positions, and their refusals to stand for refutation are personal choices. But in the *Philoctetes,* Sophocles presents a character whose refusal to listen arises from a far more complex motivation. Philoctetes refuses to listen to reason because he has been educated by the duplicity of those in power and has come to see reason as merely a cover for force. For Philoctetes, the law of the universe in which the powerful rule is that everything and everyone exist only as an instrumentality to be used as the needs of the powerful dictate. In such a world, to refuse to be an audience is, in part, an act of courage, but it is also, in part, an act of self-destruction. Philoctetes' dilemma raises questions as to whether rhetoric can be a viable practice in worlds such as ours, where the configurations of power make all discourse suspect as either conscious or unconscious manipulation.

In the *Philoctetes* public discourse has been so debased that it may not be possible to recover a public trust or discover a language that can nourish and sustain a community. The initial abandoning of Philoctetes by his Greek companions and his subsequent betrayal by Neoptolemos destroy his capacity for trust. The problem for rhetoric created by the tragedy is how to recover this trust needed for civic life when Philoctetes' experience confirms that the city or at least those who control the city deal strategically and not honestly with the citizens. Philoctetes' plight engenders and supports a skepticism that may not be livable but is certainly reasonable, and this skepticism entails a breakdown within public discourse that is so severe that a public trust cannot be recovered by normal rhetorical practice. In Neoptolemos's final appeal to Philoctetes, Sophocles creates a powerful logos, only to have it prove ineffective. The momentum of the play's skepticism cannot be arrested and leads to a conclusion that is both the natural culmination of the events but also an impossible ending for the play, for it diverges from the traditional myth, which claimed that Philoctetes played an important role in the destruction of Troy.

The situation can be saved only by the direct intervention of a god, and, in a troubling ending that involves the only use of the *deus ex machina* in one of his extant plays, Sophocles resorts to the divine *muthos* of Herakles to effect a transformation in Philoctetes' desire since the logos of Neoptolemos could not persuade him.[1] However, as R. P. Winnington-Ingram suggests, such a resolution of the difficulties may take care of the immediate problem of bringing the play's ending in line with the myth, but "the question which arises is whether the 'second ending' is more than a mechanical negation of these consequences," namely, the consequences of the initial cruel act and its implications for the heroic code (*Sophocles*, 302). Whatever else the second ending may accomplish, its recourse to a divine muthos suggests at the very least that the rhetorical crisis in the play may be incapable of human resolution, and the implications of that suggestion raise questions as to the ability of rhetoric to constitute or maintain a polis in a world in which public trust has eroded. A special urgency attaches to these questions once Philoctetes' situation is understood to be not exceptional but paradigmatic for normal daily existence. The *Philoctetes* is nothing less than a skeptical inquiry into the viability of rhetoric, and, as with any skeptical inquiry, any adequate response to it cannot simply cite the normal success of a practice, for it is the legitimacy of that success and those practices that is being challenged.

Sophocles intentionally creates a situation in which rhetoric in its normal modes of operation proves incapable of addressing an audience because trust in public discourse has been shattered by the past practice of that discourse. Philoctetes' experience argues for the reasonableness of a rhetorical skepticism that views all discourse as manipulation and as a cover for deceit. He has been victimized by a policy that conceives of him only in strategic terms and by a discourse that serves this policy. When his suffering interfered with the peace of the Greek camp and disturbed the normal order of their lives, the Atridae abandoned him on Lemnos. They assumed that Philoctetes was an inconsequential character who had become inconvenient. The Atridae used their power to deal with this inconvenience. Now that they need Philoctetes, they are haunted by their past practices, and they find themselves unable to address him openly. By the time a sincere persuasion is attempted, public discourse has been so discredited that Philoctetes cannot give credence to anything he hears. This is the play's rhetorical crisis. An aporia opens that requires not merely a reform of rhetoric but a reinvention of the grounds of public discourse. For if the *Philoctetes* is about the reintegration of Philoctetes and Neoptolemos into society and their acceptance of their particular roles, such a reintegration is inextricably entangled with the need for a new rhetoric that can both acknowledge the cynicism that destroyed the possibility of a public life and provide a narrative sufficiently powerful to contend with and overcome this cynicism. Further, this narrative needs to be sophisticated enough to provide an alternative life in a world in which manipulation and disregard of others remain ineluctable elements.

The *Philoctetes* begins during a period in which the consequences of a policy that reduces all concerns to matters of strategy have become manifest. The campaign against Troy has stagnated, and the army, bogged down in pursuit of a goal that has exhausted it, has relinquished its vision of and for itself. As Neoptolemos's report to Philoctetes makes clear, the cost of the war has been considerable: many of the noblest Greeks have perished, while those less heroic have somehow managed to survive. Philoctetes' despairing comment that it is difficult to remain pious when one sees the good dying and the bad being spared reflects the spiritual fatigue that has grown out of the war. The absence of Achilles and the presence of an Odysseus committed to victory at any cost represent the current degeneration of the Greek army from an institution animated by a concept of nobility to one that merely provides an occasion for self-interest.[2] The prolonged siege of Troy has eviscerated the heroic tradition of Greek nobility and led to a present in which a larger social vision has given way to a private perspective whose horizon is defined by a series of ad hoc attempts to meet whatever exigencies arise.[3] Paradoxically, in a play in which one key speaker for the state, Odysseus, defines himself as one committed totally to the success of the state, the possibility of public life has been lost.

As the play opens, a solution to the stalemate at Troy has become available, and there is genuine cause for hope. The captured Trojan prophet, Helenus, prophesied that if the Greeks can persuade Philoctetes to come to Troy, then he and Neoptolemos will capture the city. The prophecy, however, is far from a simple assurance of Greek prosperity. Rather, it creates an opportunity for the Greeks to address or redress a recent history in which their failure to succeed is a consequence of a rupture within their ethical and political tradition. What the prophecy does is set the Greeks a challenge: can they read their current practices as the actions of a polis that has become unmoored in a pursuit of glory, that has abandoned a vision of its own nobility, and that cannot achieve success until it recovers a sense of nobility to guide and limit its policies and pursuits?

One apparent reading of the prophecy denies the need for such serious political reform and treats the prophecy only as an imperative to obtain Herakles' bow. On this reading the bow would provide a weapon that could ensure military superiority, and the stalemate would be resolved through a battlefield victory. This reading understands the cause of the current impasse not as the product of social malaise but as a consequence of the lack of appropriate technology — which is to say that the problem has been strategic all along and that the bow is simply another means, although a vastly superior one, to be deployed. At times it seems that Odysseus understands the prophecy this way, as if the bow in its capacity to always hit its mark would offer the Greeks a technological advantage that would guarantee victory.[4] The competing reading sees the prophecy as requiring the Greeks to come to grips with their past practices and to undo injustices that they have perpetrated in the belief that their own power authorized them to do whatever they wished.[5] This reading, as Neoptolemos comes to realize, recognizes that the Greeks must persuade Philoctetes to return voluntarily to an army that ignominiously cast him off in his pain. This means that the Greek army would need both to acknowledge what it had done and to find a language that could offer someone whom it had cast off a reason for again trusting it. What such a society would need to do is to discover a way of speaking to those injured by past injustice and to offer them a way in which they might pursue a life with honor, if they returned to society. But to reconstitute the public trust, the army, and by implication the larger society, would first have to cease to treat its citizens strategically and then convince them that such a change was not simply another strategic move. The very conduct of political life would need to be transformed radically. The necessity for such an action and the almost insurmountable difficulties that attend it are at the heart of Sophocles' play.

To understand the necessity and difficulty of reintegrating Philoctetes into the Greek army, it is necessary to understand the nature of his injuries. For he is a twice-injured character: once by the gods and once by the commanders of the Greek army. Philoctetes' first injury, when he inadvertently trespassed on a sacred shrine of Chryse and was bitten by the serpent guarding the shrine, seems to have been a product of bad luck.[6] There is little in the play to suggest that Philoctetes' trespass is somehow an expression of his character or tied to any personal excess. And while the bow and the wound do seem to be intimately connected, their connection does not establish any impiety initially committed by Philoctetes that would merit punishment. As the play's ending argues, it is better to accept the suffering as a fact of life or a condition for heroism than to seek an explanation for it that would make sense of Philoctetes' suffering. He is a character to be pitied, as the chorus pities him when they first hear his story and speculate that he may be well born and from an ancient house. And while Neoptolemos argues that the hand of a god ordained this affliction on Philoctetes, even he does not attribute the affliction to anything that Philoctetes did. If the suffering is necessary, it is also undeserved. The importance of the suffering lies in its consequences and not in its cause.

It is in response to the suffering that the political issues that engage the play arise, and it is political activity that shapes character and determines even the spiritual crises within this tragedy. As D. H. F. Kitto says, Sophocles' "theme is to be not the way in which the gods treat men, but the way in which men treat each other" (*Greek Tragedy,* 301). The significance of Philoctetes' injury is that it demands a response from others. The snake's poison leaves Philoctetes with a chronic ulcerating sore. The smell from the wound is repellent, and Philoctetes' cries of pain disturb the normal functioning of the Greek army. The intrusiveness, repulsiveness, and resistance to treatment combine to make Philoctetes' pain a problem with which the Greek army must deal.

They respond to this first injury by inflicting a second and greater injury that isolates Philoctetes in his pain from all others. For the Atridae, Philoctetes' pain was primarily an annoyance, and they dealt with it accordingly. Having waited until the paroxysms of his pain produced in Philoctetes the stupor of an exhausted sleep, the Greeks flee Lemnos, leaving him to a life of pain and isolation. Sophocles clearly intends the Greek response to be a register of their ethical debasement. The isolation of Philoctetes is a Sophoclean innovation in the traditional story.[7] Although Sophocles was well aware that Lemnos was not a deserted island, he transformed it into a desolate place in which Philoctetes has no human companions. Odysseus's initial description of Lemnos emphasizes the island's inhospitality to human life. In effect, the island is a prison or, perhaps, some sort of asylum. It functions to remove Philoctetes and his pain from human sight, smell, and hearing. But if the Greek response does nothing to alleviate Philoctetes' condition, from the army's viewpoint it has dealt with the problem of Philoctetes most effectively by rendering him and his suffering imperceptible. Although he will continue to suffer, his suffering will no longer intrude on the Greek army, for it has, in effect, eliminated Philoctetes and his suffering from its presence. And Philoctetes and his suffering, once removed from the army's presence, cease to count as anything. Part of the anguish that he feels when Neoptolemos feigns ignorance of him and his condition is the realization of how effectively the Greek commanders have removed him not only from society's presence but more importantly from its consciousness.

In the demands made on the Greek army by Philoctetes' pain, Sophocles creates a fundamental problem which any society must face: how does a society respond to the suffering of those whose pain is beyond treatment? It might help to understand the significance of this problem by noting the parallels between the Greeks' treatment of Philoctetes and our own treatment of the homeless, in particular those homeless people suffering from some mental illness. In both cases a society is presented with an individual in pain whose suffering is not easily remedied, if it can be dealt with at all. Not only is the suffering painful to the person who is afflicted but such suffering is also disturbing to behold, and the presence of the person suffering can disrupt normal daily life in much the same way that Odysseus claimed that Philoctetes' cries disrupted the sacrifices of the Greeks. Further, the apparent resistance of the disease to cure can undermine a society's vision of itself as capable of meeting adequately the exigencies that can befall its citizens. The suffering becomes an unpleasant reminder of the limitations of any human technology. The suffering demands a response. It issues an ethical imperative that one acknowledge the humanity of an Other, especially since the illness and suffering are in danger of making that person lose a sense of humanity, as life is reduced to a daily and unremitting repetition of pain. To understand the ethical culpability of a polis that Sophocles is raising, we need only examine our failure to include the homeless within the compass of our political and social lives and realize that, like the Greek army, we too may lack a language with which to address those who have been injured by our social practices. If Philoctetes' injury is unusual, his situation is not, and the political challenge he poses is one that all societies must face.

All too often, the problem of an Other's pain is seen not as an important moment for social solidarity but more mundanely as an annoyance to be handled with as little disturbance as possible to public tranquility. As Peter W. Rose notes, "Philoctetes becomes society's first throw-away person" (*Sons of the Gods,* 318). The easiest way to marginalize someone is to remove that person from sight, smell, and hearing. But, as the play argues, if such isolation can take the form of a physical separation from others, it can also be achieved by rendering the person suffering outside the common narrative of that society. What is important is that the individual is effectively removed from others so that his or her demands for a response are no longer felt by others. Whether the marginalization is accomplished through physical isolation or by writing someone out of a social narrative, the point is to render the individual invisible, to make that individual into a non-being.

Marginalizing the one who suffers becomes particularly attractive if suffering is viewed not as an integral element in life, and hence something with which any society that seeks to deal adequately with human existence must come to terms, but as an aberration to be dealt with the best way that one can. And the strategic elimination of the source of discomfort from the view of society need not be limited to those suffering physical diseases. Any problem that causes discomfort can be handled in such a way by rendering the cause invisible. Hence the appropriateness of Ralph Ellison's title, *Invisible Man,* for his powerful analysis of how racism has functioned in American society.

To see the problem of dealing with the suffering of others as only a problem of managing them is to choose to deny what one does not wish to see. It is the product of a political vision that refuses to countenance that life can assume tragic dimensions, that the feeling of division or of the presence of an irremediable suffering is a fact of human existence. Rather, a strategic politics assumes an infinitely malleable universe in which all problems can be dealt with eventually by an individual who is sufficiently inventive. Such an approach to an Other's pain assumes either that the marginalized are not really needed in the society or that, if they are needed, they can be dealt with as the occasion demands. Behind either assumption is the belief that history can always be rewritten and that language will always provide resources that allow one to deal strategically with any problem.

Such an understanding comes uncomfortably close to rhetoric's recognition of the radical indeterminacy of the world of human purposes and actions. In such a view, power resides not primarily in physical force but in control of an ideological apparatus. Hence Odysseus's preference for words over actions, guile over physical force. Any audience can be moved. It is particularly appropriate that Odysseus is the one who handles the problem of Philoctetes for the Atridae, for he is the master strategist — the man who sees the world as permitting unlimited rearrangement. Bernard M. W. Knox argues that Odysseus has a clear link to the practice of rhetoric as it had emerged in the late fifth century: "But the Odysseus of the *Philoctetes* is conceived along entirely different lines [from the more noble Odysseus of the *Ajax*]; he resembles the Odysseus of Euripidean tragedy, a fast-talking, cynical politician. In the last years of the Peloponnesian war the Homeric hero appears often in the plays of Euripides as a type of the new political extremists, who, armed with sophistic rhetoric, dominated the Athenian assembly with their ferocious policies of repression and aggrandizement" (*The Heroic Temper,* 124). Odysseus's plans — first, the desertion and consequent marginalization of Philoctetes and, second, the conquering of him by guile — embody a political attitude and practice sufficiently close to rhetoric's understanding of the world as a place of action that no serious challenge to Odysseus's methods can avoid exploring how a rhetorical approach to politics might lead to and support such practices.

To be sure, Odysseus's practice of rhetoric is a clear abuse of the art and should not be taken as action that is endorsed by the standard defenses of rhetoric or that necessarily follows from them. But if there is no necessity that prompts this abuse, rhetoric certainly affords some large temptations for such abuse. And this abuse does create a problem with which rhetoric must deal. For the play is not concerned primarily with the initial desertion of Philoctetes but with the consequences that follow upon that desertion. This is a tragedy that seeks to come to grips with history and to ask how the past may determine the possibilities for present discourse. This tragedy begins with past actions that now require deceit. Since any present discourse will always take place in a context that has been historically determined in part by previous political acts, the past abuse of trust becomes the problem with which a theory of rhetoric must deal. Does the reality of this world as it has been determined by history require the rhetor who would be effective to resort to misrepresentation? Sophocles' *Philoctetes* takes seriously the issues that will later be raised by Machiavelli in *The Prince,* as misrepresentation is offered as the only rhetoric sufficiently complex to deal with the world as it is.

The most common defense offered against the charge of an immoral rhetoric is that it is not the art itself but its practice by an individual that makes it either ethical or unethical. This defense assumes a certain autonomy or freedom for the rhetor, but the situation of past injustice on which Sophocles focuses challenges this notion of autonomy, for one enters a world determined in large part by injustices that have destroyed the possibility for straightforward discourse. As we saw earlier, Aristotle acknowledges such a possibility when he defines rhetoric not as the art of persuasion but as the art that locates the best available means of persuasion in any given situation, but he does not work through the possibility that such means might have been almost totally preempted. He seems to view the failure of rhetoric to find an appropriate means to be the exception rather than the rule. Aristotle's assumption of the natural tendency of justice to prevail allows him to avoid dealing with skepticism because it rules out the fact of inherent injustice — which is the very fact that skepticism feels so powerfully. Sophocles' placing of rhetoric within a particular political history defined by past injustices raises the question of skepticism by challenging the possibility of there being a normal rhetorical practice. Since no act of rhetoric can ever claim an absolute beginning, the historical abuse of discourse constitutes a problem that cannot be dismissed as one to be dealt with strategically by, say, a set of reforms, for such abuse goes to the very possibility of the public trust necessary for any rhetoric. Given this context, any rhetorical project arguing for a literal or sincere use of logos can seem hopelessly naive.

The murkiness of the historical past in all of its ethical ambivalence is personified in the character of Odysseus. Critics have read him in a variety of ways. Bernard Knox sees him as a truly devious character, consciously manipulating all others in pursuit of his own glory. Martha C. Nussbaum analyzes Odysseus not as a character who is personally corrupt but as one who adheres to a false ethical understanding. She sees him "as a man who accords ultimate value to the state of affairs, and specifically, to the state of affairs which seems to represent the greatest possible good of all citizens. He gives his approval to any action which he believes will best promote the general welfare, and resists the argument that there are certain acts which should be done by an agent because of his character and principles, decrying this view as a form of squeamishness" ("Consequences," 30). She argues that Odysseus represents an ethical understanding that Sophocles wishes to undermine first by showing its initial attractiveness and then by showing its incoherence. James B. White sees Odysseus as a character who operates from a "classic form of ends-means rationality, which naturally focuses on the possible and the impossible, on the probable and the improbable, and regards everything in the world, including itself, as an instrument to obtain the ends that it is given" (*Herakles' Bow,* 8).[8] G. M. Kirkwood warns against reading Odysseus as a simple villain and stresses that he is a representative of the state and needs to be understood in that role. And Cedric H. Whitman adds: "whatever [Odysseus] does, good or bad, he has the full sanction of the Greek host and their leaders; he is their representative, and to them he is responsible" (*Sophocles,* 180). When the chorus argues with Philoctetes, it makes a similar point that Odysseus is not acting in a personal capacity but as a political representative, and as one who can cite a divine sanction. Winnington-Ingram offers the sensible suggestion about a particular action of Odysseus that could be applied productively to his entire conduct: "There has been much argument about the intentions of Odysseus at this point [when, having obtained the bow, he threatens to leave behind the obstreperous Philoctetes]; and it could be that Sophocles did not intend his audience to be certain of them" (*Sophocles,* 293). The spread of critical opinion would seem to support Winnington-Ingram's point and lead to the conclusion that the internal ethical life of Odysseus is not at all obvious, for although he does put forth certain views (and they are clearly statements that Sophocles wants his audience to reflect on), it is difficult to project an ethical psychology from these views.

It is more helpful to read his character in terms of his role. That role would have been obvious to a fifth-century Athenian audience. Odysseus is the embodiment of rhetoric; his ethical ambivalence is its ethical ambivalence. Charles Segal points to the design of Odysseus as a character: "For Odysseus language is a carefully crafted tool to attain definite ends. In this aspect it reflects some late fifth-century Sophistic theories of language as an amoral medium for winning one's case, a *technē* or skill to be exercised without regard for law or justice" (*Tragedy and Civilization,* 333). In his practice and in the articulation of a theory of action, Odysseus stands for certain discursive practices and the political attitudes that they entail, and it is in this light that he is most productively read.

Odysseus first justifies his actions by claiming that he was acting within a public role, that he had orders for what he did. Then he attempts to justify these actions by claiming that Philoctetes' cries disrupted the sacrifices of the Greeks. This justification has been read variously: some critics seeing it merely as an excuse to cover a disreputable action; others regard the problem as a genuine one, even if the response was disreputable.[9] Again, the disagreement itself is important, for it suggests the difficulty if not impossibility of recovering Odysseus's motives. As an individual, he is elusive, and the attempt to understand his actions as products of private reason are doomed to prove unsatisfactory. This is true, in large part, because he is a rhetor, and the self that appears to the other characters is a rhetorical construction and not an unmediated expression of some personality. One of the most striking qualities of Odysseus is that he takes nothing personally; rather, all considerations are strategic and depend upon particular circumstances. Who he is and what he must do are a function of what problem must be addressed. This protean and uncentered agency is not a product of some psychological or ethical aberration but a principle of rhetorical commitment to the particularity and individuality of the problems that present themselves in the political world.

One way to survive in this world is to be adaptable; the other, of course, represented by Philoctetes, is to be inflexible. An Odyssean flexibility at least seems to acknowledge a historical dimension to human existence, for its commitment to flexibility is a recognition that change is a fundamental part of life. Part of the reason that Philoctetes' existence is so archaic follows from his unwillingness to acknowledge historicity, as he willfully clings to a strict code of conduct that refuses to acknowledge or accommodate change. Certainly part of his savageness comes from his refusal to admit the possibility of change. His death-grip on his interpretation of the past is equally a statement of the profound anxiety over dealing with uncertainty that goes with any understanding that one cannot control the future. Odysseus at least credits the possibility of change, and he seeks to be effective in a world that has no essential character and hence is a place in which final ends that order a polis are at best irrelevant and at worst suicidal. In the absence of an overarching purpose, he seeks to act. For him any situation will provide sufficient clues to determine a possible course of action. All is capable of reinterpretation and even such a concept as nobility is subject to change — not because one is devious but because different situations demand different kinds of action. To conquer by physical force is noble when situations permit such actions, but to conquer by guile is no less noble when situations demand deceit. The indeterminacy of language and of value is simply an acknowledgement of their radical particularity, of the fact that words and values do not have ideal abstract meanings that exist independent of contexts but that rather their meanings are produced by particular human actions in particular circumstances. Such a world is not one without value but one whose value is constantly being discovered in the social and political clashes that new situations create.[10]

Nor is Odysseus without some abiding and stable values. He is loyal to and committed to serving the Greek army. He holds this value firmly, and if he is willing to treat any other virtue provisionally, loyalty appears to be an unquestionable good for him. Loyalty is what he first appeals to in Neoptolemos:

> Son of Achilles,
> our coming here has a purpose; to it be loyal
> with more than with your body. If you should hear
> some strange new thing, unlike what you have heard
> before, still serve us; it was to serve you came here. (50–54)

Although this speech is to prepare Neoptolemos to accept a line of conduct that violates his personal sense of nobility, its reasoning is appropriate for the situation. If an army is to succeed, it needs loyalty. Orders are not to be questioned but obeyed. The argument from loyalty also appeals to the same logic of rhetoric's standard defense: the loyal individual is not a source of ends but only an ethically neutral instrument concerned with the effective achievement of the ends that are determined elsewhere. Odysseus does not see himself or Neoptolemos as an independent agent pursuing private ends but as part of a larger enterprise, and it is their job to carry out and not make policy. Nor is Odysseus simply following orders blindly. Later he will claim that he is doing the will of Zeus (989–90), and the chorus will support him when it argues to Philoctetes that Odysseus has only pursued the will of the Greek army:

> A man should give careful heed to say what is just;
> and when he has said it, restrain his tongue from rancor and taunt.
> Odysseus was one man, appointed by many,
> by their command he has done this, a service to his friends. (1140–44)

Neoptolemos feels strongly the claims of the Greek army on him, even after he has defied their plan and returned the bow to Philoctetes. As might be expected, Philoctetes has no use for this line of reasoning, but his failure to understand the claims of the polis and the authority of something larger than personal friendship is a failing that Herakles needs to correct before Philoctetes can seek to fulfill his destiny.

Also, the positive force of Odysseus's position must be felt if Neoptolemos's initial decision is to be appreciated. If he is not simply a naive young man who was duped by a crafty character, then it is reasonable to assume that Odysseus's argument that loyalty can require guile is capable of being entertained as a possible statement of an appropriate nobility. Public and private morality may make different and even incompatible demands on an individual. The argument for the legitimacy of guile gains especial force if the past tradition of nobility seems unavailable in the conditions in which the characters of the tragedy now find themselves. Achilles, the embodiment of the heroic tradition of *bia* (force), has perished. The organic link between father and son has been broken by the events of the war, and Odysseus represents a way of acting that has managed to survive at a time when heroic conduct has not succeeded. The crisis of nobility may very well demand a realignment of values and the invention of a more effective way of acting. Simply by virtue of having survived, Odysseus has the right to claim a kind of authority, one that can teach a young Greek how to act in the world as it is.

He first appears in the play in the role that has striking parallels to a teacher of sophistry or rhetoric. He has been entrusted to educate a young noble Greek, and he promises Neoptolemos an education that will allow him to be a productive citizen capable of achieving his own personal ends. He will offer him an art that pursues private glory while leading to the greater public good. Odysseus's instruction will tie a successful achievement to proficiency in speaking well, offering Neoptolemos a way of acting that is appropriate for a world in which power is connected intimately with speech.

Indeed, the education in rhetoric offered by Odysseus seems quite similar to the education that Meno received from Gorgias. In each case, the problem of education arises in part because of the difficulty or impossibility of transmitting traditional values. In *Meno* the virtuous appear incapable of educating their sons in virtue; they are unable to pass on the tradition that has structured their lives. In *Philoctetes* the death of Achilles dramatically marks a rupture in the heroic tradition. The problem for education, then, becomes how to constitute actors in a world in which the acquisition of virtue or of a virtue grounded in traditional values is no longer possible.

In both *Meno* and *Philoctetes* the alternative to an education in virtue is an education in rhetoric. This education has the advantage of being available and of proving effective in the present world. In *Philoctetes* there are three options for dealing with others: bia, *peitho* (persuasion), and *dolos* (guile). Depending on the situation, any of the three might prove effective, but Odysseus's first lesson is that the situation and the nature of the particular audience determine the choice of method. To be successful in this world one needs to be flexible and to read accurately the possible ways of moving an audience. Neoptolemos's wish to use either force or persuasion displays his abstract understanding of nobility and what it requires, for it is an understanding that dictates actions without having investigated the demands of a particular situation. Such understandings of ethics today are often labeled as academic, implying their lack of familiarity with the exigencies of the world of praxis. Odysseus will try to complicate Neoptolemos's notion of nobility through the rhetorical insight that there is no absolute standard for nobility but rather that the noble is a consequence of action's being successful, and that such success requires the actor to be adaptable and to meet each situation appropriately. In defense of his choosing his method depending on the circumstances in which he finds himself, Odysseus explains that he does not seek to be immoral but adaptive:

> If I had the time, I have much I could say to him.
> As it is, there is only one thing. As the occasion
> demands, such a one am I.
> When there is a competition of men just and good,
> you will find none more scrupulous than myself.
> What I seek in everything is to win. (1047–52)

What he offers Neoptolemos is a way of being effective, and fundamental to such success is being flexible.

He argues further for the superiority of speech over physical force. Odysseus's faith is in the power of ideology and not in the efficacy of brute strength; it is deception and not active repression that governs most effectively. And he characterizes the heroic tradition, which valorizes physical prowess, as immature, as not understanding the true source of power. His argument for the superiority of speech is empirical:

> Now as I go forth to the test, I see
> that everywhere among the race of men
> it is the tongue that wins and not the deed. (97–99)

Rather than starting from an abstract principle, Odysseus will base his practical education on the nature of the world. He will teach Neoptolemos how to use his tongue because speech has proven more powerful than physical force.

What Odysseus offers Neoptolemos is what Gorgias offered Meno—not instruction in virtue but instruction in speech. Odysseus rejects both force and persuasion as ways of dealing with Philoctetes: force will fail because Philoctetes has the bow that never misses, and persuasion cannot succeed because Philoctetes has good reasons not to believe the Greeks. Critics have raised questions about the accuracy of Odysseus's claim that persuasion would not have worked, and there is room for doubt here. But his conclusion that persuasion would fail is very much in line with a probabilistic reasoning that a rhetor would use, and although Philoctetes may be generous in his initial reception of Neoptolemos, he also shows a deep and abiding hatred for the Greeks. So Odysseus's choice of guile can be justified as reasonable because it is demanded by circumstances.

Philoctetes also shares with *Meno* a recognition of the complications that beset a rhetorical act and that make a rhetorical education necessary. In both works the binary opposition between a rigid understanding and a flexible perspective that eschews commitment mark the two extremes of a discursive space. The rigidity of Anytus finds a corresponding unwillingness to yield in Philoctetes' hatred of the Greeks. Both represent a noble tradition that is unwilling to engage in the necessary reflective reform to meet the world as it is. Both only assert; neither discusses. Both are beyond the reach of persuasion; both are in opposition to sophistry. The protean flexibility of Meno finds its counterpart not so much in Neoptolemos, who, despite his impressionability, does balk at certain actions, but in Odysseus, who is willing to change actions and commitments to meet the exigencies of the different particular occasions. Like Meno, Odysseus is a character beyond refutation.

In both the dialogue and the tragedy, there is the problem of finding an opening between an intractable inflexibility and a fluid and evasive lack of commitment that would permit the undoing of a rhetorical education. Odysseus temporarily convinces Neoptolemos to assume a provisional attitude toward the world of values, so, like Meno, Neoptolemos comes under the sway of a rhetorical education. But Neoptolemos is less comfortable than Meno in this tradition, and the refutation that he undergoes is more effective. Whenever Socrates confounded Meno, Meno was always able to drop the point and return to his original concerns. He never suffered a sustained confusion that might prompt him to reassess his beliefs and his language. Neoptolemos does undergo such a refutation. When he has to confront Philoctetes as an individual who has suffered and who is generous, Neoptolemos is forced to reexamine his recently acquired belief that victory alone determines what is noble. Neoptolemos is more influenced by the heroic past, and it is his commitment to a certain understanding of nobility that allows him to feel the incoherence between the two sets of beliefs that he is currently holding. When he asks "what shall I do?" (*ti draso* [969]), an aporia has opened (Winnington-Ingram, *Sophocles,* 288). His discontent with himself is precisely the type of self-loathing that a Socratic refutation should produce. And this self-disgust leads him to abandon a set of values that have produced this self-image. He has returned to himself.

This return allows Sophocles to push his examination of rhetoric to the next level. The undoing of a current sophistic education in rhetoric turns out to be not the most difficult problem for the discovery of a new rhetoric. The refutation of Neoptolemos is a fairly straightforward process. Having been convinced of the shamefulness of using guile, Neoptolemos turns to a persuasion that is a sincere communication of what he believes. But such persuasion fails miserably and proves ineffective in moving Philoctetes. Again, a standard account of rhetoric is being subjected to a skeptical doubt that raises questions not about particular failures but about systemic impossibilities. For if Neoptolemos is no longer corrupt, he is still naive and lacks the resources to deal adequately with Philoctetes. His refutation may have advanced his ethical maturation, but it has not enabled him to acquire the power necessary to make this ethical advance politically significant. His ineffectiveness argues that the problem of rhetoric cannot be reduced to the problem of ethics, nor can rhetoric be defended by arguments that are based on the conscious intentions of rhetors.

Some critics have claimed that had Neoptolemos originally attempted to persuade Philoctetes, he might very well have succeeded.[11] But the design of the play discourages such speculation. If its inquiry into rhetoric and the viability of public discourse is to be adequate to the historical reality in which rhetoric must operate, then it is imperative that the play address an audience that resists persuasion. The issue is not one of a missed opportunity but of the possibility of action after a crushing disillusionment. It is important that Philoctetes becomes more savage as he realizes the deceit that has been practiced on him, and that the audience witness and understand that his resistance to persuasion is not merely a personal truculence but a reasonable suspicion. Sophocles wants him to be in a state of distrust that is so deep that a simple straightforward statement of belief cannot move him. Put another way, what Sophocles is suggesting is that the personal integrity of the rhetor does not end the issue over the possibility of a viable public discourse. If there were no history of injustice and each rhetorical act could take place atomistically, then maybe the viability of public discourse could be reduced to the problem of the personal integrity of the rhetor, as standard defenses do. But the point of the play is to find a public language that can speak to injustice and that recognizes a legitimate skepticism on the part of the marginalized to even sincere discourse.

James Boyd White, who also reads the play as having "much to teach us about how persuasion works, and can work, and what it means to give yourself to a life of persuasion of one kind or another" (*Herakles' Bow*, 4), argues that the problem of persuasion is a problem of sincerity. He believes that Neoptolemos learns finally to understand persuasion as "the art of stating fully and sincerely the grounds upon which one thinks common action can and should rest" (17). White goes on to hold out conversation as the model for an ideal discourse and to see sincere conversation as the mark of a true community: "Neoptolemos begins by calling upon the kind of willingness to engage in sincere conversation that has been defined by him, by Philoctetes, and by the play itself as a central feature of proper community, proper character, and proper persuasion" (17–18).

But if reform of rhetoric hinges on the issue of personal sincerity, why does Sophocles arrange events so that Neoptolemos's speech must fail? White argues that we do not finally know why the speech failed and that the point of our ignorance is to underline the uncertainty that is an inescapable element in any rhetorical situation. What the play then teaches is that the only genuine possibility for rhetoric to promote a viable public discourse is "to recognize the freedom and autonomy of another" and "to leave room for the exercise of that freedom and autonomy in ways you do not wish" (23). The problem with reading the play this way is that it solves the problem of rhetoric by eliminating rhetoric. It offers the transparency of intention as a rhetorical standard and conceives the audience not as historical beings who have suffered injustice but more as Kantian agents who are defined by autonomy of the will and personal freedom. But if one views the audience in this way, rhetoric becomes irrelevant, for discourse must aspire to the impersonality and transparency of reason. The only obstructions that can be recognized are those that prevent reason from acting fully in accord with itself. Hence the demand for sincerity — for Kant's goodwill. But in what way is the Philoctetes who resists Neoptolemos's persuasion a free and autonomous agent? The entire design of the play is to constitute him as someone who has become savage because of injustice done to him. It is his determination by historical circumstances that prevents him from being persuaded.

Further, the play establishes that the problem of persuasion is greater than Neoptolemos's recovering from a momentary loss of his true self. Sophocles takes Philoctetes' skepticism seriously in a way that White's reading does not. The tragedy wants the audience to understand that Philoctetes is justified in resisting Neoptolemos's sincere words, for, as he points out, the Greeks have not changed. History has taught him a lesson, and that lesson is that injustice will be an abiding problem and that, while personal sincerity may resolve a particular individual's ethical difficulties, it cannot be the source of an answer for the more complicated and messy problem of finding a way of talking in a situation in which public discourse has been debased. The freedom and autonomy of the individual provide an inadequate solution to a problem embedded in a historical abuse.

For White the problem of evil is finally only an apparent problem and he sees the disappearance of Odysseus as evidence for the illusionary power he held: "The ultimate fact about Odysseus is his disappearance into nothingness at the end. Once Neoptolemos faces him down, he evaporates off the stage, to reappear only as a possible target for Philoctetes. The man whose great claim is to be a source of competent energy ends up literally nothing at all. The power of evil is only apparent, for in the realm of character and community it has no force, no actuality, against an integrated mind" (20–21). But Odysseus does not simply disappear. He leaves with a promise to return with the Greek army. His defeat is far from final, and if he has withdrawn, it is only a strategic or prudential withdrawal; Neoptolemos takes his return and the claims of the Greeks seriously. It is only Philoctetes, trapped by his own hatred into an impoverished understanding of the world as a place of private concerns, who does not take the threat seriously. One reason for the design of the play with its second ending is to show that one historical consequence of past injustice is the creation of a cynicism toward the possibility of a meaningful public life and then to criticize this cynicism as limited and injurious. Far from evil evaporating, injustice endures and is sufficiently protean that one cannot engage it in a contest that could achieve a final victory. If rhetoric is to be recovered, it must begin by acknowledging that injustice will persevere and that political life is a more complicated affair than can be managed simply by personal sincerity.

The solution of sincerity fails for another reason: it is an unrhetorical solution to a rhetorical problem. If all that is needed is sincerity, then rhetoric with its concern for a stylized discourse that invents an appropriate ēthos, logos, and pathos is at best irrelevant and at worst contrary to the ideal of a conversation rooted in the sincere expression of the discoursing individuals. What White has done is to collapse or translate the problem of rhetoric and a viable public discourse into a problem in Enlightenment ethics that emphasizes the internal disposition of the individual agent or will. He has made the focus of the play Neoptolemos's coming to understand his error. But Sophocles sees this understanding as only part of the problem. The drama of the play revolves around Philoctetes' corruption, which is a more entangled and complicated affair than Neoptolemos's simply being tricked by a wily Odysseus.

Simon Goldhill argues that tragedy does not resolve issues of value and offer straightforward solutions to the significant problems besetting fifth-century Athens but instead deliberately magnifies and plays with these difficulties:

> Rather than simply reflecting the cultural values of a fifth-century audience, then, rather than offering simple didactic messages from the city's poets to the citizens, tragedy seems deliberately to make difficult the assumption of the values of civic discourse. And it is precisely this unsettling force of the tragic texts that makes certain critics' assertions of the necessarily simple, clear, and straightforward nature of the texts for performance quite so insufficient. Indeed, it would seem more appropriate to claim that it is exactly the refusal to accept the simple, clear, and straightforward that constitutes the extraordinary force of the tragic drama of Athens. ("The Great Dionysia," 124)

Goldhill sees the subversion of the values of civic discourse as a fundamental feature of a Dionysian discursive form. Dionysus is the god of paradox, and his theater is a place in which the social norm is subjected to a questioning. This approach to tragedy helps explain Sophocles' skeptical interrogation of rhetoric, for it argues that tragedy is a discursive form whose purpose is to present the political as a philosophical problem.

Goldhill shares with John J. Winkler and others a design to relocate tragedy in its civic context and to understand its dramas as part of a political ceremony that functioned to support the civic ideology of the newly emerged democracy.[12] Arguing along the same lines, Vernant and Vidal-Naquet claim that one needs to see tragedy as a cultural artifact that arose at a specific historical time and performed a specific social function. They situate tragedy between the older discursive forms of epic and lyric and the soon-to-emerge discursive form of philosophy (*Myth and Tragedy,* 29). For them, the tragic hero is offered not as a model to be imitated but as a problem to be explored, as the hero, now presented in a language that more closely approximates ordinary speech, becomes a subject not for admiration but for debate. This debate is political, for "the true material of tragedy is the social thought peculiar to the city-state, in particular the legal thought that was then in the process of being evolved" (25). Tragedy gives form to a crisis in political theory — one that is given iconographic representation in the *Philoctetes* by the presence of Odysseus and the absence of Achilles. What has prompted this crisis is the citizen interrogating the mythic tradition. But this interrogation does not presume the unquestioned superiority of the civic present over the mythic past; instead, it posits the political as a problem:

> But it is not only the world of myth that loses its consistency and dissolves in this focus. By the same token the world of the city is called into question and its fundamental values are challenged in the ensuing debate. When exalting

the civic ideal and affirming its victory over all the forces from the past, even Aeschylus, the most optimistic of tragic writers, seems not to be making a positive declaration with tranquil conviction but rather to be expressing a hope, making an appeal that remains full of anxiety even amid the joy of the final apotheosis. The questions are posed but tragic consciousness can find no fully satisfactory answers to them and so they remain open. (33)

This openness seems especially true for Sophocles, and especially for his *Philoctetes*. Rose argues that "Sophocles' career might be seen in its entirety as thoughtful questioning of democratic ideological hegemony by an informed participant, . . . a questioning haunted by a profound nostalgia for the lost Pindaric vision of society ruled by the innately superior scions of the old propertied families" (*Sons of the Gods*, 271). Rose reads *Philoctetes* as an attempt by Sophocles to appropriate some of the insights of the new sophistic thought that had bolstered democratic political thought as a basis for a new existential foundation for an aristocratic ideology (273).

Rose's emphasis on the positive ideological thrust of the play would get an argument from Goldhill and from Vernant and Vidal-Naquet, but they would certainly agree that it problematizes fifth-century civic ideology. Charles Segal argues that "*Philoctetes* reflects a mood of mistrust in the declining democracy. The failure of *logos* between men here is the expression of a deeper rift between the personal and the social *logos*, between barren social forms and the need for individual bonds of trust, friendship, communion" (*Tragedy and Civilization*, 339–40). At the center of the play's questioning is the current struggle between an aristocratic and a democratic ordering of the state. This conflict takes the particular form of the competing claims of *oikos* (household) and polis. The troubling and unsatisfactory decision of Neoptolemos and Philoctetes to abandon their responsibilities to the polis in favor of a friendship based in the loyalties of an oikos not only violates the myth but also is in direct opposition to a democratic ideology that was seeking to redefine loyalty in civic rather than in familial terms. The age and occupation of Neoptolemos make him paradigmatic for the Athenian youth who would be making the transition from ephebe to hoplite. As Vernant and Vidal-Naquet show, this transition is a move from a type of military conduct appropriate to border fighting to a new type of discipline required by the organized formations of hoplite warfare. This is a movement from a fighting in which deceit and trickery are legitimate tactics to one in which a premium is placed on following orders and performing as a member of a group (*Myth and Tragedy*, 161–62). The core of the play is the assumption of a certain kind of citizenship, and it is the possibility of a democratically organized city that becomes the open problem for the play.

This problem is twofold. If Goldhill and Vernant and Vidal-Naquet are correct, then one of its dimensions is the proper training of youth so that the young can assume and perform their civic responsibilities. In part this involves learning a proper stance toward authority and cultivating a disciplined loyalty, and in part it involves mastering a discourse appropriate for a democracy. This is an issue in military training and its consequences for citizenship and an issue of civic participation, which makes it an issue in the conduct of civic discourse. The play addresses these concerns through the conflicts of Neoptolemos.

The play addresses the other and more difficult dimension of the problem of democratic discourse through Philoctetes' situation. Here it raises a question as to the adequacy of a democratic discourse to deal with a polis's past. If the viability of a society depends upon that society's ability to educate its young, it also depends upon that society's ability to deal with its past, for such a past is never really past but is brought forward into the present as an often inconvenient obstacle that must be dealt with. The tractability, innocence, and decency of Neoptolemos mitigate the problem of his miseducation and subsequent correction. If he can be momentarily diverted from his true self by a contemporary ideology that emphasizes a strategic approach to social life, he is not so formed that such a mistake cannot be undone when he sees the consequences of this ideology in operation. But Philoctetes, because he is intractable, offers a greater problem. Unlike Neoptolemos, who has yet to be shaped by history and hence can change easily, Philoctetes has been formed by a set of experiences that have created a powerful and cynical authority that no longer believes in the possibility of a noble life within contemporary political institutions. He is no longer moved by images of noble political possibilities because past injustices make him see the world as a place barren of possibility, and the only concern that moves him is a retreat to an actively defended private life in which the demands and injustices of public life can be excluded.

Sophocles designed his play to highlight the inadequacy of a democratic logos in dealing with the issues raised by Philoctetes' marginalization and subsequent mistrust and rejection of any public discourse. Earlier versions of the story by Aeschylus and Euripides present a simple plot in which Odysseus succeeds in obtaining the bow. Apparently Aeschylus had Odysseus resort, at least initially, to cunning. Dio Chrysostom labeled the play old-fashioned, and Kirkwood speculates that the tragedy was "the working out of an ordinance of fate or deity" (*A Study of Sophoclean Drama*, 37). Euripides' version was a much more political play and matched an Odysseus skillful in persuasion against some Trojan envoys in a contest for the bow. Odysseus's triumph was a victory for persuasion.

In Sophocles' version the triumph of persuasion has become its defeat. He

has complicated these earlier versions by his innovations of adding Neoptolemos and of having the political logos fail. Both innovations work to make
rhetoric a problem. By organizing his play as a movement from Neoptolemos's
corruption by a rhetorical education, to his refutation, to the recovery of his
personal integrity, to the failure of a discourse originating in this personal
integrity, Sophocles argues that the deeper and more troubling problems of
democratic rhetoric are not products of personal corruption or the abuse of
rhetoric but inhere in a history that transcends the intentions of any particular
speaker or citizen. The problems raised by personal corruption are practical
problems that can be addressed; the problems raised by past injustice are
tragic in the terms formulated by Goldhill and by Vernant and Vidal-Naquet
—they are open questions that create a particular tragic consciousness that
recognizes that "words, values, men themselves, are ambiguous, that the universe is one of conflict" (Vernant and Vidal-Naquet, *Myth and Tragedy*, 43).
For if tragedy and rhetoric share a set of topics (Goldhill, *Reading Greek
Tragedy*, 236), Sophocles' *Philoctetes* poses a tragic interrogation of the possibility of a viable democratic rhetoric.

If we hear Philoctetes' history, we witness the final violation of his trust. The
tragedy shows him becoming savage, and if his initial isolation seemed to
return him to some precivilization state of nature, his subsequent betrayal by
Neoptolemos suggests that savagery is not a state prior to civilization but a
fate that civilization entails on certain of its citizens. It is hard to avoid the
temptation to read this play anachronistically as a critique of Rousseau. There
is no return to nature, for when one departs or is excluded from civilization,
that individual is determined by a set of moral categories that will, in turn,
influence the way in which nature is read. As Kenneth Burke remarked, the
fact of language has separated us irretrievably from our natural condition
(*Language as Symbolic Action*, 13). The landscapes that we view will be, in
part, landscapes that we project, and these projected landscapes will inevitably
be tropes for our understanding of the moral universe and not innocent descriptions of a physical place. The Lemnos of Sophocles is the "soulscape" of
Philoctetes (Segal, *Tragedy and Civilization*, 323). The hatred with which he
populates the island creates an environment with an ethical charge that is
lacking in a natural environment in which the drama is one of survival and not
one of revenge.[13]

The Lemnos that is presented at the opening of the play is a wild nature far
removed from any pastoral associations (Vernant and Vidal-Naquet, *Myth
and Tragedy*, 165–66). There are no tilled fields or any other marks of civilization. Neoptolemos's brief catalogue of what he finds in Philoctetes' cave
confirms the primitive life on the island in which human existence has been

reduced to the minimum of mere survival. Further, the "sea-girt" island is isolated. In this nature, life is brute and precarious, dominated by a rhythm of pain and momentary relief from pain. What marks this island more than hostility to human purpose is indifference to that purpose. If Philoctetes has managed to survive, he knows that he too will someday feed the animals who have fed him. In exposing him on Lemnos, the Greeks deprived him of the nurture that civilization offers in its cultivation of fields and friendships.

It is surprising when Philoctetes first appears that he is so gentle. Like a beast tamed by hunger, he approaches Neoptolemos with a need for sustenance. He has been able to scratch out a rudimentary physical existence, but he is starved for human companionship. It would be a mistake, however, to see his initial openness and even his genuine pity at the fate of his noble companions at Troy as indicating a psychic health underlying his wild appearance. For in the barren land of Lemnos, Philoctetes has cultivated a hatred for Odysseus and the Atridae — his abandonment and subsequent isolation have provided a fertile soil for the growth of that hatred. The strength of will that allowed him to endure has channeled this energy into a deep desire for revenge. The mere mention of Odysseus and the Atridae is enough to inflame his passionate denunciations. His strength and nobility now manifest themselves in an implacable loathing for those Greeks who abandoned him. A nobility that could not be cultivated in the absence of others has undergone a distorted, if somewhat magnificent, growth into a flourishing passion for revenge. The physical starkness of the landscape embodies the moral starkness of an imagination fed by a sense of the injustice committed.

Philoctetes' personal metamorphosis also is emblematic of the larger transformation of the aristocracy that has occurred during the Trojan war. The nobility that had distinguished Greek civilization has been decimated by the war. With Achilles and so many others dead, Philoctetes becomes the surviving remnant of that tradition. He is the existing alternative to the political life embodied in Odysseus. But Philoctetes is an injured nobility — one whose vision has shrunk from its recognition of the political as the field of the noble to a narrow focus on private friendship. Because of the debilitating consequences of his injury at the hands of the Greeks, Philoctetes cannot offer Neoptolemos a viable political alternative. The traditional nobility has undergone a contorted growth, becoming an obsession with its own injury that has rendered it incapable of fulfilling its social function. The bow, the symbol of Herakles' civilizing a brute nature, is employed no longer as a defense against Greece's enemies but in the private business of Philoctetes' survival (Segal, *Tragedy and Civilization*, 318–20). In an environment that does not properly nurture heroic virtue, that virtue does not simply disappear but rather becomes distorted, and energy that might have been directed to a common good instead is diverted into an intractable private hatred that makes the recovery of a noble public existence even more difficult. The noble tradition of the past has proven inadequate to deal with the changes in a present that do not afford opportunities for traditional noble actions, and it has become a festering private resentment of injustice and a despair at the changes wrought. It is no longer a source of political or intellectual fruition.

The strength of character that has allowed Philoctetes to endure a barren Lemnos is expressed as willed resistance to any yielding. If Philoctetes passionately desires discourse, he vehemently rejects any discourse that would require him to expose himself to risk. It is worth asking whether Philoctetes even before the betrayal by Neoptolemos would have or could have participated in a conversation in which disagreement occurred. Part of the reason that his initial conversation with Neoptolemos works so well is that Neoptolemos is telling him what he wants to hear. Even Philoctetes' genuine pity for the fallen heroes of Troy is an expression of his underlying despair at the prospect of justice — the events of the war confirm his experience and opinion that this is a world in which only the unprincipled thrive.

The strength of Philoctetes' resistance to persuasion reveals the depth of Sophocles' insight into the consequences of Philoctetes' marginalization by the Greeks. The hatred, the iron will are necessary for his survival. When the Greeks abandoned him, they denied him the possibility of maintaining his virtuous nobility. The transmogrification of virtue into hatred is not a personal failure on the part of Philoctetes but rather Sophocles' recognition that consequences of the kind of injury suffered by Philoctetes are even deeper and more troubling than they initially appear to be. Philoctetes' unwillingness to be persuaded is not a personal obstinacy but a defensive position that he has found to be essential for his own survival. Hence the issue of persuasion cannot be dealt with as one of personal intransigence, as if Philoctetes could voluntarily abandon his resistance.

Bernard Knox has seen Philoctetes' unyielding as a Sophoclean expression of heroic will, and he recognizes the unsettling paradox in this play that a victory for the heroic will is also a defeat for that will (*Heroic Temper*, 138–39). Philoctetes' resistance to adversity has lost a noble objective, and his stubbornness is not directed toward some noble if tragic action but to "inaction, to ineffective suffering" (*Heroic Temper*, 140). There can be little doubt that Philoctetes' rejection of the mission at Troy is tantamount to accepting the prolongation of his suffering and finally a death that is not glorious but only a surcease of pain.

But even a healthier Sophoclean tragic hero in his or her resistance to bending is troubling for a democratic society in which compromise is essential. Oedipus, Antigone, Creon, Ajax, and Electra are all difficult individuals who in their inflexibility can seem to border on the inhuman. Nussbaum has argued for the value of yielding in *Antigone,* and the speeches of Haemon to Creon claim that he who is unyielding will end up ruling a desert very much like the barren tract represented by Lemnos.[14] Philoctetes in his intransigence embodies a serious threat to democracy. How can a democracy with its commitment to communal decision making reintegrate into the polis those citizens who have been excluded? It cannot resort to the physical force (bia) that distinguished the authority of the old aristocratic order of nobility, and there appears to be an inherent instability involved in manipulating others by guile, for at a certain point the society simply destroys the capacity for trust. Persuasion is an internal necessity for democracies, so if there should be situations in which persuasion fails, then rhetoric as a problem ceases to be an issue of locating a technical means of assisting a democracy and becomes a search for a crucial space in which the possibility of democracy must be secured.

Because the possibility of persuasion is central to this tragedy, the action that we witness begins with strategic speeches that play on the trust and fellow-feeling of Philoctetes. For the situation to become tragic and not just regrettable, circumstances need to be brought to the pitch that the audience feels both the desirability of persuasion and its impossibility. Knox suggests the force of this feeling when he notes, "For the first time in Sophoclean tragedy we want to see the hero give in" (*Heroic Temper,* 135). But we also know that it would be wrong if he did so, that it would be a defeat for nobility and a victory for Odysseus and the Atridae.

After Neoptolemos has left with Odysseus in preparation for the return to Troy, the chorus and Philoctetes remain and the chorus, speaking as a friend, seeks to persuade Philoctetes to accompany the Greeks. Some critics have seen this chorus as ethically shallow, as "sanctimonious," seeming to endorse the rightness of Odysseus's argument and failing to give sufficient heed to the suffering of Philoctetes and the callousness of the Greeks.[15] But there is no reason to doubt the genuineness of the chorus's feeling, for its members, like Neoptolemos, have seen Philoctetes' pain and have felt pity for him. Their words sound trite but are nevertheless true, and their import is reasonable: Odysseus is not a simple villain; Philoctetes' suffering was the will of the god; and his suffering persists because he so wills it. The problem is that this assessment, though reasonable, does not do justice to the injury and hence is not satisfying for either Philoctetes or the audience — both of whom seek justice. It is no longer simply self-interest and justice that are opposed; it is reason and justice that are opposed, and this is why persuasion is so difficult.

The most powerful act of rhetoric is reserved for Neoptolemos. Sophocles has the young warrior defy Odysseus, break his oath to the Greeks, and return the bow to Philoctetes. There can be no doubt that he has been moved to act by the demands of both friendship and justice and that he is not acting from self-interest. His current actions undo his earlier deceit and demonstrate clearly that he seeks only Philoctetes' best interest. If anyone could be persuasive, Neoptolemos should succeed. When he speaks, it is friend addressing friend.

Sophocles has written a strong speech for Neoptolemos. Neoptolemos begins his address by thanking Philoctetes for his praise of both his father and himself. Like a good rhetor, he then proceeds to define the issue. Making no mention of the treachery of the Atridae and Odysseus, Neoptolemos focuses on the necessity to bear the sufferings that the gods inflict. He next picks up a theme argued earlier by the chorus that an individual who will not give up his obsessive concern with his suffering finally gives up his claim to the pity of others. What Neoptolemos is trying to do is to get Philoctetes to understand why continuing to nurture his hatred now represents the greatest obstacle to his cure. It is not his isolation for the last decade, nor even the austerity that reduced his life to mere survival that has made him savage, but his own anger. The final injury inflicted on him is that the injustice that he suffered has now made him injure himself, for he has lost any sense of a world larger than his own pain and injustice. Such a world no more permits trust than does the world of strategic manipulation that Odysseus thrives in. Neoptolemos tries to make Philoctetes see the radical and reductive opposition into which he has fallen. His world had been simplified into friends, defined as those who say what he agrees with, and enemies, defined as those who say something he doesn't want to hear. Like Odysseus, Philoctetes has created a world in which loyalty stands in place of trust. Philoctetes has made himself into an audience that is outside the boundaries of persuasion. This is his reversion to the savage state, for as Rose mentioned in the sophistic account of human progress, it was the move to persuasion that allowed humans to survive as a group (*Sons of the Gods*, 290–302). Philoctetes' hatred is what keeps him isolated.

Having set the issue, Neoptolemos challenges Philoctetes' reductive conception of friendship by telling him something he doesn't want to hear. The attempt at persuasion is thus an offer of a healthier and fuller friendship that manifests itself in a willingness to refute the friend. Neoptolemos states the situation straightforwardly: Philoctetes' illness was sent by Zeus. The relief from that suffering, however, can be found within a polis—the army has the resources to rid Philoctetes of his pain.

Neoptolemos then provides the authority for this claim, an authority intended to deal with the problem of mistrust. He knows the truth of what he speaks because it is divinely sanctioned, having been prophesied by Helenus, who gave the prophecy and declared that the Greeks could kill him if he were wrong.

Neoptolemos is now ready to ask Philoctetes to act. His speech to this point has been to prepare Philoctetes to do one thing: yield. Philoctetes' savagery is expressed in his incapacity to yield. For Philoctetes to be cured, he must yield. Only if he yields can he regain the humanity that he has lost in his reaction to the injury and injustice that have been perpetrated against him. What might appear to be an action — his abandoning the Greeks at Troy and returning to Oeta — is merely a way to shift the scene of the suffering. It is not a response but a retreat. Sophocles is challenging any simple equation of assertion and action and redefining action not as the concerted effort of an individual will but as a mode of social engagement that opens one to the words of an Other. To become human again, Philoctetes must risk trusting another.

Neoptolemos's final inducement to yield, the glory that will be gained by taking Troy, almost seems an afterthought. In part, this is so because public acclamation no longer interests Philoctetes, so glory cannot function as a reason for his acting. Neoptolemos knows that the issue is not the achievement of glory but the recovery of trust. Still, he must use whatever authority his friendship offers to try to break the self-maintained isolation of Philoctetes.

Philoctetes is moved by the speech and he opens himself to the refutation. His response is confusion and indecision. His resistance relents, and he seriously considers yielding. Clearly, Neoptolemos has spoken as a friend, and his friendship has authority. Philoctetes is led to the key question, "what shall I do?" (1350). An aporia has opened. Even to entertain this question is to have traveled a considerable distance. But as he reflects on his choice, he is led back to an irrefragable point and one that Neoptolemos was silent on because he could not speak to it. The Atridae and Odysseus have not changed, and there is no reason to assume that they have learned anything from their dealings with Philoctetes, except, perhaps, that they will have to be yet a little cleverer next time. Philoctetes is willing to let go of his hatred, but he cannot abandon his knowledge. The desire to break free from the debilitating confinement of his illness is not enough. History is not so easily gotten over. Philoctetes is willing to trust Neoptolemos, to open himself to an Other, but he knows that this trust also opens him to the Atridae, and their world is unchanged. To give himself over to them violates what he has learned about the world. Trust might be possible among friends, but history argues that it is incompatible with the operation of political power. It is not some perverse desire to keep cultivating his injury but reason that holds him back. He will not return to Troy.

Whitman argues that Philoctetes is right in his choice: "Philoctetes must decide freely to come to Troy, if he is to come. Force, guile, persuasion, all are useless; his knowledge and vision of his own heroic self must lead him to a decision to save his *kleos*. But Philoctetes has no moral ground for making that decision. He has every moral right to refuse, and refuse he does, resolutely" (*Sophocles*, 185). And Kitto sees the entire design of the scene as demonstrating Sophocles' intention that "Philoctetes . . . say No, in the face of every possible inducement" (*Greek Tragedy*, 305). Kitto goes on to make the point that Sophocles does not have Neoptolemos use such arguments as the number of Greek lives lost if Philoctetes should not return to Troy, nor does he emphasize fully the theological point that the prophecy has destined this to happen, so Philoctetes' refusal to go would be an impious deed. But even had these arguments been included, Philoctetes would have had reason for resisting, for neither of these arguments sufficiently addresses the problem of the past deception of the Atridae and Odysseus that makes it impossible to trust any action of which they are a part.

Philoctetes is not defiant in his rejection of persuasion. If anything, there is a note of regret — it is not that he will not comply but that the character of the Greek commanders makes it impossible for him to comply. Neoptolemos acknowledges this by agreeing that what Philoctetes concludes is reasonable. What the tragedy has demonstrated is the reasonableness of political skepticism. The unwillingness to trust the polis is not a personal decision or the result of a personal spite or truculence, but rather it is the only reasonable alternative that the polis has left the individual whom it has marginalized. For such an individual no argument framed in terms of a public purpose can have force. Philoctetes is no longer moved by glory; all he seeks is to be left alone. He has resigned himself to the inevitability of his current suffering; better to stick with the current pain than to open oneself to new suffering and injustice at the hands of a polis that can only see the individual as a means to be used for its ends.

Even without authority of the myth, the play shows that this reasonable position is wrong. Neoptolemos, who equally knows the treacherousness of the Greeks, continues to feel the obligation toward the polis. To abandon his responsibilities at Troy is to incur shame. Philoctetes dismisses such a possibility by saying to give it no thought, but it is not that easy. Neoptolemos then raises the objection that the Greeks will now come again and seek them out. Philoctetes replies that he will fight on Neoptolemos's behalf with his bow. Neoptolemos has no more to say, so he agrees to go with Philoctetes.

Nussbaum argues that Neoptolemos "feels himself obliged by his nature as *gennaios* and *chrēstos* to respect Philoctetes' right to make his own choice, even when the choice he makes conflicts with the general good, and indeed even his own good" ("Consequences," 47). But it is not respect that moves Neoptolemos to honor Philoctetes' choice to return to Oeta; rather, he has simply run out of reasons with which to oppose Philoctetes. Neoptolemos is clearly reluctant about the choice, but he has exhausted all his arguments against it. As Whitman recognizes, "Philoctetes is not confused. He is right in his judgment of the Atreidae and Odysseus, and he is right to refuse to help them; even Neoptolemos, in his most persuasive moment cannot deny that" (*Sophocles,* 178). The design of the play has been to produce this crisis. This is the third aporia. The personal crises of both Neoptolemos and Philoctetes have been resolved: Neoptolemos has recovered from his momentary diversion into the ethics of strategic manipulation and Philoctetes has let go of his hate. But both of these individual changes are insufficient for addressing the rhetorical crisis. The third aporia is not a gap or moment of personal incoherence but a breakdown in public discourse, for that discourse itself is now incoherent: the full recovery of his health requires Philoctetes to return to and participate in the polis, but the polis's past discursive practices argue that such a return is not possible, for he will always and only be viewed strategically by those in power. There is nothing the art of rhetoric can do in this situation; history has eviscerated the authority of logos.

Again, Knox, more than any other critic, is successful at conveying the feeling of this moment of incoherence, of skepticism: "Philoctetes has won. The heroic will here wins a victory which outshines any that we have seen in the other plays. One man's stubbornness has defeated not only the whole Greek army but also the prophecy of Helenus and the will of Zeus, which is the pattern of history. It is an extraordinary moment in the theater of Dionysus, and we know, from the descriptions we have of the *Philoctetes* plays of Aeschylus and Euripides, that for the audience it must have been utterly unexpected. It is a theatrical *tour de force,* and we no sooner experience the shock of it than we realize that the play cannot end this way" (*Heroic Temper,* 138–39). The play's apparent ending is both right and impossible. And as Segal argues: "By resorting to the *deus ex machina* Sophocles shows his recognition of this moral dilemma" (*Tragedy and Civilization,* 356). Rhetoric has run out of resources with which to address an audience that understands the duplicity of public discourse, and the personal sincerity of the rhetor, his or her refusal to countenance and participate in such duplicity, is still not sufficient to bring back someone who has been marginalized. Logos is silenced.

When Herakles enters, he will no longer employ a logos but will shift to a discourse that is based in muthos.[16] His speech does not make a compelling argument; what it offers, instead, is a narrative that makes sense of suffering without denying the duplicity of political practice. Several critics have seen the ending not so much as an artificial resolution of the play's problems as a continuance and resolution of the issues that have been set in motion.[17] Herakles is the heroic vision that Philoctetes has always had and that has been awakened by the friendship and speech of Neoptolemos. Certainly such a reading is right in recognizing that Herakles does offer to Philoctetes a sense of self that he had lost and to Neoptolemos a link to the heroic past that had been severed by the death of Achilles, and to this extent the ending realizes potentialities that have always existed within the characters. But the recourse to a divine messenger and the shift from logos to muthos argue for a sense of disruption, even in a world in which the human and divine are more interconnected than modern thought generally concedes.

Further, this second ending is not without its ambiguities. Rose views the appearance of Herakles as a "utopian element in this play [that] seems especially thin — archaic even for its own time. A vision of an all-male world of born aristocrats exercising political supremacy through martial prowess offers most of us nothing new with which to chart a course toward an ampler and more just world" (*Sons of the Gods,* 331). Winnington-Ingram notes the possible irony in Herakles' saying that Neoptolemos and Philoctetes, like two lions, will destroy Troy, and his warning to treat the altars piously, since the audience would know that Neoptolemos impiously slew Priam at one of these altars (*Sophocles,* 303). And Segal points out, "The resolution implied in Herakles' descent from Olympus and Philoctetes' farewell to Lemnos is not total" (*Tragedy and Civilization,* 355). For one thing, Herakles does not address the issue of the past action of the Atridae, and he does not attempt to effect a reconciliation between them and Philoctetes (Segal, *Tragedy and Civilization,* 348). Injustice is left as an unresolved issue.

Herakles does not offer Philoctetes justice. Instead he offers Philoctetes a narrative that allows him to make sense of his suffering by viewing it from a larger perspective. Herakles offers his own life as a paradigm of heroic behavior in which the acceptance of suffering is part of the eventual winning of glory. The speech he gives is not a particularly well-crafted exercise in persuasion, for it is not intended to argue with or persuade Philoctetes. Instead, it is designed to give him an image that can produce a heroic desire, and at this it succeeds, for Philoctetes feels a yearning when he hears Herakles' words and he will not disobey. An older and lost authority has now reasserted itself, and its return renders the actions of the Atridae and Odysseus irrelevant to the nobility that now stirs within Philoctetes.

But if Sophocles has brought his play into harmony with the mythic tradition by arguing for the necessity of that tradition if the myths are to remain coherent for the audience, his ending in its resolution leaves unanswered the situation that it was so clearly designed to produce. Is the democratic present and its commitment to a rhetoric that produces a logos doomed to incoherence that cannot be addressed but only superseded? And do the traces of irony that Winnington-Ingram detects in the ending also suggest that the recovery of the heroic tradition may not be as straightforward as Herakles' speech seems to indicate and that history is not so easily negated simply by recovering a sense of individual purpose? The ending leaves one uncomfortable. The rapidity of the change in Philoctetes ought to jar even a pious audience, who believed in the reality and efficacy of divine intervention, because so much of the problem that gave force to the play simply dissolves while questions remain. Why, for example, does Herakles or Zeus allow Philoctetes and Neoptolemos to work through a chain of reasoning that leads them to a conclusion that makes sense but is wrong? Why do they need to reach that conclusion? These questions persist, not so much as speculations about divine intent but as issues about the design of the play. Another serious problem that the ending raises is that its endorsement of an epic past is brought forward in a tragic discursive form — the resolution and discursive frame are at odds.

Equally, the ending of the play raises questions about the political implications of tragic discourse. Does it represent an alternative to either rhetorical or epic discourse? Does it provide a way of joining, if not reconciling, the two forms of discourse with their commitments to two different types of political order? Does the *Philoctetes* in its skeptical refutation of rhetoric offer rhetoric as a problem in a way analogous to Socrates' refutations offering certain understandings and lives as problems? If so, what is to be made of the play's demonstration of rhetoric's incoherence?

A special urgency attaches to these questions because of the audience's complicity in the play. Sophocles has structured the play so that the audience assumes the viewpoint of Neoptolemos. Like him, we are filled in on the details of the plot by Odysseus; like him, we are in on the deceit practiced on Philoctetes; like him, we experience disgust at the deceit; and like him, we seek words to speak to Philoctetes. And most importantly, like Neoptolemos, we too are silenced and prove incapable of producing a discourse that can satisfactorily address the issue of past injustice. The play's demonstration of the incoherence of rhetoric must frustrate an audience that has participated and learned from the abuse of rhetoric, for it leaves its audience unresolved. Such an audience has been refuted by the tragedy and made conscious of its own impotence. The audience experiences its own silence and the inadequacy of its own reasoning as a crisis — its normal discourse has failed. Having been brought to silence, the audience must rethink rhetoric and possibly recover a more adequate political discourse.

Part of the play's contribution to a rethinking of rhetoric is to recast the problem of rhetoric from issue of the abuse of the art by an individual to the larger and more difficult issue of the limits on rhetoric imposed by history. It may be helpful to read the play as presenting successive stages of rhetorical incoherence. Neoptolemos is a twice-corrupted character. First he falls victim to Odysseus's education into a rhetoric that is limited only by an interest in immediate success. Then, having rejected this rhetoric and the use of deception, Neoptolemos recovers a noble and direct way of speaking. When this proves ineffective, he abandons public discourse and follows Philoctetes in his retreat to a private life. This is the second corruption, and it is more difficult to deal with to the extent that Philoctetes is a more attractive character than Odysseus and one who can claim justice on his side. His rejection of Neoptolemos's logos leads to the serious silencing of Neoptolemos, as he chooses friendship over his public responsibility. As admirable as such a choice might be, it is also corrupting, for in denying or avoiding public responsibility, Neoptolemos is as certainly violating his nature as when he practiced deceit. Only now this violation feels less like a violation than like the only reasonable course of action. It is the attractive misstep for which the tragedy has been designed. Abandoning public discourse is the reasonable impossibility. And by making it a reasonable impossibility, the tragedy raises the question whether it is possible to act responsibly in a world in which a past practice of a debased discourse has so destroyed the possibility of trust that whatever theoretical case can be made for the efficacy of rhetoric, the reality is that it cannot move back into society a marginalized audience whose trust has been destroyed. In its offer of a divine solution, the play acknowledges the recalcitrance of the problem.

The very solution, in its spiritual edification, is troubling. Can an ending that subsumes a political issue under a theological solution be satisfying to a democratic audience, when it seems to reject democratic politics and to despair at the efficacy of a human rhetoric? And even if, like Rose, following Jameson's poststructuralist Marxism, one tries the interpretive maneuver of appropriating the utopian solution for a less aristocratic project, this does not speak to the rhetorical breakdown or help generate a practical response to the skeptical thrust of the tragedy. Herakles' silence on the Atridae puts the problem of dealing with injustice outside the theological solution and leaves it as a demand to be met politically.

A rhetor committed to democracy is left with bits and pieces and acquires the task of rethinking rhetoric by using these fragments as guides. In creating a fragmentation that demands that the audience reassess and attempt to develop a rhetoric sufficiently powerful to operate in a world entangled in history, the

Philoctetes acts very much like Socrates in an elenchic dialogue. Its skeptical inquiry has destabilized the normal understanding of rhetoric and has left the audience the task of exploring its commitments and attempting to reformulate a coherent account of rhetoric.

The play's second ending does help in this project. Understanding why the muthos of Herakles succeeds where the logos of Neoptolemos failed does suggest several elements that any rhetoric that seeks to deal with the marginalized must include. First, Herakles offers Philoctetes not simply a set of reasons but a narrative that allows him to place his suffering. In offering his own life as a paradigm of heroic behavior, Herakles gives Philoctetes a coherent account of the relationship between nobility and suffering. The focus is no longer on the origin of the suffering but rather on the response of the character to the suffering. This makes suffering a problem of action rather than an experiential authority that could underwrite a political skepticism.

Second, society is now seen as a place in which the cure will be effected; the relief of suffering is not a divine task but a social one. By implication, the social is concerned with suffering — the polis is defined as the place in which action in response to suffering is to be taken. Finally, Herakles gives Philoctetes an account of the future in which a noble life is possible. The consequence of Herakles' words is that desire is stirred within Philoctetes. His obedience to Herakles is not simply compliance with a divine command but a voluntary choice to return. Herakles' speech has recovered the noble life as a viable possibility, as one that can engage the imagination and desire of a noble nature.

What a democratic rhetor could learn from this speech is the need for an image of the noble life that can compel the imaginations of the audience. Unlike a logos that is rooted in reasonable appeals to self-interest, the muthos of nobility offers an image of a life that is inherently seen as public. For the logos of self-interest the public is always a derived and instrumental good. The experience of a deep injustice then undermines the utility of a public life for a citizen whose participation in the polis is based primarily on self-interest. So a democratic rhetoric needs to invent an understanding of the nobility possible in a democratically organized society. Herakles' image of the twin lions suggests one possible way to embody such a nobility by making success not a matter of individual excellence but of corporate cooperation. Herakles mentions that each one will protect the other, and hence their success is dependent upon treating the other not merely as a means but as one whose fate is intimately tied to the individual's own well-being. For the polis to thrive, all must be protected.

The second element suggested by Herakles' speech is that a democratic rhetoric needs to give society an image of itself as a place in which relief is sought from suffering. The political world of Odysseus recognized no obligations for the state; rather, the state was powerful, and its justification came from its ability to exercise its power. All were subservient to the demands of the state's power, and social reward was limited to participation in the exercise of this power. The point of the prophecy, which is picked up in Herakles' speech, is that there is a necessity for the society to deal with its past injustices and with the suffering of its citizens. The political language should be based in the metaphor of health and not of the hunt.[18]

The play itself argues the need for such a democratic rhetoric. The heroic tradition has proved inadequate to deal with the changing world; this is the history out of which the play begins. The revamped heroism that it offers at the end also contains a hint of its instability. Herakles' admonition to treat piously the sacred altars at Troy ironically looks forward to the Greek violation of these altars and the subsequent dissolution of the Greek army after its victory. Does the aristocratic ideal of the noble warrior carry within itself the seeds of an impiety that will eventually cause it to overstep the bounds of pious behavior and bring divine wrath upon itself? If so, doesn't there need to be an alternative way of organizing a society that is not as likely in its ambition to lead to violations of divine will?

The play does not directly ask these questions, but its use of history and Herakles' admonitions raises them. The return to a mythic past is finally not an adequate response to the current problems of a democratically ordered society. Sophocles' tragedy does not so much offer solutions as relocate problems. If his tragedy resorts to an epic discourse, it recognizes that such a discourse and its implied images of nobility have proven inadequate in history. Further, in the failure of Neoptolemos's reformed rhetoric to be adequate to the political demands that arise because of history, the *Philoctetes* points to the clear difficulties that any rethinking of rhetoric must face. In placing the audience in the position of Neoptolemos, of being faced with a reasonable impossibility, Sophocles has used his tragic discourse to refute the audience. Its task now is to invent a new political language that can deal with injustice and can create a desire for political existence that the current debased rhetoric has destroyed. The audience has been shown that reason alone cannot accomplish such a reinvention and that what is needed is an image of political life that can generate the desire for such a life.

What the double ending makes clear is that without such an image there is a serious danger of factionalism as a response to injury. Neoptolemos's error that makes the first ending possible arises because he lacks a language adequate to speak to the history of Philoctetes' injury. The discourse and the social allegiances Philoctetes offers are to be constructed around the history of past injustice. When Philoctetes decides that he cannot trust the Greeks, his alternative is to deny a public discourse in which all can participate and to restrict his future association to those bound to him by private ties. Herakles' appearance challenges this move to constituting social groups on the basis of past injury by reminding Neoptolemos and Philoctetes that such an association does not offer the possibility of nobility, for it defines its members in terms of being victims of injustice and this does not provide a positive basis for action. Instead, the group imprisons and isolates itself by allowing itself to be defined by those who have injured its members in the past. The group does not respond to a political history but seeks to evade the reach of those in power. However understandable such a move may be for a group, it can only guarantee that the initial marginalization will continue.

The artifice of the ending recognizes this danger and in its theological solution does not offer a new political language for democracy. Rather, Sophocles' tragedy sets rhetoric the task of inventing an image of democratically organized society in which a life of nobility and not simply one of self-interest can revitalize the trust in the inherent value of political existence. The skepticism that the tragedy points to can be met only by the creation of a new language that can address and move those who have been marginalized by a society trapped in a language of self-interest and immediate gain. But if the play does not offer such a language, it does offer standards by which to assess such discourse. An adequate political discourse must address the issues of injustice and provide an image of nobility. In refuting its audience, the tragedy has forced the audience to see the problem of the marginalized differently and has shown how even a sincere and reasoned discourse is inadequate to speak to the mistrust that follows upon injustice. Indeed the second ending's failure to address the issue of injustice suggests the difficulty of finding a language. It simply may not be possible to speak in such a way as to be appropriately responsive to past injustices and their present injuries, but to resign oneself to silence as Neoptolemos does when he accepts Philoctetes' argument to abandon Troy and return to Oeta is to jettison the ideal of a noble life that is necessary to nurture a passionate human nature. It would prove impossible to live such a life.

The alternative to resignation is risk; a rhetoric that would revitalize a democracy that is ordered only by the demands of the private interests of the powerful must attempt to invent a new political language that can create images that can sustain the human need for purposes larger than those of self-interest. The rhetorical crisis generated by a self-interested democracy is finally a crisis of imagination, and a new democratic rhetoric must reimagine the current world and redefine nobility not in terms of acquisition or victory but in terms of a willingness to grapple with suffering and injustice. For these problems in their recalcitrance to merely technical solutions, and not some physical enemy, represent the deep challenges to political life.

5

Violence and Rhetoric in Euripides' Hecuba

While Sophocles explores the problems of crediting public discourse when the public trust has been abused by those in power, Euripides makes the possibility of addressing the powerful the central theme of his *Hecuba*. He subjects to a skeptical interrogation the possibility for noncoerced agreement in which persuasion rather than force determines action. The attractiveness of positing persuasion as an alternative to force is easy to understand. It allows reason a role in human affairs and presents an account of the world in which people have some control over their lives. Rhetoric is thus intimately connected to freedom and essential for a democratic community. If properly pursued, rhetoric aids the ongoing project of articulating a community's understanding of justice, utility, and honor. Undergirding this account of rhetoric displacing force with reason and reconciling power and ethics is the assumption that audiences can be found who are moved by persuasion. Not surprisingly, the rhetorical tradition spends little time on the problem of those audiences which are unaffected by the suasions of eloquence, for such audiences call into question the efficacy of rhetoric. But the availability of an audience is a key problem for rhetoric, and it is especially a troubling problem when an audience fails to hear a rhetor because its hold on power is sufficiently secure that rhetoric, with its concern for reasoned persuasion, is irrelevant.

Euripides, by most accounts the most rhetorical of the three major Greek tragedians, was bothered by the impotence of rhetoric in a world moved by power and chance.[1] In *Hecuba* he looks at the consequences of the failure of public discourse from the vantage point of the disempowered. He creates a protagonist, skilled in rhetoric, and places her in a situation in which those in power, insulated from the pain of others, cannot be reached through persuasion. The play undermines any easy belief in the efficacy of rhetoric and questions a straightforward opposition of persuasion (peitho) to force (bia). Further, it emphasizes the personal cost to a rhetor who seeks justice in a world defined in terms of bia and examines the instability of rhetorical solutions in such a world. Euripides, however, does not raise questions about rhetoric to impugn it but to develop a complex and sophisticated justification for it. He sees rhetoric as endangered not because force actively suppresses speech but because those in power need not heed rhetoric. For him, the paradox besetting rhetoric is that power enslaves those who hold it as well as those who are held by it.[2] In *Hecuba,* the problem for rhetoric is to find an opening for public discourse when power preemptively forecloses such discourse. In his understanding of the complex relation of power to rhetoric, Euripides again demonstrates that he is our contemporary and that his dramas speak eloquently to problems that occupy us.[3]

To argue that *Hecuba* presents a sophisticated justification for rhetoric is to challenge the play's critical legacy, which has been to read this tragedy as a portrait of the protagonist's descent into an ethical nihilism. But such a reading of the play does not value sufficiently the problem of a banal evil, nor does it understand the threat that banality offers to rhetoric.[4] Part of Euripides' contribution to rhetorical theory lies in his understanding that a monumental evil does not require an extraordinary cause, and that ethical and political existence can be threatened by commonplace failures. This insight leads his tragedy to be a profound meditation on the need for rhetoric and the precariousness of its existence.

It would not be an exaggeration to say that the play's protagonist is as much rhetoric as it is Hecuba, for the ethical integrity of rhetoric is as much at stake as the ethical identity of Hecuba. Euripides structures the play around three rhetorical agons. In the first two agons, one with Odysseus and one with Agamemnon, Hecuba's rhetoric, despite its excellence, is ineffective. Hecuba's failure with Odysseus and Agamemnon raises the failure of rhetoric as an issue for the play. Her personal crisis is inseparable from the larger rhetorical crisis that occupies a world constituted by bia.[5] In such a world there is no commitment to justice, and public discourse degenerates into public relations, which can be discarded as soon as it proves inconvenient or irksome.[6]

The play's concern with rhetoric begins with a scene that displays the discourse of power. Achilles' ghost has delayed the departure of the Greek fleet, demanding the sacrifice of Polyxena as a tribute for his actions in the Trojan war. The Greek army is divided evenly for and against the sacrifice until Odysseus persuades the soldiers that what appears to them to be a difficult and agonizing choice is, in fact, a simple problem of calculation—what is more valuable to the Greeks: the life of a slave or the honor of Achilles?

The strongest defense of Odysseus is offered by A. W. H. Adkins, who bases his argument on the logic of ethical justification used in fifth-century Athens. Adkins cautions against reading Odysseus's arguments anachronistically and ascribing to the Greeks contemporary ethical understandings or sentiments ("Basic Greek Values," 193). He argues that Odysseus's justification of the sacrifice of Polyxena accords with fifth-century Greek commitment to competitive values over cooperative ones. Adkins's analysis is important for two reasons. First, it explains why the army might embrace Odysseus's reasoning. For even if Odysseus were cynical, it is difficult to believe that the army could be so easily won over to his cynicism or, alternatively, so easily taken in by his manipulation. If his argument worked, it is reasonable to assume that it had some merit and spoke to an obligation that the Greek army could recognize as making serious claims on it. Second, Adkins's argument recovers Odysseus as a character who cannot be reduced to a simple villain and shows that he need not be an insensitive and cynical opportunist, as he is, for example, in Sophocles' *Philoctetes*. Rather he can be read as someone acting honorably and doing what the circumstances require.

The weakness of Adkins's account is that it omits precisely what Odysseus cannot see, and hence it misses Euripides' criticism of Odysseus's speech. Odysseus is untroubled by his argument, and he suffers from none of the self-division that besets the army as a whole. His loyalty is single; his concern is to ensure the strength of the Greek army. He accepts unquestioningly the ethics of competition and thus is blind to the injury that he inflicts. This is what makes him so terrifying. He is not corrupt or cynical, merely limited. His speech embodies the unreflective security that follows from an ethics of power.

Other critics make clear Odysseus's limitation (Abrahamson, "Euripides' Tragedy of Hecuba," 123–24, note 10; Conacher, *Euripidean Drama*, 157–58). For them, the sacrifice of Polyxena is an act of political expediency that violates *nomos* (law as an institution or practice grounded in convention) and consequently cannot be justified. The reaction of the chorus supports their analyses. After hearing Odysseus respond to Hecuba, the chorus draws the following conclusion: "This is what it means / to be a slave: to be abused and bear it, compelled by violence to suffer wrong" (331–32).[7] What the chorus has done is to read an ostensible instance of peitho as an instance of bia. The chorus's reading of Odysseus's speech implies that one's position in a discursive situation is crucial, that when power is held unequally, force determines the outcome, and further that the force need not actively repress speech because the inequality of the speakers has already rendered rhetoric irrelevant in the determination of the situation. This is the rhetorical crisis that Euripides seeks to dramatize in the scene.

In her inability to get Odysseus to consider her words seriously, Hecuba exemplifies the rhetorical powerlessness of a marginalized speaker. Part of Euripides' dramatic strategy in this scene is to raise questions about the viability of rhetoric by placing an exemplary rhetor in a situation where her aretē must fail through no fault of her own (Conacher, *Euripidean Drama,* 156, 164). For Hecuba had argued eloquently that Polyxena's life should be spared, appealing to Odysseus first by citing his personal indebtedness to her and next by arguing what justice requires.[8] These are both significant appeals: the first to *charis* (favor, kindness) and the second to *dikē* (justice). Her appeal to justice is particularly telling, for it challenges the appropriateness of human sacrifice and of Polyxena as sacrificial offering:

> Tell me,
> on what feeble grounds can you justify
> your vote of death?
>   Political necessity?
> But how? And do your politics require
> the shedding of human blood upon a grave,
> where custom calls for cattle?
>   Or is it vengeance
> that Achilles' ghost demands, death for his death,
> and exacts of her? But what has she to do
> with his revenge? Who ever hurt him less
> than this poor girl? If death is what he wants,
> let Helen die. He went to Troy for *her;*
> for *her* he died. (259–66)

The chorus attests to the force of her argument by proclaiming that Hecuba's speech must move anyone (296–97). That her words have no effect on Odysseus indicates the powerlessness of eloquence.

Odysseus's complacent rejection of her pleas suggests his ethical failure, and the inadequacy of his response shows that political expediency need not be a matter of personal corruption but of institutional and ultimately cultural containment. The scene's structure argues that peitho is not and cannot be effective in this situation, for persuasion depends upon the relations that exist between speakers and audiences. Odysseus permits Hecuba to speak because he knows beforehand that she will not affect his decision. Simply put, Hecuba is an aged, female slave who has no power, and without power she cannot speak in a way that might influence Odysseus. Hecuba's earlier act of charis has not enlarged Odysseus's sense of his or her humanity. This is evident in Odysseus's reductive interpretation of his obligation to Hecuba. He reads his indebtedness to her generosity in terms of a strict legalism that eviscerates the ethical force of her earlier act. Because he holds power, her words cannot touch him.[9] This is not to say that he is conscious of the heinousness of his action; rather, he remains oblivious to his own cruelty, and when challenged, he displays the testiness of the misunderstood bureaucrat who is being asked to enlarge his understanding of what a situation requires of him by someone suggesting that he does not see the relevant ethical issues. It is not surprising that when he feels that Hecuba does not appreciate his largess he retreats to the assertion that he is in charge: his is a strategy of dealing with an annoying petitioner who obstinately refuses to understand the reality of her situation and in her irrationality does not appreciate the kindness offered her.

Realizing that Odysseus cannot be reached by rhetoric, Polyxena chooses to preserve her integrity and does not even attempt to supplicate him. Her heroic rejection of supplication and her embrace of death appear to offer the integrity of self-determination as an alternative to Hecuba's attempt to act through a compromised and ineffective rhetoric. Euripides, however, views her death more equivocally. He uses the scene to show that Polyxena's heroism, on the one hand, is naive and irrelevant to the larger issues of the play, and, on the other hand, abets unintentionally the brutality that it rejects.

The very purity of Polyxena's death creates an ethical ambiguity.[10] This becomes apparent in Talthybius's narrative of her death, which turns her into something both sacred and unreal. In her dying she has transcended her humanity to become an ideal figure in a ritual. In the mind of the Greek army, she has been transformed from a living person into an icon of innocence: her actions function to reaffirm her modesty and integrity, thus making her a perfect candidate for the sacrifice. The scene, as narrated, has the solemnity of another world, one that has transmogrified the horror and brutality of human sacrifice into the heroic offering of innocence. Her death in its beauty becomes a transfiguring lie that allows power to rest comfortably in its own brutality.

Polyxena's understanding of evil is limited. She welcomes death as a way of avoiding the demeaning life of a slave. It is as if she knows that should she continue to live, the kind of heroism that is now possible for her will no longer be available.[11] The purity of her action is dependent upon her not being contaminated by knowledge of the world (Arrowsmith, *Hecuba,* 6). The naïveté of her purity is emphasized as she is led to her execution, by her assurance to her mother that her brother, Polydorus, lives. Since the play began with the ghost of the murdered Polydorus, the audience knows that she is mistaken. The scene's irony suggests that her vision, if heroic, is naive and that, in a world of power, innocence and purity can be yet another form of blindness, as personal integrity can prove irrelevant in dealing with ethical and political reality.

Finally, the sense of closure and the very discreteness of Polyxena's death are evidence that it provides an inadequate model for ethical heroism. In the larger world surrounding her death, nothing is brought to a satisfying conclusion. Rather, the moral world of *Hecuba* is irremediably episodic: the fall of Troy did not end the suffering or the brutality of the war; nor will Polyxena's heroism have more than a passing effect on the moral quality of the universe. The relentlessness of this episodic structure becomes manifest in the next scene, when Hecuba is not even permitted the comfort of an uninterrupted burial of her daughter. As she makes preparations for her daughter's burial, she suffers a new blow, for the dead child brought to her is not her daughter but her son. This world in the banality of its evil has contained and rendered irrelevant Polyxena's ethical heroism. Her death has no consequences for the subsequent action of the play.

Rather, it is in the opposition to a bureaucracy which refuses to recognize the legitimacy of her claims to justice that Hecuba discovers a more complex heroism. She refuses to submit to its power and to acquiesce in its cruelties. In a world that by its very indifference to her pain has told her that she does not count, she can, nonetheless, feel an ethical obligation to act. In particular, she can be moved to seek justice on behalf of her murdered son, Polydorus (Abrahamson, "Euripides' Tragedy of Hecuba," 128; Lusching, "Euripides' *Hecabe*," 227). In this debased universe claims of justice are translated inevitably into a need for revenge, as the willingness to undertake revenge becomes an act of resistance and an assertion of dignity. In her pursuit of revenge, Hecuba refuses to accept the right of the powerful to disregard the humanity of those without power.[12] In her revenge she proclaims that Polymestor cannot with impunity harm her or her family, that such crimes will have consequences. This proclamation is so important that Hecuba is driven to seek the assistance of one of her greatest enemies.[13]

Agamemnon offers Hecuba a different rhetorical problem than did Odysseus, for he is not closed in advance to her pleas, but, as she discovers, he fears the army's censure, so is reluctant to act on what he knows is just. Hecuba's pleading with him becomes her search for a motive sufficient to make a cowardly leader willing to take a principled public position. Again, Hecuba must confront a commonplace problem of bureaucracy. Agamemnon will claim that despite his personal belief in the justice of Hecuba's arguments, his hands are tied, and although he would help her if he could, there is, given the reality of the situation, nothing that he can do—like everyone else he is not an independent actor but a servant of forces beyond his control.[14] The need to maintain his power requires that he not exercise it in a way that might jeopardize it.

In an attempt to make him see his power as legitimate only if it serves the will of Zeus, Hecuba appeals to Agamemnon on the basis of a nomos that stands above even the gods and that guarantees a moral order to the universe. She claims that this moral order demands a minimum of respect even for slaves if there is to be any possibility for justice in this world. Her characterization of this nomos, which Guthrie characterizes as "curious and thought-provoking" (*The Sophists,* 22), argues that there is a connection between human action and universal moral order. Like Sophocles' Antigone in her confrontation with Creon over the burial of Polyneices, Hecuba is attempting to ground political action in an understanding of a moral order. For if on the one hand, nomos is universal and stands above even the gods, human justice depends upon acknowledging nomos as a moral order. Thomas G. Rosenmeyer describes dikē in terms that make it similar to nomos: "Actually, Dike does not so much answer an abstract principle of justice prescribing an ideal course of action—comparable to the Platonic 'good'—as it corresponds to the notion of the social norm, of regularity, of things turning out as they usually do" ("Gorgias, Aeschylus, and *Apate,*" 256–57). Dikē is tied to ordinary experience. Hesiod notes the closeness of dikē and nomos, using nomos to designate behavior in the broadest sense, and dikē to distinguish between human and animal behavior (Ostwald, *Nomos and the Beginnings,* 21). In general, nomos designates an "order that ought to be regarded as valid" (Ostwald, *Nomos and the Beginnings,* 54; also see Guthrie, *The Sophists,* 55). Nomos is the crucial link in establishing a human responsibility for a world created, in part, by human actions. Hecuba's appeal to nomos is thus an appeal to a standard by which a culture can be judged. What distinguishes a claim to justice from an edict issued by force is its willingness to be contested in terms of nomos.

In appealing to nomos Hecuba is appealing to a source of rhetorical authority. As Susan C. Jarratt has argued, "in epistemological terms," nomos "signifies the imposition of humanly determined patterns of explanation for natural phenomena in contrast to those assumed to exist 'naturally' or without the conscious intervention of human intellect" (*Rereading the Sophists,* 42). A commitment to nomos is a commitment to the world's intelligibility, and to argue from nomos is to argue that Zeus's dikē does order that universe and that justice and not bia guarantees this order. As Hugh Lloyd-Jones has pointed out, Euripides does not charge the gods with being unjust; rather, he always acknowledges their justice, even though he recognizes that at times this justice is difficult to see (*The Justice of Zeus,* 152–54). The task of rhetoric, and also the task of tragedy, is to make this justice visible. Nomos is crucial in this undertaking, for as a concept it embodies both the conventionality and the necessity of law. It militates against a single understanding of law and argues for plurality, and it maintains that if human laws are to be genuine, if diverse, embodiments of dikē, then they must be capable of being contested in terms of nomos. Hecuba argues that disregarding nomos is equivalent to subscribing to injustice:

> I am a slave, I know,
> and slaves are weak. But the gods are strong, and over them
> there stands some absolute, some moral order
> or principle of law more final still.
> Upon this moral law the world depends:
> through it the gods exist; by it we live,
> defining good and evil.
> > Apply that law
> to me. For if you flout it now, and those
> who murder in cold blood or defy the gods
> go unpunished, then human justice withers,
> corrupted at its source. (798–806)

Euripides is less concerned with the violations of nomos than with how the community responds to such violations. When humans accede to violations of nomos, then human justice dies. *Hecuba* assumes the existence of evil; what it seeks to explore is the adequacy of human response to evil. Whatever the source of evil in the world (and the play will argue that it arises from people and not from gods), people are compelled to respond to it if they do not wish to call into existence a world of pure expediency in which all are governed by bia. The problem of justice is the problem of just response, and the philosophical force of this problem arises because bureaucratic structures allow individuals to inure themselves from the pain of others by disavowing any personal responsibility for their actions or omissions. The ethical problem for such a world is not primarily to avoid doing evil, for evil will come, since the world is not completely under one's control; rather, it is to deal with the unbidden evils in such a way that justice can live. Hecuba's situation, if extreme, is also ethically representative, for no one has sufficient power to be immune from the intrusion of evil from the outside (Nussbaum, *Fragility,* 407). The human condition is one of dependence, and only in a world governed by nomos, which embodies an understanding of human interdependence, is justice possible, for finally what such an understanding embodies is the fact of human interdependence.

Hecuba emphasizes this fact of interdependence by ending her speech with an image of herself. She asks Agamemnon to assume that he is a painter and to try to gain a perspective on her, to see her as she really is. What she offers him is a new pair of eyes that will allow him to see a nomos that at present eludes him. The image that she invents for herself is that of the victim of fortune who has been denied everything on which a human life depends. Her plea is metonymic: displacing the argument from nomos into a more concrete image of a woman totally dispossessed from the normal ties that make nomos possible. But, powerful as this image is, it fails, for Agamemnon prefers to remain unmoved rather than risk opening himself to the demands of nomos that might lead to the charge that he was favoring an enemy. The failure of Hecuba's rhetoric signals that this is a world ruled by those with no regard for nomos.

After this failure, Hecuba cries out either to or for peitho:

> Why, why
> do we make so much of knowledge, struggle so hard
> to get some little skill not worth the effort?
> But persuasion, the only art whose power
> is absolute, worth any price we pay,
> we totally neglect. And so we fail;
> We lose our hopes. (814–19)

This is a crucial outcry. The most obvious reading of these words, and the one almost universally given, is that they are evidence of Hecuba's embrace of a cynical rhetoric (Buxton, *Persuasion in Greek Tragedy,* 179, 182–83; Conacher, *Euripidean Drama,* 160–63; Kirkwood, "Hecuba and Nomos," 66–67; Lusching, "Euripides' *Hecabe,*" 231; Nussbaum, *Fragility,* 415–16). Hecuba's words, however, are not a cry for assistance from peitho, for she is not requesting anything. Rather, her words lament the absence of persuasion. She is bemoaning the fact that people do not pursue rhetoric, for if they did, a new kind of action would be possible. Rhetoric could empower people if they chose to practice it, for its practice would entail a continuous articulation of nomos. Her experiences have shown her, however, that rhetoric is not practiced, and that the absence of rhetoric has rendered her powerless to deal with the current difficulties.

Still, Hecuba tries another appeal to Agamemnon, in which she argues from his relationship with Cassandra to his obligation to help her. This plea is equally cited by critics as evidence of Hecuba's new degradation (Conacher, *Euripidean Drama,* 162; Lusching, "Euripides' *Hecabe,*" 232). Her cynicism seems to be transparent in her employing a language based on barter for Agamemnon's sexual exploitation of her daughter. Without denying that her words are, in part, a desperate attempt at barter, I want to suggest that Hecuba's plea is overdetermined and that she also is driven by another motive — and that this second motive is more important and allows us to make better sense of her plea.

Having failed to move Agamemnon, Hecuba seeks to show that these events do touch him and that they need to be seen in human terms. Cassandra is that point of contact. For if Agamemnon has any genuine feelings for Cassandra, it would be reasonable to assume that he could be moved to act on behalf of her brother. That sort of appeal, at least, has a chance of success, while an appeal based on the presumption that Agamemnon will be willing to pay for the sexual advantages that he acquired as the spoils of battle is absurd.

Indeed, if Hecuba is trying to move Agamemnon to act on her behalf, then stressing the relationship between him and Cassandra is not wise. Agamemnon is so sensitive on this point that he desperately wishes to avoid the appearance of helping her. His fear of public disapproval is so strong that he will not act on her behalf even when he believes that Hecuba's case is just. At best, Hecuba's mentioning Cassandra is a blunder and not a masterstroke of cynical manipulation, for she has raised the one point most decisive for Agamemnon's not acting. Why would a smart rhetor miscalculate so badly? Possibly out of desperation. But it is equally possible that her concern to tie Agamemnon to the case on a human level has led her to risk this dangerous point.

But the point about Cassandra, however read, is not Hecuba's final petition. Many critics ignore her subsequent plea and assume that her securing Agamemnon's implicit cooperation in her revenge can be attributed to some smarmy advantage she has acquired by exploiting Cassandra's concubinage. But apparently because mentioning the relationship has not moved Agamemnon, she reverts to the topic of rhetoric, and now she specifically wishes for a kind of rhetoric. She longs for her body to be able to voice her plea, for she is seeking desperately a way to communicate her pain and to make her cry for justice felt. She needs an opening that will allow her words to touch Agamemnon. In her anguished pleas for a rhetoric that can display her pain effectively, she creates a new image of herself. She moves from earlier visual appeal to a spoken appeal — her cry is not to be pictured but to be heard. This final appeal is more intimate, as Hecuba offers a new image of herself by having Agamemnon hear her body (835–40). She is no longer the fallen queen who appeals to pathos; she is now revealed in her full dependence. The claim that she has on Agamemnon depends finally on no personal relationship between them — she is nothing and can claim no relationship, not even a debased and extended connection through Cassandra; rather, her claim must rest wholly on Agamemnon's understanding the commonality of all people as it is revealed to him by Hecuba's image of herself as a body in intense anguish. To see her body is to hear a cry of pain. In its moral force her plea anticipates Wittgenstein's insight that the best image that we have of the human soul is the human body. In her acknowledging her total dependence on Agamemnon, she has made his choice one of either acknowledging or denying her pain and, by implication, her humanity and ultimately his own. Her supplication is the most forceful plea to nomos possible.

Her appeal does not succeed, for finally Agamemnon cannot free himself from his fear. Hecuba appeals mistakenly to him, as if he were capable of self-determination, but he has no such power, for who he is will always be a consequence of what he believes the mob will desire or at least tolerate.[15] The scene recalls the discussions between Socrates and Callicles in *Gorgias*. Appropriately, their discussion begins with a disagreement over the power of nomos. For Callicles, a justice based in convention is merely a pietistic cover for weakness. For him, true justice requires the courage and ability to dominate others. He desires proficiency in rhetoric, for its power allows speakers to manipulate others. Socrates counters that if one desires power, then he or she must recognize that there is an order to the world beyond an individual rhetor's will, and that this order establishes limits on human desire because the pursuit of a given purpose demands that one respect the structure of the universe. He argues further that those who base their power on control of the mob unintentionally and paradoxically become its servants and turn out to have the least power of anyone, for they are slaves to a capricious and irrational thing. An unjust rhetorical practice is a contradiction, and when it becomes a way of communal life, it precipitates a rhetorical crisis in which action is impossible because discourse has become incoherent.

Agamemnon offers ample proof of Socrates' claim. His cowardice opens Hecuba's eyes as to why rhetoric has failed in this world. For if Agamemnon, the general who commands the Greek army, cannot act on what he knows is just, then this is a world where all are slaves:

> Then no man on earth is truly free.
> All are slaves of money or necessity.
> Public opinion or fear of prosecution
> forces each one, against his conscience,
> to conform.
>   But since your fears make you defer
> to the mob, let a slave set you free
> from what you fear. (864–69)

This is one of the most important, if paradoxical, insights of the play: those in power are not free but are, in fact, the most deeply enslaved.[16] Her recognition of their slavery leads Hecuba to a realization of her own freedom and power. Agamemnon's cowardice has allowed her to see enslavement less as a question of domination by an outside force than as a consequence of capitulation to private interest or to an unreflective understanding of ethical codes. The masters in this universe are *chrēmata, plēthos poleos, nomov graphai,* and *tuchē.* And the play will argue that the only way to escape being a slave is to submit to nomos and to direct one's actions in accordance with justice.

Polymestor is ruled by greed (chrēmata), and Agamemnon by the city's mob (plēthos poleos). Both are cases of self-enslavement in which either a despicable purpose or a craven fear becomes the ruler of one's judgment. The case of Odysseus is less straightforward. Although he could be read as a slave to the indictments of the laws (nomon graphai) since he justifies his actions against Polyxena as demanded of him because he has promised to give honor to the best soldier, an allegiance to such a promise is not a case of simple self-enslavement in the way that being ruled by greed or fear of public opinion is. It can be argued that Odysseus's promise was made from a worthy motive. What can be said against Odysseus, however, is that his legalistic reading of his promise and of his debt to Hecuba hides the ethical ambivalence. His interpretation of what it means to honor his promise or to respond to charis is fixed, rigid, and incapable of the openness needed to respond adequately to another's rhetoric. This is, of course, a description of his imaginative containment as a consequence of his unreflective allegiance to the exigencies of bureaucracy.

Tuchē is a master of a very different order from the first three. Whether tuchē is read as either luck or necessity or both, it is a master for which the slave bears no responsibility — or at least no responsibility for incurring the condition. All are subject to tuchē, even those who serve other masters in the belief that this frees them from tuchē. The universal rule of tuchē makes human responsibility a matter of how one responds to its workings, as one shows one's worth by the quality of this response.

The positive irony of *Hecuba* resides in its reversal of a tragic pattern that arises from Hecuba's response to tuchē. Hecuba begins the play defeated. She appears initially as a character given to self-pity and seeking the support of others. But as the catastrophes follow upon each other, Hecuba becomes more active and less passive. She ceases lamenting her fate and tries to do something about it. It is not too much to claim that this play could be read as the recovery of Hecuba rather than as her defeat. Rhetoric is central to this recovery, for above all, Hecuba seeks justice for her son, and this ties the possibility of action to the production of a persuasion that is not coerced. Hecuba realizes that the enslavement of the other characters has destroyed the possibility for her to act justly. The characters in authority have acquiesced to the accidental structure of power relations that currently dominates their world. However, the moral chaos of the world becomes not an argument for nihilism but evidence for a human failure and a responsibility for that failure.

This moral chaos sets the conditions for Hecuba's action. In a world that disregards nomos, there are no good alternatives. This creates the paradox that Hecuba must face: to move to a just solution, Hecuba must violate her own ethical sense and temporarily abandon peitho for dolos (deceit) and bia. Hecuba does not have the luxury of Polyxena's early and pure death. Instead she must forsake her integrity as a mark of her freedom, and such a choice is as complete a rejection of slavery as Polyxena's earlier choice to prefer death to degradation. Hecuba's situation is more complex than Polyxena's, and her willingness to act within this complexity makes her, and not Polyxena, the heroine of this tragedy.

Hecuba acts according to the rules of this world and seeks her revenge on their terms. The charge that Hecuba deals as a cynical rhetor when she entraps Polymestor misses the point (Grube, *The Drama of Euripides*, 225). A cynical attitude is possible only if there is an actual ruling value to be cynical toward. But the refusal of Agamemnon has made it clear that this is a world in which value, in any reasonable sense of the term, is absent. Worshiping power, people have enslaved themselves. The only ethical aspiration in this world lies in Hecuba's desire for revenge, for this is an act of resistance in a world that denies the worth of those without power. If she were truly cynical, Hecuba would follow Odysseus's advice and resign herself to accept what she was powerless to change. The relevant noncynical question that confronts Hecuba is how best to achieve her revenge.

In the blinding of Polymestor and the slaughter of his sons, Hecuba effects that revenge, but she does more than merely discharge an obsessive passion. She makes Polymestor feel the consequences of his actions. Up to this point of the play, all in power have disregarded Hecuba's words, confident in their invulnerability to this aged, female slave. Hecuba's revenge has undermined such confidence and has set the conditions for the first serious rhetorical agon in the play. The importance of Polymestor's blinding is not that Hecuba accomplishes her revenge but that she forces those in power to acknowledge her publicly. Such an acknowledgement is the beginning of the recovery of a public discourse in which the aretē of the rhetor can be effective.

To understand the importance of the last rhetorical agon, it is necessary to ask why that scene is included in the drama. If the play were only a charting of Hecuba's ethical disintegration in her obsession with revenge, then the play should end with her gloating over her victory. *Medea* ends in such a fashion.

But Hecuba's blinding of Polymestor leads to his crying out publicly, demanding retribution. He is now in pain and needs another's help if he is to satisfy his desire for retribution. Her brutality has thus produced a situation in which it might be possible to conduct an agon over justice, for someone in power must now attempt to act publicly through speech if he is to achieve his end. His power is no longer adequate by itself. And Polymestor's cries for help have an additional important consequence. His seeking a public vengeance for his injury means that any argument that he makes must be put in terms of a claim that could justify punishment. The public voicing of his desire for revenge has inadvertently and inescapably raised it as an issue of justice. For the first time, Hecuba has moved an issue that effects her into an arena in which she can have a hope of action.

The role of Agamemnon as judge in the final agon is troubling (Abrahamson, "Euripides' Tragedy of Hecuba," 126–27; Collard, "Formal Debates," 65; Lusching, "Euripides' *Hecabe*," 233). Having earlier agreed to be silent and, in effect, to endorse Hecuba's revenge, how can he possibly be an impartial judge of her claims to justice? To answer this question, we need to see whether Hecuba's actions have made any change that would allow Agamemnon to espouse her cause safely in public. He feared to do so originally because his men saw Polymestor as a friend and Polydorus as a possible enemy. Sensitive about charges that his infatuation with Cassandra had influenced his judgment, Agamemnon wished to avoid appearing as if he were willing to put her interests before those of the Greek army. If Agamemnon hesitated earlier to give his support to Hecuba, he has no reason to give that support now. And it is far from clear that Agamemnon feels bound to Hecuba by agreeing not to interfere in her revenge. His fear of public opinion makes any commitment that he undertakes always provisional, always subject to its approval by the mob.

More surprising than Agamemnon's accepting the public role of judge is Polymestor's admitting the need for an agon. He does not assert the prerogative that he is a king and Hecuba only a slave, that they are not equal, and therefore that a summary judgment ought to be entered in his favor. Instead, he feels the need to offer some sort of justification for his actions. That he feels so is a tribute to Hecuba, for the powerful do not need reasons for their actions; all they need is power. Hecuba has changed that. She has forced power to justify itself.

Polymestor's justification is revealing in its weakness, and the transparency of his deceit undermines his case.[17] Polymestor's awareness of the inconsistency of both agreeing to take Priam's child and then fearing for Agamemnon's safety is partly shown when he drops this line in favor of an extended appeal to pathos by means of a detailed narrative of his blinding. When he returns to his claim that he murdered Polydorus for Agamemnon's sake, the disingenuousness of his words shows that he believes he need only provide Agamemnon with an excuse to act in a case in which the issue was already a foregone conclusion. The thinnest of pretenses should be sufficient to allow Agamemnon to acknowledge the power relations by ruling in favor of the king and against the slave.[18]

Hecuba's answer is powerful, both in its immediate response to Polymestor and in its philosophic development of the role for rhetoric.[19] She begins by acknowledging the truth that recent events have taught: actions count more than words. But she then gives this truth a new twist, and actions become words, for they reveal the ēthos of their author:

> the evil we do should show,
> a rottenness that festers in our speech
> and what we say, incapable of being glozed
> with a film of pretty words.
>   There are men, I know,
> sophists who made a science of persuasion,
> glozing evil with the slick of loveliness;
> but in the end a speciousness will show. (1189–93)

She thus redefines the world of power relations into a world of rhetoric; bia is now subject to peitho. Having done so, she attacks a specious rhetoric that uses deceit to hide the true nature of an action. And in a claim that echoes Medea and several other characters in Euripides, Hecuba argues that words finally cannot clothe the real nature of an action (*Medea,* 579–83; *Herakles,* 236; *The Phoenician Women,* 469; *The Bacchae,* 266).[20] The task for Hecuba's subsequent speech is to set Polymestor's actions forth so that they contradict his words.[21] The rhetoric that Hecuba will practice will challenge the false science of persuasion that sees peitho only as a handmaiden to power. And if Hecuba can demonstrate Polymestor's evil, justice will follow. There will be a movement from *is* to *ought,* as the rhetorical process will compel action.

Euripides endorses Hecuba's arguments by having the chorus comment on the justice of Hecuba's case and congratulate her on her rhetoric (1237–39). The chorus then goes on to make a point complementary to Hecuba's earlier one: if your cause is just, then you will not lack for good arguments. This is not to absolve Hecuba from the ethical opprobriousness of her actions, for in pursuing her revenge of Polymestor, she did abrogate her ethical integrity.[22] But the chorus makes clear that in doing so, she was acting on behalf of justice, and that such action can be defended with logos.

The ineptness of Polymestor's rhetoric provides Hecuba with another opening. Since her case is so overwhelming, she can say to Agamemnon that if he does not rule according to justice and condemn Polymestor, then he will reveal himself to be as ethically bankrupt as Polymestor. Once the quarrel between Hecuba and Polymestor has become public, Agamemnon can no longer pursue a policy of quietism. Without appealing to Agamemnon or attempting to induce him to act virtuously, Hecuba has maneuvered him into a place where he must act responsibly. If he is not forced to be impartial, he is at least required to give publicly acceptable reasons for his decision, and these reasons must address nomos, because Polymestor's crying out made the agon into a contest over justice. Hecuba has so maneuvered Agamemnon that his allegiance to a Calliclean manipulation of the mob now requires him paradoxically to aid justice.

Euripides uses the judgment of Agamemnon to show the power and the consequences of rhetoric. Rhetoric can lead to just results independent of the ethical character of the judge if an issue can get a public hearing. However much one may privately disregard nomos, a public statement must conform with nomos to be credible, since nomos is the precondition of a public life. Ostwald contends that Euripides helped erode the power of nomos (*Nomos and the Beginnings*, 36–38), but it might be more accurate to say that Euripides complicates and recovers the authority of nomos by reconstituting it as a rhetorical *topos*.

The authority of nomos and the relevance of rhetoric are precisely what Polymestor cannot see. Because he believes only in the reality of power relations, he cannot see the verdict as anything other than his defeat by a slave.

Hecuba does not accept this characterization. She argues, instead, that he was justly condemned, and she claims a victory not for herself but for justice.[23] Through her rhetoric she has returned the issue of Polymestor's guilt and necessary punishment from an act of revenge carried out through dolos and bia to an act of justice accomplished through peitho. The issue has not been the innocence of Hecuba but the guilt of Polymestor. If brutality was necessary to force a brutal world reluctantly to engage an ethical issue, rhetoric was equally necessary to transform the brutal world to which she had acceded back into a world in which one could at least debate claims about justice. When Polymestor is pronounced guilty of violating the *xenia* relationship, this is a victory of justice and not merely a triumph for personal revenge (Meridor, "Hecuba's Revenge," 29–32, 34–35). Hecuba has forced the community to take a stand on the injustice of her son's death. She has not merely injured Polymestor but confirmed publicly the humanity of her son by making the redressing of his murder a matter of nomos.

The play's justice is human justice, and it does not and cannot have the integrating and absolving force of divine justice. Effecting a divine harmony is beyond the scope of a forensic rhetoric; rather, it has the more modest, but still significant, goal of promoting a discourse about nomos. Such a discourse helps maintain civil order not simply by transplanting potentially violent disputes from the realm of private vendettas to the area of public discussion but by transforming these disputes into rhetorical agons for communal self-discovery. These agons become the soil that nurtures the growth of nomos. Even if Polymestor does not accept Agamemnon's verdict, the Greek army does, and civil peace is thereby maintained. Finally, the judgment against Polymestor neither excuses nor sanctions Hecuba's actions. The play does not absolve Hecuba by claiming that what she did was just, even though it recognizes that what she did was necessary.

Rather than negating the achievement of justice, the lack of full ethical closure requires the audience to come to terms with the untidiness and incompleteness that are part of a human justice. The incoherence of its response places the audience into a state of doubt equivalent to that following upon a Socratic refutation. The audience is drawn into an agon with the play that becomes an inquiry into the justice of the play's resolution. Euripides will not diminish the episodic reality of everyday life by a telos that suggests some sort of final harmony. In place of a final resolution, he shows both the achievement and limitation of a human rhetoric.

The play's resolution only temporarily curtails the violence, which breaks out anew even as the play ends. Avenging furies are not transformed into beneficent and watchful guardians; rather, Polymestor defies the verdict and effects a kind of revenge on Agamemnon and Hecuba in his triumphant pronouncement of prophecies that foretell evil to them.[24] Instead of being included in some reconstituted community that understood justice, he is gagged and banished to a remote island. His reduction of human action simply to a strategic deployment of power permits no integration with any idea of justice. He is beyond the reach of rhetoric. In his unmitigated hatred, he damns himself to the self-imposed isolation from which Herakles freed Philoctetes. The difference between Polymestor and Philoctetes resides in Philoctetes' having a prior sense of the noble that could permit him, with Herakles' help, to recover his social identity. Polymestor is bereft of any such nobility, since private interest and personal power are everything for him. The only way to deal with him is to remove him forcefully from society.

Hecuba is equally incapable of integration into a society. Her resistance to an indifferent power structure has exacted a price. Euripides is fully aware of the cost to the individual who must spend a life in opposition to an unresponsive bureaucracy. When one struggles continuously against an indifferent power structure to proclaim one's right to just treatment, it is difficult, if not impossible, to retain one's openness. Hecuba's murder of Polymestor's sons, her willingness to accept the injury of the innocent in pursuit of justice, is evidence of her own increasing blindness to the pain of others. Such blindness may be necessary to deal with an unjust world, but it has caused Hecuba to become closed personally in a way that parallels the institutional closedness of Odysseus and Agamemnon. Although the two types of closedness are different in kind, each undermines a character's ability to hear the words of another. The cost of Hecuba's securing justice has been a self-brutalization that has inured her against being touched by further events. But such touching is a precondition for rhetorical openness.[25] She is as isolated humanly as Polymestor will be physically. The ethical indifference that she has fought has reduced her and will eventually transform her into a stone.[26] Her prophesied future should be read not as a punishment but as a recognition of the personal cost of opposition. Hecuba cannot be included in the justice that she has helped to inaugurate.

The play's ending is relentlessly episodic, frustrating any attempt to close a situation by finding a telos. This episodic structure is an acknowledgment of human responsibility for nomos. Justice and injustice are human achievements and failures. Appropriately, the glib and deceitful Polymestor is the character who mouths the cliché that human troubles are the products of inconsistent gods (957). Euripides will have none of this evasion of responsibility. His play argues that the human neglect of peitho is the source of human problems. This is not because peitho is all-powerful as a despairing Hecuba would like to believe, but because the choice for humans is a stark one between worlds ordered by violence and those ordered by words.

But if such a dichotomy represents the choice that must be faced, to see violence and justice as simply in opposition is finally too tidy for Euripides: argument can be a mask for bia, as in the case of Odysseus, and in a world without nomos, bia may be needed to create an opening for rhetoric. In an unstable world ruled by power, the logical opposition of peitho to bia is undermined by the ethical failures of those in power who believe that, because of their power, they are untouchable. As long as those in power remain indifferent to suffering, rhetoric will lack an opening. The role of violence in *Hecuba* is to challenge this indifference by making those in power feel pain. For once they feel pain, they will cry out and demand a response to their pain. This demand is ultimately a demand for justice. It requires that the character in pain make a case for justice, and such cases are ultimately appeals to nomos. This is rhetoric's opening.

Hecuba argues that to believe in a world of words is to believe in a world of relatedness and that this means that one cannot avoid a relationship of dependence on others. When others deny such a relationship, one's own ethical integrity can be undone (Nussbaum, *Fragility,* 417). The achievement of *Hecuba* is to dramatize the sacrifice necessary to convert a world of brutality into a world in which rhetoric is possible. This is to realize that the authority of rhetoric does not arise from an original act that persuades power to submit to reason but is occasioned by a crying out that is ultimately a demand for nomos.[27] Further, Euripides argues that the rhetorical achievement is always endangered by a hierarchy of power relations that serves to inure those in power from the pain of others. The play shows that the cost of rhetoric can be the self-destruction of the character who would confront the brutality to move it to discourse. For *Hecuba* rhetoric is not a cynical strategy adopted when appeals to nomos fail; rather, it embodies the aspiration of those who would be free and just.

There is, of course, no final or stable achievement of justice. Justice remains always a goal and a standard against which to measure any action. It is important as the play closes that the threats of Polymestor echo in the audience's ears or reverberate in the reader's mind. For, like the unsettling implications of pending impiety at the end of the *Philoctetes* and the angry threats of Callicles and Anytus in the dialogues, Polymestor's prophesies underline how precarious and temporary any achievement of justice will be. The rhetorical skepticism of Plato and the tragedians positions itself against a violence and injustice that are continually reasserting themselves. What Plato and the tragedians offer is a skeptical vigilance that seeks to refute the polis and to make it recognize those whom it is presently excluding. This legacy of refutation is what antiquity's skeptical rhetoric has bequeathed to the moderns and postmoderns.

PART II

Classical Skepticism and Postmodern Rhetoric

Briefly Rethinking the Fate of Rhetoric

The legacy of skeptical rhetoric has had little impact so far on the contemporary theory and practice of rhetoric. In part, this is because the mainstream tradition followed Aristotle and conceived of rhetoric as an art of practical discourse that, while subject to occasional and individual abuse, was justified by its social utility. Then too, the skeptical legacy has made little impression on current rhetorical theory because its history has yet to be told. Finally, its limited effect may be a consequence of the stance of some postmodern historians who seem to consider any pre-Enlightenment rhetoric as irrelevant to modern theory and practice. Such historical understanding is by no means universal, and indeed, there has been a flourishing of interesting scholarship on classical rhetoric, some of which has used the rhetorical tradition as a resource with which to think about such contemporary concerns as feminist inquiries into discourse theory and practice.[1] But even this scholarship does not cite Plato and the tragedians as a source of emancipatory thought, nor does it look to the ways in which a productive skeptical stance toward rhetoric is embodied in imaginative and critical work occurring after the rise of the modern paradigm of the foundational subject and the challenges to that paradigm. So the case needs to be made for both the continuing presence and the relevance of a skeptical rhetoric grounded in a concern with an enduring injustice.

As I mentioned in Chapter 1, the argument for the absence and irrelevance of either a mainstream or skeptical rhetorical tradition is put forth by John Bender and David E. Wellbery in their historical sketch of the return of a postmodern rhetoric ("Rhetoricality"). They tell the history of rhetoric's flourishing, eclipse, and return. In their account, classical rhetoric, as a theory and practice of political and aesthetic discourse, was displaced because new attitudes toward the production of discourse arose in the periods of the Enlightenment and Romanticism. The new forms of social life that emerged during this time were rooted in a different authority than those of previous eras, and this new authority conceived of discourse differently: "The cultural hegemony of rhetoric, as a practice of discourse, as a doctrine of codifying that practice, and as a vehicle of cultural memory, is grounded in the social structures of a premodern world. Conceived in its broadest terms, then, the demise of rhetoric coincides with the long and arduous historical process that is often termed modernization: the replacement of a symbolic-religious organization of social and cultural life by rationalized forms, the gradual shift from a stratificational differentiation of society to one that operates along functional axes" (7). This new social organization would situate authority not in the realm of persuasion but in the realm of truth. Science would pursue a discourse of truth determined by the objects of its inquiry. Scientific discourse rejected rhetoric's concern with the particularity of the audience. Both speaker and listener (or more appropriately writer and reader) would no longer be defined situationally. Rather, both would assume a role in which the individual acted as a universalized and rational subject, emptied of the particular content of his or her life.

Poetry, in its broadest sense, would eventually understand its mission as the realization of subjective truths. In place of the universal and abstracted author-subject of science, poetic theory would put the individual genius of the poet. The path to a universal and transpersonal truth would be through particular investigations that deepened rather than abstracted from personal experience. However, like scientific discourse the new poetic discourse would reject traditional topoi of invention and figures of expression as antithetical to an authentic or natural presentation of subjective understanding. Rhetoric, as a practice of artificial contrivance, could only prevent the subject seeking either objective or subjective truth from reaching a genuine understanding.

The factors contributing to the demise of the rhetorical tradition were multiple; Bender and Wellbery list five: objectivism, subjectivism, liberalism, literacy, and nationalism. Notwithstanding the heterogeneity of this list, many of the cultural factors derive from or share in a new sense of the subject. The Cartesian cogito thus becomes the key moment in the shift of discursive paradigms, for it postulates a subject capable of being present to itself: "The cogito, the unshakable foundation of certainty, generates at once the impersonal or abstracted subject of science and the creative, self-forming subject of Romanticism" (11). In contrast to a rhetorical understanding that sees subjects as constructed in and by discourse, the self-present subject of Descartes allowed language to be seen as either a potentially transparent medium that would permit the formulation and communication of objective truth or as a medium able to embody and communicate an inner subjective experience. Depending on the emphasis, language was capable of universality or of immediate particularity or of both.

Bender and Wellbery argue that the instabilities and contradictions within the new discourses of truth exerted increasing pressure on the possibility of a purely objective or authentically subjective truth. As modernist understandings emerged, rhetoric came to be seen not as an aberration that needed to be eliminated but as an inescapable element of any discourse. Modernism rethought the five conditions that had undermined the rhetorical tradition: the objectivity promised by positivist inquiry was seen to be impossible as the theories of uncertainty argued that the perspective of the subject could not be eliminated; the centered subject was displaced by the disciplines of social sciences; the rational subject of politics was complicated by the clear evidence that political debate is not a rational exchange but a stylized contest; print as the predominant media was challenged by the emergence of new electronic media; and the nation as the center of cultural production was contested by the international character of the late capitalist marketplace ("Rhetoricality," 23–24).[2] Of all these developments within modernism, the most significant for the return of rhetoric was the decentered subject. For the development of the decentered subject was tied to a shift in the understanding of language. What made rhetorical understanding again relevant was the contemporary insight that thought cannot transcend the language in which it is embodied. The recognition that language is not merely a medium that is employed by thought but that language is inescapably constitutive for thought returned contemporary understanding to the insights of the sophists. What had been recovered was the world as task rather than as object of knowledge.

But as Bender and Wellbery make clear, the recovery of rhetoric was not a return to the classical tradition. The discontinuity between the lapse of the tradition and the return of rhetoric is significant. In its modern or postmodern recovery, rhetoric is conceived less as a technē or a bios and more as marking some deep aspect of our condition. "Rhetoric is no longer the title of a doctrine and a practice, nor a form of cultural memory; it becomes instead something like the condition of our existence" ("Rhetoricality," 25). To distinguish this shift in the understanding of rhetoric, Bender and Wellbery call the modern age one of "rhetoricality." Nietzsche's thought becomes paradigmatic for this new rhetoricality in that his "philosophy can be characterized as the thought of a generalized rhetoricality, of a play of transformation and dissimulation, that is the condition of truth and subjectivity" (27). Rhetoricality is the recognition that language will always exceed thought and hence cannot be fully thought out or through, and that it marks "the name of the rootlessness of our being" (29).

The history of the rise of a postmodern rhetoric is, then, also the history of the virtual disappearance of a classical rhetoric. Their only point of convergence is a shared name ("Rhetoricality," 25). But what if one, in good postmodern fashion, sees this lack of convergence not as marking the disappearance of classical rhetoric but as signifying its difference from modern or postmodern rhetoric? Need the otherness of classical rhetoric consist only in its irrelevance to a world ordered in ways radically different from a Greek polis, or might it consist in an alternative stance to language and power? The glory of postmodernism — its insight that language precedes and makes thought possible — is an insight that seems to lead it to a new formalism that plays out as an iteration of the impossibility of knowing. The impossibility of knowledge, in turn, renders action problematic. Thus postmodernism's guiding insight returns it to the problem that generated the skeptical critique within the classical rhetorical tradition. But it is a return with a difference, for the classic skeptical thread within the rhetorical tradition located action as problem not by locating the impossibility of knowledge but by confronting the inescapability of injustice. By locating formal and material conditions for discourse and exploring their interpenetration, this focus allowed classical skeptical rhetoric ways to avoid the unsatisfactory conclusion of a formalism that could not secure action. The self-identified activity of this skeptical rhetoric was refutation that sought to uncover confusions and contradictions by instigating a public drama or dialectic of identity. In bringing the classical skeptical thread of rhetoric to bear on postmodern rhetoric, we pursue the same sort of refutation, asking postmodern rhetoric to declare its wisdom and in the dialectic encounter to discover (partially and provisionally) its historical identity and the political commitments that inhere within that identity.

But even before undertaking such a refutation, it is important to ask whether the rhetorical tradition disappeared as completely as the modern and postmodern account might suggest. If the mainstream rhetorical tradition seemed to move more toward becoming a conservative pedagogy concerned with training its students for the new discourse locations of office and laboratory, this does not mean that either the themes of skeptical rhetoric or its insights into the necessity for and the difficulty of rhetoric withered away. If, as

Bender and Wellbery argue, the rise of the foundational subject undermined rhetorical thought, then it might be possible that the reactions to the rise of the foundational subject would have brought forward the concerns that animated the skeptical thread within the classical rhetorical tradition. If so, then we would have to look to these sites of resistance to find the heirs of skeptical rhetoric. That such writers might not identify themselves as rhetorical theorists would not disqualify them from being seen as carrying forward the set of concerns that we have identified as skeptical rhetoric. In disclosing the material and formal dynamics that underlie their social and cultural criticism, the insights of a classical skeptical rhetoric provide a set of interpretive concerns that allow an appreciation of the force of certain imaginative and critical works as rhetorical inquiries. Part of our task, then, is to construct (or begin the construction of) a new history of post-Enlightenment rhetoric that shows how the abiding problem of injustice was taken over and given a particularly modern or postmodern form.

The two texts—Jane Austen's *Persuasion* and Jean-Paul Sartre's *What Is Literature?*—that introduce and situate my discussion of modern and postmodern rhetoric are not ones that are normally found in the histories of rhetoric.[3] Further, neither *Persuasion* nor *What Is Literature?* puts itself forward as an effort at rhetorical theory. Nor do I want to claim that with these two works I have somehow produced a new complete history of an alternative modern rhetoric. So it is reasonable to ask: why a focus on these two works? My answer is that each is a particularly rich investigation of themes that are central to classical rhetorical skepticism, and together they suggest the direction and richness of a new history of rhetorical thought. *Persuasion* and *What Is Literature?* share a concern for the ways in which discourse is endangered by the conditions that make it necessary for a just society. Like Plato and the tragedians, both these works raise questions about normal discourse practices, and their authors are led to insights that are equally skeptical. What makes them into a frame for considering modern and postmodern rhetoric is their understanding that the problems of rhetorical preclusion are tied to a shift in modern material and discursive conditions. Each work is a response to the problems of autonomy, and each is also a response to a capitalist reorganization of modern economy and society. And for each work, nihilism is a central concern that is tied to the possibility of pursuing a public discourse that capitalist ideology has put at risk.

To return to issues raised by Michel Meyer, these works of Austen and Sartre are philosophical rather than technical explorations of rhetoric because they make rhetoric into a question: Can there be a way of speaking and writing that can effectively challenge the marginalization and dehumanization of people in a world in which traditional structures of authority that made discourse coherent have vanished or, at least, are seriously and irretrievably eroded? To put the question in this way is to see these two works as developments out of and interrogations of the Enlightenment, for what they put into question is the adequacy of an understanding of rationality that sees reason as potentially universal and hence as a sufficient ground upon which to reconstitute a society that can no longer give its adherence to older forms of social authority.[4] In place of a universal reason, each work seeks to establish the ways in which persuasion or communication is a function of specific and local communities. And this insight acquires its skeptical force as the works explore the erosion of the traditional social organization that insured authority to local communities. How does one speak or write in the absence of an established community? *Persuasion* and *What Is Literature?* both seek to give this question force and to suggest tentative courses of action. Both are aware of the need for a new rhetorical understanding and practice and of the difficulty and uncertainty that such understanding and practice can be achieved. They become part of the modern recovery of skeptical rhetoric, then, not because they operate from a conscious or explicit recognition of the classical rhetorical skepticism but because they find themselves engaged in inquiries that parallel the concerns of the classical skeptics. For all of her conservatism, Austen is the more radical of the two, unsentimentally challenging autonomy and offering only a future of risk. Sartre, on the other hand, fails to achieve a stable resolution of the themes that generated his work on writing as praxis, and his failure becomes emblematic of the split that marks postmodern rhetorical theory.[5]

If Jane Austen has not been viewed as a rhetorical theorist, she has appeared in at least one history of rhetoric as an index to the state of rhetoric during the crisis that marked the movement of traditional rhetoric to the intellectual margin. Thomas M. Conley opens his discussion of nineteenth-century rhetoric's "Janus-like characteristic of looking both backward and forward at the same time" (*Rhetoric,* 253) by quoting from *Northanger Abbey* to show the persistence of a prevailing theory of discourse as a mode of politeness during a period of momentous historical change. This passage from the novel depicts the gulf, which will widen even more during the course of the century, between an increasingly formal and academic rhetoric and a world undergoing large social and economic change. The passage portends both the diminution of rhetoric as an intellectual force and its centrality to a culturally conservative pedagogy. Rhetoric's turn toward politeness begins a movement to the dead end of the rhetorical tradition that Bender and Wellbery argue marks the discontinuity between traditional and postmodern rhetoric and necessitated the later return of the more radical energized modern and postmodern rhetorical theory that followed in the wake of Nietzsche and others.[6] Conley sees Austen's passage as embodying the incipient irrelevance of the dominant conception of rhetoric to its historical time: "In the background [of the cited passage], we have, on the one hand, the world of polite conversation and learning — the world of Blair, in fact — and on the other, the disturbances and repression of insurgents, the strife that overtook all of Europe in the aftermath of the French Revolution. . . . Austen's polite world, a world created by the imagination of the Enlightenment, was all but shattered during the next century by political and social revolutions" (*Rhetoric,* 236). Austen's work becomes pivotal in the history of rhetoric not because it attempted any explicit formulations of rhetoric but because it so sharply portrayed a moment of crisis (even if the contemporary theorists and practitioners of rhetoric were oblivious to the crisis) in that history.

But Austen's work may have even greater relevance for the history of rhetoric than suggested by Conley's useful citation. If one reads Austen's later work as a serious revision of her earlier novels, she becomes not simply a novelist who accurately recorded certain aspects of a historical period but an artist engaged actively in exploring a crisis in discursive practice and in searching for alternatives to the rhetorical tradition that she had inherited. Indeed, nineteenth-century rhetoric begins to look a lot more interesting if novelists like Austen are read not simply as indexes to the mood of the times but as participants within that history who contribute to an understanding of the role of discourse in community.

Tony Tanner's work on Austen provides substantial support for reading her novels as original and perceptive responses to the intellectual and political marginality of rhetoric occurring in the nineteenth century. Having shown Austen's awareness of current history, Tanner goes on to characterize her as a writer for whom language was the central preoccupation: "The overriding concern of Jane Austen's novels — and of many of her heroines — is the nature of true utterance. Language, to state the obvious, is the most important distinguishing mark of the human. But, equally obvious, it is everywhere abused, often to cruel and terrible ends. Jane Austen enacts and dramatises the difficulties, as well as the necessities, of using language to proper ends" (*Jane Austen,* 6). Tanner then argues that Austen was also a more astute and profound social critic than has often been perceived: "Her novels never simply, complacently celebrate the social *status quo*. At its best, society has to be purged and reconstituted. At its worst it has to be rejected and abandoned. Jane Austen's novels do not 'perennialise' society: they problematise it" (10). This is especially true of *Persuasion,* which is a novel that "arises precisely out of the thwarting and 'negating' of her first (and earlier type of) novel" (212).

Central to the negating and revision of this earlier Austenian novel is a reassessment of persuasion. The word *persuasion* occurs fourteen times in the novel (210). So if one is looking for a rupture within the traditional understanding of rhetoric and a response to that rupture, *Persuasion* becomes an important text, one that self-consciously interrogates both the efficacy of an inherited understanding of discourse and criticizes the emerging discourse of autonomy. If what marks theory is a reflection on or thought about a problem of knowledge or action, then Austen's work deserves to be read as a theoretical work, for it is a work that thinks hard about the possibility of discourse. That it does not explicitly identify itself as a work of theory no more diminishes its richness as a source for thought about rhetoric than does the fact that the tragedians used dramas to explore problems in rhetoric and that Plato found it necessary to write dialogues rather than treatises to adequately engage theoretical issues.

What places Austen within the tradition of classical skeptical rhetoric and marks her as an innovator within this tradition is her rejection of prudence as an adequate justification for rhetoric and her thematization of the problem of rhetorical preclusion. Her role within the tradition arises not because of any conscious attempt to engage with Plato or tragedians, or because she engaged in any explicit theorization about rhetoric, but because she saw the ways in which contemporary social organization silenced or marginalized some speech and she understood the ways in which discourse is constitutive of community. She saw both the opportunities and the new dangers that arose when a social order based on aristocratic privilege rooted in ownership of the land was replaced by a social order determined by the modern forces of economics and history. *Persuasion* takes up in a modern context the themes that were so central to the tradition of classical skeptical rhetoric at the same time it attempts to formulate an account of discourse that can be adequate to the flux and fragmentation that characterize modern or postmodern life.[7]

If Jane Austen articulated the new problems that were to engage a modern rhetoric, it was Jean-Paul Sartre who explicitly engaged these problems through critical reflection as he sought to define the work of the modern intellectual.[8] As Anna Boschetti comments, Sartre was a major midcentury influence on French — and on European and American — intellectual life: "Sartre's enterprise is undeniably one of the most extraordinary successes in French cultural history. During the fifteen years which followed the Liberation, he held undivided sway over the entire realm of French intellectual life as no one has since. To find a comparable dominion, we must go back to Hugo, or even to Voltaire" (*The Intellectual Enterprise*, 1). Fredric Jameson agrees: "It is safe to say that Sartre's work as a whole has left its mark on every French intellectual experience over the last twenty-five years; its enormous ideological impact may be measured by the position of Sartre in French intellectual and literary life today, a position that has no equivalent in any other recent national experience" ("Three Methods," 97). Mark Poster argues that it was in the work of Sartre and the *Arguments* group that "the tentative beginnings that might result in a major new social theory" (*Essential Marxism,* vii) were being discovered.

One of Sartre's most significant contributions was to engage publicly the issue of the social responsibility of the writer. The task that Sartre set himself was to justify writing as a mode of political action that avoided the apolitical revolt of the Dadaists and escaped from being simply an instrumentality for a Stalinist Marxism. What Sartre wanted to know was how one could write so that he or she did not further but rather combated injustice. Jameson argues that Sartre's concern with the consequences of prose aligns him with a rhetorical study of literature: "Sartre's originality, among contemporary critics of style, lies in his treatment of literary style as an objective rather than a subjective phenomenon. As against those for whom the work of art is the privileged occasion of contact with a deeper force, with the unconscious, with the personality, with Being, or with language, Sartre takes his place among the rhetoricians. The work of art is a construct designed to produce a certain effect; the style of the work of art is the instrument with which a certain illusion is conveyed" (98) And even if Sartre never referred to himself as a rhetorical theorist, his work on prose is a serious modern attempt to achieve the rhetorical goals of analyzing the ethical and political effects of prose and of providing some guidance as to how to produce these effects. If Sartre has now been displaced from the central position of intellectual authority that he had occupied in postwar Europe through the late sixties, it is his effort and his inability to resolve the problems that he located that best introduce the issues that have shaped contemporary directions of postmodern theories of rhetoric.

According to Sartre, the modernist writer in a late capitalist society faces a peculiar problem of having readers but no public (*What Is Literature?* 240, 259). Before pursuing his or her task of naming and consequently revealing the world to the reader, the writer must invent a reader who can be a public, that is, who can read the writer in an appropriate way. Without such a reader, literature, which Sartre defines as a dialectical creation of a world of human freedom, loses its force, for the writer's work will not be read as an exigency and a gift, but at best will be seen as either another commodity or an object that self-destructs in a flight from commodification. The inherent need of a writer for a reader makes Sartre's analysis of the situation of the modernist writer a potential rediscovery of antiquity's skeptical insight into rhetorical preclusion. The modernist writer's position is precarious not because he or she is subject to being misunderstood but because unless a reader is willing to cooperate in the appropriate recreation of a discursive text, the writer is denied the possibility of being a writer. Writing involves an essential commitment to the Other, and there is a limit as to what the writer can do to bring this Other into a potential community. To see preclusion in these terms is to translate the classical rhetorical concern for the way in which power preempts rhetoric to the modernist problem of trying to coherently reground a political life working from subjects who are defined by the paradox of being, on the one hand, private selves and, on the other, rational agents governed by the transpersonal laws of a universal reason.[9] Sartre's importance to the contemporary study of rhetoric arises from his recognizing the historical origins for the modernist crisis in writing, but despite his insight into the historicity of the self, he himself remains contained within the values of the Enlightenment and at a key moment abandons a rhetorical understanding of discourse toward which his existentialist critique of writing was stumbling in favor of a hermeneutical one that vests authority in a universalizable rationality.[10] Sartre's insightful articulation of the modernist problem of writing, then, does not lead him to move beyond that problem, but, in his failure to grasp the rhetoricity he uncovered, he shows unintentionally the need for a new paradigm that must return discourse to an appreciation of refutation.

6

Persuasion: *Jane Austen's Philosophical Rhetoric*

The interrogation of rhetoric by classical skepticism always returned to the location or recovery of moral responsibility for the polis. Plato, Sophocles, and Euripides directed their skepticism at the contexts within which rhetoric must act. Plato argued for a human embeddedness in language; Sophocles explored the way in which a history determined by past acts of injustice foreclosed the possibility of public speech; and Euripides looked to the ways in which the present configurations of power precluded rhetorical action. For all three, the underlying and abiding problem was injustice. In this concern for an injustice that was irremediable, they differed from the traditional defenses of rhetoric, which might acknowledge difficulties faced by rhetoric, but which located those difficulties in the incidental corruption of individual rhetors rather than arguing that the very conditions that made persuasion imperative also made it impossible or at least very difficult. This need for and impossibility of persuasion was the central concern to which the skeptics found themselves returning. This skepticism was given its most explicit theoretical formulation in Plato's account of Socratic refutation, which argued that refutation provided a means to resist injustice without assuming that such injustice could ever be vanquished finally.

Political existence was a given for antiquity. Even characters who shunned a conventional political life were resolute in affirming their inherent political identity. In the *Crito,* for example, Socrates prefers to die unjustly rather than to live in exile from Athens. But it is the givenness of political existence that became a problem in the modern turn to a liberally organized society. Rousseau's theory of the social contract is emblematic of a new understanding that saw the original mythic human condition as one of private individuals who only belatedly acquired a social identity. Community was no longer a given, as philosophical investigations and economic reorganizations undermined the inherited social order. On the one hand, this reorganization was liberating, providing opportunities that had not existed before, but on the other, it was a new source of alienation, as the very ways in which people could meet underwent change. A rethinking of rhetoric would seem to follow naturally from such a change, but no such rethinking occurred among mainline rhetorical theorists. As Michael Ryan claims, liberalism saw itself as an antirhetoric:

> Few social theories so actively demonstrate the power of rhetoric in the construction of social reality as liberalism. Yet few social theories so strive to refute rhetoric's claims. Liberalism presented itself originally (in the late seventeenth century) as a rational social system; it placed itself in direct contradiction to the irrational exercise of force that characterized feudal social relations. Yet this rationality was formal and ideal, universal and transcendental, rather than democratic and material, or substantial and egalitarian. It privileged logic over rhetoric, and it guaranteed rights only in a formal or abstract sense, not in a realized material one. (*Politics and Culture,* 134)

One needs to look elsewhere to find innovative understandings of the relation of speech to community. As Bakhtin argued, it was the novel that explored the heteroglossia of human languages and put the consequent ideologies into play. In this inquiry into language, the novel assumed the role that ancient tragedy had earlier taken, engaging a theory of rhetoric by displaying major conflicts within its practice.

The modern dissatisfaction with prudential rhetoric and turn to a rhetorical understanding informed by insights analogous to those of the classical skeptical tradition occurs within the work of Jane Austen. *Persuasion* marks Austen's break with her earlier novels, as she seeks to defend rather than suppress a feminine discourse. The economic and social changes either accompanying or following from the emerging liberal conception of society provoked Austen to reimagine the rhetorical paradigm for feminine speech that she had inherited. As the certainties of the older economic and social order gave over to the new role of fortune, two significant reorganizations appeared. On the level of the individual, the modernist self acquired a distinctly economic cast — what made one a man was the ability to rise to and master the fluctuations of fortune. The new economic order was seen as a product of the will of men capable of exploiting the accidents of fortune. Captain Wentworth is a model of the new self-made man (Tanner, *Jane Austen*, 228). On the level of community, the older order of set classes into which one was born was being dissolved by the rise of the new individuals who defined themselves instead of being defined by an inherited set of social distinctions. The older notion of community was disappearing and had yet to be replaced by a new modernist version. Kellynch Hall, as an aristocratic home that was to be let to a character with a newly made fortune, reflects this new social instability.

These two social transformations meant that a traditional rhetoric based in established social mores was becoming obsolete. This had particular consequences for feminine speech. In the past the function of rhetoric for women had been to offer an appropriate education (chastisement) in which they learned how to suppress their voices as women. However, it now became necessary for women to discover how to speak in a world in which the established order was changing. What they had to learn was how to invent the new communities that could offer them a meaningful life in the emerging economic and social order. One shape that this problem took was that of the refiguring marriage from an economic necessity to a rhetorical opportunity. The traditional marriage of Austen's earlier novels worked to ensure that a socially responsible couple would prudentially administer the neighborhood, as such couples had in the past. But such a marriage was now no longer an appropriate model. The social situatedness of life had given over to a new and more fluid set of possibilities. There thus had to be a new kind of marriage, and this meant that there had to be new ways for men and women to speak to each other. This was a particularly difficult problem because of the new image of the masculine self. The new economic understanding had created a complementary image of man as autonomous, and this new image ran counter to the new speech that sought to reground human relatedness. Wentworth's deliberate refusal to hear Anne is paradigmatic of this protective closure. Before such an audience could appreciate this new rhetoric, it had to be refuted and shown the value of a gendered diversity.

Austen's dissatisfaction with the rhetorical opportunities available to women becomes clear in the shift from the problems that occupy her earlier major heroines, Elizabeth Bennet and Emma Woodhouse, to those that occupy her later heroine, Anne Elliot. In both *Pride and Prejudice* and *Emma* the problem of rhetoric for women was conceived as a question of how to bring wayward female protagonists back into line. In these novels the heroines undergo a standard comic education (which is really an education in rhetorical reformation), in which certain personal extravagances are abandoned in favor of a more prudential attitude toward the place of women in the world. This is essentially a conservative education designed to preserve a set of past patriarchal practices. A female imagination that flaunted social convention and claimed an independence for itself needed to be taught the realities of the social order and brought to an appreciation of the proper way for women to speak and act.

Although Elizabeth Bennet and Emma Woodhouse begin from quite different economic situations — Elizabeth deeply dependent on the goodwill of others and Emma excessively independent — the two heroines are presented as needing to learn the same lesson, namely how to curb their tongues. In each case a future husband serves as tutor, providing an education that allows the heroine to outgrow an immature way of speaking that is pronouncedly feminine and considered undisciplined and to begin to speak more like a man; that is, she will become more prudential as her judgment is educated so that she can act the role of mistress in her respective estate. The heroines' initial corruption arises not from an illicit quest for power but from a failure to appreciate the seriousness of their position in society. Both have grown up in households in which there has been a lack of parental guidance. As a result, neither character has had the natural vivaciousness of her imagination tempered by an appropriate discipline. Because of this neglect, they have remained girls, but as they have now reached a marriageable age, they need to become women. The frivolity of their speech is a sign of their immaturity. Their natural wit needs to be checked, and they need to learn the decorum appropriate to the discourse of a landed gentry. The path of this education involves a key moment of humiliation in which the heroine's understanding of the social world changes. When Elizabeth reads Darcy's letter and when Emma is corrected by Knightley after her behavior at Box Hill, each heroine reassesses her conduct and reforms her rhetoric, tempering her wit with a new prudence. Each can then assume her proper place within a social order that has managed to reestablish itself by proving the rightness of its hierarchy and categories.

How different is the situation of Anne Elliot. The security of the life of the landed gentry has passed, as the overextended and unproductive aristocrats are now letting out their homes for rent. Austen seems to have little regret for the aristocracy now in decline, for clearly characters like Sir Walter Elliot and his daughter, Elizabeth, have long given up any moral claim to social authority. Not acquiring capital but living off it, they are a historic and economic anachronism, even as they persist mistakenly in believing that they are a genuine social center. In their place, a new economic class is emerging, and a new vigor and common sense seem to be taking hold. Although neither Admiral Croft nor Captain Wentworth is tainted by having made his fortune through trade, both are self-made men. Each has risen through his talent to his newly acquired economic status. They are representatives of new money, and like their brethren in trade, their money is better described in terms of fortune rather than in terms of wealth. They have not inherited money but have acquired it through a propitious combination of fortunate circumstance and personal resourcefulness. The economic order of the earlier novels is already consigned to the past. The aristocratic and even courtly associations embodied in a name such as Knightley have given over to a frankly economic surname in Wentworth. There is no place for a Knightley or Darcy in *Persuasion*. Contingency is the new order of the day, and what is required is not the decorum of aristocratic judgment but the daring and force of personality that allows one to capitalize on what fortune happens to hand one. Although Austen focuses on private lives, the nature of this new world is Machiavellian, as Fortuna is the reality with which the characters must deal. The task of bringing order from chaos, however, does not fall to a prince but to a woman who is currently condemned to a diminished life of relative solitude.

Anne's task cannot be to fit into preexisting economic and social order, for such an order is disappearing; instead, she must find her way in a changing world. Nor does she stand in need of the traditional Austenian education undergone by earlier heroines. She certainly does not need to learn how to curb her tongue, since no one listens to her. And although Anne clearly has a sense of humor, she is not a witty character, nor is her speech marked by the playfulness of either Elizabeth Bennet or Emma Woodhouse. Hers is not an imagination that is out of control. When the novel opens, Anne is a character of mature judgment. She begins the novel as a character who has heeded traditional advice and suffered for it. But for all of her quiet accommodation to those around her, Anne had learned to think for herself:

> Anne at seven and twenty, thought very differently from what she had been made to think at nineteen. — She did not blame Lady Russell, she did not blame herself for having been guided by her; but she felt that were any young person, in similar circumstances, to apply to her for counsel, they would never receive any of such certain immediate wretchedness, such uncertain future good. — She was persuaded that under every disadvantage of disapprobation at home, and every anxiety attending his profession, all their probable fears, delays, and disappointments, she should yet have been a happier woman in maintaining the engagement, than she had been in the sacrifice of it. . . . How eloquent could Anne Elliot have been, — how eloquent, at least, were her wishes on the side of early warm attachment, and a cheerful confidence in futurity, against that overanxious caution which seems to insult exertion and distrust Providence! (32–33)

She has seen that the old ways no longer work, and she is positioned to revise her understanding of what is important. She is a character poised on the cusp of change. Her experience has inclined her to be eloquent, but her situation denies her the possibility of speaking. What she must find or invent is a new way of speaking that allows her to assert rather than negate herself.

Although Anne's disparagement of caution and support for exertion may make her sound like an early apologist for a free market, her situation is not one of new opportunity but one of new estrangement. Anne does not need an education in how to conform to a dominant discourse; instead, she needs to find an audience that will credit her excellence. Rather than learning the lessons of a prudential rhetoric, Anne must confront a rhetorical preclusion. For all their marked differences, Hecuba and Anne Elliot share the same rhetorical problem. Both are characters distinguished by their ability to speak, yet each finds herself in a situation in which her rhetorical excellence is beside the point. Both, in effect, are silenced. The subjecthood of each is created by her exclusion from the discursive community, and in this exclusion each points to the politics of her construction, for as Judith Butler argues: "For the subject to be the pre-given point of departure for politics is to defer the question of the political construction and regulation of the subject itself; for it is important to remember that subjects are constituted through exclusion, that is, through the creation of a domain of deauthorized subjects, presubjects, figures of abjection, populations erased from view" ("Contingent Foundations," 13). Such erasure is precisely what has happened to Anne Elliot and to Hecuba. For Hecuba it is the invulnerability of those in power to the pain of others that renders her speech ineffective; for Anne, the banality of the evil is even more pronounced. She is silenced by triviality. She must contend not so much with a bureaucratized system of power as with an endemic stupidity and vanity. Nihilism has moved from a problem of extreme political situations to a fact of ordinary domestic life.

With Anne Elliot's silencing, Jane Austen has brought forward the skepticism of classical rhetoric and resituated it as a problem of everyday life in a modern liberal society. And like her skeptical predecessors, she offers a serious alternative to the standard defense of rhetoric. In Anne's exchange with Captain Harville, she explicitly challenges a gendered literary tradition and argues against the masculine value of a modernist self that is defined by the self-determination of an individual will. In a wonderful reversal of the Austen educational paradigm, a female character now educates a male character and demonstrates the inadequacy of the modernist self to the rhetoricity of human existence.

Persuasion opens with Anne Elliot, who should be valued by anyone with genuine discernment, displaced from the Elliot family circle by the sycophantic and ambitious Mrs. Clay, who has become the intimate companion of Elizabeth. As Elizabeth confides to Mrs. Clay, "Anne is nothing to me" (137).

And Anne will remain nobody as long as she is confined to the vapid and vain society of the Elliots. Whatever problems the emerging social order brings, it is clear that the older order has lost its claim to authorize a meaningful life. For what Kellynch cannot give Anne is the conversation that will nourish her intelligence and imagination and that will allow the expression and reciprocation of her passion. Without such conversation, she will continue to wither, as she has done for the seven years following her broken engagement to Wentworth. To have a chance at the life that she merits, Anne must create a new community, and she must create this community in a situation in which any direct communication of her passion has been foreclosed. Unlike the deconstructive rhetorics that see the problems of discourse to follow from deluded attempts to achieve a final closure, Austen confronts the devastation that attends to a discursive creature who can find no opening and hence cannot locate a community that will respond to her. For Austen this is the form that nihilism takes as a philosophic problem — one becomes nobody when there is no audience that will listen to her speech, and her solution will be to recover rhetoric as the art of community.

Anne's search for community is a search for her Other. The problem is not simply that such Others are rarely available, but that because we are creatures of passion, we often attach ourselves accidentally to the wrong partners. Fortune has supplanted the extravagance of wit as the ethical obstruction to a good marriage. Austen emphasizes the role of accidental attachment by ending *Persuasion* with the assertion that the reality of passionate relationships runs counter to any ethical theory arguing for a rational basis for marriage: "When any two young people take it into their heads to marry, they are pretty sure by perseverance to carry their point, be they ever so poor, or ever so imprudent, or ever so little likely to be necessary to each other's ultimate comfort. This may be bad morality to conclude with, but I believe it to be truth" (233). If selves are inherently social, then one's identity is inescapably tied to those Others with whom one is most intimately associated. If passion creates the opportunity for a peculiarly rich life, it also brings great peril. When those Others to whom one is tied are trivial, one's own self is inevitably diminished.

An inadvertent inauthenticity becomes the fate of those nonreflective characters who live in communities in which the other characters are not their equals. In a novel that acknowledges that most marriages are products of accident, the marriage of Mary Elliot and Charles Musgrove shows why an intelligent character might choose to remain single rather than condemn himself or herself to an existence based on an escape from an adult world. Their marriage embodies the ethical loss that follows upon an accidental attachment, and it inverts the novel's ideal of marriage as a continuing conversation between equals. For Mary and Charles are not equals, and in the absence of an equality capable of promoting a sharing and consequent growth, Mary has retreated to hypochondria, and Charles into triviality, his only serious pursuits being recreational. They truly have nothing to say to each other.

In a world in which accidental attachment plays such a determinative role, it would seem reasonable to value prudence, but Austen is more concerned with the dangers of overvaluing prudence than with those occasioned by its absence.[1] Anne's prudence has led to a severely diminished life that has left her intellectually and passionately malnourished. For if prudence minimizes the possibility of a misstep, it does so by offering only a defensive strategy for living. The alternative offered by a purely prudential universe is one of human detachment, a truth that experience has taught Anne: "She had been forced into prudence in her youth, she learned romance as she grew older — the natural sequence of an unnatural beginning" (33). Unlike either Elizabeth Bennet or Emma Woodhouse, who need to learn prudence, Anne's needs are more profound, for she needs to be saved from a miseducation. The problem that occupies *Persuasion* is not that of individual reform but that of a new appreciation for the value of a discourse that has been suppressed by prudence. Maturity is no longer aligned with prudence, but instead it involves a return to or recovery of a self that can be denied when it is informed by a prudential discipline. The novel emphasizes how much Anne has lost by being prudential: the ideology of caution, of making a good deal, has purchased her security at the cost of emotional well-being. The dictates of economic good sense or the demands to preserve the patriarchy cannot be reconciled with the psychological needs of a passionate creature. The considerations that determined the marriages of Elizabeth Bennet and Emma Woodhouse can no longer operate in the changed circumstances of *Persuasion*. In a world governed by fortune, the new stability cannot be economic but instead must become psychological and ultimately rhetorical. The problem for the modernist self is not that of disciplining itself to fit into a society and economy that have a fixed and stable order but of discovering the new orders of community that can nurture people in the absence of an abiding tradition. What this new community requires is a new way of speaking.

Austen's concern with the overvaluing of prudence and the underappreciation of passion is reminiscent of Plato's *Phaedrus,* which, as Martha C. Nussbaum has argued, inquires into eros as a viable philosophical motive (*Fragility,* 200–233). In *Phaedrus* Lysias, in the guise of the nonlover, supposedly not moved by passion, argues that a relationship founded on a prudential detachment is the best means that a beloved has for safeguarding his interests. What the nonlover offers the beloved is a friendship based on rational self-interest and aspiring to a reciprocal respect. The lover, on the other hand, caught in the throes of passion, is a dangerous and irrational creature whose relationship with a beloved is unstable and almost surely injurious. But in the recantation preceding his second speech, Socrates challenges this account of eros and affirms the divine status of passion. For Socrates, Eros is a god, and the madness that he offers is superior to a safe and calculative human reason. Because of the divinity of Eros, only an erotic relationship opens a self to the possibility of achieving wisdom. Eros propels one toward one's Other, and in the experience of this passionate enthusiasm, the philosophic quest for beauty, and ultimately for wisdom, begins. In Socrates' account of the growth of the soul, the particular personal beauty of the beloved provokes the lover's soul to a philosophic reverie, and this reverie, in turn, leads the lover to wish to educate the beloved. The beloved then grows to become a soul equal to or at least capable of promoting a corresponding and reciprocal growth on the part of the lover. The best that a nonlover can offer a beloved is a kind of human cleverness (256e).

A philosophically erotic relationship would be conducted, in the main, through conversation. The lovers would mature as their conversational interchanges became a dialectic, and the dialectic would acquire its own rhythm in which the erotically charged selves would be the medium. Such selves would abandon the careful control and concern with avoiding injury for a madness in which the self was risked so that it could discover the divinity within. This dialectical conversation would shape itself into the highest and most fulfilling form of human intercourse. Such conversation would nurture selves whose identities would then be consequences of the mutually conducted discourse.

Only in such conversation can Anne's intellect and passion find fulfillment. But Plato's lover and beloved were both men, and whatever difficulties might attend their developing relationship, both were at least given freedom to speak. Anne is without such an opportunity. Further, she must act in a situation in which an older order of values is now out of synch with the new social realities. If Anne is to find someone with whom she can talk, she needs to redefine the Elliots' insistence on an "alliance of equality" from its preoccupation with social position into an ethical concern with creating a community in which she can, through conversation, find her Other. The alternative for Anne, if such a community cannot be created, is to remain a nobody.

The seriousness with which *Persuasion* views this alternative indicates the depth of Austen's insight into the origin of ethical skepticism. Anne Elliot faces a nihilistic future as devastating as that of any hero or heroine of modern or postmodern fiction. That Anne does not despair is a mark of her courage, but it should not lessen our appreciation for the ethical nihilism following from her discursive isolation. *Persuasion* labels such nihilism as nothingness, and it sees this nothingness as the condition in which a character finds herself when she is unable to enter a discursive community. The abyss that confronts Anne is not a product of either metaphysical or epistemological inadequacy but a consequence of the nature of a self whose identity is deeply tied to membership in a discursive community. Such communities are no longer given historically. Accident (fortune) and not tradition determines the new and changing social order, and consequently this is a universe in which it is very possible for lovers not to meet.

In the section at Uppercross, Austen makes explicit the problem of nothingness: Anne "had never been staying there before, without being struck by it, or without wishing that other Elliots could have her advantage in seeing how unknown, or unconsidered there, were the affairs which at Kellynch-hall were treated as of such general publicity and pervading interest; yet, with all her experience, she believed she must now submit to feel that another lesson, in the art of knowing our own nothingness beyond our own circle, was become necessary for her" (43–44). In her isolation Anne has learned the rhetorical truth that there is no transcendental reconciliation of viewpoints in some Kantian city of ends but only a collection of communities, each of which "dictates its own matters of discourse" (45). If the vanity-induced myopia of Sir Walter and Elizabeth can blind them to their own triviality and lead them to believe that the universe is centered on their interests, Anne, who has been forced to look at communal life from both the margin and the outside, can appreciate the truth that a self is relative to membership in a discursive community.

The bleakness that Austen sees is evident in the absence of conversation for most of the novel.[2] The design of *Persuasion* emphasizes both the importance of conversation and the rareness of its occurrence. Anne's plight at Uppercross demonstrates how limited a speaker is in her ability to present herself to an Other. Because of the broken engagement, Anne and Wentworth can no longer meet innocently, for their relationship has a history that is currently one of "perpetual estrangement." Like Neoptolemos, Anne must try to speak to an audience whose trust has been violated. As a speaker, she is embedded in history. And in his preemptive deafness about their previous engagement, Wentworth refuses Anne the opportunity to be eloquent about her continuing love for him. Further, Wentworth's implicit interdiction of any serious conversation cannot be challenged by Anne because the social constraints placed on her gender restrict her only to certain appropriate discursive roles, and these roles do not allow her to initiate the conversation that could lead to the resumption of their engagement. Again, Anne's situation is different from that of Austen's earlier heroines. Neither Elizabeth Bennet nor Emma Woodhouse lacked for discursive openings. Each was free to speak; each found audiences at hand; each began with a clear recognition of her right to speak. Mr. Bennet encouraged Elizabeth to exercise her wit, and Mr. Woodhouse exercised no control over Emma. The heroines' tongues were free — both in the sense of having little constraint over them and in the sense of having little regard for the cautions of conventions. When these two heroines get in trouble, their difficulties are not from any preclusion of their voices but from their own indiscretions. Having been indulged earlier, they need to be educated. These heroines must reform their speech, finally making it more acceptable to the men whom they would marry. Anne needs no such education, for her speech is marked by a sensibility and maturity, and even more, Austen has put the moral authority of the past social order in question, so Anne need not seek some sort of accommodation with a prudential rhetoric. Anne's problem is that the excellence of her speech is irrelevant because she lacks an available audience. There is no personal nor technical reform that can address this problem.

The marginality of her position at Uppercross also contributes to Anne's silencing. The Musgroves have only a limited appreciation of Anne's excellence, and it simply never occurs to them to regard Anne as anything more than a useful supernumerary. It is not that the Musgroves are insensitive — they are amiable enough, and Anne has a genuine affection for them, but they are taken up with their own concerns in which Anne plays only an insignificant part. However much Anne may clothe herself in the concerns of Uppercross, she is valued only for her utility in dealing with Mary and for service as a musician at the dances. Even if Anne were included more in the life at Uppercross, that would not solve anything, for that community is limited in what it can offer her. Mrs. Croft's judgment of the Musgrove daughters — "Very good humoured, unaffected girls" (90) — in its faint praise suggests what is lacking at Uppercross. It is not a community of large passion or discriminating intelligence.

If Uppercross is not closed by the triviality and vanity of Kellynch, its easygoing sentimentality breeds its own set of dangers. In its lack of discrimination, it carelessly cedes to accident the authority to determine events. It neither understands nor respects Fortuna. None of the community's principal actors, for example, sees the danger of allowing chance to decide whom the Musgrove daughters marry. Because there is so little thought on the part of anyone in this community except Anne, who is not listened to, Wentworth and Louisa drift into an undeclared and, on Wentworth's part, unintended attachment.

Wentworth is peculiarly susceptible to such unintended entanglements because of his confidence in his own abilities.[3] He is a very different male protagonist for an Austen novel. He is not a member of the upper class; nor is he a paragon of virtue. The potential husband is no longer an Olympian figure who brings the gift of wisdom to his future bride. Rather he is a more rough-and-ready type who finds fulfillment in action. Austen's decision to make him a candidate for comic education shows some of her misgivings about the new directions in which society was going. If Austen can applaud the initiative of such a character, she can see clearly the dangers in the new myth of the new man. Because such a character is not born into an established order of privilege, it is easy for that character to reduce all problems to those of individual decisiveness. Wentworth's deluded sense of autonomy arises from a faith in the invincibility of the human will. Although in his naval career he has bested Fortuna, he has little understanding of the constraints that Fortuna can impose. More than anything else, Wentworth is naive.

Wentworth's blind faith in the autonomous and active self and his subsequent and unintended entanglement with Louisa point to the way in which a character can lose control over a situation by assuming naively that one's commitments are under one's conscious and rational control.[4] Although Wentworth acknowledges the role that luck played in his military successes, he has the inflated self-esteem of the self-made man. His overvaluation of a fixed and firm mind is the misperception of a complicated world by an actor who has succeeded too well too early. Wentworth is paradigmatic of a new economic actor. Although his is a naval and not a commercial career, his personal qualities are very much those of venture capitalist. Fortune is his handmaiden, and he seems to thrive in a world that requires one to be alert to the opportunities that will come his way. His high estimation of his own worth is emblematic of a rising individualism that sees success or failure as a consequence of a personal initiative. Wentworth, and not Anne, becomes the character in need of comic education, as a new type of foible — the false assumption of autonomy — has arisen with the newly organized liberal economies.

Wentworth's easy and straightforward success has allowed him to view the world as a place that responds unproblematically to will and action and has blinded him to the fact that a social universe is more complicated and that in such a universe no one has complete control over how actions are read or how words are taken. In particular, Wentworth misses the important truth that one commits oneself as much by action as by explicit statement. The human condition is inherently rhetorical. Actions speak; attentions are read by the community as intentions, for the community determines character by reading words and actions. By frequently appearing with Louisa, Wentworth commits himself to her, even if he is not conscious of undertaking this commitment. It is only when his heart begins to return to Anne that he suddenly finds out that the rest of the community conceives of him and Louisa as engaged. In his inadvertent entanglement, he is finally brought to understand that in a social universe no self is autonomous, for all selves are products of that community's discourse. This is to learn that what is needed is not a resolute will but a rhetorical sophistication that appreciates the role of communal discourse in determining human freedom and happiness.

Austen opens rhetoric as a philosophic problem by showing that the ethical difficulties of having a viable self are the rhetorical problems of constituting a community. In contrast to ethical theories like Kant's, which posit an agent who is autonomous, an ethics like Austen's, rooted in the discursive and communal nature of the self, emphasizes the dependence of an ethical agent on Others, and it makes clear the role of a discursive community for the constitution and sustenance of the individual self.[5] The rhetorical difficulties in *Persuasion* arise not because of a poststructural imprisonment in the infinite regress of figurality but from a preclusion of certain topoi. Where the epistemological skepticism of deconstruction casts doubt on the finality of any closure, the ethical skepticism of *Persuasion* worries about the absence of an opening. In arguing against the possibility of skepticism as an alternative that anyone could live, Stanley Fish tries to calm what he takes to be a false theoretical anxiety created when a referential understanding of knowledge is abandoned: he claims that there is nothing to worry about because it is impossible to find oneself outside a discursive community (*Is There a Text?* 356–61). But Anne's isolation argues that the theoretical worry is not a mere chimera; far from being an empty theoretical fate, being positioned outside any discursive community is a real and serious possibility. For Fish, our necessary enclosure in some language guarantees that there will be no skeptical opening and makes epistemology a function of rhetoric. For Austen, the problem is that because we are creatures of discourse and because any understanding is necessarily internal to our shared conventions, we can exclude from our hearing, either deliberately or inadvertently, those voices we do not admit to our conversations. This is the problem of justice as Plato developed it in the *Gorgias*. And as Socrates made clear in the *Gorgias,* this problem cannot be solved through either a more rigorous ethical discipline on the part of the individual or by a technical reform of rhetoric. The problem is not that our knowledge or will fails us but that we lack an available Other with whom to talk or that we fail to make our conversations available to Others. This problem of the Other's availability makes rhetoric, for Austen, inherently ethical, and it puts her very much in the company of the classical rhetorical skeptics.

The problem of available conversation is also intimately connected to the problem of misreading appearances. The most obvious example of misreading is, of course, the Elliots'. Their vanity is emblematic of a centripetal hermeneutics enclosed in the self-satisfaction of its own privilege. Their interpretive horizon is bounded by one text, the *Baronetage,* which for them is the "book of books," and their reading of Others involves an uncomplicated appeal to two signs: class membership and physical appearance. These two signs serve them as infallible guides for determining a person's worth, and to the extent that Sir Walter and Elizabeth constitute social authority for Kellynch, these signs ensure the continuing triviality of a world whose beginning and end is vanity. By determining in advance both the topoi and standards for discourse, this hermeneutic code guarantees that the universe of vanity remains invulnerable to criticism from the outside. History as change and not simply as a neatly plotted duration is alien to them. Their identity is fixed for eternity and is symbolized in their ability to escape the wrinkles and ravages of age because their life is outside of time. Their misreading of Anne merely follows from their code. Her concerns with social responsibility and human excellence are precluded from the community's discourse: she is without significance.

Misreadings, like those of the Elliots or even Lady Russell, are fairly straightforward. But a deeper and more interesting type of misreading separates Anne and Wentworth, for they are passionate readers, and their passion creates difficulties. If passion draws a self to an Other, it also plays a role in how interpreters see both themselves and Others. Austen recovers Aristotle's concern with rhetoric and the role of appearance. Like him, she realizes that the serious problem of an uncriticized passion is that it can distort how the world is seen and that, as a felt, personal response to that world, such passion can have a privileged authority. But where Aristotle would solve the problem of passion and distorted appearance by attempting to limit the role of passion, Austen is more Platonic and offers passion as the correction to passion.

Wentworth's interpretive failure is the more apparent of the two and easier to deal with. Still smarting from Anne's having ended their initial engagement, he has come back determined to misvalue her. His infamous comment about Anne having changed so drastically that he could hardly recognize her is, in fact, a description of his strategy for reading her so that she will not be available to him. He does not want to open himself up to Anne. Determined to keep their meetings confined to the occasional banalities of polite conversation and to avoid any mention of past experiences or present feelings, Wentworth has constituted himself as an audience who is not available to hear Anne's pleas, profit from her understanding, or share her feelings. Further, Wentworth is confirmed in his truculence by his recent successes in the navy. In his overvaluing of firmness, he is a walking paradigm of the new economic virtues of risk and decisiveness. And he exhibits another modern predisposition of those who favor economic explanation in that he tends to simplify human psychology and to see difference only as inferiority. He can see Anne's complex response to a situation of competing obligations only as weakness of the will. However, in cultivating his anger, he has placed himself in a state of contradiction — Anne represents his ideal for a wife, but she is the one woman whom he will refuse to consider as a wife (Johnson, *Jane Austen*, 151). Wentworth stands in need of refutation. He does not simply need to comically reform his character, he needs to experience the fundamental contradiction that is structuring his life. He needs to be shown his own incoherence.

Wentworth's fallibility makes a striking contrast to the near perfection of Darcy or Knightley. While Darcy initially may be a little too stiff, this awkwardness is really a surface blemish. His core self is sterling, and, as the novel progresses, the quality of this self becomes more and more evident. Knightley is almost inhuman in the maturity of his wisdom and the correctness of his judgment. Both characters become standards by which to judge the female protagonists. Further, both characters confirm male superiority, and this superiority forms a bedrock for the novels' sense of value. Patriarchy assures the continuance of a sane and sensibly sensitive world. Wentworth's fallibility shows Austen's rethinking of patriarchy. He is currently on top because of a fortunate coincidence of accident and ability that he misperceives as an instance of personal merit. He partakes not of wisdom but of delusion.

Instead of opening himself to a conversation in which two interpretive perspectives could encounter and modify each other, Wentworth persists in valuing a firm and unpersuadable temper whose chief value is a conviction of the rightness of its own judgment. But because a self can know itself only in conversation, Wentworth's choosing not to talk to Anne is also a choice not to know himself. Like many of the characters that Socrates must deal with, Wentworth rests comfortably in his self-deception, unable to know himself because he refuses to open himself up to refutation. As part of his willed self-deception, Wentworth has foreclosed the possibility of such refutation by limiting the topoi on which he and Anne can talk. Because he will not give her an opening in which she can bring up their shared past, the past is closed as a topic.

Anne's interpretive failure is more insidious, for, in her misreading, a self-inflicted injury masquerades as a virtue. Anne's mistaken belief that Wentworth is right and that she should now discipline herself to feel less allows Austen to recover Plato's understanding in *Gorgias* that the problem of injury is a problem for rhetoric not because a rhetor actively seeks evil but because he or she pursues a mistaken good. Anne is in danger of granting a male character the authority that Austen had conferred on them in the past. Anne too stands in need of refutation. Unlike Wentworth, she acknowledges her passion, but her openness to this passion causes her to undervalue herself, to grant Wentworth an authority that he does not deserve, and to overinterpret his gestures. Although Anne has often been read as if her vision were that of an objective or, at least, clear-sighted interpreter, Austen does not exempt her from the limitations that inhere within any interpretation.[6]

Because things matter, Anne's sight is filtered through her passionate involvement. And in the absence of any open exchange of thoughts or feelings, she tries to interpret Wentworth's discourse and action as an index to his passion, but in her uncertainty and anxiety she succumbs to the all-too-human tendency to doubt her own worth. For example, when Wentworth comes to Anne's aid at Uppercross, she reads Wentworth's behavior as a sign of indifference: "His kindness in stepping forward to her relief—the manner—the silence in which it had passed—the little particulars of the circumstance—with the conviction soon forced on her by the noise he was studiously making with the child, that he meant to avoid hearing her thanks, and rather sought to testify that her conversation was the last of his wants" (79). Although Anne's is certainly a plausible reading of Wentworth's actions, it is by no means the only reading. Indeed, it is a suspect reading because Anne has accepted Wentworth's cruel misstatement that she has changed for the worst as if it were the truth: " 'Altered beyond his knowledge!' Anne fully submitted, in silent, deep mortification. Doubtless it was so; and she could take no revenge, for he was not altered, or not for the worse" (61). But in granting Wentworth this authority over her, Anne is wrong, as Austen makes clear when she gives us our only access to Wentworth's mind to show that Wentworth does not know his mind or feelings. In his comments on Anne he was not offering an opinion but exacting a revenge. Thus, when Anne accepts his opinion and begins to try to compose her feelings accordingly, she injures herself. If Austen's other major heroines need to learn to accept a male authority, Anne Elliot needs to learn to reject such authority and come to value appropriately a feminine authority.

Stuart Tave has argued that *Persuasion* sees submission as a virtue (*Some Words*, 269–71). But Anne's submission to Wentworth's unfair and mean characterization of her encourages her to pursue a strategy of desiring "nothing in return but to be unobserved" (71). In pursuit of this strategy, Anne begins to instruct herself in how to feel less. Convinced that Wentworth is indifferent to her, Anne repeatedly tries to do the prudent thing and repress her own passion. The apparent virtue of submission would, if successful, damn Anne to a world of isolation. The danger for Anne is that she will succeed in her misreadings, accept Wentworth's current contradiction as a state of true passion, and thus prudentially invent a lesser universe of controlled and re-stricted feeling in which she will then be condemned to live.

Anne begins to heal only when she learns to value herself. Her good judg-ment after Louisa's fall (when Wentworth succumbs to hysteria) is essential during this trying period. She effects a role reversal and challenges the myth of male competence and female helplessness. Even more important, Anne de-velops an ironic appreciation for both herself and Wentworth: "Anne won-dered whether it ever occurred to him now, to question the justness of his own previous opinion as to the universal felicity and advantage of firmness of character; and whether it might not strike him, that, like all other qualities of the mind, it should have its proportions and limits. She thought that it could scarcely escape him to feel, that a persuadable temper might sometimes be as much in favour of happiness as a very resolute character" (113). Anne finally gets a healthful look at the clay in the feet of the divinity she had worshiped and to whose judgment she had subjugated herself. Austen anticipates later ideological critiques by exploring how available social and economic under-standings can cause the individual to subjugate himself or herself. Like later theorists of ideology, Austen must find an opening for action in a world in which the operation of ideology is inescapable. She needs to find a power that can contend with ideology. To find such a power, she will turn to passion and to eloquence.

Anne is saved despite her initial bow to male authority, for she cannot force her feelings to submit to rational control. Unlike Wentworth's anger, which closes him to Anne and himself, Anne's feelings are marked by a generosity that opens her to an Other. Generosity rather than prudence becomes the novel's central virtue. If Anne's openness contributes to her vulnerability, it is also what allows her to grow and to know what she needs. Anne's continual efforts at acknowledging and doing justice to other characters, even to Went-worth after he has cruelly wounded her, are motivated by her generous feel-ings. If certain passions may abet a willed ignorance and create hermeneutical difficulties by allowing characters to see only the world that they want to see, a generous passion will serve as a reliable guide by attaching a character to his or her Other. This is the lesson of Romance. The generosity of her feelings allows Anne to escape most of the dangers and misunderstandings that threaten the other characters. And if she is in danger of isolating herself by seeking to repress her feelings for Wentworth, she is never in danger of attaching herself inadvertently to the wrong person, however attractive that character may appear to others. Because Anne's feelings are generous, her judgment is secure.

The role of William Elliot is to make clear the epistemological worth of generous passion. With his cultivated manner and sense of social propriety he is a character who has mastered the appearance of being a gentleman. His prudence, uncompromised by any passion and consequently at the exclusive service of self-interest, easily fools other characters in the novel, even characters who are intelligent, like Lady Russell. But he never poses a serious threat to Anne. The shallowness of his feeling, his ability to dissemble, his lack of openness, and his facility at pleasing everyone are sufficient to make Anne unsure of him, even if she cannot bring any specific complaint against him. All she has to do is imaginatively call him to mind, and even the temptation of being Lady Elliot loses its force. Anne has already made her mind up not to accept any proposal from him, should he offer one, before Mrs. Smith unveils his true character.[7] Austen forgoes the potential drama of Anne's almost falling victim to his schemes because it would distract from the more insidious dangers occasioned by Wentworth's jealous misperceptions. It is as if Austen argues, through a narrative strategy of frustrating the conventional expectations she raises, that the real, if less dramatic, danger for Anne lies in Wentworth's not knowing himself. Austen no longer requires a Wickham who in his oily smoothness can cause an improvident heroine to misread him initially and thus show her need of education at the hand of a male intelligence, for the problem of *Persuasion* lies not in a female infatuation but with a willed male ignorance and a female authority that momentarily gives this ignorance a credence. In *Persuasion* gender stands in the place of the bureaucratized power that foreclosed rhetoric's openings in *Hecuba*. In each work the rhetorical failure does not arise from personal inadequacy or lack of discipline but is embedded in the very conditions that structure the society and determine the possibilities for discourse.

It is within the context of Austen's intentionally undercutting external drama that the role of Mrs. Smith is best understood. Austen's handling of Mrs. Smith has been considered a flaw in the novel, and critics have charged her with mismanaging the dramatic presentation of crucial material (Harding, "The Dexterity," 208; Tave, *Some Words,* 268–69). But if Austen's concern with the epistemological role of the passions is taken into account, then the anticlimactic structure of having Mrs. Smith bring forth damaging information about Mr. Elliot only when he is no longer a threat is required if the constancy of Anne's feeling, and of true passion in general, is to be accorded its proper power. If Anne were moved by William Elliot's appearance and saved only by the plot's unraveling as she comes to learn of her mistake, then the passions should not finally be trusted as a guide in human relationships. If this section of the novel were to exploit the dramatic possibilities inhering in Mrs. Smith's revealing information essential to safeguarding Anne's judgment, then the novel's action would, in effect, be arguing that knowing romance, one should learn prudence. This would be to return to Austen's earlier novels.

But Anne is not a heroine who needs protection. What she needs is a rhetorical opening. For even an open and frank temperament is no assurance that a character can communicate his or her passions. After Wentworth has finally admitted to himself that he loves Anne, he and Anne have a difficult time declaring their passion for each other. Although they meet several times at Bath and move closer to an understanding, these meetings do not bring them into a final communion, for Anne and Wentworth still lack an appropriate opening for serious conversation. To know each other truly, they need to converse with each other. In Wentworth's confusion, Anne sees signs of his returning affection for her, but the appearances by themselves are not enough to convince her. "If she could only have a few minutes conversation with him again, she fancied that she should be satisfied" (170). It will be the "power of conversation" that will eventually enable them to acknowledge their love for each other.

If passion is essential for a full life, it is not sufficient by itself for that life. It needs the assistance of eloquence. In a world that is inescapably discursive, relationships between people are too complicated, both by accident and by human limitations, to permit anything as straightforward as a natural expression of passion. In a discursive universe, rhetoric is the art of community. By the use of her language, a rhetor makes a self available to an Other. And in a world in which community is often not available because of self-regard or sentimentality, the rhetor's role is to risk herself by giving that self generously to the Other to read.

Alistair M. Duckworth's insight that *Persuasion* shows the world as "lacking a public syntax" and that it requires a new and private nonlinguistic means of communication would seem to argue against the novel's endorsement of rhetoric (*The Improvement of the Estate*, 199–204). He argues further that the novel has lost faith in the public sphere and turns instead to private and personal relationships. What Duckworth has seen is the rhetorical crisis within the novel: *Persuasion* is a world without community, a world beset by the increasing value of the private. His reading suggests that the novel enacts the historical shift that Laufer analyzed in his account of the rise of liberalism. While there is much to Duckworth's insight, he has moved too quickly from the absence of an existing community to the private character of Anne and Wentworth's relationship. Austen does not simply emplot the crisis of rhetoric but responds to it. Rather than abandoning her concern with community, Austen is suggesting the way in which a public must be reconstituted. Given the prominence of accident and the new moral investment in the autonomy of the individual subject, the rhetor acquires the task of not simply guiding a community's particular decisions but of inventing the community itself. The social disorganization or reorganization has created gaps, and one of these is that human excellence cannot be seen and heard. Anne's intelligent social concern belongs neither to the older aristocratic order that neglected such responsibilities nor to the arising individualism that makes a firm will the chief virtue. Anne must now exert her genius to begin to assemble a community anew that can appreciate human excellence. The originality of Anne's new community is embodied in her rejection of the male-dominated literary tradition that has accorded men's passions a privileged place. Anne argues for the superiority of women's feelings in terms of their greater tenderness and endurance. In effect, she is challenging Wentworth's earlier praise of decision and firmness and advocating the importance of a flexible receptivity. The new community that Anne is making will be one founded on generosity. And however significant her actions, it will be by her words that she creates this community by moving Wentworth to speak on behalf of his passion. Discourse will not simply be the medium of community life; it will be the origin of that life.

Appropriately, the conversation that opens up the possibility for the resumption of Wentworth's and Anne's engagement is one that deals with true feeling. Anne eloquently defends the permanence of women's feelings, and her eloquence reopens passion as a topos by signaling to Wentworth her own continuing affection for him. Central to Anne's defense of woman's passion is her claim that such passion endures. To make such an argument is to reopen the past as a topic. In a world in which accident is a serious and troubling source of instability in human relationships, passion is offered as a source of stability. Anne's speech does not glorify personal deeds nor valorize personal advancement but instead argues for the value of commitment and concern. Not personal ambition, but rather concern for an Other will govern this community. Anne's eloquence in testifying to the force of her passion becomes an ethical proof in which her language functions as a sign of her feelings. It also shows her generosity in her unprotected opening of herself to Wentworth. She shows a courage that he lacks until her words enable him to act, for Anne's defense of passion creates the opening that allows Wentworth to express his passion and to propose a new engagement.

Anne's conversation is a masterpiece not only of eloquence but also of indirection.[8] On a literal level, she provides a general defense of woman's passion, but her words are themselves a figurative expression that declares her love for Wentworth. Her use of figure, of indirection, creates the opening that will enable Wentworth to risk the declaration of his passion for her. As any good rhetor must, Anne seizes the occasion of her discussion with Captain Harville and transforms it into an opening toward Wentworth. She knows that a discourse is not only heard but overheard. For though she speaks to Harville as her immediate audience, she directs her discourse to Wentworth. *Persuasion* has shown through Wentworth's entanglement with Louisa that being overheard is as much a part of discourse as being heard and that in a discursive universe language is not a private possession but belongs to the community. No speaker possesses a simple or exclusive control over his or her own words. The best that one can do is to exploit those moments that accident throws one's way. In slightly different terms, rhetoric is the art of a creature who is historical, and it is thus an art that deals with the contingent. As Anne's final judgment about the rightness of her following Lady Russell's advice shows, she understands the contingency at the heart of human existence. Her appreciation of the importance of using the moments that fortune gives allows her to discover a way to be heard when her situation in society denies her direct access to initiating certain kinds of conversation.

The power of Anne's eloquence is demonstrated by Wentworth's impassioned letter. To understand the distance that Austen has traveled in her reconception of the problem of discourse, one has merely to compare this letter of Wentworth's with the earlier letter of Darcy. The Austen heroine is not undergoing education but encouraging the hero to move beyond a rhetoric of the individual will, with its valuing of a decisive and firm judgment. Anne's speech inaugurates a new rhetoric that is self-consciously female. And her rhetoric has accomplished what good rhetoric does: it has called forth eloquent discourse in response to it. Anne's speech and Wentworth's letter bear out the truth of the *Phaedrus:* passion begets eloquence, which, in turn, calls forth more passion and more eloquence. The lovers' discourse is beginning. But contrary to Socrates' recommendation, Wentworth abandons speech and resorts to writing. Part of the reason for Wentworth's writing has to be that a crowded room would not allow him to speak his passion to Anne. This, however, can only be part of the reason because Anne has just managed to communicate her passion to Wentworth in the same room. The greater significance behind Wentworth's writing is that he consciously gives up control of his discourse. One of Socrates' chief objections to writing is that the writer gives his words over to an Other, and consequently he can no longer control their meaning. Since the rhetor is not immediately present, he cannot correct misreadings. For Wentworth to give up such control is his ultimate act of faith in Anne. It is a generous gesture that announces his understanding of the rhetoricity of a true community.

The superiority of Anne's and Wentworth's second engagement is the superiority of a rhetorical to an accidental relationship. The marriage of Anne and Wentworth then becomes a celebration of the value of genuine passion. A relationship that was founded on the good luck of two people who were right for each other and who accidentally came together at the right place and time ("he had nothing to do, and she had hardly any body to love") has been replaced by a rhetorical relationship that is grounded firmly in passion eloquently communicated and in a recognition of the discursive nature of the self. Fortuna has given place to rhetoric. The second engagement represents an ethical understanding of the communal nature of the self and of the role of passion and discourse in communal life.

Conversation itself becomes the distinguishing mark of a genuine community. Anne makes this clear: " 'My idea of good company, Mr. Elliot, is the company of clever, well-informed people, who have a great deal of conversation: that is what I call good company' " (142). Only in such a company can a person achieve a full life, for what such company makes possible is a serious sharing and a genuine openness. While describing the concert at Bath, Austen begins by comparing the happiness of Elizabeth and Anne, but she stops herself because she believes that the two happinesses cannot really be compared. She goes on to claim that the origin of Anne's happiness was her "generous attachment" (175). This is a good characterization of the richness of a communal existence. Characters can trust in their feelings and be led by them to meet and discourse with Others. These meetings are marked neither by the vanity of the Elliots, nor by the sentimentality of the Musgroves, nor by the calculations of William Elliot, but are instead open sharings of feelings and thoughts. The possibility of genuine conversation makes the marriage promised by the second engagement superior to the marriage that would have followed upon the accidental first engagement. The good marriage founded on a generous attachment becomes a continual conversation.

But if Anne triumphs, Austen uses her triumph to point to the difficulties and recalcitrance of a world of accidental attachment. This world is complicated by misreadings that foreclose the topoi needed to acknowledge an Other and by rigid gender categories that equate courage with firmness rather than with generosity. Thus Austen shows us the precariousness of an ethical self and its need for community. In beginning her final chapter with the wisdom that human nature does not conform to the simplistic rationalism of ethical theories that are grounded in the idea of an autonomous self, Jane Austen seeks to place the ethical understanding behind *Persuasion* within a heterogeneous and contingent human experience. This ethical understanding becomes a justification for a rhetorical sophistication that can affect human concerns because humans are not only passionate and historical creatures but also discursive ones. *Persuasion* becomes an eloquent pleading for "a cheerful confidence in futurity" (33), and that is an argument for an ethical stance. As Anne shows, one should meet a world generously, not because the world will necessarily respond to that generosity but because such a stance is necessary if a character is to open herself or himself to the Other through whom a discursive communion will lead to a full and vital existence.

With *Persuasion,* Jane Austen offers her critique of the modernist self in which rhetoric stands in opposition to an understanding of the world as an arena for action where individuals through the agency of their wills strive to advance themselves by mastering contingency. Instead, contingency is seen as inhering in any situation, and a rhetoric grounded in passion is offered as the best way to deal with such contingency. Older certainties have given over to new uncertainties, and to act rhetorically is to assume responsibility for creating a new and more adequate social order and to testify to a confidence in human resources to deal with the uncertainty that is an ineradicable element in any life.

7

Refuting Sartre
Modernism's Equivocation on the Reader

In *Persuasion,* Jane Austen explored discursive preclusion as a theme of a novel that set forth a rhetorical crisis evolving from the social, economic, and philosophical reorganization of liberal society. Sartre moves the problem of preclusion from a theme that literature explored to a condition that threatens and defines the possibility of literature, or at least the future of prose. Sartre argues that the crisis of writing in the mid-twentieth century derives from the larger historical problems of alienation and abstraction that have undermined both the community and the individual.[1] In *What Is Literature?* he attempts through both inquiry and polemic to address this problem of the absence of community. He conceives the task of the contemporary writer as creating a public, which means creating the conditions for a genuine community, one founded on a critically reflective socialism. A Sartrean writer then stands to the modernist public much as Neoptolemos stood to Philoctetes. Each must speak in a situation where the very possibilities of public discourse have been put into question; each begins in a world that is marked by discontinuity; each must discover a new authority. For Sartre this will be a problem of authenticity, but for Sophocles, as we have seen, individual authenticity, while desirable, cannot resolve the problem of the public, for the issue is not individual integrity but the possibility of acting in a situation in which a deep skepticism is the most reasonable position. What distinguishes Sophocles from

Sartre is their differing commitments to the individual in history. For Sophocles, we are inescapably political; for Sartre, we are alienated from politics. The modernist subject may aspire to political commitment but is finally defined not by participation in politics but by participation in reason. The demands of this reason to the authority of a universal rationality fate Sartre to abandon the rhetoricity that he discovers and that is at the heart of Sophocles' productive skepticism.

Sartre's concern with the preclusion of discourse because of the unavailability of the audience marks him as a fellow traveler with the rhetorical skeptics of antiquity. Sartre's particular contribution to rhetorical theory resides in his analysis of the radical subjectivity at the center of the modern writer's crisis. His existential and Marxist impulses in their pragmatic thrust make his thought a rich resource for exploring the possibilities of a modernist rhetorical theory. When Sartre argues that the alienation of individual subjects is the problem of modernism, then the possibility of any genuine rhetorical community is brought into question. This understanding leads him to frame writing as a problem of action without a meaningful purpose and to investigate the motives available to a writer who begins from and within an alienated universe. But his inability to move beyond the crisis of the subject is indicative of an incoherence within modernism that provokes the inquiries that have come to be known as postmodernism.

Sartre's search for a motive for the writer that is sufficient to allow him or her to escape from an alienated and abstract subjectivity reopens a question that Plato had addressed in the *Phaedrus*. In that dialogue Plato reconsiders the aspiration to self-sufficiency and revises his assessment of the philosophic value of passion. There he does not argue that the problem of unscrupulous manipulation at the hands of corrupt rhetors can be solved by the cultivation of philosophical selves who are invulnerable to illicit appeals based in pleasure or founded on deception.[2] Rather the dialogue reexamines this position and, in a serious revision of the middle dialogues, acknowledges a directive role for eros in the philosophical life (Nussbaum, *Fragility,* 202). In the Platonic revision, eros becomes a legitimate rhetorical motive: our love for another urges us to speak to him or her and thus creates a dialectical opening for community that is equally philosophical and erotic, although a tension between the two still remains. The rational detachment of the nonlover ceases to be a value marking a self under emotional control but instead becomes a personal deficiency that prevents a particularly full form of human relationship. Because the nonlover is not possessed by eros, he or she cannot offer wisdom (which is divine in origin) but only a limited human cleverness. This is the cleverness of sophistic rhetoric in which others exist only as a means for the rhetor's private end. Without a passion that makes one's Other an end in himself or herself, the calculation of *phronesis* becomes indistinguishable from the manipulation of sophistry.

Plato's reformulation of passion as a positive and directive force in human relations has the apparent advantage of locating philosophic activity in a social and potentially communal relationship. The love for another person becomes one motive for a life of wisdom, and this pursuit of wisdom requires that the lover try to engage his or her beloved equally in such a search. A proper passion becomes the origin of ethical constraint by determining the rhetor to act in the interest of the beloved. Still, the erotically motivated rhetoric that is depicted in the dialogue requires, at least initially, the physical presence of both the rhetor and the beloved. In the dialogue, speech displaces writing as the written text of Lysias gives way to the speeches of Socrates.[3] Indeed, the relationship between lover and beloved involves an intense and reciprocal intimacy originating in a private and exclusive physical gaze that can sunder the lover and the beloved from their normal ties to the world or to others outside of the relationship. Rather than the solipsism of the modernist subject endangering discourse, private friendship becomes the obstacle to participation in communal life. Plato has thus placed this pair of lovers in a situation parallel to Neoptolemos and Philoctetes before the divine discourse of Herakles recalls them to their social responsibilities. For even if one or both parties to the Platonic relationship based in eros give openly of themselves, their love remains rooted in the particular partner and does not generalize to others (Nussbaum, *Fragility,* 218).

The consequence is that erotic discourse is potentially corrosive for public life, for the erotic relationship of Plato in the *Phaedrus* is ultimately private. In the dialogue, writing becomes a problem because of its inherent tendency to become public. One of Socrates' key objections to written discourse is that it gives up the direct contact between two souls, with a consequent loss of vitality for the discourse. Socrates also objects to written discourse because it can be disseminated to a large audience and thus the writer cannot exercise any control over who receives the discourse or how they make sense of it. Socrates sees written discourse almost as a kind of wantonness, and he compares it to the activity of an inartistic farmer who sows seeds indifferently in all kinds of soil. The seeds root where they may and grow where they will. Socrates prefers speech because the speaker can choose and limit the audience, with the ideal audience being restricted to the beloved. The motive for community is opposed, in effect, by the desire for an exclusive intimacy, and it is unclear how the partners might move from their personal affection to a discovery and participation in a larger community. So while eros may be the source and sustaining drive for a significant personal growth, there is no reason to assume that this personal growth will lead to the development of communal virtues. If a political role for rhetoric is to be recovered, the erotically based philosophical rhetoric of the *Phaedrus* needs to undergo refutation. Plato offers such refutation twice: once in Diotima's speech in the *Symposium,* when eros is argued as the point of entry to a philosophic life that transforms that eros from a concern with another individual to a concern with the larger organization of the intellectual life; and once in the *Phaedrus,* when the form of the dialogue demands the reader actively revise an initial understanding of its content.

The erotic rhetoric of the *Phaedrus* was a challenge not only to Plato but to other rhetors who sought a role for passion in rhetoric. Augustine would attempt to displace eros by charity and recast rhetoric as an instrument to be deployed for the salvation of others. And Sartre would displace charity by the secular passion of generosity. This movement from eros to charity to generosity offers, in miniature, a recapitulation of the history of the Western subject from its necessary if ambivalent political identity through Christianity's spiritual reformulation of this identity, to the Enlightenment and post-Enlightenment attempts to reground this spiritual identity in reason.[4]

Augustine seeks an apparent escape from the erotic containment of private relationships by reconceiving passion as the movement of the soul toward God. He alters the Platonic paradigm for rhetoric by beginning from a self that has a spiritual rather than an erotic identity. In *On Christian Doctrine* he inverts Plato by conceiving spiritual passion as an unmediated relationship between soul and God and then argues that the rhetorical relation between rhetor and community is mediated rather than immediate. In Augustine's revision utility and enjoyment replace power and eros as the two fundamental rhetorical motives. A rhetor's relation to this world is of interest only to the extent that it helps or hinders the project of personal salvation. The fundamental human task is to love things appropriately. This is primarily a hermeneutical rather than a rhetorical task, for it involves an individual in learning how to read the world appropriately. For Augustine, one begins as a reader and not as a writer, and although rhetoric is important for Augustine, especially in the practice of charity, the production of discourse is a second-order interest that follows upon the ability to read well. This ordering is a good index of how far rhetoric has moved from its grounding in either a Platonic eros or an Aristotelean phronesis. An Augustinian rhetor does not invent the material of the discourse but uses his or her words to aid an audience in reading the central text that God has created. Rhetoric is justified by its theological and not by its political utility.

The Augustinian self is a hermeneutical subject, existing in a world comprising things and signs, or put differently, in a world of things that is available to human selves only as a world of signs (*On Christian Doctrine, 7*). Faith has replaced either eros or phronesis as a guide to human life, and the problem is no longer constructing an adequate civic ethos but being true to whom one really is. In Augustine's Christianity, the modernist self is born, or at least gestated, awaiting Descartes to transform its inherent self-doubt into the very principle of its new authenticity. For Augustine, if one is to be saved, one must learn to read. In such a world it is incumbent on the self to be able to read the signs correctly; however, this kind of reading is deeply problematic because a sign's meaning can never be authenticated by an appeal to an external and prior point of reference. Signs simply generate other signs, and there is no exit from the semiotic circle. Reading is not an epistemological enterprise but an ontological activity in which a self moves toward or away from an authentic relationship to the Divine — the one thing in the universe that is to be loved for its own sake. However, since God is ineffable, a human self can never know God; rather, the standard for successful reading is not an alignment between a sign and a referent but is authorized by the reader's motive. A reader can approach a thing with one of two acceptable motives: either to love the thing in itself and therefore to enjoy the thing, or to love the thing for the sake of something else and therefore to use it as a means of reaching that which can be loved for its own sake. Since only God merits love for its own sake, all other things must be loved for the sake of reaching God. It is the appropriate love of others that moves an individual from the hermeneutical task of reading to the rhetorical responsibility to produce a discourse that can aid others in their quest for salvation. The rhetor is moved to speak to others not because of an immediate passionate or political interest in them but because they are to be used as yet another thing to bring the rhetor nearer to God. Such interest Augustine calls charity, and charity supplies the motive for rhetoric. For Augustine, any reading that arises from a charitable motive and that seeks to increase charity is valid, and the motive itself becomes a generative source for being. When reading gives over to speech, hermeneutical discoveries guide the deployment of rhetoric.

In such a rhetoric the communal must always be a secondary and derivative concern, because, for a serious spiritual reader, the important world is always the world to come and not the material and historical one that one happens to inhabit. The essential relationship is not that of person to person or person to community but of self to God. This relationship of self to God lays the ground for the modernist subject of Cartesian thought. The self is inherently private, and its most important concern is being authentic to those internal spiritual passions that drive it. Although the rhetor is moved by love, this love is mediated through a more essential concern for spiritual authenticity. Indeed, this self is neither naturally nor essentially social and does not properly seek other selves except for the command of charity. For the self to do otherwise is for it to promote the reign of cupidity, of eros, and such a kingdom is one that leads the self away from a love of God to a love of other things for their own sake. And that would be to enter a humanly inauthentic world. A Platonic rhetoric is not simply mistaken but is a serious spiritual danger. An Augustinian community, instead, is a sharing in and of divine love, and it is this spiritual kingdom of charity that the rhetor seeks to bring about. But even when successful at achieving appropriate love, the Augustinian subject does not transcend the private to become a public and dialectical self. Salvation is a deeply personal concern.

In his *cogito* Descartes took the uncertainty of the Augustinian self and made it the new basis for a modernist philosophy. His skepticism, however, was different in kind from that of classical rhetors. He was concerned not with the problem of an ineradicable injustice but with the problem of discovering a secure ground for knowledge. What Descartes bequeathed to the Enlightenment was the subject as the new foundation for knowledge and political life, while shifting the authority for this subject from a theological to a rational base. And although Descartes would still vest an authority in God, in the modern philosophic discourse he initiates eventually God would no longer provide the assurance that an interpretation was meaningful; rather, human reason would underwrite the new epistemological and political orders. As Thomas M. Conley comments, the impact of Cartesian philosophy on rhetorical theory was tremendous: "As far as the history of rhetoric is concerned, it is generally held that virtually every important position on the nature of rhetoric enunciated since Descartes can be seen as extensions of, or reactions to, a few basic principles in his philosophy" (*Rhetoric,* 171). The rational subject who in his or her rationality could discover a certain or at least more secure truth by the formal operation of reason alone made rhetoric, at best, irrelevant and, at worst, dangerous.

This conception of the subject would prove to be incoherent. The inability of reason to provide a final authority for itself would eventuate in the crisis of modernism.[5] But even before it would encounter problems of coherence, the idea of the subject was deeply troubled. For one thing, with the loss of God as a guarantee of the meaningfulness and the relatedness of the individual subject to a larger whole, the isolation of the self became a pressing problem. Rather than being part of a larger spiritual enterprise, the self was understood as locked in the prison of its own privateness. The Enlightenment promise of a new personal freedom founded on the use of reason gave way in the nineteenth and twentieth centuries to a preoccupation with the loss of the traditional communities that are necessary to sustain a self. The modernist subject ceased to be glorified as autonomous and instead was pitied as rootless. The inherent isolation of the modernist subject became a preoccupation of the existentialist movement.

That is the intellectual context for Sartre's *What Is Literature?* Sartre conceives of a world of selves that share Augustine's problem of authenticity but for whom the temporal and spiritual cannot be separated, for the human condition is essentially historical. Sartre's immediate historical context for his study of writing is World War II, and in particular the activity of the French resistance in a Nazi-occupied France. What separates Sartre from Augustine is, on the one hand, the birth of the modernist subject defined by reason rather than by a relationship to a divinity, and, on the other, a historical situation in which action was demanded but also problematic because the evil of Nazism seemed to negate the possibility of a meaningful ethical choice. The political opprobriousness of the Nazis' occupation of France threw individuals back on themselves. These different contexts — one of reason and the other of history — require different understandings of the problems adhering in responsible action, and the unresolved conflict leads Sartre to a deep equivocation, as he will fall back on a modernist belief in the authority of reason to solve a historical problem rooted in a need to act in a world in which reason has lost authority.

Like Augustine, Sartre seeks a rhetoric that can operate in a world of signs and things, a world in which the relationship between a sign and a thing is not epistemological but practical and finally ontological. But since he can no longer rely on a divinity to guarantee the authenticity of a particular rhetorical act, he must develop a new understanding of rhetoric as a resource for community. To discover what writing is, Sartre focuses his questions on the relationship of writer and reader. His peculiar and unconvincing distinction between poetry and prose — that prose is an instrumental use of language that begins from an understanding of language as a system of signs while poetry treats words principally as material objects — must be read in the light of Sartre's interest in the writer/reader relationship. Sartre is trying to clarify the two types of writing by recourse to the author's motives. His question is: how does a particular writer intend to treat language?

Sartre's distinctions parallel in a rather clumsy way Kenneth Burke's categories of rhetorical and poetical motives (*Literature as Symbolic Action*, 29). Burke distinguishes kinds of discourse in terms of the speaker or writer's motive. In poetic discourse, the speaker or writer is using signs for the sheer joy of symbolicity. As symbolic creatures, we take an inherent joy in the use of symbols in a way similar to, say, a dog's intrinsic love of running. It is a natural ability that we enjoy exercising. The rhetorical motive comes into operation when we wish not simply to use language but to use it to have an effect. This is very close to Sartre's understanding of why one writes prose. Thus his definition of prose — the writing that truly interests him — returns to the rhetorical tradition's standard line that locates the purpose of discourse in its utility. For Sartre, prose is a mode of action, and the fundamental question is: why has one chosen to act in this way? His inquiry into the nature of literature is, as such, an exploration of the ethical and political motives of the writer and their ramifications for the individual and community. Whether or not he acknowledges it, Sartre's existential inquiry into writing makes his defense of prose an act of rhetorical theory that continues a long tradition of justifying discourse by arguing for its utility.

But Sartre's conception of rhetorical utility has a philosophical depth that leads him also in the direction of the skeptical concerns of antiquity. What Sartre, in effect, proposes is a rhetoric of refutation. This becomes evident when Sartre gives his preliminary answer to the question of why someone would choose writing as an appropriate mode of acting. One writes to name the world and by this naming "to reveal the world and particularly to reveal man to other men so that the latter may assume full responsibility before the object which has been thus laid bare" (18). The writer's task is to ensure that people do not remain ignorant of the world that they have helped to create and, instead, that they take responsibility for that world. For Sartre, the human universe acquires its identity through human actions and understandings of those actions. Human beings are creatures who characterize the universe in which they live, and for this reason Sartre defines "Man" as the being toward whom no other being can be impartial (18).

The problem for the writer is that the world is not properly named and stands in need of demystification. The Sartrean writer must pursue the mandate of Socratic refutation and make a community aware of the values and commitments that it has inherited and by which it lives. Sartre seeks to recover the world in its historicity as a place for human value and action. Such a world is inherently indeterminate, and at best it admits of temporary closures for particular situations. Sartre's existentialism is thus a recovery of rhetoric's basic concern of constituting a community that can act in the absence of certain knowledge. But Sartre differs from the rhetorical tradition in not having a collection of topoi from which to discover an appropriate form of action. Put another way, his rhetoric is one that eschews tradition as a resource for invention. Indeed, Sartre's understanding of the writer as a person who feels his or her lack of connection to the world becomes a central assumption from which he will construct his new rhetoric.

For Sartre, the writer's fundamental motivation derives from the human predicament of residing in a universe in which one feels inessentially linked to being. Sartre sees human reality as the great revealer of being: human beings are the source of the rich relations that exist between the different parts of being. But it is equally true that if humans reveal the dense reality of being, they are also inessential to its maintenance. If a human being ceases to be, the rest of the universe still goes on. To avoid the feeling of being inessential to the world that they have revealed, people become creators of imaginative worlds. That is, they assume the role of the producers of being. The motive common for all human creation, and consequently for all writing, is to connect oneself essentially to being by being its source. It is in and by human creation that one establishes an authenticity that parallels the Augustinian rhetor's enjoyment of the Divine. Hence the initial impulse in a Sartrean rhetoric is not political, as with Socrates, but private, as with Augustine. What has shifted is the locus of salvation. The future theological destination has given over to the material and political possibilities embodied in any present historical situation. Human aspiration is no longer toward a spiritual future outside this world but to the future spiritualization of this world.

Like Augustine's rhetor, Sartre's writer begins as an isolated self, but the isolation of the Sartrean self is considerably more profound. For Augustine, the means to salvation are available, for the world is a system of signs that selves can use to move toward God. Augustine believes that the signs are true markers of the path to God, but that, as humans, we can never know with certainty whether we have read them correctly. Still, underlying the temporal world of appearance is a genuine reality. But Sartre's rhetor can have no such reassurance. And it is precisely this lack of reassurance that makes writing into an act of faith. For him writing is an action that is always at risk and in which there is no fixed point. All the writer can do is offer his or her work and hope that it will be read in the appropriate way. But this apparently severe limitation is in fact the central rhetorical opportunity because the writer's need for a reader to achieve his or her own authenticity transforms a potentially solipsistic enterprise into an essentially communal endeavor. If the original impulse to write is not political, the hope of a purposive acting on this impulse gives the discursive act a necessarily political dimension.

The nature of writing creates the writer's need for a reader. In the act of creating an object through language, the writer is essential to the object, for the writer is now the source of the object's production. But if the writer is essential to the object, the object itself is not yet essential. The writer can always change it, for there is no fixed point that compels the revision process to end. By itself the act of writing cannot permit a writer to escape from subjectivity. As Sartre claims, a writer "can not reveal and produce at the same time" (33). A writer cannot read his or her own writing because the option to revise that text is always available to the writer. The reading that a writer does of his or her own work is different in kind from the reading of someone removed from the creation of the work, for this other reader cannot change the writing but must rather reveal what is there. For that reason the writing is objective only for the reader.

The literary object, then, does not fully become an object until it is read, as it exists only in the dialectical play between reader and writer: "The literary object is a peculiar top which exists only in movement. To make it come into view a concrete act called reading is necessary, and it lasts only as long as this act can last. Beyond that, there are only black marks on paper" (34–35). The literary object creates the possibility for a community of selves who have jointly used their subjectivity to render themselves essential to each other and to this world: "The operation of writing implies that of reading as its dialectical correlative and these two connected acts necessitate two distinct agents. It is the conjoint effort of author and reader which brings upon the scene that concrete and imaginary object which is the work of the mind. There is no art except by and for others" (37). Thus the requirements of a genuine writing transform what is originally a merely personal motive into one that is also essentially social. The truth that the Sartrean writer knows is that for his or her self to be, there must be another self that acknowledges the writer's relation to the universe that has been revealed through the writing.

But the writer cannot act in such a way as to compel this kind of reading. As Aristotle noted, all that the rhetor can do is to discover the best available means of persuasion in a given situation (*On Rhetoric*, 1355b). One cannot force a judgment, for the essence of a communal sharing is a free and unforced participation in a mutual understanding. While it is certainly possible to have people come together under other circumstances, they cannot achieve community under these circumstances. Socrates tries in the *Gorgias* to explain this fact to Callicles (508a–b). Callicles' universe of natural justice is a universe that is logically devoid of communities because it precludes a stable and enduring cooperation between people. At best, it admits temporary and insecure liaisons for purposes of mutual benefit, but an unconstrained actor moved only by appetite would undermine even these arrangements. The logical endpoint for Callicles' universe is the profound isolation of an individual self that is incapable of action but is moved solely by the appetite that is uppermost at a particular time.

The writer who seeks genuinely to be a writer acts, then, under certain ethical constraints that establish the possibility for appropriately meeting his or her reader. The writer must appeal to the reader's freedom: "As the sufficient reason for the appearance of the aesthetic object is never found either in the book (where we find merely solicitations to produce the object) or in the author's mind, as his subjectivity, which he cannot get away from, cannot give a reason for the act of leading into objectivity, the appearance of the work of art is a new event which cannot *be explained* by anterior data. And since this directed creation is an absolute beginning, it is therefore brought about by the freedom of the reader, and by what is purest in that freedom. Thus, the writer appeals to the reader's freedom to collaborate in the production of his work" (40). The work itself, as a testament to the writer's belief in the reader's good faith, becomes a means of ethical proof that the rhetor uses to move the reader to join in the production of the literary object. The act of faith in writing creates a character for the reader to assume. The writer is saying, in effect, I trust you, the reader, with the most essential aspect of my being, and I base this trust solely on my faith in your humanity.

Underlying this act of faith is generosity, the fundamental virtue of Sartre's rhetoric. The writer is moved to write because of generosity, and without this generosity, the very act of writing would be absurd. In Sartre's claim for generosity as the central virtue of the writer, the instability of his program is ensured: generosity is demanded because reason cannot supply a reason that would compel a writer to act. It is not that a writer is moved by an irrational impulse to write but that reason is beside the point. The ethical commitment of a Sartrean writer is not founded in the personal erotic relationships that Plato dramatized in the *Phaedrus* or in the divinely inspired charity of Augustine, but is rather a defiant personal gesture in favor of a humanity that does not yet exist.[6] The writer is moved to write, in part, to proclaim against a situation that makes all subjects inessential and that exploits the alienation of the subjects to maintain a system of oppression. The writer defies the order that is and names the order that should be. At the heart of the generosity, Sartre believes, is an act of will that is identical to Kant's categorical imperative. The writer in his or her freedom "takes the literary work, and, through it, mankind, for an absolute end. [The writer's freedom] sets itself up as an unconditioned exigence in relationship to itself, to the author, and to possible readers" (265). Generosity as a motive is the desire to call into being the city of ends. Such a desire springs solely from the private conscience of the individual writer and claims no other ground for its authenticity than the recognition that human beings are free and therefore must be treated as ends in themselves. Sartre's generosity thus stands in direct opposition to Austen's, which assumed social embeddedness and sought to refute the ideal of an autonomous will.

The act of writing acknowledges the reader's humanity and, equally, demands that the reader acknowledge the writer's own humanity. Sartre's rhetorical community originates in this mutually implicating set of demands: "The author writes in order to address himself to the freedom of readers, and he requires it in order to make this work exist. But he does not stop there; he also requires that they return this confidence which he has given them, that they recognize his creative freedom, and that they in turn solicit it by a symmetrical and inverse appeal. Here there appears the other dialectical paradox of reading: the more we experience our freedom, the more we recognize that of the other, the more he demands of us, the more we demand of him" (45). The origin of the generous community, in contrast to the erotic or charitable community, can be traced to the act of writing itself. Writing, with its freedom rooted in the critical and productive powers of the mind, is the new source of human spirituality (97).

In appealing to generosity as a motive sufficient to move a modernist subject from isolation to community or, at least, to the offer of a community, Sartre collapses the problem of a transpersonal preclusion of discourse into the problem of an adequate motive for action. In his turn to good will, he has moved from his skeptical insight into injustice as an abiding problem for rhetoric and turned to the traditional domesticated version of the problem of rhetoric as one of controlling the rhetor's potentially deviant motivation. Rhetoric as a problem of action in an unjust world gives over to hermeneutics as the problem of establishing the conditions for successful communication. Sartre's misstep is paradigmatic of a modernism that admirably seeks to recover political agency but that conceives of such a recovery as requiring a determinate subject. But as Judith Butler has shown, the concern with political action need not require such a centered subject: "We may be tempted to think that to assume the subject in advance is necessary in order to safeguard the *agency* of the subject. But to claim that the subject is constituted is not to claim that it is determined; on the contrary, the constituted character of the subject is the very precondition of its agency. For what is it that enables a purposive and significant reconfiguration of cultural and political relations, if not a relation that can be turned against itself, reworked, resisted?" ("Contingent Foundations," 12–13). And Derrida has raised questions as to whether a voluntaristic and self-present subject is even possible. His exchange with Gadamer becomes emblematic for the modernist/postmodernist encounter, and Gadamer's incomprehension of the thrust of Derrida's attacks and his repeated attempts to answer such attacks by appealing to the necessary good will of the hermeneutical subject display the same equivocation that traps Sartre.[7]

It is with his concern for establishing constraints on the participants in a rhetorical exchange that Sartre's solution begins to show some of the difficulties that follow from the notion of the subject that modernism had inherited. The Enlightenment commitment to a foundation in a reason that can be universalized leads Sartre to stint the reader's active participation as a historically situated individual in the literary work. In his equivocation of the role of the reader Sartre abandons the rhetorical opening that his appreciation of the writer had created. Instead, he opts for a modernist hermeneutical authority of a universalizable reason and thus loses community as a philosophic problem. As Theodor Adorno claimed, Sartre's commitment to idealism eliminated history as a serious determinant of agency: "Despite his extreme nominalism, Sartre's philosophy in its most effective phase was organized according to the old idealistic category of the free act of the subject. To Existentialism as to Fichte, any objectivity is a matter of indifference. Consequently, social conditions came in Sartre's plays to be topical adjuncts, at best; structurally, they do hardly more than provide an occasion for the action" (*Negative Dialectics*, 49–50). Finally Sartrean writers transcend local communities and an act on behalf of an ideal of social organization that is grounded on the translocality of universal reason.

To understand Sartre's equivocation, it is necessary to explore his turn to hermeneutics and to reexamine his account of reading as creation or re-creation and to establish the particular responsibility that devolves upon an engaged reader. His own account of human spirituality as a productive and critical freedom is finally too abstract even for Sartre. His account raises two problems: one Sartre addresses, and the other he only vaguely and incompletely comes to terms with. Sartre recognizes that his initial account of the writer's appeal to the freedom of the reader proceeds as if the reader were a universal and ahistorical being. Such a conception of the reader, however, runs contrary to Sartre's major claim that human beings are creatures who exist only in particular historical situations. To reconcile his two claims, Sartre explains that freedom is a process of negativity through which one continually overcomes particular obstacles. This turn to negation looks as if Sartre is about to recover the role of refutation. The nature of the obstacle is what allows one's freedom to become functional; it is against particular historical oppressions or mystifications that one defines freedom.

Sartre goes on to say that the reader is "suspended between total ignorance and all-knowingness, he has a definite stock of knowledge which varies from moment to moment and which is enough to reveal his *historicity*. In actual fact, he is not an instantaneous consciousness, a pure timeless affirmation of freedom, nor does he soar above history; he is involved in it" (63). For the reader to become the writer's public, the writer must address the issues that confront the reader in his or her historical particularity. Writing is meaningful only if it defines a situation in which human action is significant. Writing is not a matter of getting abstract and essential truths right but of locating ways in which the contemporary world prevents humanity from fully becoming itself. To write is "to disclose the world and to offer it as a task to the generosity of the reader" (54). This is to understand writing as analogous to Socratic refutation. At those points when Sartre conceives of the reader historically, he grasps the problem of injustice as it is conceived by the skeptical thread of the classical tradition. Writing is a mode of saying no. At these times, Sartrean generosity comes very close to Socratic courage, as a virtue that recognizes injustice even while it refuses to countenance such injustice and that sustains action in the absence of a reason that would ensure or argue for probable success of such action.

Sartre, however, is not completely clear on what would constitute a generous response by a reader, and his ambiguity creates problems for his understanding of what the reader does, of what generosity entails, and of the dialectical nature of the rhetorical community. He finally ends by simplifying the reader's activity, and this simplification endangers the possibility of community. At this point, Sartre trips over his unresolved relationship to the Enlightenment. And his recovery of a potentially radical rhetoric begins to look uncomfortably like a Habermasean turn to a countertradition within the Enlightenment, as rhetoric and hermeneutics turn out not to be truly reciprocal activities for Sartre but to appeal respectively to a historical and to a universal and ahistorical reason.

Sartre conceives of reading as a synthesis of perception and creation in which a reader discloses a world through the creation or re-creation of an object (37). In such a process both the object and subject are essential. Sartre claims that the object is transcendental in that it creates the structures from which the subject must disclose the object, and the subject is essential because the object can exist only if it is disclosed. Initially, it appears that Sartre is giving the reader an equal if different role in the creation of the object: "If he [the reader] is at his best, he will project beyond the words a synthetic form. . . . From the very beginning, the meaning is no longer contained in the words, since it is the reader who allows the significance of each of them to be understood; the literary object, though realized through language, is never given in language" (37–38). The reader must invent the text that he or she is reading. The text is encountered as a silence, and it acquires a voice only as the reader lends it his or her person in its totality. Clearly, Sartre believes that each reading is the creation of a new object and not merely the repeated instantiation of a fixed essence. But he also wants to call the reading process "directed creation" in which the reader brings the text into existence by acts of induction, interpolation, and extrapolation. This account of the reader suggests that the meaning of the writing exists in potential and is actualized by the reading process. But such an understanding of the reading process raises the questions: In what sense is the reading an open and free action? Is there finally a transcendental, if indeterminate, structure that authorizes the various readings? Is the reader really a free and equal participant in the dialectical act that constitutes the literary object if the reader's task is to follow directions? And how can the dialectical play of increasing demands of reader on text and text on reader take place if the reader is bound by a transcendental structure that the writer has created?

Sartre shows a partial awareness of these questions when he addresses the tension between the transcendental and historical demands of the work: "Reading should not be mystical communion any more than it should be masturbation, but rather a companionship. On the other hand we recognize that the purely formal recourse to abstract good wills leaves each one in his original situation. However, that is the point from which we must start; if one loses this conducting wire, he is suddenly lost in the wilds of propaganda or in the egotistical pleasures of a style which is a matter of 'purely personal taste.' It is therefore up to us to convert the city of ends into a concrete and open society—and this by the very content of our works" (268). The task of contemporary literature is to unite the metaphysical absolute with historical relativity. That is, literature must invent humanity in such a way that humanity is the ground of its value. Such invention cannot be abstract but instead must deal with the historical exigencies as the writer encounters them.

Only a reader who is aware of both ethics and history can be the writer's public. Such a reader would bring a particularity with him or her. Further, to read so as to begin the dialectic that constitutes the literary object and the rhetorical community, the reader must also be situated. But if a reader brings this particularity to a work of literature, he or she transcends that particularity in a true Sartrean reading: "Let us bear in mind that the man who reads strips himself in some way of his empirical personality and escapes from his resentments, his fears, and his lusts in order to put himself at the peak of his freedom. This freedom takes the literary work and, through it, mankind for absolute ends" (264–65). To be able to read with the appropriate attention to the text, the reader must empty out his or her historical content. At this point, Sartre characterizes the ideal public as a mere formal receptivity whose questions are aimed at making present an authorial intention (68). Passion, not as an erotic push but as the willingness to receive grace, now marks the reader's stance in a hermeneutical situation in which he or she suffers, in the Christian sense, the text. The text is a power to be submitted to. Sartre's stress, despite the earlier concern with invention, is on reception. In this stress, he misses the dialogic tension and its potential for emancipation that Bakhtin analyzed:

Both the authority of discourse and its internal persuasiveness may be united in a single word — one that is *simultaneously* authoritative and internally persuasive — despite the profound differences between the two categories of alien discourse. But it happens more frequently that an individual's becoming, and ideological process, is characterized precisely by a sharp gap between these two categories: in one, the authoritative word (religious, political, moral; the word of a father, of adults and teachers, etc.) that does not know internal persuasiveness, in the other the internally persuasive word that is denied all privilege, backed up by no authority at all, and is frequently not even acknowledged in society (not by public opinion, not by scholarly norms, not by criticism), not even in the legal code. The struggle and dialogic interrelationship of these categories of ideological discourse are what usually determine the history of an individual ideological consciousness. ("Discourse in the Novel," 342)

Don H. Bialostosky's account of Bakhtin's dialogism argues that there is "no systematic or historical limit to the voices that may find a place in a dialogue" ("Dialogics as an Art," 790). Hence there is always the possibility for novel and unanticipated openings in a reading that allow a repressed or marginalized position to be voiced. On this understanding of reading, one can escape the problems of the writer as a Sartrean universal intellectual, for the writer ceases to be an exclusive and determinative voice who speaks for those he or she would represent (Poster, *Critical Theory,* 44–45). For Bakhtin, the active clashing of the reader's language permits creativity and ultimately the discovery of an individual identity:

When someone else's ideological discourse is internally persuasive for us and acknowledged by us, entirely different possibilities open up. Such discourse is of decisive significance in the evolution of an individual consciousness: consciousness awakens to independent ideological life precisely in a world of alien discourses surrounding it, and from which it cannot initially separate itself; the process of distinguishing between one's own and another's discourse, between one's own and another's thought, is activated rather late in development. When thought begins to work in an independent, experimenting and discriminating way, what first occurs is a separation between persuasive discourse and authoritarian enforced discourse, along with a rejection of those congeries of discourses that do not matter to us, that do not touch us. ("Discourse in the Novel," 345)

Sartre loses this possibility when he first takes reading outside of its particular historical context. He has, in effect, capitulated to monologism. For him, reading becomes a two-step process: initially there is the transcendental understanding of the absolute; then there is the application of this understanding to history. Sartre has to emphasize the importance of the second step because it is logically possible in his account of reading for the reader to stop after the first step and to remain at the level of abstraction. There is nothing in the act of reading, as Sartre has conceived it, that compels the return to history. Indeed, Sartre writes as if he has to remind the reader to return to history because the act of reading has taken the reader outside of history:

> But in order for this ideal chorus [of readers] to become a concrete society, it must satisfy two conditions: first, that readers replace this theoretical acquaintance with each other, insofar as they are all particular examples of mankind, by an intuition, or, at the very least, by a presentiment of their physical presence in the midst of this world; second, that, instead of remaining solitary and uttering appeals in the void, which, in regard to the human condition in general, affect no one, these abstract good wills establish real relations among themselves when actual events take place, or, in other terms, that these non-temporal good wills *historicize* themselves while preserving their purity, and that they transform their exigencies into material and timely demands. (265)

The second set of obligations, however, can be meaningful only if the act of reading has failed to allow the reader and consequently the writer to escape from his or her subjectivity. In effect, Sartre is acknowledging that the dialectical act of literature, as he has conceived it, does not in itself allow the individual participants to escape from their subjectivity. At most they transcend their individual empirical selves for a full — and finally empty — transcendental subjectivity of mere formality. Adorno sees Sartre as trapped by a notion of the subject from which he could not escape: "The absolute subject cannot get out of its entanglements: the bonds it would have to tear, the bonds of dominion, are as one with the principle of absolute subjectivity. It honors Sartre that this shows up in his plays, against his philosophical chef d'oeuvre. The plays disavow the philosophy with whose theses they deal" (*Negative Dialectics*, 50). This transcendental subjectivity transforms generosity from a practical virtue into a formal precondition. Literature has reenforced rather than challenged the human misstep into abstraction.

In his appeal to a universal reason as the guarantee of a good will, Sartre has stumbled onto the path that Habermas would so diligently explore.[8] For all his concern with history, Sartre is led finally to postulate a reader that looks like one member in a Habermasean discursive community. Such a member is defined precisely by a lack of historical content and political situatedness.[9] Responsibility is not an issue bequeathed to discursive participants from history but a formal condition that is embodied in the apositional (because universalizable) stance of the participants. Despite its purported interest in community and politics, Sartre's is an apolitical discourse of reason that just happens to be mediated through participants to the conversation. Again the potentially troubling insight of skepticism into an injustice that abides is domesticated by a reform that seeks to redress any discursive difficulties by a set of constraints on the individual participants.

Sartre encounters his particular difficulties because he has drifted away from the rhetorical paradigm that he used initially to characterize the act of writing and turned to a Kantian understanding of aesthetic judgment. Sartre's feeling that he needed an absolute to ground value in history created the need for something like a Kantian ethics, which had then to be modified so that it would be tied to history.

It is easy to have sympathy for Sartre's wanting to escape the trap of ethical relativism that sees value as a product solely of history. Such an understanding of value seems to create a skeptical opening in which one can no longer distinguish genuine from illegitimate claims to value. But a Kantian ethics need not be the only response to this problem. The rhetorical tradition has long held that the universe prior to the action of the rhetor exists as a situation of contending values in which there are no absolute standards from which to discriminate between the competing claims. Indeed, the problems that the rhetor will ask a potential community to deliberate upon do not exist as problems until the rhetor so establishes them. Cicero emphasizes this understanding when he stresses the importance of taking control of the issue as the key rhetorical move (*De Inventione,* 21). The problems that rhetoric poses for deliberation are capable of plural formulation, and different rhetors will frame different problems because they wish to constitute or reconstitute different communities. Certainly, the rhetors will be limited, in part, by potential communities' current beliefs and particular passions, but these beliefs and passions cannot be restricted to one correct determination.

The plurality of the initial conceptions of the problem is compounded by the plurality of solutions. In the rhetorical deliberation the community's future is created through an act of invention rather than recovered through a historical reconstitution and subsequent interpolation. Rhetoric begins from a recognition of indeterminacy and asks, in a plurality of ways, how an individual and a community can locate a reasonably grounded value. At issue is the character and quality of communal meeting. If this meeting can be conducted in such a way that it is part of an ongoing process in which the community reflects upon its commitments as they are embodied in its discourse, then it is possible to offer a serious alternative to the historical relativity of value without having recourse to a moral absolute. The rhetors would reaffirm the underlying plurality of problems even as they moved the community to a determinate and temporary closure of a situation. The community would constitute itself through the process of rhetorically reinventing itself and thus acquiring a history. The community's life would be grounded in deliberation and would embody the plurality of a continual becoming.

Equally available to Sartre was the skeptical rejoinder to this account of rhetoric in which refutation and not persuasion was the featured activity. In the Sartrean writer's initial need to name the world and thus to hand it over to the reader as a task is the theoretical insight that could have led to an understanding of the need for refutation. Such an understanding is so much more consonant with generosity as a rhetorical virtue, because this generosity would mark the position of the writer as someone offering a gift to the polis that could not be commodified or seen as instrumental or useful to some particular end. Generosity, like Socratic courage, would then suggest an order of political discourse that was intended not to be pragmatic but rather to be philosophical. While such discourse would be inescapably positioned in history, it would not seek a positive outcome but would induce communal reflection on injustice and lead to communal assumption of responsibility for it.

The best example of such a communal inquiry is the dialectical writing of Plato. If the erotic-philosophic relationship that Plato dramatized in the *Phaedrus* seems to close off community, the way in which Plato develops the materials of his dialogue creates an opening for community. Form refutes content. Plato's stance as a writer is itself an invitation to a reader to open himself or herself to the words of another. His rhetoric is an inherently ethical way of encountering other selves. In the *Phaedrus* Socrates worries that when one's words are written, one gives up control over who will have access to them. One, in effect, opens oneself up to misunderstanding. Socrates has located a serious problem, for the rhetor who uses written discourse gives up the possibility of clarifying or expanding the discourse in a direct response to a question, and, as any writer knows, his or her words can and will be read variously. But Plato is willing to undertake this risk, and he is willing to do so because of the opportunity for community opened up by written discourse.

Plato's offer of himself as a writer opens up the philosophical inquiries for his readers. The dialogue form becomes a rhetorical resource in which Plato creates situations that invite reflection. If the *Phaedrus* can be read as a Platonic recantation on eros, the dialogue itself creates the opportunity for a communal recantation and refutation of Socrates' position on writing by forcing the reader to deal with the apparent contradiction of a written discourse dismissing written discourse as a serious activity. In this way, the dialogue opens up writing as a problem for reflection, and the writing itself is an enactment of a philosophical rhetoric.

As pieces of writing, the Platonic dialogues move beyond a Socratic discourse grounded in the private relationship between lover and beloved. Plato constructs his dialogues not as an extended enunciation of a system but as a series of occasions that begin usually in simple encounters and whose solutions, when and if they are reached, are tied to their development within the situation. Plato emphasizes the need for generosity by making his dialogues into problems that open to the reader rather than by presenting his philosophical dramas as successful models to be imitated. He offers the linguistic agon that Bakhtin sees as essential to dialogic understanding. Plato's mode of writing provokes the reader to respond by putting his or her language into play. Indeed, if he had chosen to render his dialogues as successful resolutions of the problems, he would have undermined his fundamental premise that one is moved to assume political responsibility for injustice through refutation, because he would have demonstrated what the properly constituted self should look like. He would thus have fixed permanently what he must leave open to future refutation. For Plato, the community does not exist prior to the dialogue but rather either constitutes itself or fails to constitute itself in the discourse that comprises the dialogue. The reader does not simply witness an enacted drama but participates actively in it (White, *When Words*, 108–9).

In the *Gorgias* Plato shows how a dialectically constituted rhetoric could induce its participants into entering a community, grounded in a shared discourse and committed to a particular understanding and valuing of the human universe that both accomplishes temporary closure and creates an opening for further discovery and reconstitution of themselves as a community. Socrates begins the dialogue with a simple question that he has his stand-in, Chaerephon, ask Gorgias. Socrates wants Gorgias to declare who he is by saying what he does. As the dialogue proceeds, it becomes clear that Gorgias is not able to answer Chaerephon's question to Socrates' satisfaction, for Gorgias has not seriously explored the nature of his art or understood its relation as an art to the interests of the larger community. In a sense Gorgias does not know who he is, nor do his students, Polus and Callicles, know who they are. Their failure is in part a failure of generosity, which manifests itself, especially for Polus and Callicles, in an unwillingness to trust the dialectic that is structuring the dialogue. Although it is unclear exactly how Gorgias would have acted if his students had not intervened in the dialogue, it is clear that neither Polus nor Callicles is seriously willing to risk his understanding of what constitutes rhetoric. They enter the dialogue with fixed positions that see rhetoric only in terms of personal effectiveness, and they try to defend this understanding at all costs rather than engage seriously and openly with a historical understanding that represents the current point of the community's dialectic progress. In this rigid determination, the consequence in part of a desperate self-love that fears a full investigation of its beliefs because it may not be who it wants to be, Polus and Callicles contrast with Socrates, who is continually willing to be refuted (White, *When Words,* 102). Their fear destroys the courage — the shameless-ness — that is necessary for a generous giving of the self to the dialectic. Socrates demonstrates his generosity by his willingness to treat his understanding as something that must always be open to challenge. He can be only to the extent that he is generous. He does not conceive of his positions as personal property but as places or points of community to which he has been led by past dialectics. It is fitting that Socrates closes the dialogue not by an assertion that his conclusions are true but that they represent the community's best effort at making sense of its situation (White, *When Words,* 103).

The conclusion of a Platonic dialectic, even if it is not grounded in a tran-scendental absolute, makes a serious claim on the members of the community: they cannot, without contradicting themselves, act contrary to that conclu-sion. If they do act in disregard of the conclusion, they destroy the possibility for that community and render themselves incoherent — which, of course, they may in fact do, for people often live in contradiction.[10] But if the dialectic has been genuine, then the conclusions that are reached by the community of speakers are based on the values of the individual speakers as they have been communally played by the dialectic. The community's dialectically reached understandings thus have the same force as the absolute transcendental grounds that Sartre was seeking. Both make legitimate demands on an individ-ual that can be ignored only at the cost of self-contradiction. So when someone who has participated in the dialectic disregards these conclusions, it is not simply a case of voluntarily refusing to enter a community that he or she finds unsatisfactory for some reason; rather, it is a case of refusing to pursue the implications of his or her values, and that is not the exercise of an option but the commission of an error.

Sartre seeks to address this kind of closedness by arguing that, if the reader is to be truly open to the writing, then he or she must assume initially a role of generous receptivity for the dialectic of writing and reading to take place: "The belief which I accord the tale is freely assented to. It is a Passion, in the Christian sense of the word, that is, a freedom which resolutely puts itself into a state of passivity to obtain a certain transcendent effect by this sacrifice" (44). Sartre's way out of the problem of disruptive personal interests is to require the reader to assume a position that is marked by the empty formality of an absolutely good will. But, as we saw earlier, this solves the problem of obstructing interests only to create the problem of abstract understanding. In the *Phaedrus* Plato offers a different, and more promising, solution to the problem of private interest. Socrates and Phaedrus make progress toward a genuine exchange because they share a common love and possess a mutual trust. Their particular interests (they are both lovers of discourse) bring them together and provide a serious starting point for their exploration of discourse and love. Unlike Polus and Callicles, Phaedrus is willing, almost eager, to be refuted, for he is not in love with a particular and fixed position on love but is a devotee of beautiful discourse, and this provides an opening for dialectic. Socrates fails to achieve a community in the *Gorgias* because no one is willing to pursue the dialectic to its conclusion. His three opponents all have a vested interest in the outcome being a certain way that they are unwilling to give up. Phaedrus, on the other hand, compels Socrates to remain and to complete his speech. Phaedrus is concerned enough about love that he does not wish for either Socrates or himself to leave before they have fully explored love as a problem. The two participants in the dialogue are willing to explore their current understanding because they possess a faith in each other that together they can constitute a discursive community that will show them what their words mean.

But the dialogue itself points to the difficulty and uncertainty of an erotically based community because such a community is so rooted in the physical attraction of soul mates. If the *Phaedrus* opens the possibility for a community that would be grounded in discourse, it finally does not show the achievement of that community. Indeed, Phaedrus is almost too open to suggestion. His openness seems a kind of indiscreetness: first Lysias convinced him, then Socrates' first speech convinced him, and then Socrates' second speech convinced him. His apparent openness to refutation is perilously close to an unreflective passivity. And such passivity itself prevents serious refutation because it does not permit an active enough contest for there to be a real risk.

The failures of the rhetors in the *Gorgias* and the *Phaedrus* to be equal to the task of engaging in a communal dialectic suggest the character that is necessary to participate in a refutation. Such a character is itself not fixed but rather exists in a dynamic tension between passion and action. The generosity of such a character manifests itself in the character's gift to the dialectic of his or her person in its totality. This giving is, on the one hand, a serious willingness to listen to the words of another and, on the other hand, an equally serious willingness to contest those words. And although this contest must be rigorous, the character's interest is not in a personal victory but in advancing the discourse and hence the community. The combination of being open yet willing to contest the words of another creates a character who is capable of using discourse to search for his or her true interests. And, as the two dialogues show, the rhetor's particular interests, be they power, eros, or whatever, are inevitably entangled and implicated in a stance toward discourse itself. What is required for such refutation is that the parties involved have commitments that they are willing to put into play. The characters most likely to undertake such risks are those who are passionate about discourse. The dialectic that Plato, through the demands of his writing, enables us to see is one in which we initially meet another because our language reveals our personal interests and commitments, which then become the basis for our attempt to form a community by the refutation and public reconstitution of those interests and commitments in a mutually sustained discourse.

In contrast to Sartre's characterization of the generous reader as an individual who both gives himself or herself to the literary work in his or her totality and at the same time abstracts from any personal or historical content to the level of a transcendental subjectivity, it is now possible to reconceive this reader as a properly interested reader. A generous but interested reader would approach a literary work in the spirit of a rhetorically open participant in a Platonic dialogue. The generosity of the reader would be manifested in a trust in the text that would show itself by a willingness on the reader's part both to refute and to submit to refutation. The question that any genuine literary work or reader would ask the Other is: "Who are you?" The answer to this question would then initiate the dialectical process that Sartre considers to be the mode of existence of a literary work: "There is then established a dialectical going-and-coming; when I read, I make demands; if my demands are met, what I am then reading provokes me to demand more of the author, which means to demand of the author that he demand more of me. And, vice versa, the author's demand is that I carry my demands to the highest pitch. Thus, my freedom, by revealing itself, reveals the freedom of the other" (50). What the act of literature demands in demanding generosity is that the reader be willing to allow his or her commitments to be questioned by the text and equally to contest with the text for the communal understanding. The dialectical play, which is the literary object, becomes the communal exploration of the commitments of the members of the community. Since these commitments are the product of a life lived in history, they are not fixed, and this is what allows each reading to be a new event. There is not a set answer for the generous reader to the question, "Who are you?" Indeed, the answer to this question will come only in the temporary closure achieved at the end of the dialectic, and such an answer will inherently be both individual and communal. It will also be historical, so there will be no need for the kind of ethical reattachment of the self to history that Sartre worried about because there has been no gap opened up through a transcendental abstraction. The act of literature would then be less an induction, interpolation, and extrapolation — a kind of figuring out what is there — and it would, instead, be analogous to a philosophical conversation.[11]

Literary being would exist as the rhythms of a dialectic between the reader and the text. And, as some deconstructionists have argued, reading would finally be an act of writing.

To acknowledge that freedom is the issue and the criterion by which engaged conversations are distinguished does not mean that such conversations are easily or securely recognized. In fact, a certainty about one's discourse prevents the necessary openness to potential refutation. Rather, one enters these conversations to see whether they will develop into a meaningful discourse on freedom, and there can be no advance knowledge or guarantee that they will. This is what makes generosity so important. For the generous participants act out of a faith in openness that becomes an invitation for the Other to be open. Each participant must bring his or her interests and commitments in the hope of either finding a mutuality of interests and commitments, which can then be communally investigated, or discovering that what appears to be one's interests and commitments, are, in fact, not one's genuine values. Such a conversation requires above all else generosity. This generosity is evidenced in the willingness to be open to the conversation and in the commitment to rigorously follow the conversation wherever it goes. This commitment goes back to the Sartrean concern with literature as a mode of disclosure. The generous reading is the recovery of the universe as if it had its origin not in necessity but in freedom.

But such an encomiastic account of generosity itself needs to be refuted. For the very language of generosity has a tendency to reinstaniate the problem of justice as the problem of the authenticity of the individual. Sophocles' *Philoctetes* is always there to remind us that however admirable a generous intention within a discursive exchange is, such an intention does not settle the possibility of there being a just discourse. If generosity is required for refutation, an endemic political injustice cannot be redressed through the personal generosity of either the writer or the reader. Generosity needs to be understood not as a personal disposition but as a recognition for the continual need for reopenings in the activity of writing. Generosity is the giving up of personal control while diligently assuming political responsibility.

The writer's and reader's identities are never essentially fixed but rather emerge anew with each reading. Generous reading is a continual exploration of the possible relationships and commitments inhering in a discourse. This kind of reading makes impossible the modes of literary history that Sartre so loathes. There is no longer a universe of courtesy in which two beings who know themselves and know each other meet in a reading with a nod that conveys that all is set and all is understood (85). This notion of generous reading as a philosophic conversation would allow Sartre's project to open up history in a way that Sartre had not conceived. History would cease to be a determined record and instead become a dialectic between readers and texts. Paul de Man argues that such reading is in fact what literary history should be (*Blindness and Insight,* 165).

Such an understanding of the historical nature of literature suggests that the crisis of the public cannot be solved through a transcendental appeal but must somehow be dealt with in terms of the particular historical conditions that have created the current crisis. The central condition prompting the crisis is the abstraction of a piece of writing from the particular conditions that called it forth. Thus Sartre complains that the BBC radio production of his banned play made it available to a larger audience but that this audience was one that could not attend properly to the work, so that the work could not seriously speak to them (238). This is to claim that literature has become a possession of the world at large and that is the same thing as saying that it has ceased to belong to any particular community. That is the contemporary crisis of the public. Only in a particular community in which the writing addresses pressing problems will an engaged public be capable of responding to literature in an appropriate way. Detached from these communities, an international literature cannot function as a negativity that leads to a genuine freedom.

To meet this crisis Sartre suggests that writers avail themselves of the greater avenues of access to public consciousness that technology has opened up. But he knows that simply disseminating one's work on a larger scale will not seriously address a problem that originates from a different sense of the work's unavailability. The deeper problem is how to make readers into a public that truly understands its own interests and needs, especially since this community can no longer assume a preexisting set of local concerns that could become topoi for the invention of appropriate communal actions. The only answer is, finally, to require the writer to act from a faith in his or her potential readers in the hope that such a faith will provoke an equal and corresponding act of faith from the reader. Such a faith, for both writer and reader, arises from their feeling of being currently inessential and their need to challenge such a feeling.

Sartre's utopian vision of literature suggests two distinct tasks for writing that correspond to refutation and persuasion. First, there is the negative task of demystifying language. The writer must show the reader in what ways language is a product of historical oppression. In this task, the writer parallels the Socratic dialectician's negative phase in which he or she revealed the commitments inhering in the community's unreflective possession of or by language. The second task is constructive. The writer must present the world as a place in which the reader has power to act. If the writer can free readers from a false consciousness and enable them to see themselves as people capable of effecting their own destiny, then the writer will have a public who can make demands on him or her that can lead to a genuine self and community.

Both of the writer's tasks to create a public rest upon the writer's ability to invent an issue that gives the reader a suitable choice. This task would be relatively straightforward if writing were still localized in particular communities whose traditions, history, and resources would create the exigencies from which to discover appropriate issues and courses of action. To some degree such communities still exist, and the history of recent protests show that communities can be mobilized through the power of discourse. The civil rights movement, the antiwar movement, and the feminist movement testify that discourse can play a crucial role in forming a community and changing a world. But Sartre's utopian vision of writing pushes him to worry about a nonlocalized community that can become congruous with all humanity. The task of persuasion leads again to the demand to abandon rhetoric for the philosophical authority that the Enlightenment invested in a universal reason. The new global community that a universal persuasion would engender is embodied in Sartre's ideal socialist society. And the question that he must face is: how to create a public that would make this community a possibility?

But this may not be the right way to ask this question, for it would involve the rhetor in a search for an absolute that is outside history. Rather than conceiving of a socialist universe as a goal to be pursued, it might be more productive to treat it as a standard against which to measure any particular community's relationships among its own members and between that community and other communities. This returns it to a role in refutation. Such an understanding of the question is more in keeping with rhetoric's skeptical thread, which understands the universe as a place of praxis. Rhetoric's concern with particularity and indeterminacy is a commitment to a universe of unremitting plurality that is rooted in the localness of community. People are not bound together abstractly to form a community but rather reside in communities because they hold interests in common. The notion of a universal community that encompasses and structures all local communities into a just hierarchical arrangement can then be a negative ideal that allows any given community to assess the justice of its dealing with its members or with other communities. The nature of the historical world would resist being fixed into a universe structured by a community of communities, for such a universe would finally make rhetoric and history superfluous. Part of the function of rhetoric is to continually challenge and undermine the various attempts of communities to claim this architectonic global capacity. In other words, persuasion is an ongoing temptation for rhetoric.

More than anything else, what distinguishes the various postmodern approaches to rhetoric is their skepticism concerning persuasion. This skepticism follows two paths. When the formal possibilities of persuasion are called into question, a deconstructive understanding of rhetoric emerges. In such an understanding the inherent movement of language to undermine itself is embodied in the claim that all language is tropic, that acts of language do not close but simply turn. When the operations of power in language are the focus of investigation, then the role of ideology comes to the fore. The problem is no longer the tropic possibilities of language but the implication of language in the maintaining of oppressive political orders. The incoherence of Sartre's modernist subject caught between reason and history becomes the split between form and power that separates the two major postmodernist rhetorics. Both of these rhetorics stand in need of refutation, and the service of the skeptical thread of ancient rhetoric is to recover the connection between form and power by returning postmodernism to the problem of an irremediable injustice as the origin of rhetorical thought.

8

Refuting de Man

The formalist impulse within postmodern rhetorics perhaps can be seen most clearly in the work of Paul de Man. In a casual aside in the essay "Semiology and Rhetoric," de Man offers a working definition of rhetoric as "the study of tropes and of figures (which is how the term *rhetoric* is being used here, and not in the derived sense of comment or of eloquence or persuasion)" (*Allegories*, 6).[1] So considered, rhetoric would be a formal study of linguistic transformations. De Man takes this definition to be sufficiently self-evident and noncontroversial that he feels no need to justify or elaborate on it. Rather, he proceeds as if traditional definitions of rhetoric, which often consider persuasion and not the study of tropes and figures to be the guiding purpose of rhetoric, are simply beside the point. Their justifications, however complex, for conceiving rhetoric primarily in terms of persuasion apparently do not merit consideration.[2]

Still, de Man's indifference to the rhetorical tradition may not be quite the perfunctory dismissal that it at first appears to be; he may have felt no need to elaborate on his definition since in his late essays he is always discussing rhetoric. He might have reasonably assumed that anyone at all conversant with his work would realize that this casually offered definition was simply an encapsulation of an understanding that pervades his thought. In his late essays he often uses rhetoric as a name for describing textual instabilities that he uncovers. Rather than cooperating with or following from grammar, rhetoric marks those elements of the text that disrupt meaning. Rhetoric is what reading discovers, as it reveals that the text's language is both saying what it intends and at the same time undermining this intention by saying something it does not intend. For de Man the key issue for rhetoric is not how language might function as a medium for communication but how language as a system of meaning or a medium for knowledge turns upon itself. His preoccupation is with the necessary epistemological failure of figurative language and with the consequent problems of cognition. Still, it is troubling, especially given his concern with the semantic drift inherent in language, that de Man asserts so unequivocally a contested definition of rhetoric without even addressing the contest. One cannot help but feel a de Manian impulse to ask why such a sensitive and subtle critic would treat a complex tension (the relation between figure and persuasion) as if its hierarchical ordering were a settled fact.

The lack of an explicit and elaborated contest over the definition of rhetoric is especially to be regretted because such a contest might help illuminate tensions that are central for understanding the rhetorical tradition. For even if de Man does not explicitly address the rhetorical tradition, his exploration of irony and allegory can help highlight a tension inherent within the rhetorical tradition which is not accidental but essential to that tradition. Or to put it differently, far from establishing the priority of figure over persuasion, de Man's definition of rhetoric opens up the relation of persuasion to tropes and figures. In turn, an investigation of de Man's position on rhetoric has enormous consequences, for it raises the issue of whether refutation or deconstruction is a better model for critical reading. But if de Man's conception of rhetoric is to contest traditional accounts or to advance a more complex understanding, then some of his assumptions need to be made explicit and their consequences need to be traced.

Since the classical period, the standard scholarship has defined rhetoric in terms of persuasion, so how are we to make sense of the claim that persuasion is the derived sense of rhetoric? Clearly, the derivation is not chronological; but if the derivation is then logical, what is its logic? Second, in its hierarchical preference of figure over persuasion, de Man's account of rhetoric posits language as a problem of knowledge rather than of action. True, his critiques, which undermine the possibility of knowledge, are extended to negate the possibility of action by tying it to epistemological failure, but this critique depends upon granting priority to epistemological questions. If, however, one starts with a concern for action rather than an interest in the adequacy of claims to knowledge, his skeptical attack on the possibility of action is less convincing, in part because a concern with action recognizes that the need to act must close off arbitrarily possibilities for the sake of making a decision.

De Man's favoring knowledge over action as the key dynamic with which to perform a rhetorical analysis leads him to end where the traditional defense of rhetoric, starting with Aristotle, begins. His skeptical discovery of indeterminacy is a recovery of a starting point for the Aristotelian rhetorical tradition, which assumed, at least with respect to action, that the world was indeterminate, and for this reason an art of rhetoric was needed. Such an understanding makes a skepticism rooted in epistemology beside the point, for traditional rhetorics see any determinate closure as inherently situational, temporary, and capable of being undone. For these accounts, rhetoric neither begins from nor ends in knowledge. Rather, it seeks to invent or discover understandings or actions that will help an audience constitute an identity by taking a position. That is, it seeks to persuade an audience.

Traditional accounts treated the relation between persuasion and tropes and figures hierarchically as one of ends and means; de Man replaces this hierarchy with a new one. He does not, however, simply reverse the ordering; he empties the term persuasion of any serious force, and one is left instead with the fact of figurative language or of the figurativeness of language. The old charge that a rhetor can delude an audience reemerges in a new form as de Man worries about the seductive illusion of language. The problem of the potential ethical and political unreliability of the rhetor has been displaced by that of the epistemological allusiveness/elusiveness/illusiveness of language in general. It is no longer the simple problem that an unscrupulous or inept individual might abuse language, but rather that the misuse of language inheres within language itself.[3] Put another way, what have been conceived traditionally as potential political and ethical difficulties for rhetoric are, in fact, the epistemological conditions that follow upon language as figure. To say this is not for de Man to deny an ethical or political dimension to language or literature, as has been sometimes charged, but to argue that an understanding of the ethical and political dimension requires first that one understand the ironic allegory that is produced by and productive of any text.[4]

The best way to get at my critique of de Man is to ask a series of questions: Does de Man have an ironized understanding of rhetoric or has he developed a position on rhetoric? Does de Man know something about rhetoric, even if that knowledge can only be negative, or does he posit something about rhetoric? (Knowing versus positing plays an important role in de Man's discussion of rhetoric, and it will be central to my critique of his discussion.) What is the status of the claim that language is figurative? Is this a truth claim, appropriately ironized, or is it a critical act that determines a field for inquiry, or is this dichotomy itself questionable and the claim about rhetoric possibly both true and performative or neither true nor performative?

De Man appears to be claiming to know something about rhetoric. In the essay "Rhetoric of Tropes (Nietzsche)," de Man develops explicitly his hier-archy of figure over persuasion. To support this claim, he turns not to the major texts of the rhetorical tradition but to some lectures on rhetoric given by a young Nietzsche. De Man credits Nietzsche with moving "rhetoric away from techniques of eloquence and persuasion *[Beredsamkeit]* by making these dependent on a previous theory of figures of speech or trope" (*Allegories,* 105). Nietzsche's claim is that the "trope is not a derived, marginal, or aber-rant form of language but the linguistic paradigm par excellence. The figura-tive structure is not one linguistic mode among others but it characterizes language as such" (105). De Man sees Nietzsche's insight into the natural occurrence of figures in language as freeing language from explanation in terms of a paradigm that conceives of reference as the primary function of language. Language is not a means to reach an end outside language, namely an understanding of a nonlinguistic world; rather, language is an autonomous system (hence a formal system) that is characterized by the presence of two forces: there is grammar, which ensures the meaningfulness of form by giving universal rules for well-formed acts of language, and there is rhetoric, which disrupts the application of grammatical rules.

De Man does not appear to be aware that in recognizing the occurrence of rhetorical operations in everyday language, Nietzsche has discovered nothing that is particularly radical. Aristotle, certainly a well-established source for the rhetorical tradition, begins his treatise by acknowledging that people have used various elements of rhetoric long before the systematic theorizing on the art of rhetoric began sometime during the fifth century BCE. He sees his rhet-oric as a systematizing and clarifying of these practices. Nor does he build his rhetoric on a belief that the authority of language is tied to a referential func-tion. He is well aware that he is dealing with how things appear and that the authority for rhetoric is vested in an audience and consequently is not a matter of knowledge but a matter of judgment. Nietzsche does, however, differ con-siderably from Aristotle in the attention that he gives to tropes. In Aristotle's *Rhetoric* tropes are discussed only in book 3, when Aristotle addresses the problem of appropriate and effective language; he clearly sees them as a means to an end. Nietzsche claims a more important and constitutive role for tropes. Again, this is a claim that does not establish itself in contest with traditional claims. Nietzsche does not argue with Aristotle or any other major figure of the rhetorical tradition; rather, his strategy is to reverse the importance of persuasion and trope by focusing on the process of reversal that he sees inher-ing in language.

De Man is particularly interested in Nietzsche's use of the figure chiasmus, as it exemplifies the process of "substitutive reversals" as the essential linguistic operation. According to de Man, Nietzsche showed how the binary polarities of cause/effect, outside/inside, before/after have been used and subsequently forgotten as a way of creating an epistemologically stable universe. De Man argues that Nietzsche shows that what was taken for a cause can be considered an effect, and that what was taken for an effect can be considered a cause. Nietzsche claims, for example, that our inner experience, which seems essential to who we are, is really a consequence of language operating on us from the outside. We have inner experience only because we turn a chronological sequence into a causal sequence; we see effects in the world (on the outside) and we postulate unseen causes (on the inside) that are the origin of the effects. Nietzsche is reminding us that we forget that we never meet the world innocently but are always meeting a situation that has been characterized. Or, as Kenneth Burke sometimes playfully comments, it is as fair to say that we are an invention of language as that language is an invention of us. The relationship between ourselves and language is tropological; it can be turned infinitely but it can never be grounded.

For de Man it is important to make clear that this insight generated from a critique of a referential epistemology does not itself escape from the deconstruction of the critique. A person who reads in an awareness of the figurativeness of language has no choice but to read figuratively. At best an awareness of the tropological nature of language allows one to be aware of the deception in all language, including one's own: "And it turns out that the very process of deconstruction, as it functions in this text *[The Will to Power]*, is one more such reversal that repeats the selfsame rhetorical structure. All rhetorical structures, whether we call them metaphor, metonymy, chiasmus, metalepsis, hypallagus, or whatever, are based on substitutive reversals, and it seems unlikely that one more reversal over and above the ones already taken would suffice to restore things to their proper order," in which they were grounded by an epistemology based on a new and more sophisticated understanding of reference (*Allegories*, 113). As readings simultaneously uncover and produce error, as they reverse one another, they create a series. But this series is not a progression in service of truth; nor a regression to a point of lexical paralysis; nor a digression that lapses into dissipation, but a repetition that is fated to perform the "deceit it denounces." The form of such a series of readings is an allegory, and what it narrates is "the story of a literally destructive but nontragic linguistic event" (116). What is endlessly reenacted is the impossibility of knowledge.

In "Rhetoric of Persuasion (Nietzsche)," de Man takes up the topic of knowing. He approaches the problem of the stability or reliability of knowledge through Nietzsche's comments on the law of contradiction that seek to show the rhetorical operations that generated the law. Nietzsche argues that in asserting the applicability of logic's axioms to the structure of the world, we have engaged in a chiasmic operation of substituting our limitations as if they were discoverable facts about the world. Nietzsche's point is not that the law of contradiction is false, but that we will never be in a position to know whether it genuinely reflects the structure of the universe because we can never escape the limitation of our perspective. Nietzsche chooses to read the law of contradiction because it is the fundamental law of logic as it has developed in the West. What is at stake in this law is the principle of identity. If our confidence in the principle of identity can be eroded, then the entire operation of knowledge as a description of the universe comes into question.

Nietzsche, according to de Man, uses his critique to tease out the obligation inhering in the claim that contradiction is a law. He does not attempt to challenge that obligation but to seek its authority. What he wants to show is that a supposedly declarative sentence is, in fact, an imperative; people, not nature, have written this law: "In short, the question remains open: are the axioms of logic adequate to reality or are they a means and measure for us to *create* the real, the concept of 'reality,' for ourselves? . . . To affirm the former one would, as already stated, have to have a previous knowledge of entities; which is certainly not the case. The proposition therefore contains no *criterion of truth,* but an imperative concerning that which *should* count as true" (120). Traditional claims to knowledge have been issued in guises that disguise their pragmatic form. If the law of contradiction is a law, then it is so as a consequence of a legislative act which declares its necessity and not as a consequence of the discovery of a necessary fact about the world. That the law of contradiction is in no way inescapable for us says nothing about its truth.

This critique is extremely important for de Man's conception of rhetoric, for it appears to open up the possibility of conceiving rhetoric as a problem of action rather than as a problem of knowledge. If in fundamental claims, truth is beside the point, then the relevance of the criterion of truthfulness and the questions as to the knowledge guaranteed by claims to truth are equally irrelevant to assessing linguistic acts. Rather, the emphasis would seem naturally to shift to an inquiry into the status of linguistic acts as acts. Rhetoric would then mark off linguistic claims as a field of praxis.

De Man explores this potential shift by looking at the opposition between "knowing and positing 'erkennen' and 'setzen' " (121). For de Man, knowing is not an action but rather a mode of accurate passivity or reception. As Rodolphe Gasché characterizes it, knowledge is "non-positional" (" 'Setzung,' " 49). A sentence involving a claim to know would not, then, be a speech act but rather something called a speech fact. The knower is making no claim to have done anything other than used language to effect a predication that mirrors a structure in the nonlinguistic world. De Man, using John Austin's vocabulary, labels such claims to knowledge as constatives. These contrast with performatives, which are acts in and through language and which depend upon the power of the agent for their efficacy.

Positing is a performative. It is not an attempt to render in language a fact about the universe but an attempt to put or place something. It is a register of human will and agency. Following Nietzsche, de Man claims that the principle of contradiction is a law that we have posited: "Classical epistemology, Nietzsche asserts, has maintained [that the identity principle is merely a fact that can be spoken] at least since Aristotle: '. . . according to Aristotle, the law of contradiction is the most certain of all principles . . . , the ultimate ground upon which every demonstrative proof rests'; it is the ground of all knowledge and can only be so by being *a priori* given and not 'put up,' 'gesetzt.' The deconstruction sets out to show that this is not necessarily the case. The convincing power of the identity principle is due to an analogical, metaphorical substitution of the sensation of things for the knowledge of entities" (122). This claim is critical, for it founds the skeptical undermining (or as de Man prefers to call it, "the ironization") of knowledge. If the principle upon which any claim to know must rest is itself not known but only posited, then there is no way to have access to a world independent of our assumptions about it. Our descriptions may or may not be accurate, but we can never know that. Further, if claims to knowledge are based on the substitution of a set of sensations, which is itself contingent, then the entire activity of thinking that is called "conceptualization" is dependent on this substitution. All thinking is the enactment of tropes: "Conceptualization is primarily a verbal process, a trope based on the substitution of a semiotic for a substantial mode of reference, of signification *[bezeichen]* for possession *[fassen]*" (122–23). We can encounter only what we have put there to begin with, but since we have forgotten that we placed it there, we take a previous speech act for a fact about the world. The world that we encounter is produced by the power of language to posit. The necessity of the law of contradiction is imperative and not declarative.

But if such a conclusion might seem to authorize understanding language as action, de Man questions whether this claim is any more stable than the claim to know. He immediately begins to raise problems for the stability of Nietzsche's insight. He looks at what Nietzsche does following the claim that language is performative and not constative. De Man argues that Nietzsche does not embrace his discovery by violating the principle of contradiction and "simultaneously affirm[ing] and deny[ing] identity"; rather, Nietzsche only "denies affirmation" (124). Nietzsche's text cannot enact what it has discovered.

De Man quickly continues that this error is not a voluntary mistake on Nietzsche's part but rather a limit that inheres within language: "This complication [being unable to enact the claim of simultaneous identity and nonidentity] is characteristic for all deconstructive discourse: the deconstruction states the fallacy of reference in a necessarily referential mode. There is no escape from this, for the text establishes that deconstruction is not something we can decide to do or not to do at will. It is co-extensive with any use of language, and this use is compulsive or, as Nietzsche formulates it, imperative" (125). De Man then goes on to use Nietzsche's work in *On the Genealogy of Morals* and *The Will to Power* to show his skeptical attack on the notion of action. First, he draws on Nietzsche's deconstruction of the subject and his consequent questioning whether there can then be a link between subject and the event that it has supposedly authored. Next, de Man analyzes Nietzsche's deconstruction of *denken,* to think, by emphasizing that to conceive of thought as an action we must employ the figure of synecdoche and treat a part of an event as if it were a distinct element that could in principle be separated from the rest of the event. Such a figurative construction would not be an error in conception but rather would constitute the grounds on which a conception of thinking were possible. We can only describe or identify thought figuratively. So the possibility of conceiving of an action depends upon figure, and figure, in Nietzsche, is tied to epistemological delusion. De Man then concludes that Nietzsche's "critique of metaphysics can be described as the deconstruction of the illusion that the language of truth *(episteme)* could be replaced by the language of persuasion *(doxa)*" (130).

In his discussion of Nietzsche on language as performance, de Man attempts to use his tropological reading to show Nietzsche's inevitable blindness to his central insight and to argue that such blindness is inescapable. Characteristically, such blindness ends up treating one element of a trope as prior, either constatively or performatively, and thus reduces the operation of the trope into an instrumentality of a particular will. This is to forget that tropes are linguistic and not voluntary operations. Tropes turn, and any conclusion arrests this turning and therefore violates the grounds of its insight. What is needed is a willingness to embrace tension in place of a hierarchical structure. De Man ends his essay on Nietzsche by offering such a tension.

He asserts that Nietzsche's "privileging figure over persuasion is a typically post-Romantic gesture" (130), and de Man will complicate this gesture by returning to the rhetorical tradition and reclaiming a role for the more mundane dimensions of rhetoric. He looks to its pedagogical past and to its role as "humble and not-quite-respectable handmaiden of the fraudulent grammar used in oratory" (130). He conceives of rhetoric as the gap, the distance, between its philosophical inquiries into language, knowledge, and action and its everyday interest in being an effective instrument for persuasion. He then concludes: "Considered as persuasion, rhetoric is performative but when considered as a system of tropes, it deconstructs its own performance. Rhetoric is a *text* in that it allows for two incompatible, mutually self-destructive points of view, and therefore puts an insurmountable obstacle in the way of any reading or understanding. The aporia between performative and constative language is merely a version of the aporia between trope and persuasion that both generates and paralyzes rhetoric and thus gives it the appearance of a history" (131).

In this pursuit of the tension that inheres within and hence constitutes rhetoric, de Man's conclusion creates another tension. This time the tension is within his own text. For if the claim that rhetoric as an art of persuasion is undone by rhetoric's constitution by figures, and if the claim that rhetoric marks the figurativeness of language is equally undone by showing its performative nature, then de Man's claim in "Semiology and Rhetoric" that the figurative sense of rhetoric is its prior sense is contradicted by his exploration of rhetoric in Nietzsche. He has erected a hierarchy in place of a tension; he has stopped the turning of his tropological understanding. This would neither surprise nor threaten de Man, because he has never claimed that he was exempt from the error that he was analyzing. Just the opposite. He continually reminds his readers that such errors cannot be avoided, that they inhere in language. He argues that this type of error is immune to refutation; rather, it is a necessary aberration. In de Man's language, it might be called a speech fact, though it is a negative one. This conclusion is what I will challenge.

One task of my argument is to demonstrate that what de Man here takes to be a necessary aberration is actually his way of not acknowledging an action that he has taken. The language of failed epistemology covers a commitment to a position, and what appears to be analytic description is, in fact, a critical choice. (I do not mean to imply that de Man is intentionally deceptive, but that he is unaware of a commitment that he has undertaken.) This is to argue that this particular inconsistency as to the priority of figure in rhetoric creates problems that cannot be addressed by simply acknowledging the inevitability of an involuntary blindness. To refute de Man I need to show that he has taken two positions that are incompatible and that their incompatibility is not necessary but a consequence of a desire to protect a particular understanding. My refutation has to show, in de Man's own terms, that he has committed himself to an incoherent position and that the incoherence arises from a failure to pursue a position to its appropriate conclusion.

If there is a central claim to de Man's understanding and to his way of reading, it is that language is figurative, tropological — always in the process of turning. If that claim encounters difficulty, then de Man's enterprise of deconstruction is shaken. This would be especially significant if deconstruction's negative knowledge depended upon a positing, an action. For if that is the case, deconstruction would not be a register of a fact about language, that is, an instance of a negative epistemology, but a critical position that has been adopted and for which one is accountable.

Much turns on how positing is understood in de Man. Juliet Flower Mac-Cannell concludes her portrait of de Man by emphasizing the importance of position: "What about 'position' in its other than technically philosophical sense that Gasché has so carefully tracked? The question is as crucial to a reading *of* de Man as it was to the reading he himself did of other critics, that is, not only not to accept a purely philosophical definition of any of its own terms, but also — more importantly — to discover how a 'philosophical' definition given in a text can be read in and through the form of the text in which it is given. Such a term is position, or positing in Paul de Man — the form of the subject, the subject of the form" ("Portrait," 70).

In "Shelley Disfigured," de Man emphasizes the violence of positioning in his argument that figure is not naturally given but rather posited by an arbitrary act of language. However, to call such an imposition an act is partly to misdescribe it, for such an imposition does not follow from the will of a particular agent but as an inexorable moment in language. Derrida makes a similar point by arguing that position is neither a psychological nor a voluntaristic concept: "Are we agreed also that there is no *effective* or *efficient* position, no veritable force of rupture, without a minute, rigorous, extended analysis, an analysis that is as differentiated and as scientific as possible? Analysis of the greatest number of possible givens, and of the most diverse givens (general economy)? And that it is necessary to uproot this notion of taking a position from every determination that, in the last analysis, remains psychologistic, subjective, moral and voluntaristic?" (*Positions*, 94). It might be better to call such imposition a language event. Such events are arbitrary in that they are not compelled by nature, but they are equally unavoidable, for they are a formal condition for language. They create a problem for de Man. For if the event of positing a figure implies a relationship between language and a natural referent and if the event is arbitrary, how is it possible for the figure to be meaningful? De Man answers that meaning is something that we impose on the figure. Figurative language comes to be in the gap between the performative act of positing and the constative recognition of meaning. Position is that which is forgotten so that a subject can engage with a figure. Position becomes that which it is necessary to repress for knowledge to be. Its erasure becomes a condition for subject's own constitution, which is a consequence of its engagement with an act of language that it treats as a text. Position is what reading must forget if it is to occur, and such forgetting can never be complete, so no reading can delude itself that it is other than an allegory.

Rodolphe Gasché reads de Man's use of position as a critique of speech act theory. Gasché argues that speech act theory is the recovery of the problem of self-reflection, and he sees Austin's relocating the paradigm of philosophical analysis from constatives and their concern with reference to performatives with their implicit recognition of an "I" who acts as returning philosophy to the problem of subjectivity. If speech acts are understood as performances in which there is a positing, then for there to be such a positing, there must be a self which posits itself. Both object and subject are consequences of this positing. The self becomes aware of itself as a subject by positing an object against which it can begin to determine its subjectivity. By such positing a subject becomes present to itself, becomes conscious of itself as an intentional being.

Although such an account of positing may seem to suggest that the self is the origin of objects and subjects, Gasché, through a reading of Heidegger, argues that a claim of positing that depends upon an original and nonempirical self is a metaphysical claim that relies upon a prior understanding of positing less as an action than as a register of what is given in the world. He works through a notion of positing as *thesis,* as that which is placed, to claim that "*thesis* is a mode of *aletheia,* of truth as unconcealing" (" 'Setzung,' " 54). Positing is an act "constitutive of presence"; it is an act of "letting come forth into what is present" (54). Since positing reveals what by its nature was concealed, what is present can be present to us only in a form other than its own. Our knowledge must always be knowledge in an estranged form. There will always be a gap; our understanding will always and necessarily be figurative and these figures will equally be distortions and disfigurations. Tropes, especially metaphor, catachresis, prosopopeia, and an asymmetrical chiasmus, are ways of registering our connection and estrangement to both the world and ourselves. Cynthia Chase reads this situation as de Man's understanding of the "linguistic predicament." The "I" who posits turns out to be both necessary and impossible, for that "I" is both a sign, which is arbitrary, and a symbol, that is tied to a referent and hence nonarbitrary: "For the sign to operate as a symbol, in signifying, is for the functioning of language as signification to cancel what allowed it to come into being in the first place, the arbitrary power of position of the sign" (*Decomposing Figures,* 94).

For Gasché, de Man's account of positing is a description of textual disruption. In this account, position is tied to concern with knowledge, with a givenness prior to language that can become available only in a distorted reflection that we call metaphor. And even though de Man will use a model of translation to show the unrecoverable origin of acts in language, he never imagines (posits) an interactive linguistic situation. That is, despite his concern with positing, de Man never conceives of the user of language as positioned. This is shown by de Man's recurring concern with cognition. Allegory, not dialogue, is his key term. An allegory, according to de Man, is a sequence that undoes what came before. For all its concern with disruption, this account never conceives of a disruption of reading by another reader. Reading, for de Man, is always serial and never dialectical. If failure is a foregone conclusion, so is success. The text may resist movement to a stable knowledge by its disfiguration, but it cannot resist the critics's attempts to read/misread it. Texts never achieve the status of being acts of subjects; rather, they are objects — things to be read, not acts of language that can interrupt an act of criticism and call a critic's language into question by alerting the critic to a position that he or she has assumed unawares. Reading always involves a particular agent engaged in a particular task (reading) with a particular text (which is unreadable). Language is the medium in which this model of sense-making (imposition of meaning) takes place, and the agent is understood to be performing an act (reading) in which he or she is removed from a situation in which one's action might elicit response from another.

The bodies in de Man's criticism are corpses, things to be given faces, surfaces on which to inscribe figures. There is a peculiar asymmetrical relationship in which the reader is agent and the text patient, albeit a difficult one. Reading is a Sisyphean task. The individual reader is fated to repeat the story of reading. This account depends upon an act of self-positing being the act that begins any reading. This is the violent opening, the questioning. This does not imply a voluntary beginning on the part of an agent but rather it marks what it means to be a reader. De Man conceives of the crucial move from speech act to trope to be an imposition by a reader "on the senseless power of positional language the authority of sense and of meaning" (*Rhetoric of Romanticism*, 117). He goes on to argue that to be in a position to constitute meaning one must be dealing with a "positional act, which relates to nothing that comes before or after" (117), so that the reinscription of the act is without a context. But this quandary follows only from a formalistic account of reading; in a positional account of reading such isolation is impossible. What this quandary marks is the arbitrary beginning that follows upon a formalistic account of language in which a temporal sequence is possible only if an artificial or violent beginning occurs. But a positioned understanding of language never needs to postulate such a beginning because it conceives of language as always already in relation.

De Man, in his analysis of Nietzsche's account of the deconstruction of action and consequently of performative language, also takes over a conception of action as a deed performed by a subject. This is what allows Nietzsche's first critique to focus on the illusory nature of subject and to tie a critique of subject to a deconstruction of consciousness. Equally, his criticism of our idea of action being the consequence of a synecdoche that we perform unawares makes the fundamental aspect of action that it exists as an isolatable and independent aspect of an event, and then Nietzsche shows such a concept of action to be an abstraction. But it is possible to frame a discussion of action not as a description of deeds of individual doers that seeks to explain those deeds in terms of a psychology of consciousness. The idea of action may frame a discourse about responsibility in which the issue is not to develop a coherent account of an internal psychology but to explore the issue of position. Such a discussion would start self-consciously from the larger notion of event and would then argue that this event should be characterized as an action or a motion. This discussion would not be an inquiry into the structure of the event (for such an inquiry would seek knowledge); rather, the discussion would seek the relationship of the audience to the event. The discussion would be a rhetorical act that sought to determine an identity for an audience by having it assume a position with respect to the event. It would assume this position by positioning responsibility within the event. This would be a claim not to know an identity but to posit one; it would not get itself trapped in an undecidable reversal between constative and performative language because its understanding of an event as a particular kind of motion or action would be an invention. Discourse about action would thus mark a way of talking about events and not be a confused presentation that unintentionally sneaked in ontological presuppositions about agents and actors. Such discussions would constitute a rhetoric of positional and not presuppositional language.

The de Manian conception of position is marked by another important blindness. It assumes that rhetorical acts must occur, even if the manner of their occurrence is an unstable and reversible turning. This is to assume an empowered reader, a reader in position to read and in position to act rhetorically. And while de Man treats the closing of rhetorical acts as problematic, as revealing their conflicts about knowing and the impossibility of knowing, he is untroubled by the difficulties that can beset the beginning of a rhetorical act. But to those without power, it is the beginnings that prove difficult or impossible. This is a problem about the possibility of action and not of knowledge. This is one of the problems that is at the core of the classical skepticism toward rhetoric and at the core of the modern recovery of this skepticism. As heroines as different as Anne Elliot and Hecuba have shown, once position is denied to someone, then rhetorical activity becomes impossible. The figure prosopopeia is especially relevant here, for as de Man reads this figure it is the positing of voice or face. De Man goes on to draw the conclusion that what prosopopeia demonstrates is the negative epistemological insight that we are always "deprived of the shape and sense of a world accessible only in a privative way of understanding" (*Rhetoric of Romanticism*, 81). He misses the more significant insight: if face or voice are given through the operation of a rhetorical figure, then one acquires a position because of rhetoric. Those who are without a voice or face, who are without position, are so precisely as a consequence of rhetoric. The bitterness of Philoctetes registers this fact. A reader or readers have figured those without voices or faces in such a way that they lack the position from which to speak. This is the thrust of Euripides' exploration of Hecuba's fate. Her disfigurement is not primarily the consequence of a necessary epistemological failure of her readers but a blindness made possible by the security of their positions.

Positing is a term that implies a relationship. I cannot posit or put something unless there is a place to put it. Positing cannot then be developed through the pseudotemporality of allegory because it is a spatial concept. It is a concept that has Otherness built into it.[5] Jacques Derrida notes this aspect of position in his comments on the pair spacing/alterity (*Positions*, 81–87, 93–96). Conceptually the notion of position precedes the idea of positing. One begins not as an agent but as a patient, that is, one is always already related. Any chronological account that seeks to develop conditions for this positionality can succeed only in rendering the concept of position unintelligible. Position is a given; this can be rephrased tautologically to emphasize Gasché's argument that what is posited is that which is concealed by saying position is posited, position is position. This is not simply linguistic nitpicking; rather, it is an argument that an account of reading should not begin from a constitutive act of positing but should start from the recognition that for us to be, we must be positioned. Our positings, then, are not originative acts but impositions, reorderings. Again, Derrida catches the doubleness of position: "Thus there are at least two concepts of the *position*. Why not leave *open* the discussion of this question of the position, of the *positions* (taking a position: position (/negation)? position-*affirmation*? overturning/displacement? etc." (*Positions*, 96). Our task is not to know this position but to deal with it. This discovery echoes Marx's critique of philosophy—the task of a positioned creature is not primarily to know but to change the world. One can never know one's position; one can only try to explore the consequences of one's position for constitution of self and others. We could label such activity refutation, and we could see such activity as necessitated by past acts of persuasion that have contributed to the current configurations of positions.

De Man's most explicit dealing with persuasion is his essay "Pascal's Allegory of Persuasion," although the essay is concerned more with the problems that surround the attempt to define allegory than with exploring the dynamic of persuasion. Indeed, persuasion seems to be a sufficiently comprehensible term that it can be used by de Man to help define allegory: "Allegory is the purveyor of demanding truths, and thus its burden is to articulate an epistemological order of truth and deceit with a narrative or compositional order of persuasion" ("Pascal's Allegory," 2). De Man then goes on to claim that in a "stable system of signification" a representation is persuasive if faithful in a manner analogous to an argument being persuasive if truthful. Thus truth and persuasion are linked, with persuasion being a function of truth. The assumption is that the persuasion is a consequence of a linguistic act's being adequate to a preexisting structure. The persuasion is successful because it articulates this structure. This connection is developed further when de Man joins persuasion with proof and uses the example of a mathematician for whom persuasion follows upon proof.

The example of mathematics is telling. De Man uses mathematics to contrast a harmony of proof and persuasion with those texts that "attempt the articulation of epistemology with persuasion." These latter texts seek to explore "truths about ourselves and the world." ("Pascal's Allegory," 2). De Man's contrast seeks to open up or point out a gap between persuasion and proof. But proof in mathematics is formal; while rhetoric employs formal reasoning (enthymemes and examples), its proof is contingent upon the accidents of the rhetor's skill, the audience's receptivity, and the timing of the persuasions. The notion of proof in a persuasion is larger than that of formal validity, and the interesting aspects of persuasion do not usually involve questions of formal validity or referential accuracy. Our everyday talk brings out this distinction: to say that mathematical theorems are persuasive seems forced. Rather, we say that they are proved; that is, we acknowledge their formal consistency but do not take a position with respect to them. Persuasion, on the other hand, is concerned with the force of reasons or figures to move one to take a position. If persuasion does not mark a moment in cognition but functions as a mode of action, then there is no preexisting structure to be faithful to. The rhetor trying to persuade an audience is attempting to get it to act, to posit itself, to position itself, to see itself as positioned. Even to see oneself as positioned is not to be faithful to a preexisting condition but to alter one's relation to the past by accepting a particular responsibility for it. Persuasion marks a mode of closure possible for indeterminate situations in which questions of formal validity or referential accuracy lack the power to close the situation. When de Man then claims that from "a theoretical point of view, there ought to be no difficulty in moving from epistemology to persuasion" ("Pascal's Allegory," 2), he is collapsing the problem of formal validity or referential accuracy with the problem of sufficient or compelling grounds for belief.

And there is a peculiar asymmetry in his terms: if the terms were parallel, one would move not from epistemology to persuasion but from epistemology to theories of persuasion, or from knowledge to persuasion. De Man seems to be eliding Aristotle's distinction between a theoretical and a practical science, between inquiries in which the end is knowledge and those in which the end is action, by assuming that knowledge is a category that structures both types of inquiry. Not surprisingly, he then sees the interesting oppositions in terms of "such traditional philosophical topoi as the relationship between analytic and synthetic judgments, between propositional and modal logic, between logic and mathematics, between rhetoric as *inventio* and rhetoric as *dispositio,* and so forth" ("Pascal's Allegory," 2). The opposition between knowing and acting is omitted.

When he discusses Pascal, the language of persuasion is placed in opposition to a language of pleasure and seduction, and the language of persuasion becomes the language that is rule-governed by the axioms of geometry. Persuasion is collapsed into logic and it becomes superfluous, something that follows automatically upon proof; that is, the demonstration of formal validity. So de Man ends with an account of persuasion that bears little relation to how the term is understood by the rhetorical tradition. For the tradition sees persuasion as an activity that functions in those areas in which the demonstration of certainty is not possible.

This discrepancy between de Man's use of the term *persuasion* and its traditional use is worth noting, for de Man's reposition of persuasion in opposition to seduction is crucial to his locating an important break in Pascal's text. De Man's wishes to see the problem of persuasion as one in which its relationship to truth turns out to be incapable of a determinate and precise formulation. What de Man will show is that attempts to develop a formal vocabulary inevitably stray beyond the strict boundaries of nominal definition and import terms that make claims about the nature of the world. Geometry is particularly appealing as an example because it seems to offer a self-contained system of formal validity only to fail to do so.

De Man quickly demonstrates that Pascal's distinction between nominal and real definitions encounters insurmountable problems. These problems arise from the unavoidable presence of "primitive words" in any geometrical system. These words, "such as motion, number, and extension," turn out not to designate a particular referent but instead function as a "vector, a directional motion that is manifest only as a turn, since the target toward which it turns is unknown. In other words, the sign has become a trope, a substitutive relationship that has to posit a meaning whose existence cannot be verified, but that confers upon the sign an unavoidable signifying function" ("Pascal's Allegory," 1–7). The consequence of the necessary inclusion of primitive terms in any geometrical system is that at a fundamental level, the system is then making claims about the world, but these claims cannot be proven, since they are put in figurative terms. As a system that claims to authorize a knowledge that is certain (because it is exclusively formal), geometry turns on itself and must suspend such claims.

De Man is interested in showing how the problems encountered by geometry are also met by other and nonmathematical languages. He takes as his example Pascal's discussion of nature and custom, in which Pascal puts the two terms into play by using the figure of chiasmus to effect an exchange between the properties of the one and the other. Nature turns out not to be original and stable but a function of custom, which ceases to be considered variable and derived. This same pattern of a reciprocal exchange of properties applies to other binary oppositions such as waking and sleeping, which is central to the debate between the skeptics and the dogmatists. For de Man, the example of waking and sleep points out the unstable but coercive nature of a chiasmic situation: "For one cannot remain suspended between the irreconcilable positions: it is clear that, by not choosing between the two poles of the polarities [being awake or being asleep], one is adopting the skeptical position. The predicament is that of the undecidable: propositional logic is powerless to decide a conflict that has to find a solution, if this logic is to survive" (16). Pascal claims that the name of this predicament is "man." To be human is to be double; to understand a human nature, one must move from a principle of radical doubt to the suspension of this doubt by a knowledge that one is doubting. But if it is the human condition to achieve a kind of self-knowledge that derives from a doubt that can suspend itself, the chiasmus that structures this knowledge is symmetrical and generates a reciprocal relation that permits an infinitive exchange between the polarities.

Such an infinitive exchange, if undecidable, at least has an internal coherence. The exchange that most interests de Man is one in which the chiasmic crossings break down. The binary pair is power and justice, and its chiasmic exchanges are disrupted at the topic of persuasion. As Pascal has analyzed the relationship, justice and power becomes structured asymmetrically. De Man comments:

> For the proper of justice to be power, and for the proper of power to be justice, they must be able to exchange the attributes of necessity and of innocence which characterize them. Justice must become necessary by might, might innocent by justice. This would accomplish and demonstrate the homogeneity of propositional statements as cognition and of modal statements as performance. But, unlike all other previous examples from the *Pensees,* the exchange does not take place. Justice refuses to becomes justessee; it remains pragmatic and inconsistent, "subject to dispute," unable to fulfill the criterium [*sic*] of necessity as cognitive persuasion. Might, however, has no difficulty whatever satisfying the criterion of necessity; it is "sans dispute" and can therefore *usurp* the consistency of cognition without giving anything in return. (21–22)

In effect, force can prove its point. This is important for de Man because he considers force as a pure instance of act or performance. Justice, on the other hand, is linked with knowledge and with cognition. There is thus a heterogeneity within language; performance and cognition, persuasion and proof cannot be brought into a stable relation: "Language, in Pascal, now separates in two distinct directions: a cognitive function that is right *(juste)* but powerless, and a modal function that is mighty *(forte)* in its claim to rightness. The two functions are radically heterogeneous. The first generates canonical rules of persuasion, whereas the second generates the eudaemonic values that are present as soon as one has to say that the claim to authority is made 'at the *pleasure* of' the despot. The first is the language of truth and of persuasion by proof, the second of the language of pleasure *(volupté)* and of persuasion by usurpation or seduction" (23). This leads de Man to conclude: "To the extent that language is always cognitive and tropological as well as performative at the same time, it is a heterogeneous entity incapable of justice as well as of *justesse*" (23). Allegory embodies this relationship.

But if this is a heterogeneous relationship, de Man's formulation is still in terms of cognition, even if these terms mark out its falseness or impossibility. And as long as his analysis persists in favoring cognition it can continue to reinscribe these allegories, but if the focus is shifted to the performative aspect of language, then the repetitive structure of allegory is replaced by a structure of history, albeit a history without a telos. De Man assumes that the heterogeneity of linguistic functions needs to be put in cognitive terms, but his own analysis undermines this necessity and instead reveals it as his choice. That is, it is a question not of knowing or not knowing but of positing. As de Man pointed out earlier with respect to skepticism, the figurative relation proves impossible to be lived and consequently demands that one take a position (16). Thus if there is a necessity, it follows not from concerns of cognition but from concerns of action. In a situation in which we cannot have knowledge but nonetheless must act, we must posit something. That is, we must take responsibility for the naming or defining. And this, of course, is to recover the original justification for rhetoric, namely to provide guidance in those situations in which we must act in the absence of any knowledge that is sufficient by itself to necessitate a course of action. The counter to force or might is not truth but persuasion. Language is a mode of power, and the problem of justice is a problem not of knowledge or of truth but of action, of assuming appropriate positions and taking responsibility for these positions.

Several interesting consequences follow. First, arbitrary and responsible cease to be in opposition to each other and instead help define each other. If a situation is undecidable, then, in one sense, any position taken is arbitrary. (That is, it cannot be final or exclusive, and will necessarily involve doing injustice to some aspect of the situation.) But because this position is arbitrarily chosen by a person, that person becomes responsible for the position. Indeed, one consequence of the original arbitrariness of any position is the unending task of trying, by positing an understanding of the situation, to do justice in some way to those aspects or people that one imposes on in the act of constituting oneself. Persuasion entails refutation.

Second, to argue the resolution of the heterogeneous functions of language in terms of performance is to embrace the claim that effective language does not rest on truth. Truth does not make persuasion. Certainly particular truths will play important roles in an audience's determination to name a situation in a particular way, but such truths will acquire force only when they are placed within a position. To put it another way, rather than language marking an infinitely postponed arrival at truth, persuasion registers the positionality of language users. To speak is to posit; it is to discover a position.

Third, to discover a position implies that one is situated with respect to other positions. The play is then between positions. Its intent is not to achieve a final structure (such as de Man's cognition might ideally seek, realizing nonetheless that such an ideal is infinitely postponed), for such a structure would freeze all positions into a totality that would destroy the very freedom that makes positions possible. If truth could be discovered, positing would be beside the point.

Fourth, and most important, we do not simply assume positions but we begin from assumed positions. The importance of history is to make one aware that these positions of our figured understandings that appear referential (nonpositional) are not neutral starting points. Our original position is not voluntary; we are born into it, for we are born into a language which is the consequence of a history of past positions. These past positions necessarily, as positions, bring with them questions of their justice and injustice. This is the insight that founds Plato's skeptical critique of rhetoric in the *Gorgias;* it is this history of injustice that is the insurmountable obstacle that a refuted Neoptolemos cannot overcome despite his good intentions. To be born into a language is to involuntarily posit an understanding of the world for which one becomes responsible even though that position is not chosen but merely assumed. This creates rhetoric's most interesting problem: how does a rhetor get an audience to see itself as positioned, and hence always already implicated in both just and unjust understandings and practices? This is the problem that Socratic refutation addressed. Such refutation assumed that the key problem was one not of epistemological suspension but of taking appropriate responsibility for one's position and impositions.

Kierkegaard labels this refutation ironic: "I have found an unknown quantity, a position that appeared to have been characteristic of Socrates. I have called this position irony" (*The Concept of Irony,* 241). Kierkegaard sees this irony as "the infinite absolute negativity" (261). It is a mode of proceeding that does not establish a new position but that challenges existing positions. Hence, Socratic irony is a position that is not positive; its concern is with calling the positivity of other positions into question: "He went around to each one individually in order to find out if that person had a sound position; nevertheless, his activity was intended not so much to draw their attention to what was to come as to wrest from them what they had" (175).

The Socratic enterprise is concerned primarily with neither logical validity nor psychological seduction but with positional play. It is an ever-continuing attempt to discover how we have been placed and how we have placed others. To proceed with a refutation, Socrates needs acts of language that represent the beliefs of those with whom he speaks. Only if someone is willing to take a position is dialectic possible. This is one of the lessons of the *Meno. Meno's* position as a handsome youth poised to inherit wealth and power makes him unwilling to put this position in play. Socrates tries mightily to engage him, but Meno frustrates such engagement simply by not seriously taking a position.

Socrates' failure is instructive. De Man's allegorical reading is directed at texts, for texts mark the way in which language must embody itself: "We call *text* any entity that can be considered from such a double perspective: as a generative, open-ended, non-referential grammatical system and as a figural system closed off by a transcendental signification that subverts the grammatical code to which the texts owes its existence. The 'definition' of the text also states the impossibility of its existence and prefigures the allegorical narratives of this impossibility" (*Allegories,* 270). Since de Man works with texts, he cannot fail as Socrates did. The failures in de Man's reading inhere within the nature of reading and are of a different order than Socrates'. Until Meno attempts in good faith to give his position as he understands it, there is no language for Socrates to work with. His critique works on language but is directed at a person. Hence, Socrates' concerns are with the ethical and political entanglements that follow upon being born into a language. Refutation is not concerned with problems of epistemology; rather, it wishes to put positions in play to make one aware of the consequences of a position. What refutation tests is not the adequacy or stability of knowledge but the character and commitments of a self. Refutation assumes that a self is never in position by itself to reflect upon its own position. Refutation is the antithesis to a practice of self-reflection, for it assumes that one can never get beyond language to a nonpositional point that could be called knowledge.

The *Meno* more than any other dialogue raises the problem of the infinite ironization of position that structures a de Manian critique of action. In the dialogue Meno tries to relieve his embarrassment at not being able to supply a definition of virtue by raising the issue of the impossibility of knowing. He says to Socrates: "And how will you inquire, Socrates, into that which you do not know? What will you put forth as the subject of inquiry? And if you find what you want, how will you ever know that this is the thing which you did not know?" (8od). Meno's questions suggest that it is impossible either to begin or end an inquiry, for we can never be certain of either our starting points or our conclusions. Socrates' refutation of this doubt is instructive. He does not seek to establish a ground that is certain, nor does he provide a demonstration that seeks to impugn syllogistically the skeptical doubt. Rather, he tells a story that is clearly a fiction. The point of the fiction is not to prove to Meno that knowledge is possible but to persuade him to adopt the position that inquiry is productive even if it falls short of knowledge. The myth of recollection is intended to function ethically and to create a character for Meno. The subsequent section that attempts to demonstrate the viability of the myth uses the slave boy and several rudimentary theorems not to develop a positive account of knowledge but to argue that we can free ourselves from particular blindnesses.

The full point of the slave boy episode becomes apparent only later, when Socrates is trying to distinguish true opinion from knowledge. Recollection is defined as a tying down, or, as we might say, the establishing of a position. This is done through repeated tests that seek to discover whether this position is harmonious with other positions held. Thus, it is through refutation that skepticism is met. Refutation cannot prove a positive thesis, but it can make progress by locating false positions. Its final test is its productiveness. A position is considered worthwhile if it provides good guidance, that is, if it allows one to discover a way or a path. As Socrates emphasizes, such guidance never reaches a final stability. It can always be brought into question, but each questioning, even if it arises arbitrarily and is an imposition, nonetheless finds itself positioned because it enters a discourse in which positions have already been drawn and which must be addressed, even if the purpose of the address is to overturn the positions.

The testing of a position is always situational. One tests a position by positioning it against another position. With luck, the two positions will be brought into an exchange that brings out that they are positions and not knowledge of a reality. That exchange is the dialectic and it leads, at best, to only a temporary closure, which must be put in play as a position as soon as it encounters another position that it will engage to risk itself in a dialectical encounter. To be able to assume new positions, to escape from a complete determination of one's life by remaining contained in the position into which one was born, is power, is freedom. Since the condition of such power is the willingness to play one's position off the position of another (and such play is possible only if one is honest and treats the other position fairly), this power is dependent upon justice. The power/justice split that characterized de Man's reading of the binary is reconciled in Socratic refutation.

The major rhetorical problem for Socrates is to persuade others that it is not position in the world that gives power, but the positing of positionality and its consequent play that mark serious power. Euripides complicates this problem by showing that those imposed on and deprived of a recognized position in a community are denied the access to power by their preclusion from rhetoric. And Sophocles shows that past acts of injustice can leave a rhetor, even a well-intentioned one, in a position without power. Since one can gain perspective on a position only if he or she is allowed to play that position off another position, freedom is a social construct tied necessarily to the opportunity and ability for rhetorical play. It follows from this understanding of position, power, and freedom that no one can ever be certain of his or her power or freedom; rather, freedom is both that which is posited and that which is sought. One cannot know this; but a skillful rhetor through refutation can persuade one of the desirability of this position.

One task of a rhetor engaged in refutation is to encourage or reconstitute an audience so that it becomes willing to risk its position to discover its inadvertent commitments and the possibilities inhering in new positions. Socrates in the *Gorgias* displays several strategies for creating such engagement: he gives respect and deference to Gorgias; he deliberately provokes Polus; and he tries to induce shame in Callicles. None of these strategies succeeds, but they do suggest that refutation must tailor itself to an identity that it offers a particular audience. Since this chapter seeks to refute Paul de Man's position on rhetoric, it needed to do several things. First, it had to try to do justice to the complexity of de Man's thought. This is no easy task, and, to be frank, I am not sure that I have fully succeeded.[6] Next, as with any refutation, this essay needed to try to uncover commitments hidden within a position that raised problems for the coherence of that position. My strategy has been to argue that what de Man took to be a negative instance of knowledge forced on him by the mode of a text's being was in fact a position that he adopted. I have attempted to turn his language on itself by showing that his definition of rhetoric was at odds with the understanding of rhetoric that emerged in his discussion of Nietzsche. Further, I have tried to show that this contradiction was not a product of the inherent figurality of language but a consequence of seeing language as primarily a matter of knowledge and not of action.

But as in any refutation, the process of discovery has gone both ways. Before writing this chapter, I felt comfortable that I understood traditional rhetoric as activity that rendered the indeterminate determinate for purposes of community or action, and I conceived of the tropes and figures as means to persuade an audience. The pressure of de Man's writings has moved me from my position on rhetoric to consider how rhetoric might be reconceived not as a hierarchy of persuasion over figure or figure over persuasion or as a gap between philosophical inquiry and pedagogical practice but as an art of position. And Derrida has enlarged my understanding of rhetoric as an art of position by suggesting that the concept of position allows us to see ideology in a new way:

> But inversely, what is perhaps in the process of being reconsidered, is the form of closure that was called "ideology" (doubtless a concept to be analyzed in its function, its history, its origins, its transformations), the forms of the relationships between a transformed concept of "infrastructure," if you will — an "infrastructure" of which the *general text* would no longer be an effect or a reflection — and the transformed concept of "ideology." If what is in question in this work is a new definition of the relationship of a *determined* text or a signifying chain to "reality" (history, class struggle, relationships of production, etc.), then we can no longer restrict ourselves to prior delimitations, nor even to the prior concept of regional delimitations. What is produced in the current trembling is a reevaluation of the relationship between the general text and what was believed to be, in the form of reality (history, politics, economics, sexuality, etc.) the simple belief that this exterior could operate from the simple position of cause or accident. (*Positions*, 90–91)

But the deconstructive approach to ideological criticism, even if it shares with a materialist critique the undoing of idealism, cannot move to serious political criticism until it engages its own position not primarily as a dance of a chain of signifiers but as a register of one's political situatedness. Even Andrzej War-minski's interesting and intriguing argument that de Manian deconstruction is materialist history could not move beyond the text, although the text is now read materially ("Ending Up/Taking Back," 20).

Warminski's essay reminds us of how truly complex de Man's thought is, and he shows how de Manian reading is the disclosure of the textual entangle-ment of ideology. But such entanglement remains a problem of knowledge (30). However, to see the world in terms of positions is to see the world as figured, and moreover it is to see the world as necessarily a place of action, a place in which we need to figure out who we are and how we have been positioned. De Man's irony can then be appropriated as part of a practical critique; it need not be limited to undoing illicit but inevitable epistemological closures but can be redirected against the ever-present temptation to assume (in part because it feels natural) the nonpositionality of one's position. War-minski's essay allows us to see this temptation and to understand the ways in which de Man's critique itself sought to comment on the political implications inhering within any act of discourse. De Man's work can be yet another re-minder of a rhetorical doubleness in which persuasion is both the goal and the problem for rhetoric. The need for irony is the need that de Man recognized in his essay "The Rhetoric of Temporality." This is the need for comedy, the need for the fortunate fall. Or, as Socrates put it in the *Gorgias:* the only use for rhetoric is to attack the ones you love. An ironic unsettling is essential if rhetoric is to open its audience to refutation. But rhetoric cannot rest simply in the repetition of overturning positions, for since being positioned is unavoid-able, one must equally always be trying to do justice to new understandings of past positions and to the consequences of newly assumed positions. Rhetoric is concerned with action, not because it is a function of the will of individual agents but because it is the play of positions.

The rhetorical tradition is marked by the play of two competing positions; this tension is central to rhetoric's constitution. The tension, however, is not the one that de Man earlier identified between pedagogical practice and philo-sophical import but rather the tension between praxis and irony, between a position represented by Aristotle and one represented by Plato.[7] To refute deconstruction is to read it as a position aligned with classical rhetorical skep-ticism yet differing from that skepticism because of its epistemological preoc-cupations, and it is to open up one's position to be read by it. If de Man has slighted the standard account of rhetoric as it is embodied in Aristotle's posi-tion, it would be a serious mistake to simply reverse and repeat this slight of de Man's position on rhetoric.

Frank Lentricchia begrudgingly concedes to de Man the accomplishment of the negative task of undermining the assumptions of the philosophic tradition that culminated in the nineteenth-century philosophies of idealism (*Criticism and Social Change,* 50). This concession trivializes the power of de Man's critique as a position because Lentricchia is unwilling to allow de Man's position to challenge his own. Lentricchia's commitment to be uncompromisingly positioned makes him unavailable for refutation. What Lentricchia fails to see is that what counts as political criticism is not self-evident. A rhetorical position that would do justice to de Man must incorporate his ironical undermining, his allegorical reading, into the histories it seeks to tell. To fail to do this would be to help bring into play a world of mere power, of positions resting content in their own rightness and unaware that they cannot escape being impositions even when their goal is the achievement of social justice.

To understand de Man's contribution to rhetoric, we might ask: when one is persuaded, what is one persuaded of? Not truth, if my account of rhetoric is right. Instead, one will be persuaded of what a rhetor has allowed a reader or audience to have figured out. The danger that de Man alerts us to is the collapse of persuasion accomplished through such figures into a claim of knowledge. For such a collapse leads to an imposition that sees itself not as violent but as respecting truth. One feels that he or she has the right position. The danger lurking in any act of persuasion is that it will be too successful—that what is a figurative understanding designed to be held in a provisional fashion and to be open to subsequent modification in response to how that figure repositions the world as a place for action will be treated as if it were a truth claim. De Manian irony would be a continual pressure on any position that would assert that it is not a position but a truth. It would be a counter to that movement inherent in language that Kenneth Burke ironically displayed by noting that as creatures of language we are rotten with perfection. If, as Gasché has claimed, de Manian deconstruction "is an invitation to endlessly and in an infinite process debunk the totalization of knowledge" ("'Setzung,'" 45), then one can understand the work of deconstruction to be necessitated by acts of persuasion and to necessitate subsequent acts of refutation. But contrary to de Man, this continual critique of ideology would be forced on us not by the epistemological impossibility of language but by the need to be responsible for the positions that we find ourselves in and which we assume. Rhetoric would thus embody and play out continually a tension between persuasion and trope, but it would do so not because we adopted a stance (a position) of knowledge but because we realized that we are inescapably positioned. This is to shift from a paradigm of deconstruction with its repetition of epistemological failure to a paradigm of refutation with its repeated attempt to do justice to a positioned world.

If de Man alerts us to the danger of collapsing position to truth, a refutation of de Man alerts us to another danger: framing rhetoric in terms of cognition rather than action. This danger is to see the world of language as a reiterated textuality rather than as a place in which human beings act and are acted upon by language. Understanding the role of persuasion in rhetoric need not commit one to seeing rhetoric as a function of the wills of individual agents; rather, it is to see that human beings are inescapably positioned creatures because they are creatures of language. This is an insight that harmonizes with de Man's undoing of binaries. For it undoes the binary of inside/outside. There is no outside of language, not because language is an autotelic formal system but because a creature who is positioned is one who is political, who has ethical interests, who negotiates various economies. To argue this understanding of rhetoric is to argue that the world is a place, and that place is a function of positions. What positions mark are human relationships, and what they pose in their positionality is the question of taking responsibility for these relationships, for seeing the world as constructed, and for seeing the human task as one of continual reconstruction guided by a goal of justice that would empower all to put their positions into play so that all could conduct and stand for refutation and thereby take responsibility for themselves and others.

9

Rhetoric and Ideology

Ideology occupies the present recovery of rhetoric in a way that parallels the rhetorical tradition's concern with the problem of individual abuse of rhetoric. At issue is the accidental or inherent distortion of meaning by the demands or operations of power on discourse. The movement from worrying about rhetorical distortion as a problem of an aberrant will to conceiving it as a problem of structural relations is indicative of the way in which the current recovery of rhetoric both moves toward the skeptical critique with its concern for the relation of language and injustice and extends the scope of the rhetorical enterprise by reformulating questions concerning the role of discourse in social mediation. The role of the individual rhetor gives place to a general property of language; rhetoric is conceived less in terms of an individual art and more as a condition marking the possibilities and limitations that follow from language as a medium of symbolic performance.

This reemergence of rhetoric as an extended understanding of the inherent positionality of any act of language leads inevitably to a concern with ideology. The linguistically veiled or dissimulated operations of power become an inescapable fact for worlds constituted by and mediated through discourse. In a linguistically dependent world it is essential to understand the force of past and present acts of language in the constitution and conception of a subject and a society. A recovered rhetoric must deal with a world in which ideology is irremediably a part.

Ideology is, of course, both a heavily loaded and a deeply contested term. Terry Eagleton begins his recent book *Ideology* by listing sixteen different uses of the term, and he announces that he will approach the "word 'ideology' . . . [as] a *text* woven of a whole tissue of different conceptual strands; it is traced through by divergent histories, and it is probably more important to assess what is valuable or can be discarded than to merge them forcibly into some Grand Global Theory" (1). Rather than settling on a definition, he provides a semantic web. To use W. B. Gallie's phrase, he shows the "essential contest" over the term.[1] Given the nature of ideology, it is reasonable to assume that any particular definition will fail to see its own partiality. So rather than attempt yet another definition of ideology, I will use the term simply to mean the mystification of power within discourse. Ideology, in this sense, is a necessary feature of a rhetoricality that sees thought itself as an effect of the continual and ineffable interplay of positions. Understood in this way, ideology brings with it the question of the relation between discourse and action. In the paradigm shift from rhetoric as the art of an agent to rhetoricality as a feature of discourse in general, the issues of justice and responsibility emerge as problems: can the world still be conceived as a scene for action once subjectivity is pluralized and diffused? This, in turn, raises the question whether rhetoricality displaces rhetoric or whether it calls for a new rhetoric that can use the classical tradition and its skeptical challengers as resources for the discovery of the possibility for action within a world constituted, in part, by and through rhetoricality.

In his essay "Ideology and Ideological State Apparatus," Louis Althusser addresses the problem of rhetoricality by reformulating the relation between ideology and materialism. He sees ideology as a "system of ideas and representations which dominate the mind of a man or a social group" (*For Marx*, 149). He shifts the question from why people need an order that intervenes between their representation of "real" conditions and their understanding of such conditions to why this relationship of individuals to their social forms is an imaginary one. This reformulated question allows Althusser to address the relation of ideology to power. He attempts to explain how subjects give free allegiance to the social orders of which they are a part. Ideology explains this allegiance because it is through ideology that the subject is constituted. Such constitution does not come about because of the intention of any individual person or group but is part of the condition of an individual being able to be a subject. Althusser argues that such subjectivity is always already there, that it is the fate of each individual, that it is crucial for how each of us understands himself or herself as a subject. At the heart of such constitution is paradox (contradiction, mystery). Ideology explains how the subject recognizes itself as subject. Individuals recognize an absolute subject, and this absolute subject, in turn, functions as a mirror in which individuals recognize themselves as subject to this absolute subject. Such recognition is paradoxically both free and necessary, and as such it creates the possibility of a subject willingly obeying a set of imperatives because those imperatives are essential to who the subject is. These imperatives consequently are not available for a normal scrutiny because they are logically prior to the subject and hence a condition of its existence. To question them is to bring one's subjecthood into question, and that is to undo one's very identity. Power need not directly intervene to enforce conformity to social norms because it already operates in the very constitution of the individual as a social subject. The individual will be his or her own overseer. Althusser underlines this rootedness of cultural power by arguing that ideology is like the unconscious in Freud.

But if ideology is like the unconscious, it differs in one crucial aspect: its origin is neither biological nor physiological but social and material. It is embodied in material practices into which one is born, and, as a system of belief, it will necessarily manifest itself in the practices that one undertakes. We are shaped in and by our practices, and this shaping infuses within us an imperative that feels natural. Ideology registers the fact that our primary relation to the world is one of acceptance rather than questioning. One does not question quotidian reality because such reality is unconsciously and naturally privileged—this is caught in the phrase "well, that's the way things are." By this mystification, history is turned into nature and this "nature" then acquires something like the force of the inevitable. One's subjectivity is experienced not as a voluntary acquiescence that is the practical conclusion to a reasoned process but as a fact.

What ideology explains, then, is the drama of the perpetually lost origin of subjectivity. Paolo Valesio develops the importance of this aspect of ideology when he argues that "the real enemy of rhetoric is not logic but ideology" (*Novantiqua*, 61). For Valesio, ideology is a form that rhetoric takes when it decays. He sees an ideology as an evasion of the inescapably linguistic nature of human understanding. Ideology is connected to a positivist impulse that "assumes that while truth and other basic values are non-linguistic in nature, they can be faithfully expressed by language provided it is used correctly" (62). When such a view is held, rhetoric must become suspect, for it conceives of language itself as playing a role in the determination of understanding and not simply as a medium in which understanding is embodied and through which it is communicated. Valesio would have trouble even with Althusser's notion of ideology, for example, because the word "real" is still functioning in Althusser's explanation. For Valesio, this is evidence of a residual positivism, and it will display itself in the special discursive role that Althusser allots to science.

Valesio argues that the political task of rhetoric is to undermine such mystification by studying the "structure of the different rhemes and their dialectical relations" (44). He would replace the idealist/materialist conflict over the priority of language by a skepticism that would seek to dialectically engage any attempt to undo the stylized play of rhetoric into a surface for some ultimate nonlinguistic referent. Antithesis is the key rhetorical figure for Valesio, and it is Gorgias's insight that we can say nothing about Being that is fundamental to a rhetorical understanding.

Valesio sees rhetoric as inherently dialectical. In a rhetorical universe there are no absolute distinctions; rather, there is a continuous interchange of positions that are adopted strategically. *Kairos*, skill in determining the appropriate moment to deploy a particular strategy, becomes central to rhetoric. There are no absolutely right or wrong, moral or immoral strategies; there are only effective and ineffective uses of the topoi and figures, opportune and inopportune moments. Rhetoric, so conceived, is the science of linguistic competence, and it discloses the resources through which we construct and reconstruct our understanding and hence our reality. Such an understanding is fluid and provisional. When this fluidity and provisionality are lost, an ideological understanding replaces rhetoric. One now believes that he or she has discovered something true about the world. Ideological mystification replaces rhetorical ontology.

In place of materialism, Valesio would adopt a "materialist attitude" (114). Rather than arguing for a particular view of material reality, this attitude derives from two assumptions: (1) total social context determines a subject's consciousness, and (2) "even [the rhetor's] unconscious is bound to collective patterns" (114). Valesio is less interested in exploring what this attitude entails than in preserving the desire for a cultural criticism. What a materialist critique offers him is the possibility of doing a historical critique without subscribing to any particular idea about any ultimate material reality. A materialist attitude would be one that would recognize the particular historical nature of conflicts that a rhetoric encounters and would recognize that this history constitutes a given in terms of material for rhetoric, but this material does not imply a direction or determine a future. Rhetoric is creative, and in the opportune deployment of the topoi and figures, a rhetorical conflict determines an understanding for a particular time.

V. N. Volosinov equally stresses the creativity of language.[2] Like Valesio, Volosinov is interested in establishing the relationship of ideology, language, and material reality. But in contrast to Valesio's materialist attitude, Volosinov develops what might be called a materialist semiotics. For him "the domain of ideology coincides with the domain of signs" (*Marxism,* 10). The ideological exists in the sign, for the sign is both a material thing and a reflection and refraction of social reality. This is so because the nature of a sign requires that it arise on "interindividual territory" (12). For a sign to exist, there must be a social organization shared by two people. Signs are properties of communities, and they are not so much stable meanings as they are sites for an ongoing struggle over meaning. Clifford Geertz would explain this struggle in terms of a cultural strain (*The Interpretation of Cultures,* 219). Ideology is both the product and the medium of such struggles, as these symbolic agons formulate the images, commonplaces, and assumptions of a political understanding that hopes to produce a social stability by grounding language. Hence Michael Ryan would revise Althusser's conception of ideology as largely a negative process of subject formation and stress ideology's inherent instability and threat to a prevailing order (*Politics and Culture,* 111–13). An ideology, then, is not so much the successful operation of power as it is a defensive action that a particular hegemonic structure deploys in an attempt to contain the threats to itself by the extension of its principles of justification to groups currently excluded from that power.

Ryan's view of ideology as an attempt to forestall a potential social revision fits in well with Volosinov's sense of the open-endedness of a sign. Volosinov argues that we should analyze problems of meaning not by focusing on the individual speaker in isolation and assuming that the fact to be explained is that speaker's relation to a reality but by realizing the dialogic nature of the sign. The crucial exchange is not between a single speaker and a physical reality but between two speakers. Further, this exchange is necessarily and exhaustively semiotic. One makes sense of a sign with another sign. Meaning for Volosinov does not precede the sign but develops out of the struggle within a concrete social situation. For if there is sharing within a specific situation there is also stratification, and a word like *justice,* for example, is going to reflect and refract very differently depending on where someone is placed socially. As different social interests vie to determine the meaning of a sign, a dialectic is generated. There is always an openness in this process that is a function of the nature of understanding. "The task of understanding does not basically amount to recognizing the form [of a sign] used, but rather to understanding it in a particular, concrete context; to understanding its meaning in a particular utterance, i.e., it amounts to understanding its novelty and not to recognizing its identity" (*Marxism,* 68). Understanding, in contrast to recognition, is always creative. This process of understanding verbal expression shapes and reshapes the possibilities for forms of experience. Volosinov calls the experience determined by the forms of expression "behavioral ideology" (91). The larger systems of ideology are "crystallizations of behavioral ideology" (91). Out of this dialogical engagement in particular concrete historical situations, an understanding emerges that is a consequence of the vital creativity of language.

Kenneth Burke equally stresses the role of language as creative mediation in particular concrete situations and the connection between ideology and language. He distinguishes two senses of ideology: (1) a primary sense that involves the study of ideas and their relation to each other, and (2) a more current sense of a "system of political or social ideas, framed and propounded for an ulterior purpose" (*A Rhetoric of Motives*, 88). Burke treats this latter sense of ideology as simply an instance of rhetoric, since it shares with rhetoric the goal of inducing people to act in a certain way. Unlike Valesio, who sees ideology as a rhetoric that has decayed into a rigid understanding, Burke is willing to accept ideologies as operating rhetorically.

If, for Burke, ideology does not represent a departure from normal rhetorical goals, it nonetheless can generate harmful understandings that necessitate an antihegemonic discourse. Burke reads Marxism as a penetrating critique of capitalist rhetoric, and he sees one of its major contributions to the study of rhetoric in its account of the mystification of an ideology of private property. In particular Burke reads Marx's critique of capitalism as allowing one to see how private property becomes a guise that "sets up a fog of merger-terms where the clarity of division-terms is needed" (109). Like Ryan, he sees ideology as reactive. On Burke's reading, Marx showed the ideological move within capitalist discourse that postulated a general psychological motive to account for the current structure of social relations and private property. Marx then argued against the general or merger-term for a division-term, and that division-term was class. In Burke's analysis a universal motive is a mystification of the underlying division of motives. The goal of analyzing a situation in terms of universal motives is to establish a common identity for all people. In contrast, a division-term like class highlights the stratification within a shared situation. The choice of merger-term or division-term will have significant consequences both for how the world is conceived as a place of action and for the nature of any action proposed to redress injustice in such a world.

Although Burke is sympathetic to the Marxist analysis and a materialist semiotics, his own analysis is too fluid to rest simply in agreement. In particular, he is interested in showing that ideology inheres within symbolicity and is not ultimately reducible to a motive rooted only in our materiality. Material conditions will certainly play an important role in the particular direction in which an ideology develops, but the key motive to ideological understanding is rooted in the nature of symbolism as a mode of action. Burke tries to demonstrate the inescapable ideology of language by displaying the fluidity within symbolic designations. In one of his many analytic reversals, he shows how an analysis in terms of a dyslogistic term like "mystification" can become positive when framed in the eulogistic language of "mystery." Burke's point is not to slide easily into a relativism in which no distinctions remain but to show that the terms of a critique are strategically deployed, that rhetoric is better understood as an inducement to action than as an aid to knowledge, and that certain motives which might appear to be located in economic activity inhere in language itself.

Perhaps the most important of these motives is the impulse to construct hierarchies. Burke sees the movement to hierarchy as following from the activity of division, or, in more postmodern terms, from the fact of difference: "The hierarchic principle itself is inevitable in systematic thought. It is embodied in the mere process of growth, which is synonymous with the class divisions of youth and age, stronger and weaker, male and female, or the stages of learning, from apprentice to journeyman to master. But this last hierarchy is as good indication as any of the way in which the 'naturalness' of grades rhetorically reenforces the protection of privilege. Though in its essence purely developmental, the series is readily transformed into rigid social classification, and these interfere with the very process of development that was its reason for being" (141). The question is whether the inevitability of the movement to hierarchy with its correlative development of a system of social privilege is rooted in language, in material practice, or in some combination of the two. For Burke, there is a logical priority of the symbolic over the economic (136). Without denying a role to material practice, Burke is emphatic that a "spirit of hierarchy" moves language from within. This spirit is a secular analogue to original sin (*Language as Symbolic Action*, 15). Ideology then is not simply an apparatus for class control but an inescapable element of linguistic existence: "Ideology cannot be deduced from economic considerations alone. It also derives from man's nature as a 'symbol-using animal.' And since the 'original economic plant' is the human body, with its diverse centrality of its particular nervous system, the theologian's concerns with Eden and the 'fall' come close to the heart of the rhetorical problem. For, behind the theology, there is the perception of generic divisiveness which, being common to all men, is a universal fact about them, prior to any divisiveness caused by social class" (*A Rhetoric of Motives*, 146). Burke goes on to claim that this divisiveness "is the basis of rhetoric. Out of this emerge the motives for linguistic persuasion" (146).

Burke appears to be moving to an insight similar to the recognition by

Bender and Wellbery that rhetoric marks some fundamental aspect of our existence. But while Burke would agree that we are deeply rhetorical, he has arrived at a very different understanding of how this marks our existence. For Bender and Wellbery, with their tie to Nietzsche, language is a limit that we cannot transcend to get at some prelinguistic reality. Hence we are destined to a rootless existence. But for Burke we are not rootless but rooted. Because we are symbolic creatures, prior to any action that we undertake is the fact of division and compulsion to hierarchy. Our rootedness leads to our rottenness. There is something like an imperialist motive within language itself. The primal contradiction or mystification develops from a denial of our division that seeks to cover over divisions by transforming them into graded orders. That is why Burke calls symbol-using animals rotten with perfection (*Language as Symbolic Action*, 16). Rhetoric becomes a strategy for dealing with the mystification of language with its organizing drive to make one out of many. Burke's ironic rhetorical play functions similarly to Socratic refutation — both seek to uncover positions that have been unconsciously assumed by people simply by virtue of their necessary participation in language.

Burke's comment that in our need for hierarchy we are in a secularly analogous position to original sin is helpful in making sense of our rhetorical predicament. Original sin marks an inheritance and locates a fundamental responsibility for the fallenness of the world that each subject is fated to deal with even though that subject did not personally commit the elemental transgression. The concept of fate is equally helpful. It is our fate to misperceive division. This does not mean that we should not try to do justice to division and to unmask past mystifications. Indeed, such activity becomes one of our fundamental responsibilities. What it does mean is that no imaginable social order can be free from this inherent tendency to an injustice begot out of a fundamental blindness that would mystify division by having us see the Other as merely some aspect of ourselves. Whatever role economic considerations may play in the current set of injustices (and Burke believes that economic considerations do figure as major components in current injustice), no economic reorganization can ever do away with injustice, even theoretically. Burke and Socrates see an ongoing need for refutation, for a rhetoric that undoes past rhetorical acts.

There is an important antiutopian strain in Burke's thinking. Like Valesio, he is committed to a linguistic skepticism. Also like Valesio, Burke's concern is retarding the move from linguistic fluidity to linguistic rigidity. Again, both of them seek to avoid an abstract and empty formalism and to develop a rhetoric that is appropriately materialist. And while both are sympathetic to Marxist analysis, both consider its commitment to an economic materialism as creating an ontology that misses the true material force of rhetoric.

Burke's complex relation to Marxist analysis can be seen in his use of the term *class*. For Burke, prior to an economic determination, class is a consequence of language: "We have said that man, as a symbol-using animal, experiences a difference between *this* being and *that* being as a difference between *this kind of* being and *that kind of* being. Here is a *purely dialectical* factor at the very center of realism. Here, implicit in our attitude toward things, is a principle of *classification*. And classification in this linguistic, or formal sense is all-inclusive, 'prior' to classification in the exclusively social sense. The 'invidious' aspects of class arise from the nature of man not as a 'class animal,' but as a 'classifying animal'" (*A Rhetoric of Motives*, 282–83). So class is a formal motive within language. The particular expression of this formal motive will be determined in large part by factors within a social, economic, or political situation, but always infused within any construction of these factors will be the purely formal motive that organizes the material in terms of class. Since this motive is formal, it will be felt as natural. Class will be the natural form in which symbol-using animals see their world. If one combines the formal motive to class with the formal motive to hierarchy, oppression becomes a natural occurrence for symbol-using creatures. It is part of our fallenness — injustice need not be understood as a consequence of particularly evil or misguided persons or groups but as a consequence of language itself.

This insight allows a Burkean analysis a greater flexibility and power than a Marxist analysis. Even the most sophisticated contemporary Marxist cannot avoid a commitment to economic conditions as central to current forms of oppression. Hence race and gender oppression must be explained ultimately as consequences of economic injustice. But while it is clear that there are important relations between economic injustice and race and gender oppression, it seems false and unduly contrived to derive racial and gender injustice from economic considerations. Burke does not need to engage in such derivations, for he can treat economic, racial, and gender classifications as three different forms of the fundamental drives to classify and order that inhere within language. All three forms represent an illicit move from difference to social privilege that Burke sees as a normal occurrence within language and that rhetoric can either bolster or challenge.

Iris Young's *Justice and the Politics of Difference* develops a theory of justice that accords well with Burke's insight into injustice as the formal mystification of class into order. She begins by challenging contemporary discussions that treat justice as a problem of distribution. Such discussions tend to focus on "end-of-state patterns" rather than processes. Also they tend to conceive of injustice as a specific wrong done by one party against another; hence, the correction is directed not at a systematic condition but at a particular aberration. Without denying that discussions of justice do at times involve issues of distribution and instances of particular individual wrong, Young argues that justice is better served if it is conceived of as a structural issue. Building on Foucault's analyses, Young conceives of power less as an individual possession to be used or abused than as a set of relations that structure social and political life. It is this structure of relationships and its consequences for people's lives that create the need for discussions of justice.

This diffused notion of power means that any account of justice will have to deal with ideology. Injustice as a structural problem is tied intimately to the work of ideology, as it is in and through ideology that subjection takes place. The subjects who both perpetuate and suffer injustice are constituted through a mirroring process in which they identify with a central subjecting power. The possibility of justice depends upon the development of a rhetoric capable of addressing such endemic and diffused injustice.

Young conceives of social justice in relation to two values: "(1) developing and exercising one's capacities and expressing one's experience . . . and (2) participating in determining one's action and the conditions of one's action" (*Justice*, 37). In keeping with Young's stress of conceiving goods in terms of doing rather than having, both values are given in the grammatical form of gerunds, emphasizing the active nature of the good. And both values are concerned with self-authorship. In Burke's terms, the possibility of self-authorship is a fundamental value for a symbol-using animal. In terms of this chapter, it is the problem of becoming a rhetor in a world of rhetoricality.

Young's two corresponding instances of injustice, oppression and domination, can be read as specific ways in which self-authorship is preempted. What is especially important about these forms of injustice is that they do not require particular agents. There can be oppression without there being a specific individual oppressor. The order in which power relations are structured in a society may oppress certain people as a consequence of their arrangement without any one party's having intended such oppression. That is the work of ideology. For Burke, this is a recognition of the formal motives to class and hierarchy that exist within language itself. The consequence for both Young and Burke is that injustice is a structural problem, and this requires that it be addressed on that level.

Part of Young's rhetorical task is to make evident this type of injustice. To shift the discussion she introduces the concept of a social group. Oppression and domination are directed against individuals because they are members of a particular social group. The problems of injustice are problems that are generated in the structure of social relations that creates social groups. Young defines a social group as a "collective of persons differentiated from at least one other group by cultural forms, practices, or way of life" (43). Social groups are, in part, a product of rhetoricality — they are socially symbolic constructions. These groups differ from associations in that group membership is not voluntary. Rather than choosing to join a group, one discovers that he or she is a member. There is a sense of "thrownness." The concept of group, then, is a recognition of the fact of positionedness. Equally groups differ from an aggregate because the members of a social group possess a special affinity with one another that is a product of social relations. This shared affinity gives rise to an identity that is reflected in a sense of history and of separateness, and this affinity can lead to distinct modes of reasoning, valuing, and expressing feeling. Finally, groups are fluid; they can come into and go out of existence.

Young distinguishes groups from classes (42). But she has in mind the Marxist notion of class as determined ultimately by economic organization. Burke's notion of class as a linguistic category is, however, in some respects very close to Young's notion of social group. Social groups involve the recognition that someone is a person of this kind rather than of that kind, and that recognition is the kind of identification involved in Burke's notion of class. Further, like Burke's notion of class that in itself does not imply a positive or negative evaluation, Young's notion of social group is descriptive — not all social groups are victims of oppression or domination, but oppression and domination as modes of injustice are directed at people because they are members of certain social groups.

Burke's notion of class, however, is broader than Young's notion of social group. In fact, his notion of class is very close to a general principle of difference. Young's social groups would be one instance of this more general principle of difference. The social dimension of this principle becomes evident in Burke as the formal motives within language push to total explanation. For Burke, inherent in each class distinction is a dialectical impulse to expand the initial distinction to a total description of the world. Such a total explanation is blind to its own partial perspective because it can undo and reformulate any competing perspective's classifications in terms of its own fundamental classes. Within language there is a formal motive to discount Otherness and to retranslate it as mere difference. This process gets one more twist. Since any language is partial, it will finally prove inadequate to rendering the whole world as a scene for action. When a language encounters difficulties with its explanations, two options are available. The language can engage in a dialectical refutation with a competing language with the hope of temporarily discovering a more adequate understanding, or it can develop a scapegoat theory. In such a theory Otherness reemerges not as mere difference but as something foreign and evil — this Otherness is outside the realm of discourse and hence must be dealt with by force or guile. It is this Otherness that provides a formal motive for the move from hierarchy to domination or oppression. Both are instances of a despair at the possibility of public discourse.

Young also argues that social groups are "both an inevitable and a desirable aspect of modern social processes" (47). Burke would again agree and claim that this insight is a recognition of the inherent motive within language of division. One important consequence that follows is that we need to reexamine the ideal of equality, which requires us to disregard group membership and to treat in the abstract each person as theoretically a free and unattached agency. For Young such a view of equality reflects the ideology of impartiality; for Burke, it is a mystification in which an abstract universal characteristic is deployed strategically to direct attention away from difference. In framing the issue as a problem of strategy, a Burkean analysis would argue (and Young would agree) that equality was a strategically important way of engaging the problem of oppression within the historical circumstances in which it arose, but that equality is not an absolute good and it needs to be critically engaged by competing goods, such as difference as a value, if it is not to lapse into a mystification and become an inadvertent obstacle to public discourse and ultimately to justice.

The problem of reconstituting an adequate public discourse, however, goes beyond the problem of recognizing the importance of social groups. Young's critical theory faces the more difficult task of recasting both the goals and the forms of public discussion. According to Young, one consequence of our evolution into a welfare capitalist society has been the effective loss of a discourse that is public. She sees this loss in the shift from regarding people as citizens to regarding them as a client-consumers. In effect, this shift privatizes all interests, and there is no longer a conception of a public. Instead, the central government is conceived of as a collector and dispenser of resources and is addressed only in that capacity. Public discussion is no longer a guide to political policy but rather an extended haggling over resources, in which all parties seek to secure their interests. Welfare capitalism has encouraged the rise of interest groups who, in contrast to social groups, function as a collective representative of private interest. The discourse of interest groups has replaced political discourse. If there is to be an adequate discussion of justice, there must first be a recovery of politics.

Young provides two accounts of politics. In one instance she characterizes it as "the process of struggle and deliberation about such rules and policies [namely, the rules and policies of institutions that produce identifiable consequences for persons], the ends they serve, and the values they embody" (211). In this understanding, politics is a deliberative public contest over the nature of public institutions. Its publicness is a function of its openness (88), and its openness means both that there is genuine access to the debate for those who will be affected by its outcome and that the debate itself is the place and vehicle for reaching the decision. "A politicized public resolves disagreement and makes decisions by listening to one another's claims and reasons, offering questions and objections, and putting forth new formulations and proposals, until a decision can be reached" (73). That is, a politicized public is rhetorical — the rhythmic play and clash of positioned discourse creates a movement that brings the positions into a new alignment that represents a collectively derived conclusion.

Young later expands her sense of politics by adding a characterization of the audience: "Politics must be conceived as a relationship of strangers who do not understand one another in a subjective and immediate sense, relating across time and distance" (234). In what way does politics require strangers? When I first read this passage, I was bothered because it seemed to remove the possibility that political discussion could occur among friends. I am still convinced that it is an exaggeration, a strategic emphasis, but I now read this passage as saying something close to Burke's account of rhetoric. Being a stranger is a consequence of social group or of Burke's notion of class. Politics thus is a mode of addressing social mystification. This mystification follows from the twin motives of division and hierarchy that inhere within language. To be in a group or a Burkean class is to be related to others and at the same time to stand in a relation of mutual mystery. This situation of difference is always threatening to become an antagonism or a hierarchy. Rhetoric is the continual attempt to negotiate mystery without reducing difference. For Burke, the division by social classes is the basis of rhetoric (*A Rhetoric of Motives,* 146), and "rhetoric remains the mode of appeal essential for bridging the conditions of estrangement 'natural' to society" (211). Young's politics by strangers is Burke's rhetoric.

Young's account of politics has another important affinity with rhetoric. In her attempt to develop a nonessentialist definition of difference, she argues that "one is more likely to avoid the dilemma of difference in doing this if the meaning of difference itself becomes a terrain of political struggle" (*Justice,* 169). In Burke's terms, this is to recognize that we are classifying animals before we are class animals and that we need the skills of courtship to translate continuously the mysteries of class without inadvertently structuring them into the order of a hierarchy. Both Young and Burke point to the role of the agon in rhetoric and the primarily comedic goal of rhetorical exchange. Rhetoric embodies a desire to seek agreement through the play of disagreement. The vitality of rhetoric involves a continual achieving and risking of agreement, and this means that rhetoric in order to continue must paradoxically seek difference.

The need to keep difference in play is essential if rhetoric is to continue. This is a formal imperative. It is what keeps rhetoric from being a mere instrumentality that is employed to seek advantage or from simply being an analysis of "the material effects of particular uses of language in particular social conjunctures" (Eagleton, *Walter Benjamin*, 101). Burke argues that "there is, *implicit in language itself*, the act of persuasion; and *implicit in the perpetuating of persuasion* (in persuasion made universal, pure, hence paradigmatic or formal) *there is the need of 'interference.'* For a persuasion that succeeds, dies. To go on eternally (as a form does) it could not be directed merely toward attainable advantages" (*A Rhetoric of Motives,* 274). Young's concerns with the ideology of equality and community reflect a similar recognition that the collapse or assimilation of difference would not be a political triumph but would signal the end of political existence. In terms of my argument, the need for refutation follows, in part, from the need of persuasion to remain vital.

Young sees as a well-intentioned error the current recovery of community as an alternative to the bureaucratic order of the capitalist welfare state. The trouble with community as an ideal is that it wishes to reduce heterogeneity and multiplicity to unity. It seeks only persuasion and not refutation. For Young, community exemplifies the logic of a metaphysics of presence, and "whether expressed as shared subjectivity or common consciousness, on the one hand, or as relations of mutuality and reciprocity, the ideal of community denies, devalues, or represses the ontological difference of subjects, and seeks to dissolve social inexhaustibility into the comfort of a self-enclosed whole" (*Justice,* 230). Community would not only mean the loss of social groups but finally it would entail the implosion of the subject, as the multiple, interwoven, contrasting tensions that constitute a subject by their continual play were reduced to the fixity of an achieved identity. In the many becoming the one, they would cease to be many and hence the one would be not an integration but a homogenization that destroyed an essential tension.

There is a further problem with community. Could any community do justice to the heterogeneity of interests and needs, or would its unity be purchased at the cost of excluding some interests and needs that could not be reconciled with others? Would the unity of a community finally depend upon the exclusion of some? If one acknowledges the possibility that all needs and interests cannot be reconciled, then community leads inevitably to hierarchy and to normative transvaluing of difference. Such transvaluing inevitably follows the paths of power, and this means that the unity of community is procured at the sacrifice of the interests, values, and identities of those with less power. However well intentioned, assimilation cannot help being imperialistic. That is, injustice becomes a fundamental requirement for community to be.

In place of community as a political ideal, Young would put the democratic city. Her ideal politics would be a politics of urbanity. The flux, energy, diversity, and creativity of the city would be the qualities of her ideal polis. Young lists four virtues of city life: (1) social differentiation without exclusion, (2) variety, (3) eroticism, and (4) publicity (*Justice*, 238–40). Three of these political virtues — social differentiation, variety, and publicity — seem straightforward, but Young's account of eroticism is more troubling, and it suggests a deeper problem that inheres in stressing difference exclusively.

Young locates the erotic as a "wide sense of an attraction to the other, the pleasure and excitement of being drawn out of one's secure routine to encounter the novel, strange and surprising" (239). She sees the erotic as the obverse of the communal, for it places the discovery of difference in the place of the security of identity. Her examples of erotic experience are aesthetic pleasures of encountering Otherness. The city is a collection of sights, sounds, tastes, textures that offer "delights and surprises." Absent from these examples are abiding human relationships. The risks and pleasures of eros seem to have nothing to do with commitments to other human beings, with approaches to intimacy in which the self is risked. Young seems to offer a self who is an enclosed and atomic being rather than a creature who can be moved by and can need Others. Young's eros seems almost to be a form of consumerism; she seems to imagine the city as an inexhaustible marketplace. Without denying the pleasures of such a marketplace, I want to argue that eros and its risk to identity manifest themselves not only as an infinite sampling of Otherness but also as, in Plato's *Phaedrus,* a force compelling a kind of exclusive attention. Young misses the play of difference and identity made possible by eros by overemphasizing the pleasures of difference. Put another way, eros is a site of the mysterious paradox of identity within difference, and its occurrence makes community a more complicated political problem.

The political dimensions of the problem of eros and community inhere in the very activity of persuasion. For the Greeks, the goddess Peitho was a handmaiden to the goddess Aphrodite. Eros was both a motive to and a source of persuasion. Hence when Kenneth Burke worked up a modern account of rhetoric, he connected persuasion, identification, and courtship. If difference was a source of rhetoric, community, in the form of identification, was one of its goals, and the way to achieve community was through courtship. Burke argues that identity and difference are interwoven: "In pure identification there would be no strife. Likewise, there would be no strife in absolute separateness, since opponents can join battle only through a mediatory ground that makes their communication possible, thus provides the first condition necessary for their exchange of blows. But put identification and division ambiguously together, so that you cannot know for certain just where one ends and the other begins, and you have the characteristic invitation to rhetoric" (*A Rhetoric of Motives*, 25).

The invitation to rhetoric is the continual need to adjust to the demands of unity and separateness, identity and difference, persuasion and refutation. The urgency of maintaining difference follows, as I mentioned earlier, from Burke's notion that division and hierarchy are motives that inhere within language. The need for identity arises out of the situation of difference. If political discourse is to proceed by a process of public deliberation, then part of that process involves making interests, values, desires, and needs count. Even if participants differ, they will talk only if they understand a common interest in working for a solution. Political discourse is supposed to have consequences in the world, and this requires that it be capable of staking its participants so that their endorsing a conclusion means that they are willing to act on it. Eros would then signify that Others are not merely curiosities for us but are people for whom we should care. Identification is crucial for such investment. Burke claims: "You persuade a man only insofar as you can talk his language by speech, gesture, tonality, order, image, attitude, idea, *identifying* your ways with his" (*A Rhetoric of Motives*, 55). Identification does not mean collapsing one's ways into the ways of another, but it means that a genuine persuasion requires the speaker to establish a common ground with the audience. If the rhetor is interested in persuasion and not manipulation (a rhetoric that embraced manipulation would violate Young's condition of openness by entailing that participants not merely stylize their positions but disguise them), then the rhetor is obligated to try to see the audience's interests as the audience sees them. The rhetor does not have to agree with or accept the interests, but he or she must understand how these interests speak to the audience. This means that a rhetor must attempt, at least imaginatively, to occupy the position of the audience. To persuade an audience a speaker must show how a given position is in the audience's best interest.

The rhetorical interchange in which positioned speakers try to do justice to both their own positions and those of the other parties moves to resolution by identifying a course of action that seems best for that particular assembly. The rhetorical interchange makes the contending parties into a community because they have for that particular situation formed a common identity by their public deliberation. They have not achieved the kind of community that Young opposes — there is no metaphysical discovery of a shared essence, or of some sort of enduring reciprocity. But amid the continuing differences there is also a sharing that unites the parties. Such a community is unquestionably provisional, but it is nonetheless a community in that it is publicly determined through a deliberative process. To the extent that it is seriously committed to the deliberative process, it will be continually exploring and redefining itself, not because it is moving closer to its true nature or telos but because the accidents of history will continually demand creative responses, and these responses themselves will have an impact on future possibilities.

For Burke, the art of community is the art of courtship. He considers courtship as "the use of suasive devices for the transcending of social estrangement" (*A Rhetoric of Motives,* 208). To court someone is to acknowledge both the worth and the mystery of that individual. To conceive of political discourse on the model of courtship is to grant the dignity and power that Young has shown is necessary for a just social order. It is to recognize oneself as a petitioner. The petition is not for the addressed party to grant a private favor but for the addressed party to cooperate in the creation of a public that does not currently exist. It is an invitation to join in deliberation.

But if the erotic urge to identification is necessary for politics, it is also potentially disruptive. Experienced as a deep attraction to another particular individual, eros can be both a compelling force for a social relationship and at the same time a major solvent of social bonds, as the exclusivity of the relationship renders others at best marginal and at worst as potential threats to the relationship. Within the erotic there is always the pull toward anarchy.

Perhaps nowhere is this shown better than in Plato's *Symposium.* The speeches dialectically attempt to place the erotic urge to private and exclusive relationships in an appropriate public context. Just how disordering eros can be is seen in the chaos that is threatening to undo the dialogue. Equally the creativity arising from eros can be seen in the dialogue's continually rescuing itself from impending chaos by flexibly reordering itself. The dialogue's structure argues that the ordering/disordering play of eros cannot be ordered into a final stability. Socrates' attempt to dialectically transcend the erotic by transforming the private/political tension into a hierarchical ascent from the somatic to the philosophic is undercut by the action within the dialogue. Socrates' retelling of Diotima's speech looks like a conclusion that addresses and places the concerns of the preceding speeches into a hierarchy that philosophically unifies and transcends their plurality, but at the end of his speech the dialogue is wrenched from its apparent resolution by an unplanned intrusion from the larger world. Politics, embodied in the unbridled energy of Alcibiades, simply obliterates the moment of calm philosophic ecstasy produced by Socrates' speech on love. The erotic, deeply entangled with the political, has forced its way back into the dialogue, and its entrance has disordered the pattern of rational ascent emplotted in the progress of the various speeches on love.

Alcibiades' praise of the practice of Socrates replaces, redirects, and reconcludes the earlier discursive competition in praise of eros. But Alcibiades' praise of Socrates stresses his unique and almost inhuman quality, and by the end of the speech it is not clear whether, given Socrates' magnificence and his uniqueness, the human situation is philosophically comic or tragic. The dialogue leaves as undecidable whether our lives are best understood in terms of the community of comedy or the isolation (the emphatic assertion of difference) of tragedy. One thing that is clear is that a Socratic transcendence into philosophy is not available to us. The drama of the dialogue makes this clear as Socrates' audience proves incapable of sustaining the rigors of philosophic conversation and finally succumbs to sleep just as Socrates is explaining how a truly philosophic character could write both comedies and tragedies.

The structure of the dialogue's dramatic action suggests that Socrates' political education of his audience resides not in a dialectical recovery of a philosophic position but in that position's being contested by practice. Diotima's speech gives over to Alcibiades' speech; a philosophic account of eros is superseded by an account of an erotic philosophic life. Dramatically, theory is challenged by practice, philosophy by politics. On the one hand, Alcibiades, as student of Socrates, gives the speech. This raises the immediate question of the efficacy of a Socratic education for the state, for if ever there were a deeply problematic and disruptive political personality, it was surely Alcibiades. On the other hand, the praise of Socrates' life can be seen to follow from and modify the theory of philosophic eros that Socrates delivers in Diotima's speech. Socrates, the character, has not followed a path of transcendence in pursuit of an ecstatic and spiritualized eros that would lead to the isolation of a philosophic mysticism that his speech seems to endorse but instead has practiced a politics of sorts both in his dialectical education of young men and in his modeling of nonexploitative relationships. The dialogue becomes an inescapable play of identity and difference as any attempt to produce a final hierarchy between theory and practice is undermined by the dialectic between theme and action within the dialogue.

What, then, does the dialogue teach, and how does it allow for an understanding of the place of eros within a community? Its education is simultaneously theoretical and practical. Its play of theory and practice forces a critical activity on the reader. Reading the dialogue does not lead to recognizing a position but entangles the reader in attempting to understand the dialogue's position. Volosinov suggests that such activity is at the heart of language:

The basic task of understanding does not at all amount to recognizing the linguistic form used by the speaker as the familiar, "that very same," form, the way we distinctly recognize, for instance, a signal that we have not quite become used to or a form in a language that we do not know very well. No, the task of understanding does not basically amount to recognizing the form used, but rather to understanding it in a particular, concrete context, to understanding its meaning in a particular utterance, i.e., it amounts to understanding its novelty and not to recognizing its identity.

In other words, the understander, belonging to the same language community, also is attuned to the linguistic form not as a fixed, self-identical signal, but as a changeable and adaptable sign. (*Marxism,* 68)

Socratic education is a continual exercise and reflection upon the condition of being linguistically situated, of being a creature who uses language. Such education is political because it seeks to keep us alive to rhetoric. Hence, Socrates' claim in the *Gorgias* that he is the sole practitioner of politics is intended to be both nonironic and yet provoking. What it seeks to provoke or invite is refutation. The material of his politics is the current ideological understanding, whatever it happens to be.

Socrates' rhetoric works to recover and display cultural strains that have been mystified as they have been taken over uncritically in the ordinary practices and assumptions of those he interrogates. In a Burkean sense, Socrates attempts to provoke the class struggle — he is one of Gramsci's organic intellectuals who both has a class function of criticism and attempts to heighten awareness of the mystified classes so that his interrogatees are brought to question that the world is how they see it. Socrates' refutations are paradigmatic rhetorical acts in that they are calculated and contrived uses of language designed to undo understandings that have acquired the status of being natural and essential in their self-evidence. His discourse is ideological criticism that not only challenges a particular ideological position but also makes ideology as an inherent condition within discourse available to reflect on and act within. His practice is a self-conscious artifice that calls attention to its own contrivance but which cannot be reduced to or dismissed as manipulation. In an ideological world, rhetoric as refutation becomes a mode of empowerment, as it returns the apparently natural back into a province for human action. Socrates' challenge to an unreflective understanding is the rhetorical creation of a tear in the fabric of ideology. Socrates' initial questions are the teasing out of a seam from which he can unravel the whole cloth of ideological understanding. In the give-and-take of refutation Socrates recovers the possibility of a genuine political discourse.

Refutation is the process of bringing to consciousness that which has become mystified because it has come to structure the self-evident categories of normal recognition. Refutation is the deliberate attempt to undo persuasion and to recover difference, not simply for the sake of the play of difference nor for the production of some ultimate transcendence of all difference, but for the purpose of exploring what differences can be brought into productive community. Eros is the motive that underlies refutation. As Socrates claims, the purpose of a rhetoric is to attack the ones whom one loves. As Burke would argue, it is an instance of pure persuasion, of persuasion shorn of advantage seeking. In a delicious irony, pure persuasion requires refutation. However much such eros longs for union, it also longs for difference; the activity and object of eros are always in tension. A rhetorical eros is thus double: the refuting rhetor is in love both with the form of persuasion (with persuasion as a form) and with the particular audience. Paradoxically, the rhetor seeks both union with and separation from this audience. Refutation is a political discourse that seeks to provoke the play of difference. It marks a kind of discourse that is seriously political but not immediately practical. That is, it is not so much concerned with the resolution of an immediate and pressing practical issue as it is in generating a stable political ēthos. This ēthos is in service of a good that is only available in a political situation — namely the erotic pleasure of political discussion. It is this joy that is missing and maybe not possible in Young's urbane but noncommunal meetings.

The urbane encounters of strangers are occupied with the problems of mediating particular differences. The goods that they offer are different in kind from the goods produced by the play of communal refutation. These goods of communal refutation are goods that arise out of philosophic reflection on one's political situation. Such reflection can take place only in the company of others with whom one feels a shared situation because the risk undertaken is potentially very great. Obviously some such discussion takes place in Young's social groups, and she values it as important to a sense of self-worth for the members of the group. But such discussion can occur outside social groups. One place to look for such a community is in the acknowledgments of Young's own book. She mentions both organizations and individuals who contributed to the development of her ideas. I want to claim that some of these discussions were communal. They were not communal in the senses that trouble Young but communal in the sense that persons who cared about each other shared in common the discussion of a set of issues and that the people were not all members of the same social group. In the discussions was an ongoing stability, an identity of sorts, that merits the name community. It is primarily in the presence of such communities that the goods of philosophic reflection about political life are available. For the genuine risks that such discussion requires one must have a confidence in the others involved that allows one to risk an understanding of a current identity in an open-ended play of difference.

Without such communities even an idealized urbanity will be politically deficient, for an important good will be missing. Young herself acknowledges the value of such communities (although she resists her insight by setting off the term in quotation marks): "By 'city life' I mean a form of social relations which I define as the being together of strangers. In the city persons and groups interact within spaces and institutions they all experience themselves as belonging to, but without those interactions dissolving into a unity or commonness. City life is composed of clusters of people with affinities — families, social group networks, voluntary associations, neighborhood networks, a vast array of small 'communities' " (*Justice*, 237). It is not surprising that Young summarizes her list of intermediate organizations as communities. She feels the need to add quotation marks because the notion of community against which she has been defining her social ideal of urbanity is singular, overarching, and imperialistic. But a community need not take that form. The equation of a community with the public that troubles Young can be replaced by a notion of community that is not essentialist. Community can be conceived of as a pluralized, temporal, provisional form of sharing. Community in this sense marks a public space in which people feel secure enough that they are willing to put in refutative play their identities as a way of perceiving and taking responsibility for their own ideological constitution. The value of community lies in its providing a shared situation or activity in which identity can be risked and possibility reconstituted; such a community must seek and value difference as a condition for its functioning as a community.

Unlike membership in a social group, communal membership is not socially defined, and that is part of its special value. One does not have a choice whether to be or not to be a member of a social group. There is a logically prior act of social classification. One's political tasks then become to engage in a creative and ongoing discovery of the possibilities for human achievement available to members of the group and to attempt, when necessary, to ensure that group membership does not entail oppression or domination by others. In the "thrownness" of a social group, there is a social fate. Community is different. One always has the option of leaving a community. However a community begins (and its origins are heterogeneous), a community continues as a community only to the extent that its members persist in conceiving themselves as having situations genuinely in common and in believing that their shared commonness matters. Rather than having a fixed identity, a community is continually adjusting or changing identity as circumstances change. The role of rhetoric is to bring such change under deliberation, to make the constitution of a community a product more of choice than of chance. The goods of such a community are possible only if difference is respected, for the goal of such a community is to explore new richness for all its members, so that the members voluntarily continue to desire to explore these goods in common.

The continued vitality of these pluralized, temporal, and provisional communities is determined in the ongoing contest between ideology and rhetoric. If, as Althusser claims, ideology explains the lost origin of subjectivity, in that one becomes a subject by subjecting oneself to a prior absolute subject, then ideology remains an inherent threat to any community. Young analyzes the particular current ideological form of this threat as the denial of difference in the postulation of the abstracted self of an idealized equality. The consequence of this ideology is the particular form of subjection that leads to the denial and denigration of those people who are members of nondominant social groups. As Burke claims, the ideological move is the disguising of difference by an overstressing of some universal motive or characteristic.

In a wonderfully lucid essay, Robert Wess analyzes recent developments in the Marxist understanding of ideology and suggests the need to move beyond a discussion of ideology to the formulation of a Marxist rhetoric ("Notes Toward"). He centers his discussion on the work of Althusser and the responses which that work provoked. Wess argues that Althusser opened an important new direction for Marxist thought when he introduced the concept of "structural causality." In particular, this concept allowed Marxist analyses to move beyond the mechanical model of base and superstructure and created the possibilities for a more complicated account of social determination. Wess argues further that Althusser was never quite able to rid himself of a bias to frame issues of ideology in terms of an epistemology, and this frame inevitably reintroduced the old models of causality that Althusser had sought to reconceive. The most unfortunate consequence of Althusser's inability to move beyond a conception of ideology in epistemological terms is that his account of the subject remains stuck in a determinism that withholds any agency from the individual subject. Wess proposes to correct this shortcoming by conceiving the subject as a "signifying practice." A subject "is constituted in the field of signifying practices involved in the multiple alignments and divisions characteristic of any complex social formation" ("Notes Toward," 144). Such a subject would be both determined and capable of determination. Further, because the field of signifying practices embodies the identities and divisions within a culture, the subject would exist in a fluid state that reflected and embodied the tensions, histories, and contradictions of the larger culture or cultures. These tensions would be a source of freedom that was neither absolute, for it is historically determined, nor abstract, for it is very much the product of specific relationships and understandings. Wess sees this subject as possessing relative autonomy, and because of this autonomy it is open to persuasion. Rhetoric thus becomes essential to a Marxist understanding because it offers an important resource for directing class struggle.

Terry Eagleton and Frank Lentricchia are two critics within the Marxist tradition who have attempted to develop explicit connections between a Marxist criticism and rhetoric. Both critics claim that criticism is political, and they recognize that such a starting point aligns them with the rhetorical tradition. For both critics, rhetoric is the discipline that has sought to investigate the relations of discourse to power and to develop ways of using discourse to achieve and deal with power. Eagleton goes so far as to claim that "historical materialism is itself a 'rhetoric,' in the fundamental sense that it is unthinkable outside those suasive interests which, through trope and figure, project the world in a certain controvertible (falsifiable) way" (*Walter Benjamin,* 112). But the relationship between rhetoric and historical materialism is a bit more complicated for Eagleton, and, indeed, a paragraph later he is already moving to a standard outside rhetoric with which to determine the direction and shape of rhetoric. He calls the standard "justice," but it is a justice that shares a transdiscursive stability with Plato's (if Plato is not read as a rhetor) concept of justice. Without its being explicitly argued, historical materialism is functioning again analogously to the idealist tradition as the guarantee of an essence that precedes practice.

Eagleton's move to a transdiscursive point of reference is his attempt to accommodate the deconstructive insight of the inescapable figurativeness of language yet to avoid the apparently debilitating consequence that discourse is trapped in a process of futile repetition, in a mere perpetual play of difference. He wishes to both acknowledge what Bender and Wellbery called rhetoricality and yet retain the prior function of rhetoric. He wants to establish the way in which a critic through the pursuit of rhetoric can conceive and challenge the effects of the currently dominant discourses. In his turn to rhetoric, he seeks to discover not merely a subject but an agent, not merely a condition of language but an agency. This is an admirable attempt, and one whose goal I share, although I have a different way of trying to achieve this goal.

Lentricchia is also moved to such an attempt. *Criticism and Social Change* is an extended effort to use Burke's work on rhetoric as a resource with which to think through the challenges that deconstruction offers to a criticism that argues for the necessity of political, and, in Lentricchia's case, revolutionary criticism. His book provides an excellent place to explore the possibilities for a Marxist rhetoric, and in particular to get clear on the relation of rhetoric to a sophisticated historical materialism that has arisen from the work of Gramsci and Althusser.

Lentricchia develops a friendly and nuanced reading of Burke that is sympathetic to Burke's project, that attempts to do justice to the complexity of the project, but that also engages critically with Burke. Reading Burke serves Lentricchia as an occasion to reflect on the general problem of the relation of the intellectual to political action: "In its most general intention, this book is about culture, intellectuals, the authority and power of intellectuals—how intellectuals in their work in and on culture, involve themselves in the political work of social change and social conservation" (6). Even more, his reading of Burke allows Lentricchia to obtain purchase on his own role as a teacher and writer. Through his attention to Burke, Lentricchia can reflect upon his situation—the situation of a person concerned with justice and social change whose work is primarily the production of reading and writing—and discover the particular possibilities and forms of action available to someone whose worksite is a university. The university as workplace has become a problem for him precisely because of the emergence of rhetoricality—the specific form that he feels he must contest is de Manian deconstruction. Like Eagleton, he would like to move beyond the recognition of rhetoricality to the recovery of a contemporary rhetoric. His abiding concern is to recover the possibility for a revolutionary criticism.

History is the key critical term for Lentricchia as he reads Burke. Rather than give central place to Burke's theory of dramatism, which Lentricchia believes is uncomfortably essentialist in its leaning, he argues that Burke's most important contribution arises from his understanding of history: "Dramatism is Burke's official program, the name he has given to his system. *Attitudes Toward History,* the title of his fifth volume, gives us access to what I think is a more fundamental Burkean activity—one that contemporary literary intellectuals have consistently shied away from: a process of formulating, exploring, making, forays—in so many words, the various acts of reading and writing" (55). For Lentricchia, Burke's attitude toward history expresses itself most pronouncedly in his resistance to systematic thought with its tendency toward essentialism.

But if the historical attitude is triumphant in Burke, it is never uncontested. Burke is never purely historical, and this, at times, appears to distress Lentricchia. He cautions against reading Burke as someone who is firmly a nonfoundationalist thinker: "These two strategies [a historical essentialism and a historical commitment to heterogeneity] of interpretation are at work in Burke's books from the beginning. And though in his two interpretations of interpretation he clearly elevates one over the other, neither such valorization nor the mere fact of high-level hermeneutic self-consciousness permits him to master the essentializing impulse in his writing" (59–60). Lentricchia's Burke is a writer wavering between synchronic and diachronic explanation. In its claim to explain human action in terms of five essential motives that are necessary for any account of action, Burke's dramatism developed a formalism that shares much with structuralism. But as Lentricchia is quick to acknowledge, a Burkean formalism is never a simple affair, and the constant and scrupulous play of Burke's thought deconstructs his key terms. For example, as Burke pushes against the term *action,* its independence and the implied autonomy of the subject of an action become problematic, as Burke argues that actions require motives but that motives can inhere in a situation, and thus the actor is acted upon by the situation. What appears to be a paradigmatic instance of the expression of will of a subject turns out to be inherently undecidable — boundaries between scene, purpose, act, agent, and agency are permeable and mobile.

The restlessness of Burke's mind leads him to return inevitably to a historical attitude. Burke's grasp of what he calls "the muddle" allows him to see the heterogeneity and instability within any understanding. These two factors are crucial for Burke's undoing the deterministic understanding that often haunts structuralist thought and developing instead the grounds for an antihegemonic discourse. Lentricchia argues that Burke's recognition of the inherent openness and fluidity of language allows key terms of a hegemonic discourse to be appropriated and strategically redeployed against those who are the agents of domination and oppression: "Another sign of the structural instability is that, unlike real estate, the language of privilege and authority is not private property of any person or class. The linguistic symbols of authority, like 'rights' and 'freedom,' are appropriable — they can be seized by a collective and turned against those who last appropriated them in order to dispossess yet earlier appropriators. . . . This process, described by Burke as 'the stealing back and forth of symbols,' is the beginning of any hegemonic education and rule. The point is clear: no hegemonic condition is fatally fixed because no hegemonic condition rests on natural or God-given authority" (79).

But if Burke's work manages to develop an account of the instability and fluidity of language, Lentricchia sees Burke as coming dangerously close to foundering on another essentialism. This danger is best understood if the structure/history pair is replaced by another and more fundamental opposition: the aesthetic versus the political, form versus power. If Burke's definition of form, the instrument for generating and then satisfying an appetite in an audience, looks rhetorical in its understanding of the particularity and temporality of form, Lentricchia believes that Burke's rhetorical understanding is undermined by his subscription to a traditional notion of audience that has maintained there is a transhistorical and universal subjectivity characteristic of people as such. Lentricchia traces this understanding as far back as Aristotle's *Poetics,* and he sees its particular expression in the contrast of modes of representation: on the one hand, poetry and philosophy, which are universal in that they represent necessary or highly probable types of characters; on the other, history, which must deal with characters in their localness and particularity. Lentricchia argues that this distinction inaugurates the tradition in which the aesthetic is set against the political. Lentricchia believes further that Burke falls victim to this tradition because he accepts a Kantian anthropology that postulates a potentially shareable (universalizable) subjectivity as characteristic of the aesthetic and that relegates the particular, interested (politically constituted), and historical to the nonaesthetic — whatever its appeal, it is not formal. What Lentricchia objects to is the idea of a nonhistorical subject.

Lentricchia treats this aspect of Burke's work as an inability to break free from the powerful attractions of modernist aesthetic, with its desire to flee the contamination of political life. It is Burke's residual modernist aesthetic, with its understanding of the inherent appeal of form, that threatens to undo the political force of his rhetoric: "By bringing a potentially dangerous rhetorical theory into the fold of modernist thought, by enclosing rhetoric, which historically never had any fear of the so-called *outside* of literature (Yeats' 'externality') in the symbolist sanctuary of subjectivity itself, Burke becomes modernism's cagiest champion. That, I believe, is the strongest political case that can be made against the work of Kenneth Burke. With friends like Burke, rhetoric needs no enemies. Not content to leave the rhetorical and the political to men of will, modernism in Burke would overreach to aestheticize rhetoric itself" (93). The charge, in effect, is that Burke in his recontaining any emergent politics within the aesthetic is becoming de Man.

Lentricchia's exculpation of Burke from this charge involves a return to the term *action.* Burke's aesthetic considerations must be read in the context of his larger frame: the human being is a creature who acts symbolically. Lentricchia reinscribes a modernist elevation of subjectivity as an aesthetic principle by reading it in Marxist terms. On such terms, the valuing of subjectivity becomes a mode of resistance — in particular, a resistance to a reduction of all value to use value. Read this way, modernism can be understood as a historical phenomenon that manifests a critical spirit of rejection. Habermas argues that the resistance of modernism began in art (*Legitimation Crisis,* 78). However, Lentricchia argues that because such rejection did not follow through on its impulse to a full action that would have broadened its contest with capitalism and its degraded aesthetics, it doomed itself, as an act, to self-trivialization. What Burke's stress about the nature of action would have and could have taught the modernists is that their rejection should not have been directed against use per se, for anything can be appropriated for use, but rather it should have challenged an appropriation of language, experience, art, and the processes and products of representation that diminished freedom and reenforced hegemonic categories. If modernists had heeded the insights of the shifts and instabilities that Burke located in his essential terms for dramatism, they would have realized that a retreat to a pure anything was logically impossible and could at best be a delusion.

What the focus on action uncovers is the inherent connection between form and ideology. Lentricchia argues that Burke's understanding of the fluid, unstable, and overdetermined nature of symbolicity leads him to realize that the politics will always appropriate form, that power seeks form both to express and secure itself. Ideology designates this motive within power, and Burke's rhetorical/aesthetic definition of form both explains the operation of ideology and opens up the possibility for an antihegemonic discourse:

> This power is born in the linkage of form with ideology in its two psychosocial domains: ideology, in other words, both as overt "culture," however "upside down" — a common, normalizing and socializing space, a conscious nodus of beliefs, attitudes, and judgments — and as the sort of unconscious that Althusser called a "lived relation to the world." In neither sense is ideology deterministic and homogeneous, free from the stresses of internal contradiction, which means that in the combined sense of the term, the possibility of struggle and resistance is never in advance eliminated. In the moment of linkage, form would seize and direct ideological substance, transform it into power over the subject-audience; it would turn our ideology, in both senses, over to a disciplinary intention that would utilize and subjugate us. The aesthetic moment of linkage, then, is the manipulative moment at which the subject-audience is submitted ("subjected") to the productive force of ideology. And the act of linking form with ideology is what inserts the writer into the process of sociopolitical education and activates us as his political "subjects." So defined, form is "correct" — Burke, an aesthetic pragmatist, means that it works — when it controls as it gratifies the needs it arouses. Form can both gratify and control those needs, however, only if it properly engages and represents what readers consider desirable and only if the readers' overt ideologies are in some way "respected." Only then can those ideologies be manipulated in the engagement with form so that the power effect touched off by that engagement will engender two ultimate political effects of aesthetic power: the domination effect or its contrary, the effect of resistance. (103–4)

The potential conflict between political and aesthetic impulses, then, is finally not, for Lentricchia, a conflict because the nature of action implies a hierarchy of motives. In place of essential definition, the fluidity of the symbolic situation permits relative definitions, and the relation between power and form is then defined as agency and instrument. Any autonomous motive within form will always and necessarily be transformed or reformed to meet a logically prior concern of the structured power relations in which the formal impulse arises.

What Lentricchia has done, in effect, is to undo the very heterogeneity that makes antihegemonic discourse possible. In his recontainment of the aesthetic within the political, he has assumed a translatability between motives and he has also posited the code, the inherently political motive within a situation that is its most central element, that directs the flow of the translation. Put somewhat differently, he has tamed Burke's potential heretical deviance by rewriting a tension as a hierarchy. He has rescued a political Burke at the cost of an aesthetic Burke, but such a rescue represents a way of refusing Burke's important political insight and equally displaces the necessary centrality of rhetoric for Burke. And it needs to be kept in mind that simple binary oppositions never remain so simple for Burke. Burke's concern with form differs from the modernist tradition of aesthetics that begins with Kant's definition of the aesthetic as a judgment recognizing the quality of purposiveness without purpose in a particular beautiful object. For Kant, aesthetics and rhetoric are opposed categories: aesthetics deals with disinterested judgments; rhetoric is decidedly interested and manipulative, using stylistic appeal to distort or undermine the operations of reason. But for Burke rhetoric is valued precisely because it is a stylized appeal, and aesthetics for him is simply an instance of pure appeal. The formalism of his aesthetics is grounded in the rhetoricity of language, and it is, in effect, pure rhetoricity. Such a possibility would seem contradictory to Kant.

Form, for Kant, is the judgment rendered when the faculties of the understanding and imagination are brought into an uncoerced harmony. Kant's aesthetics deals with judgments that are abstracted from the contents of the object that is judged. This is another way of saying that they are disinterested, and in their disinterestedness they mark off a special field called aesthetics. In contrast, Burke's aesthetics are grounded not in the harmonious relations of certain human faculties, but in the arousal and satisfaction of appetite (*Counterstatement,* 31). His aesthetics are derived from the rhetoric of symbolicity, as the questions that he asks about form are questions about the way in which the artist aroused and satisfied desire. A pure or formal motive in Burke, then, does not place aesthetics as a disinterested concern over against, say, the political as an interested concern; rather, the formal motive registers the pressure that inheres in any situation in which a symbol-using creature acts. The most rhetorical of situations contain formalist motives; hence, the entelechial drive toward pure persuasion requires rhetoric to intervene, complicate, and finally undermine the closure of a particular persuasion if the possibility of further persuasion is to remain. The drive to pure persuasion entails refutation. The move to purity entails the suspicion of purity, as a formal matter. This brings Burke very close to Socrates. Form both seeks perfection, and, as a matter of self-preservation, seeks to undo perfection.

The move to hierarchy is a formal consideration for Burke, but he is deeply aware of the political consequences of this formal motive. Burke's appreciation of the aesthetics of symbolicity necessarily returns him to politics, and his appreciation of imperialism as a formal motive within language leads him to look for ways to interfere with this motive. His insight into the formal dynamics of symbolicity makes him cautious about the potential tyranny that inheres within any act of language.

While Lentricchia has done an excellent job of showing Burke's continual effort to situate writing within the political context, he has slighted Burke's equally urgent and insistent skepticism. Comedy is a strategically chosen goal for Burke because he is so attuned to the possibilities of tragedy that do not merely follow from the particular and historical developments within culture but reside within the formal motives of language itself. Lentricchia sees the problem as resolving or negotiating between two discordant impulses within Burke: "This is the inevitable question: How are we to put together, in a coherent theory, the social implications of Burke's fable of indolent school children with the radically individualist/anarchist/Emersonian impulse of his version of democracy, a celebration of the antiprogrammatic, isolated, self-reliant, discordant voice that refuses to enter into the chorus of collectivity?" (109). But why is there a need for a final coherence, for a theoretical coherence? Certainly, when dealing with a thinker who values perspective by incongruity and who continually delights in reversing and "joycing" assumed ways of discoursing, a pursuit of coherence might be a mistaken effort.[3] Rather than seeing a final incoherence as troublesome, as a weakness to be tolerated or an apparent inconsistency to be reasoned away, it might be better and truer to Burke's spirit to treat his incoherence as a healthy disrespect for a deadening and unrhetorical totalizing that theory is prone to adopt. He may well be Whitman's compatriot who rejoices in his own contradiction as a sign of his richness and vitality. The lack of a comfortable coherence may be the necessary consequence of seeing symbolicity as fluid, overdetermined, and unstable, and it may be the necessary form of a rhetoric committed to a radical indeterminacy and immediacy that believes that if we are driven by needs for freedom and justice, neither freedom nor justice is self-evident but must be continually rediscovered or reinvented in an ongoing rhetorical process.

To understand why the tension between form and power, between the aesthetic and the political, should be played with rather than resolved into a hierarchy, it is necessary to return to Burke's concept of situation. If a situation is a source of motives and hence a constitutive element in any action, then that action will manifest the character of the situation. In particular, if a situation contains a heterogeneity of motives — that is, if a situation does not have a preexistent identity but is, in part, a product of rhetorical construction, then the heterogeneity may well make itself felt in terms of a collection of motives that do not form a coherent whole. There will be motives that we characterize as political; some others may be theological, physiological, or even aesthetic. The rhetorical art will involve a search for commonplaces and it will seek strategies that will allow an identity to emerge by appropriately addressing the various motives. This means that a translation of sorts is possible, a provisional identification can be effected, but this translation and identification need not follow any particular course. This is especially true if key terms are themselves fluid, unstable, and overdetermined. The path of the contest will depend on a variety of factors from the material circumstances of the situation to the genius of the individual rhetors.

Burke's description of his project as symbolic action emphasizes that there are at least two central sources of motives: one from the constraints of action — itself not a logically stable concept — and one from the constraints of symbolism. To argue for a reading that subsumes form under politics is to reduce the duality of Burke's conception to a monism. The symbolic, the aesthetic, the formal are, however, for Burke, as essential to his project as the practical and, by extension, the political. Further, a formal appeal need not commit Burke to assume a universal subjectivity in the audience but only to assume that in a situation in which one set of motives is a consequence of sheer symbolicity, this set of motives will have an effect that cannot be reduced to the material circumstances in which they occur. There is, for example, a formal appeal in most athletic contests simply to execute the conventional moves of that game as well as possible. This formal appeal exists independent of the particular material conditions under which a game is played. Undoubtedly the material conditions will play a role. For example, if one team or player is far ahead in a game, that team or player may stop playing hard in order to avoid humiliating an opponent. In such a case, the formal motive would be violated to some degree. Equally, a team that has no chance of winning might still play hard simply out of respect for the formal possibilities of the game. Or, to borrow Burke's example, a scientist might well feel compelled (as a consequence of the motive inhering the particular mathematical language to bring it to completion) to finish a set of calculations, even though those calculations predicted disaster for the world. That a formal motive never exists in isolation and that a formal motive can never be an exclusive motive does not alter the fact that the formal motive is as elemental and nonreducible as the political motive.

In a friendly but rigorous analysis of Burke's dramatism, Fredric Jameson worries whether the form/power dialectic is as fully developed by Burke as it should be. In particular, Jameson is concerned with the short shrift given "purpose" in *A Grammar of Motives*. He argues that Burke has restricted the term "purpose" so severely that it can permit discussion of a work only in terms of formal strategies and cannot accommodate an analysis of a work in terms of ideology that enable it to be and in which consequently it participates:

> We must therefore take the passage just quoted as evidence for a discouraging reversal in Burke's critical strategy: his conception of literature as a symbolic act, which began as a powerful incitement to the study of a text's mode of activity in the general cultural and social world beyond it, now proves to have slipped back over the line and, passing from the generalized sense of the word Purpose to its immanent and strategic, restricted sense, now to furnish aid and comfort to those who want to limit our work to texts whose autonomy has been carefully secured in advance, all the blackout curtains drawn before the lights are turned back on. ("The Symbolic Inference," 83)

Jameson thus believes that Burke's symbolic analyses lead finally to a "strategy of containment" (82).

Burke has responded with passion to Jameson's reading of him. Unfortunately for my purposes, Burke was concerned primarily with dealing with what he considered to be Jameson's slighting of his discussion of ideology. Burke spends little time on the issue of the scope of purpose. This is to be regretted, for I feel, like Jameson, that Burke's account of purpose is too brief and needs to be rounded out.

Jameson in his response to Burke's response ends by trying to clarify the differences between them: "Here, too, then, we return to one of the central motifs of the exchange between Burke and myself; and here, too, I am content to remain within my initial diagnosis. Burke's too immediate celebration of the free creativity of human language (in its broadest symbol-making sense) overleaps the whole dimension of our (nonnatural) determination by transindividual historical forces. This realm of alienation, which is to history what the unconscious is to individual experience, is, however, a space which will not ignore us, however we may prefer to ignore it" ("Ideology and Symbolic Action," 422). Jameson turns to the binary of the free creativity of language versus determination by the transindividual forces of history. But this is not an either/or dichotomy. Burke's importance for rhetoric arises from his stressing that both elements of the dichotomy are present for symbolicity. His commitment is to heterogeneity. This heterogeneity does not do away with Jameson's rightful concern with ideology, nor does it reduce ideology to false consciousness. Rather, it locates both language and history as sources of ideology and suggests that ideology will always be a problem for symbolic creatures.

If Lentricchia can show, as he does, that form can be appropriated for political ends, it is just as easy to do a Burkean reversal and to show that politics can be appropriated for formal ends. Burke engages in a somewhat analogous project in his essay "Poetics in Particular; Language in General" (in *Language as Symbolic Action*), when he defends Poe's account of his theory of composition by deriving the subject matter of an elegiac lyric from the demands of the elegiac form.

This emphasis on the elemental nature of form as a motive is not an attempt to argue that Lentricchia's effort to see Burke's serious contribution to literary study as the recovery of criticism as a political activity is wrong. I think that he is right about that, but also that Burke's account is more complicated because it is more rhetorical than Lentricchia is willing to concede.

Part of the reason that Lentricchia does not see a more rhetorical Burke is Lentricchia's own commitment to justifying a revolutionary rhetoric in an academic climate in which the flourishing of traditional and deconstructive criticism seems to have aligned teaching and scholarship in the humanities with the conservative function of validating and perpetuating certain political attitudes that either directly or indirectly promote injustice. Lentricchia feels the urgency of justifying revolutionary criticism: "But—and this is the question—can we choose which critical power we will align ourselves with? Can we choose to align ourselves within an emergent rather than a residual culture? With the future, rather than with the past? The choice of the emergent—or, more dramatically yet, of a rupturing culture—is always the choice of the revolutionary. But what if that choice is never open to us as such, in any innocent way, what then of revolution?" (*Criticism and Social Change*, 117). Such a question does not trouble Burke—not because Burke is unsympathetic to revolutionary change (Lentricchia does a good job of showing how sympathetic Burke is), but because the question is asked from a position that a rhetor never occupies. Lentricchia's posing the question has made the choice of acting a choice of defending an absolute beginning, for the urgency of the question arises because the questioner feels outside of the situation and is seeking an entry.

The situation of Lentricchia's revolutionary critic is reminiscent of Sartre's modernist writer. But to start from a symbolic creature so alienated is to misconceive how situation works for Burke. Lentricchia himself makes a similar point when he discusses how Burke deconstructed the concept of action to show how only God was capable of acting or of having action as a philosophic quandary because creatures like ourselves could never get in a position where we were not always already acted on by our situations. Burke would not privilege revolutionary criticism as a goal because he knows that our situations will act on us in a variety of ways and that we will adopt, for strategic reasons, a variety of responses. Sometimes we will seek to rupture a tradition; sometimes we will seek to encourage it. If someone wants a rhetor to answer in advance the question under what conditions, then, would we or should we be revolutionary, a Burkean would have to reply that it depends. To enter all situations with the determination to be revolutionary is to be rotten with revolutionary perfection, and such rottenness will ultimately undermine the revolutionary aspirations to freedom and justice.

Lentricchia's need to justify revolutionary criticism may also indicate a certain lack of faith in the revolutionary project. He fears that the forces in play within the established literary institutions are so strong and pervasive that one must ask "how to avoid being professionally constituted as a conservative" (*Criticism and Social Change*, 119). Burke shows no such anxiety — possibly because he never occupied a position as centered as Lentricchia's, but more importantly, I think, because he understands the issue not as achieving a particular political destination but as the more mundane problem of how to trip up himself and others when they stray, either advertently or inadvertently, from the rhetorical insight that our position is and must be always intermediate, somewhere in the muddle, and assume that they have discovered knowledge. This is the concern that Valesio shares when he argues that ideology is decayed rhetoric. The desire for a position outside of the rhetorical flux can allow one some sense of confidence in the perspective discovered, but it is precisely such confidence that rhetoric denies. Rhetoric has the potential to be revolutionary not because it seeks to be politically revolutionary but because it seeks to be sensitive to the instability and flux within a situation. It has the potential to turn the ideological defenses that Michael Ryan analyzes against themselves by exploiting the materials within ideology that suggest its precarious stability. When a particular project is committed to perpetuating a fixed point of view, to seeking hegemony, a Burkean rhetoric will see that project as undermining its revolutionary possibility, despite its explicit commitment to accomplish a revolutionary end.

Again, Lentricchia, who so astutely recognizes that Burke's rhetoric decentered the subject, tends to smuggle the centered subject back in when he asks his questions about whether it is possible for a writer who is inextricably a product of a tradition to "*be* a power and, in however modest a fashion, to *make* alternative history" (138). The problem with this question is that it is really a request for knowledge: is there a way that I can act so that I know that I am not contributing to but opposing a tradition? This assumes a notion of the writer as subject that is far more coherent than Burke's rhetoric will allow. If, as Lentricchia showed, action is not an autonomous and independent element, neither is the agent as subject. The subject as writer is moved within a situation, a situation which penetrates and permeates without fully defining his or her subjectivity. The upshot is that one is never in a position to know. It is not a question of knowledge or the possibility of action dependent upon knowledge; rather, it is a matter of recognizing that one is necessarily and multiply implicated in any situation, and the issue is not how to act but how to react, how to respond, and then how to respond again. This is Burke's essentialism: to see us as symbolic creatures is to see us as creatures who possess an ethical and political responsibility because of our participation in symbolicity. Such an essentialism is not epistemological or, to use Burke's term, scientistic, but political, ethical, and hortatory.

Such a reading of Burke accords well with much of what Lentricchia says. It lends support to Burke's claim, which Lentricchia seems to endorse, that rhetoric is irreducible (*Criticism and Social Change,* 146), and it explains the inherent link between rhetoric and politics. Only a conception of rhetoric that treats formal motives within language as possessing the same imperatives as the material motives within history can do justice to the role of class in rhetoric. The movement to difference and hierarchy that arises within symbolicity is what makes a skeptical stance toward hierarchy and class an essential task for rhetoric. Only an understanding of the importance of form for rhetoric will justify Lentricchia's claim: "To exist socially is to be rhetorically aligned. It is the function of the intellectual as critical rhetor to uncover, bring into light, and probe all such alignments. That is part of the work of ideological analysis. Only when such political work of identification is understood, when our various and devious 'identities' are put on the table, when our involvements are brought thus bluntly before us, in all their repugnant detail: only then can the rhetorical work of transformation realistically begin" (149).

Calling the work of rhetoric transformation underlines the role of form within rhetoric. What rhetoric transforms is the present operation of past persuasions (that we call ideology) into a receptive tentativeness that can allow us to explore the shape or form of our positionedness and to reform those positions to better deal with the injustice that is uncovered. Rhetoric might well be labeled the politics of form, and, as the rhetorical tradition has emphasized, persuasion, in contrast to force and guile, is the only genuine form of political life. And as the skeptical tradition has added, such persuasion must always be contested. Inhering within the political transformation effected by persuasion is the danger that the transformation will seek to perfect itself. Such transformation in its move to perfection will inevitably constitute a new hierarchy that obfuscates class even as it reenforces class relations within its hierarchy. A skeptical rhetor, then, must always be on the lookout for what a particular transformation includes and excludes, and he or she will need equally to explore the hierarchy within the inclusion. This is rhetoric's need to recognize the fact of ideology at the very time that it contests particular ideological operations. The obfuscation of class as a consequence of ideology necessitates refutation. If we transform ourselves, in part, by the strategic choices of our languages, a rhetorical skepticism must maintain a vigilance so that these transformations are seen as strategies for action and not as discoveries of truth. In this sense, transformation designates a necessarily ongoing and open-ended process. Only in this way can we negotiate the ideologies that we inherit and in which we must live.

Ideological analysis, then, becomes for Burke the investigation of the ways in which we have been formed directly and indirectly through symbolicity. There is both a direct and indirect use of discourse and discursive institutions to secure and maintain power, as Althusser and others have observed. And there is an inherent tendency within symbolicity itself to degenerate into fixed and hierarchical ideological understandings, as Valesio, Burke and others have shown. The postmodern recovery of rhetoricality as a feature of language or as a condition of our existence as language-using creatures is a discovery of the inescapable ideological basis of our identities. As Eagleton and Lentricchia have understood, our resource for dealing with rhetoricality is rhetoric. To contend with the inherent tendencies to ideological constitution, those who value community must develop a new rhetoric that preserves a sense of difference, challenges the unreflective but constitutive classifications and hierarchies following from the formal motives within language itself, and restores a sense of agency to both persons and groups. Such a rhetoric would contest the imperialism within any language as a formal system. This formal tendency takes its particular direction from material circumstances and from the synthetic products of the formal motives of language and materialist history in which ideological classifications of social privilege and their justifications mask formal and materialist motives by characterizing them as natural.

A new rhetoric would do well to borrow one additional insight from Marxist accounts of ideology. Both Althusser and Volosinov treat ideology as a site of class struggle (Althusser, *For Marx*, 140; Volosinov, *Marxism*, 23). Volosinov sees in the multiaccentuality of the sign an inherent dialectic that keeps language vital and, in moments of crisis, available for revolutionary change. He treats the struggle over the meaning of a sign as a class combat in which a dominant class seeks to fix the meaning of a sign and thereby to secure its hold on how reality is perceived. Volosinov does not argue that such an intention need be consciously held by any person or group; rather, it seems to be a motive inhering in the very exercise of power. Establishing a fixed meaning for a sign extends control over a heterogeneity that is always threatening a dominant class by undoing and redirecting the very signs through which it creates the subjectivity of its subjects. Volosinov's understanding of the sign as the site of class struggle is very close to Burke's "the stealing back and forth of symbols." Both see the concern for meaning as a struggle for power following from the fluidity and overdeterminedness of language that seeks to characterize the world as a particular kind of place that necessitates a particular kind of action.

Where Volosinov and Burke differ is in their account of the origins of ideology. Volosinov traces them back ultimately to economic conditions, while Burke argues for both a material and formal origin for ideology. This difference is over how to conceive class. Should class be an economic term, or should it designate a property within language itself? The advantage of choosing Burke's approach is that it allows for a heterogeneity of classes and hence for the possibility of heterogeneous sources of domination and oppression. Further, it enriches the class struggle by increasing the fluidity of class itself, and it allows rhetoric a way of dealing with forms of domination and oppression that do not yet exist but that may evolve in response to the accidents of history. We could call the new rhetoric, grounded in Burke's understanding of the material and formal origins of social discourse, a rhetoric of class.

This new rhetoric of class would share with the classical rhetorical tradition a belief that the agon was essential for the ongoing activity of rendering the indeterminate determinate, and it would equally share with classical skepticism about rhetoric the belief that such rhetorical understanding has a tendency to reify into truths that, in turn, must be undone. This new rhetoric would turn to the classical tradition to understand the strategies available in the contests over how to define a situation for purposes of action. And without needing to postulate particular agents having consciously designed the current understandings, the new rhetoric of class could use the strategies of classical skepticism as critical devices to expose the exercises and deformations of power operating as a set of structured relationships. The foe for a new rhetoric would be the unreflective but insistent operations of power that it would challenge by showing their rhetoricality. A rhetoric of class would be a rhetoric of refutation.

A rhetoric of class would seek both to debunk particular forms of mystification and to provide resources for all people constituted by ideology to listen to and talk with those positioned variously on one of the many social hierarchies. This rhetoric of class would acknowledge the "rhetoricality" that the contemporary rediscovery of rhetoric has argued marks a fundamental aspect of our existence, but it would also draw from rhetorical tradition with its stress on the agency of the rhetor. And from the skeptical challenge to that tradition it would argue that injustice remains the abiding problem for rhetoric. A rhetoric of class would emphasize continually the need for transformation — for new symbolic strategies to open us to the consequences of class and its symbolic encodings. And such a rhetoric would caution us against reading any transformation as a final placement of class. For a rhetoric of class, the rhetorical tradition would have more than a historical interest. It would represent an understanding of the world as a site of agency. Such an understanding would not involve an uncritical taking over of earlier models of rhetoric and assuming anachronistically their relevance in dramatically changed discursive circumstances; rather, such an understanding would engage the rhetorical tradition rhetorically. It would, as rhetorical skeptics in antiquity did, contest the tradition from its new location and in this contest it would seek to discover what it shares with the work of Plato, Aristotle, Gorgias, Cicero, and others. It would seek to refute the dominant tradition and the skeptical challenge to that tradition with the intent that the tradition and its skeptical challenge would, in turn, refute it. Such refutation would allow a new rhetoric to challenge and undo its own postmodernity by recovering the postmodern as simply another position, as one rhetorical option, and it would prevent the inherent tendency to translate imaginative rewritings of history as if they were epistemological discoveries. Finally, such refutation would call into question its own conclusions as constructions and thus provide a continual critique of its own ideology. In Socratic fashion it would not reject understandings by recovering their ideological basis but rather convert them into resources, into renewed topoi that would permit the ongoing reevaluation that is necessary for any person, group, or community that aspires to do justice in the worlds that it inherits and to which it must respond.

Notes

1. Refutation: Rhetoric as a Philosophical Problem

1. What I am calling the classical thread of rhetorical skepticism should not be confused with the philosophical skepticism of antiquity that began in Plato's Academy in the third century BCE. Such philosophic skepticism is rooted in a concern with the reliability of sense perception as a guide to reality, but a rhetorical skepticism arises from a concern for the ways in which language as both a formal system and as a historically developed mode of action promotes injustice.

2. See Simon Goldhill, "The Great Dionysia and Civic Ideology"; Oddone Longo, "The Theatre of the *Polis*"; and John J. Winkler, "The Ephebes' Song: *Tragoidia* and *Polis*"; all three essays are in *Nothing to Do with Dionysos? Athenian Drama in its Social Context,* edited by John J. Winkler and Froma I. Zeitlin. Also see Josiah Ober's *Mass and Elite in Democratic Athens: Rhetoric, Ideology and the Power of the People.*

3. Two recent works that help correct our understanding of Plato's theory of rhetoric are Seth Benardete's *The Rhetoric of Morality and Philosophy: Plato's Gorgias and Phaedrus,* and C. Jan Swearingen's *Rhetoric and Irony: Western Literacy and Western Lies.*

4. Hugh H. Benson's *Essays on the Philosophy of Socrates* provides a good introduction to recent work on Socrates, and it also has an excellent bibliography of current scholarship on Socrates.

5. Meyer himself does not appear to appreciate fully the interrogative thrust of the elenchus (*Rhetoric, Language, and Reason,* 69–70).

6. Meyer believes that Plato shares Aristotle's feeling about rhetoric and that they

differ primarily in that Aristotle can distinguish dialectic from science (*Rhetoric, Language, and Reason,* 63). But to read Plato this way is to collapse the Plato that some see as the author of the middle and late dialogues with the decidedly nonmetaphysical Socrates of the early dialogues. If one takes his or her cue from this Socrates, Plato's entire corpus looks far more tentative and rhetorical.

7. For an example of the diffusion of power and its operation on subjects, see Foucault, *Discipline and Punish: The Birth of a Prison,* 135–225.

8. See Berlin, "Revisionary History: The Dialectical Method," 136–37.

9. I have not discussed Aeschylus's tragedies, although clearly rhetoric as a theme is developed in the *Oresteia.* Originally I had read that trilogy as a dramatic celebration of a community's move from the violence of retribution that was required by the ties of blood to the discursive agon in which a contest of words displaced violence and contributed to the stability of a more or less just resolution. After completing my study of tragedy, I came across J. Peter Euben's *The Tragedy of Political Theory: The Road Not Taken.* His chapter on Aeschylus has convinced me that the *Oresteia* is considerably more ambivalent toward the stability of its conclusion, and that Aeschylus, even if more optimistic than either Sophocles or Euripides, shares in their skepticism toward rhetoric and its role in a democracy.

10. In "A Reply to my Critics," Habermas provides a concise account of communicative action: "The theory of communicative action is based on an analysis of the use of language oriented to reaching an understanding. With the concept of communicative action, the action co-ordinating, binding effect of the offers made in speech-acts moves to the centre. Through these offers, the participants in a communication establish interpersonal relations through intersubjective recognition of criticizable validity-claims" (269). It is not surprising, given this definition, that Habermas lacks sympathy for the aims and methods of rhetoric: "This [namely, an action orientation] is not even true in the standard case of the rhetorician who wants to convince the audience through means of persuasion. The rhetorician knows, at least in retrospect, when and how he or she wanted to manipulate the public. The Janus face of rhetoric, which is mirrored in the ambiguous meaning of the word 'persuasion', arises from the perspective of the addressees, not from that of the speaker" ("A Reply to my Critics," 266–67). Habermas's model requires the parties in a conversation to bind themselves through a set of mutual obligations. The tragedians question whether such mutuality is possible, given the unequal distribution of power that occurs in a society.

11. See, for example, "Remarks on the Concept of Communicative Action," 153–54.

12. Recent historical studies of rhetoric have begun to challenge the domination by Aristotle. C. Jan Swearingen's *Rhetoric and Irony* establishes the case for a Platonic rhetoric. Takis Poulakos's collection, *Rethinking the History of Rhetoric: Multidisciplinary Essays on the Rhetorical Tradition,* shows some of the ways in which the tradition is being rewritten.

2. *In Defense of Plato's* Gorgias

1. Edwin Black and David S. Kaufer are two rhetorical theorists who have developed interesting and nonreductive readings of Plato's positive contributions to rhetorical the-

ory. Both Black and Kaufer see *Gorgias,* however, as the more negative of the two dialogues on rhetoric and as intended primarily to point out abuses in current rhetorical practice. They believe that *Phaedrus* represents Plato's mature and more fully worked-out theory of rhetoric (Black, "Plato's View," 368; Kaufer, "The Influence," 73). Although I find much to agree with in both of their readings, their accounts of *Gorgias* do not provide a sufficient defense of the dialogue, and, in particular, the authors do not deal with the problems of Plato's apparent historical distortions in the Pericles section.

The other recent major discussion of Plato on rhetoric and writing is Jacques Derrida's "Plato's Pharmacy," which focuses more on *Phaedrus* and says little explicitly about *Gorgias.*

2. All citations of *Gorgias* refer to Terence Irwin's translation.

3. Mary Ellen Waithe in her discussion of Aspasia makes a similar claim: to take Plato's use of history seriously does not require that we assume the historical accuracy of every detail but demands that we ask how the events are used in the dialogue ("Aspasia of Miletus," 79).

4. Even so, John Stuart Mill shows that Plato's comments can be telling when they are assumed to be directed against the intentional corruption of a practice ("Grote's Plato," 400–403).

5. Barbara Herrnstein Smith makes a parallel argument for the possibility of serious discussion of value within critical theory without the need for a standard outside history (see *Contingencies,* 150–84, esp. 175).

3. Persuasion and Refutation: Meno's Challenge

1. For a recent discussion of Plato's understanding of writing that also emphasizes his interest in rhetoric, see Swearingen, *Rhetoric and Irony,* chapter 2, "Rhetor and Eiron: Plato's Defense of Dialogue," esp. 62–64.

2. See Derrida's "Plato's Pharmacy."

3. See de Man's *Allegories of Reading;* also see de Man's "Rhetoric of Temporality" for his analysis of Derrida's misreading of Rousseau, another literary philosopher.

4. Thus Plato's writing escapes Rorty's binary of edifying and serious philosophers.

5. For evidence that refutations, when successful, make the refuted gentle, see, for example, *Theatetus* 210c, *Sophist* 230b–c, *Republic* 354a, and *Phaedo* 83a.

6. Most scholars consider the early dialogues as the ones displaying refutation. However, refutation is also a key concern of the later dialogue, *Sophist,* in which Socrates wonders whether the eleatic stranger is a refuting philosopher. See Rosen's *Plato's Sophist* for an account of the dialogue as an extended trial of Socratic philosophy.

7. Part of the importance and fruitfulness of Vlastos's account of the elenchus can be seen in the number of essays that his recent writing on the elenchus has provoked. See for example, Richard Kraut, "Comments on Gregory Vlastos"; Hugh H. Benson, "Meno, the Slave Boy, and the *Elenchos,*" "A Note on Eristic and Socratic Elenchus," "The Priority of Definition and the Socratic *Elenchos,*" "The Problem of the Elenchus Reconsidered"; Richard McKim, "Shame and Truth in Plato's *Gorgias*"; Roland M. Polansky, "Professor Vlastos's Analysis of Socratic Elenchus"; and Thomas C. Brickhouse and Nicholas D. Smith, "Socrates' Elenchic Mission," "Vlastos on the Elenchus." Vlastos's essay and

book, along with Richard Robinson's work, are the scholarship to which one must turn when beginning to explore Plato and refutation.

8. Brickhouse and Smith's excellent essay points out that scholars have neglected the elenchus's role in examining lives. They note Kenneth Seeskin's *Dialogue and Discovery: A Study in Socratic Method* as one work that does take Socrates' examination of lives seriously. James Boyd White's essay on *Gorgias* in *When Words Lose Their Meaning* should be added as another work that explores refutation as an activity directed against people and not propositions.

9. The issue between the constructivists and the nonconstructivists is whether the elenchus is capable of providing some sort of knowledge. The constructivists argue that Socrates seeks to use his refutations not only to debunk an interlocutor's unexamined beliefs but to make some positive progress toward a moral knowledge. The nonconstructivists see Socrates' refutations as a skeptical enterprise that cannot move beyond the negative achievement of bringing the positions that it challenges into doubt. Vlastos is a good example of a constructivist position; Benson is a representative of a nonconstructivist line of interpretation.

10. See the discussion by Sternfeld and Zyskind of the opening of *Meno* for a good account of how the setting of the dialogue introduces key issues (*Plato's Meno*, 20).

11. For a fuller account of the distinction between eristic and dialectical refutation, see Benson, "A Note on Eristic and Socratic Elenchus."

12. For the importance of understanding the character whom the dialogue addresses, see Rosen's account of the role of Glaucon in the *Republic* (*Quarrel*, 110–14).

13. For an account of misology as a serious danger and hence an important concern for a Platonic philosophy, see David Roochnik, *The Tragedy of Reason*, especially 68–69.

14. As J. Peter Euben argues: "This subject of how language and culture constitute each other is an implicit concern of virtually all Platonic dialogues and the explicit preoccupation of several" (*The Tragedy of Political Theory*, 210).

4. Sophocles' Philoctetes *and the Crisis of Rhetoric*

1. As Charles Segal notes, "by resorting to the *deus ex machina* Sophocles shows his recognition of this moral dilemma" (*Tragedy and Civilization*, 356). Segal goes on to argue that the appearance of Herakles signals the presence of the divine within human events, and that in Sophocles' work such a presence is "always disturbing" and "never fully circumscribed by human terms." Since my focus is on rhetoric, I am less interested in Herakles' divinity than in the shift in his mode of discourse and its implications for the invention of a more adequate rhetoric.

2. For a discussion of the fifth century's understanding of Odysseus and Achilles as representing contrasting worlds of thought and feeling, see Knox, *Heroic Temper*, 121–22.

3. Whitman (*Sophocles*, 178) and Bowra (*Sophoclean Tragedy*, 286–87) see parallels between the situation enacted in the *Philoctetes* and the political climate of Athens in 409 BCE.

4. Odysseus's exact understanding of the prophecy cannot finally be known. Some critics, like White (*Herakles' Bow*, 19–20) and Nussbaum ("Consequences," 35), assume Odysseus incapable of grasping fully the prophecy and capable only of reading it as a

demand to get the bow. Knox believes that Odysseus has understood the prophecy fully but relates it to Neoptolemos in the incomplete way that he does because Odysseus plans to capture the bow and ultimately the glory for himself (*Heroic Temper,* 126–29). Although I don't agree with Knox's reading of Odysseus, he does offer good reasons for assuming that Odysseus is not simply incapable of seeing what the prophecy means. What is clear is that Sophocles has made Odysseus a character who is inaccessible to the audience's understanding. He is a strategic character, so we are not supposed to ever be certain what his true and unfeigned understanding is, for he can never be met except in one of his guises.

5. Charles Segal explains how Greek society needs to be reordered if the prophecy is to be fulfilled (*Tragedy and Civilization,* 328).

6. For a good discussion of the wound as a paradigm for the "arbitrary-seeming circumstances that stamp a human life with its peculiar destiny," see Segal, *Tragedy and Civilization,* 318.

7. Rose, *Sons of the Gods,* 282; Segal, *Tragedy and Civilization,* 307–8; and Vernant and Vidal-Naquet, *Myth and Tragedy,* 163–64.

8. Notice how the categories that will prove ethically problematic for White are, in fact, central considerations in normal rhetorical practice.

9. Bowra, for example, grants that something had to be done about Philoctetes, but he reads Odysseus's justification as a feeble attempt to account for his actions. Bowra mentions the particular obligations that soldiers felt toward each other (*Sophoclean Tragedy,* 290–91). Whitman seems to accept Odysseus's account that Philoctetes' constant cries made sacrifice impossible (*Sophocles,* 174).

10. Rose has some interesting comments on the anti-idealistic materialism of sophistic thought and its relation to relativism (*Sons of the Gods,* 273–79).

11. See, for example, Knox, *Heroic Temper,* 137.

12. See also Rose, *Sons of the Gods;* Vernant and Vidal-Naquet, *Myth and Tragedy;* and especially *Nothing To Do with Dionysos?* edited by Winkler and Zeitlin.

13. For a good account of Philoctetes' imaginative population of the island, see Winnington-Ingram, *Sophocles,* 291–92.

14. See especially Nussbaum, *Fragility,* part 1, chapter 3.

15. The label is White's (*Herakles' Bow,* 15). But there is disagreement over how to read the chorus, and Winnington-Ingram, for example, sees it as a collection of "sympathetic realists," (*Sophocles,* 293).

16. See Winnington-Ingram, *Sophocles,* 299; Podlecki, "The Power of the Word," 244–45; and Segal, *Tragedy and Civilization,* 333–40.

17. Segal, *Tragedy and Civilization,* 337; Whitman, *Sophocles,* 187; and Wilson, *The Wound and the Bow,* 232.

18. For a discussion of the language of hunting see Segal, *Tragedy and Civilization,* 300–301; and Winnington-Ingram, *Sophocles,* 287.

5. Violence and Rhetoric in Euripides' Hecuba

1. Aristophanes saw Euripides' use of rhetoric as functioning politically and pedagogically. In *Frogs* the character Euripides justifies the practice of his art and hence his right to return from the underworld by arguing that his tragedies educated the Athenians

in public speaking (905–9). For a discussion of rhetoric in Euripides' drama, see Conacher, *Euripidean Drama,* 156, note 25; Finley, *Three Essays,* 6–7; Kerferd, *The Sophistic Movement,* 169–71; Lesky, *Greek Tragedy,* 133–37; G. Murray, *Euripides and His Age,* 23–27; R. L. Murray, "Persuasion in Euripides"; Solmsen, *Intellectual Experiments,* 49–62: and Thomson, *Euripides and the Attic Orators.*

2. For a similar argument that force enslaves both the powerful and the disempowered, see Simone Weil, "The *Iliad,* or the Poem of Force."

3. In its dramatization of the failure of discourse, *Hecuba* examines how a secure audience can permit a speaker a great deal of freedom because the audience knows beforehand that nothing the speaker says can compel it to act. The grant of freedom is made because the speaker is powerless; however, the grant of freedom allows the audience to conceive of itself as generous or benevolent. A similar kind of self-flattery can manifest itself in our congratulations and defenses of the First Amendment. We allow freedom of speech in part because we know that we don't have to listen. To say this is not to argue against the First Amendment but to argue that the First Amendment has not settled the issue of freedom of speech. Rather, if the First Amendment is to be a meaningful protection of speech, it must impose an ethical obligation on us as audience to critically examine the ways in which our own security deafens us to the voices of those at the margin.

4. Hannah Arendt's *Eichmann in Jerusalem* (subtitled *A Report on the Banality of Evil*) is the most influential modern study of this problem.

5. A. M. Dale has argued that Euripides' characters are not psychological portraits but rhetorical constructions in which an ethos is displayed strategically (*Euripides: Alcestis,* xxvii–xxviii).

6. That a Euripidean drama produced in 425 or 424 BCE would be located in a rhetorically debased universe is not surprising, and several scholars have noted the parallels between the situation depicted in *Hecuba* and the recent and future actions of Athens (Arrowsmith, *Hecuba,* 5; Nussbaum, *Fragility,* 404). James Boyd White has argued that Thucydides' *History* charts the drift into incoherence of Athens's public discourse during this period (*When Words,* 59–92).

7. All quotations are from William Arrowsmith's translation of *Hecuba.*

8. In *Iphigenia in Aulis* Clytaemnestra is equally unsuccessful despite the power of her arguments to prevent the sacrifice of her daughter.

9. For a discussion of the powerlessness of words in a world of bia, see Weil, "The *Iliad,* or the Poem of Force," 328.

10. For an alternative reading of the play that sees Polyxena as the ethical center of the play, see Conacher, *Euripidean Drama,* 154–55.

11. Polyxena is typical of the Euripidean innocent whose integrity depends on having avoided an extended contact with a corrupt world. She resembles Iphigenia in *Iphigenia in Aulis* and, to some degree, Hippolytus.

12. Like Antigone's plea for Polyneices' burial, Hecuba's arguments on behalf on Polydorus are grounded on a law that is prior to any particular political consideration.

13. For a discussion of the ethical compromise of this supplication, see Conacher, *Euripidean Drama,* 162.

14. See Arendt's discussion of bureaucracy as the rule of nobody, *Eichmann in Jerusalem,* 289.

15. In *Iphigenia in Aulis* Agamemnon is led to a similar insight (449–50).

16. For a discussion of freedom and slavery in *Hecuba,* see Daitz, "Concepts of Freedom," 217–26.

17. Buxton (*Persuasion in Greek Tragedy,* 182) and Lusching ("Euripides' *Hecabe,*" 233) claim that Polymestor loses because he is now weak, but their readings fail to do justice to the force of Hecuba's argument, and they fail to observe that Agamemnon's judgment is finally accountable to the Greek army.

18. The arrogance of power is a mark of such ethically disreputable characters in Euripides as Jason or Coprus in *The Heracleidae.*

19. For an opposing view, see Conacher (*Euripidean Drama,* 163) and Grube (*The Drama of Euripides,* 227), who do not believe that Hecuba's final speech is a good work of rhetoric.

20. Pietro Pucci makes a similar point about the relationship between false character and bad speech in *Medea* (*The Violence of Pity,* 107–8).

21. Adkins argues that the play's originality lies in its suggestion that motive is relevant in the assessment of Polymestor's innocence or guilt ("Basic Greek Values," 207–9). I would extend this argument and claim that it is Euripides' exploration of forensic rhetoric that opens up the issue of motive.

22. Her situation is parallel to Orestes in *Electra,* 1244.

23. Hecuba's pleas echo similar claims by Clytaemnestra, Orestes, Antigone, and other characters from Greek tragedy who justify their actions as demanded by justice.

24. For a good discussion of the relation of *Hecuba* to the institution of justice in the *Oresteia,* see Nussbaum, *Fragility,* 416.

25. The theme of touching another is important to Euripides. See Nussbaum, *Fragility,* 409; Zuntz, *The Political Plays,* 9–10. Individual plays that deal with the issue of touching are: *Andromache,* 420; *Medea,* 1323–60; *Suppliant Women,* 288.

26. For a discussion of how force turns those who use or endure it into stone, see Weil, "The *Iliad,* or the Poem of Force," 328.

27. See the opening section of Cicero's *De Inventione* (7) for an account of the myth of a rhetor founding a society through an eloquence that persuades private power to submit to a public interest.

Part II Introduction: Briefly Rethinking the Fate of Rhetoric

1. See, for example, Jarratt, *Rereading the Sophists: Classical Rhetoric Refigured.*

2. Bender and Wellbery may have overestimated the demise of nationalism. Benedict Anderson makes a compelling argument for the continuing importance of nationalism. See *Imaginary Communities.*

3. Neither is mentioned, for example, in Bizzell and Herzberg's *The Rhetorical Tradition: Readings from Classical Times to the Present* or treated as theoretically consequential in Conley's *Rhetoric in the European Tradition.*

4. For a discussion of the fundamental incoherence at the heart of the Enlightenment's effort to reconcile freedom and reason, see Rosen's *Hermeneutics as Politics,* especially 3–49.

5. For an extended account of Sartre's centrality to contemporary social thought, see Poster's *Existential Marxism in Postwar France: From Sartre to Althusser,* which charts Sartre's decades-long effort to reconcile his existential insights with a theory of social praxis.

6. For a discussion of rhetoric and politeness in the eighteenth century, see Potkay, *The Fate of Eloquence in the Age of Hume,* especially chapter 2.

7. If this claim seems a little grandiose, it is helpful to again turn to Tanner and his discussion of Austen's *Persuasion* as, in part, an exploration of what, following Barthes, he labels the "sociolect": the fragmenting of society into separate discourse communities, he observes, "could portend a society which is no longer truly a society in any meaningful sense but rather an aggregate of contiguous but non-communicating groups or just families (or even just individuals), with no *real* connections, no overall coherence, no single structure, binding them together. Separate 'commonwealths' with neither 'wealth' nor anything much else held in 'common': 'Dictate-orships' perhaps (Jane Austen's words carry a weight of possible irony) of one kind or another. To a large extent this is our 'society' today" (*Jane Austen,* 221).

8. See Poster, *Critical Theory and Poststructuralism: In Search of a Context,* 36.

9. See Rosen, *Hermeneutics as Politics,* 3–49. Also see Meyer, *Rhetoric, Language, and Reason,* 37–38.

10. For a discussion of Sartre as a universal intellectual, see Poster, *Critical Theory and Poststructuralism: In Search of a Context,* especially, 36–38.

6. Persuasion: *Jane Austen's Philosophical Rhetoric*

1. Auerbach, "O Brave New World," 116; and Johnson, *Jane Austen,* 148.

2. See Tave, *Some Words,* 259.

3. Butler, *Jane Austen and the War of Ideas,* 275.

4. For a reading that sees *Persuasion* as sharing the anti-Kantian insights of contemporary philosophers who argue for a consequentialist ethics, see Hopkins, "Moral Luck and Judgment in Jane Austen's *Persuasion.*"

5. For an account of the problem of the overestimation of autonomy, see Poovey, *The Proper Lady,* 199.

6. For an account that argues for Anne's vision as objective, see Crane, "A Serious Comedy," 185.

7. For an account that considers this section an artistic failure, see Harding, "The Dexterity of a Practised Writer."

8. For a discussion on indirection and women in Austen, see Poovey, *The Proper Lady,* esp. 192, and for a specific discussion of indirection in *Persuasion,* see Duckworth, *The Improvement of the Estate,* 205–6.

7. *Refuting Sartre: Modernism's Equivocation on the Reader*

1. See Romain Laufer, "Rhetoric and Politics," for an analysis of the crisis of legitimacy besetting liberal politics.

2. Although I will differ with her reading of the *Phaedrus* in certain key places, my reading of the dialogue has been influenced by Martha C. Nussbaum's excellent analysis in *The Fragility of Goodness: Luck and Ethics in Greek Tragedy and Philosophy,* 200–233.

3. For an alternative reading of the relationship of writing and reading in the *Phaedrus,* see Jacques Derrida's "Plato's Pharmacy."

4. For a good account of the incoherence of this regrounding, see MacIntyre's *After Virtue.*

5. For a thoughtful response to this crisis that argues for the recovery of rhetoric, see Pangle's *The Ennobling of Democracy: The Challenge of the Postmodern Age.* But where Pangle would undo the doubt of postmodernism, I would refute it and make it a resource with which to deal with injustice.

6. For a discussion of the role of the writer in creating a community through language, see White, *When Words,* x.

7. See *Dialogue and Deconstruction: The Gadamer-Derrida Encounter,* ed. Michelfelder and Palmer, for the exchange between Gadamer and Derrida. The essays that comment on the exchange provide a broad range of response and help sharpen the points of disagreement between deconstruction and hermeneutics.

8. See "Remarks on the Concept of Communicative Action," "A Reply to My Critics," and "What Is Universal Pragmatics?"

9. At times Habermas appears to appreciate the historicity of discourse: "The reason operating in communicative action not only stands under, so to speak, external, situational constraints; its own conditions of possibility necessitates branching out into the dimensions of historical time, social space, and body-centered experiences" ("An Alternative Way," 325–26). But the sentence following subordinates history to reason: "That is to say, the rational potential of speech is interwoven with the *resources* of any particular lifeworld (326). The key to communicative action is that speakers are constrained by "claims to truth, correctness, and sincerity" (324), which are the conditions necessary for the bonds of reason. What Habermas's theory of communicative action requires is the rational subject who is bound by the transpersonal force of reason.

10. Plato is fully aware that individuals can and do fail to follow the conclusions of a dialectic. The *Gorgias* dramatizes this truth, for Socrates does not persuade any of the participants to act according to the conclusions that the dialectic has reached, and he experiences a crisis of the public as deep as Sartre's. There is a sense in which Socrates ends the dialogue incomplete, for he is now without an order to aid him in the conduct of further dialectics. The dialogue ends as a register of communal failure.

11. Rorty in *Philosophy and the Mirror of Nature* has argued that we should understand the philosophic enterprise as an ongoing conversation. However, critics like Lentricchia have argued that Rorty's account of the conversation is too free of any grounding or context to permit it to become significant as anything other than an enterprise that simply perpetuates itself (*Criticism and Social Change,* 15–16). Lentricchia argues that a philosophic conversation must be socially grounded to become meaningful. I argue that generosity as a rhetorical virtue, despite Sartre's various equivocations, goes in the direction of meeting this demand.

8. Refuting de Man

1. De Man does not consistently maintain any tight distinction between trope and figure, but tends to use the terms interchangeably, both denoting the figurative nature of language. For a brief account of the distinction between trope and figure, see Vickers, *Defence*, 315.

2. Aristotle's characterization of rhetoric as an art that seeks to discover the best available means of persuasion in a particular situation indicates the practical interests that drove a study of rhetoric.

3. Plato had a similar insight, and his argument for the necessity of refutation follows from this insight. De Man, however, takes the insight in a different direction.

4. It is especially relevant, given the discovery of de Man's wartime journalism and the problems that it raises for reading him, to realize where his work was moving at the time of his death. As I read de Man, I see an increasing willingness on his part to raise political and ethical issues. In an interview with Stephan Rosso, de Man explained that his work on the rhetoricity of texts was preliminary and necessary to an inquiry into ideology or politics:

> I don't think I ever was away from these problems [of ideology and politics], they were always uppermost in my mind. I have always maintained that one could approach the problems of ideology and by extension the problems of politics only on the basis of critical-linguistic analysis, which had to be done on its own terms, in the medium of language, and I felt I could approach these problems only after having achieved a certain control over those questions. . . . I have the feeling that I have achieved some control over technical problems of language, specifically problems of rhetoric, of the relations between tropes and performatives, of saturation of tropology as a field that in certain forms of language goes beyond that field. (*The Resistance to Theory*, 121)

5. For a discussion of the importance of Otherness for De Man, see MacCannell, "Portrait: de Man."

6. MacCannell credits Gasché with having developed a cogent philosophical understanding of de Man, yet she argues that such an understanding does not capture de Man's position. In effect, a position becomes transformed into a thesis and loses the particularity of its form. De Man's rhetorical understanding highlights this resistance to restatement by claiming that all such attempts are ultimately translations that demonstrate the impossibility of recovering an original statement. The value of such translations resides in their contribution to the allegory of a text or a position, which constitutes its mode of being. A position is constituted by the plurality of its readings. The importance of Gasché's reading is both what it makes clear and what it obscures about de Man's position. MacCannell's comments on Gasché can serve as a caution for any reading that believes it has done justice to de Man or any other writer. Justice is always a criterion that necessitates further action rather than being the achievement of a fixed understanding.

7. For a fuller treatment of irony in Plato, see Swearingen's *Rhetoric and Irony*, 58–79.

9. Rhetoric and Ideology

1. See *Philosophy and the Historical Understanding,* 157–91.

2. Volosinov was apparently a name under which Bakhtin published.

3. Ruechert's "Some of the Many Kenneth Burkes" is an excellent discussion of just how varied Burke's work is. As he mentions in his conclusion: "Burke is more than his system. He is more than any part of his system, and he cannot be reduced to any one of his books" (30).

Glossary of Greek Rhetorical Terms

aretē excellence, virtue, nobility, the goodness of a person, animal, or of an art
bia force, power, might, bodily strength
bios life, livelihood
charis grace, favor, kindness, a sense of thankfulness, gratitude
chrēmata goods, property, money
chrēstos good services, benefits, kindnesses, a good person
dikē custom, law, right, justice
dolos guile, craft, cunning
doxa notion, opinion, judgment
empeiria experience
ēthos character
gennaios high-born, noble by birth
kairos the right point in time, the proper time or season
kleos rumor, report, good report, fame, glory
logos word, reason, thought, discourse
muthos speech, a tale, a narrative, a legend, a myth
nomos law, custom
nomov graphai written laws
oikos household
pathos emotion
peitho persuasion
phroneis prudence, good practical judgment

plēthos poleos a great number of citizens, a crowd, a mob
polis city
technē an art, skill, or craft
topos place
tuchē luck, necessity, that which happened
xenia the rights of a guest, hospitality

Bibliography

Abrahamson, Ernst L. "Euripides' Tragedy of Hecuba." *Transactions of the American Philological Association* 83 (1952): 120–29.

Adkins, Arthur W. H. "Basic Greek Values in Euripides' *Hecuba* and *Hercules Furens*." *Classical Quarterly* n.s. 16 (1966): 193–219.

———. *Merit and Responsibility: A Study in Greek Values*. Oxford: Clarendon-Oxford University Press, 1960.

Adorno, Theodor. *Negative Dialectics*. Translated by E. B. Ashton. New York: Continuum Publishing Co., 1973.

Althusser, Louis. *For Marx*. Translated by Ben Brewster. London: New Left Books, 1977.

Anderson, Benedict. *Imagined Communities: Reflections on the Origin and Spread of Nationalism*. London: New Left Books, 1983.

Arendt, Hannah. *Eichmann in Jerusalem: A Report on the Banality of Evil*. New York: The Viking Press, 1964.

Aristophanes. *The Frogs*. In *Three Greek Plays for the Theatre*. Translated and edited by Peter D. Arnott. Bloomington: Indiana University Press, 1961.

Aristotle. *On Rhetoric: A Theory of Civic Discourse*. Translated by George A. Kennedy. New York: Oxford University Press, 1991.

Auerbach, Nina. "O Brave New World: Evolution and Revolution in *Persuasion*." *ELH* 39 (1972): 112–28.

Augustine. *On Christian Doctrine*. Translated by D. W. Robinson. New York: Bobbs-Merrill, 1983.

Austen, Jane. *Persuasion*. Edited by John Davie. New York: Oxford University Press, 1990.

———. *Pride and Prejudice.* Introduced by Mark Schorer. New York: Houghton Mifflin, 1956.

Bakhtin, M. M. "Discourse in the Novel." In *The Dialogic Imagination: Four Essays.* Edited by Michael Holquist. Translated by Caryl Emerson and Michael Holquist. Austin: University of Texas Press, 1981.

Barilli, Renato. *Rhetoric.* Translated by Giuliana Menozzi. Theory and History of Literature 63. Minneapolis: University of Minnesota Press, 1989.

Benardete, Seth. *The Rhetoric of Morality and Philosophy: Plato's Gorgias and Phaedrus.* Chicago: University of Chicago Press, 1991.

Bender, John, and David E. Wellbery. "Rhetoricality: On the Modernist Return of Rhetoric." In *The Ends of Rhetoric: History, Theory, Practice.* Edited by John Bender and David E. Wellbery. Stanford: Stanford University Press, 1990.

Benson, Hugh H. *Essays on the Philosophy of Socrates.* New York: Oxford University Press, 1992.

———. "Meno, the Slave Boy and the *Elenchos.*" *Phronesis* 35 (1990): 128–58.

———. "A Note on Eristic and Socratic Elenchus." *Journal of the History of Philosophy* 27 (1989): 591–99.

———. "The Priority of Definition and the Socratic *Elenchos.*" *Oxford Studies in Ancient Philosophy* 8 (1990): 19–65.

———. "The Problem of the Elenchus Reconsidered." *Ancient Philosophy* 7 (1987): 67–85.

Berlin, James A. "Revisionary History: The Dialectical Method." In *Rethinking the History of Rhetoric: Multidisciplinary Essays on the Rhetorical Tradition.* Edited by Takis Poulakos. Boulder: Westview Press, 1993.

Bialostosky, Don H. "Dialogics as an Art of Discourse in Literary Criticism." *PMLA* 101 (1986): 788–97.

Bizzell, Patricia, and Bruce Herzberg. *The Rhetorical Tradition: Readings from Classical Times to the Present.* Boston: St. Martin's, Bedford, 1990.

Black, Edwin. "Plato's View of Rhetoric." *Quarterly Journal of Speech* 43 (1958): 361–74.

Boschetti, Anna. *The Intellectual Enterprise: Sartre and Les Temps Modernes.* Translated by Richard C. McCleary. Evanston: Northwestern University Press, 1988.

Bowra, C. M. *Sophoclean Tragedy.* Oxford: Clarendon, 1944.

Brickhouse, Thomas C., and Nicholas D. Smith. "Socrates' Elenchic Mission." *Oxford Studies in Ancient Philosophy* 9 (1991): 131–59.

———. "Vlastos on the Elenchus." *Oxford Studies in Ancient Philosophy* 2 (1984): 185–96.

Burke, Kenneth. *Counter-Statement.* 2d ed. Berkeley: University of California Press, 1968.

———. *Language as Symbolic Action: Essays on Life, Literature and Method.* Berkeley: University of California Press, 1966.

———. "Methodological Repression and/or Strategies of Containment." *Critical Inquiry* 5 (1978): 401–16.

———. *A Rhetoric of Motives.* New York: Prentice Hall, 1952.

Butler, Judith. "Contingent Foundations: Feminism and the Question of 'Postmodernism.'" In *Feminists Theorize the Political.* Edited by Judith Butler and Joan W. Scott. New York: Routledge, 1992.

Butler, Marilyn. *Jane Austen and the War of Ideas.* Oxford: Clarendon, 1975.

Buxton, R. G. A. *Persuasion in Greek Tragedy: A Study in Peitho.* Cambridge: Cambridge University Press, 1982.

Cavell, Stanley. *The Claim of Reason: Wittgenstein, Skepticism, Morality, and Tragedy.* New York: Oxford University Press, 1979.

Chase, Cynthia. *Decomposing Figures: Rhetorical Readings in the Romantic Tradition.* Baltimore: Johns Hopkins University Press, 1986.

Cicero. *De Inventione; De Optimo; Genere Oratorium.* Translated by H. M. Hubbell. Cambridge: Harvard University Press, Loeb, 1949.

Collard, C. "Formal Debates in Euripides' Drama." *Greece and Rome* 22 (1975): 58–71.

Conacher, D. J. *Euripidean Drama: Myth, Theme, and Structure.* Toronto: University of Toronto Press, 1967.

Conley, Thomas M. *Rhetoric in the European Tradition.* New York: Longman, 1990.

Crane, Ronald S. "A Serious Comedy." In *Jane Austen: Northanger Abbey and Persuasion, A Casebook.* Edited by B. C. Southam. London: Macmillan, 1976. Originally published in Ronald S. Crane, *The Idea of the Humanities and Other Essays, Critical and Historical* (Chicago: University of Chicago Press, 1967).

Daitz, S. G. "Concepts of Freedom and Slavery in *Hecuba.*" *Hermes* 99 (1971): 217–26.

Dale, A. M. *Euripides: Alcestis.* Oxford: Clarendon Press, 1954.

de Man, Paul. *Allegories of Reading: Figural Language in Rousseau, Nietzsche, Rilke, and Proust.* New Haven: Yale University Press, 1979.

———. *Blindness and Insight: Essays in the Rhetoric of Contemporary Criticism.* 2d ed. Introduced by Wlad Godzich. Theory and History of Literature 7. Minneapolis: University of Minnesota Press, 1983.

———. "Hegel on the Sublime." In *Displacement: Derrida and after.* Edited by Mark Krupnick. Bloomington: Indiana University Press, 1983.

———. "Pascal's Allegory of Persuasion." *Allegory and Representation.* Edited by Stephen Greenblatt. Baltimore: Johns Hopkins University Press, 1981.

———. *The Resistance to Theory.* Minneapolis: University of Minnesota Press, 1986.

———. *The Rhetoric of Romanticism.* New York: Columbia University Press, 1984.

Derrida, Jacques. "Plato's Pharmacy." *Dissemination.* Translated by Barbara Johnson. Chicago: University of Chicago Press, 1981.

———. "Positions: Interview with Jean-Louis Houdebine and Guy Scarpetta." In *Positions.* Translated and annotated by Alan Bass. Chicago: University of Chicago Press, 1981.

———. "Three Questions to Hans-Georg Gadamer." Translated by Diane P. Michelfelder and Richard E. Palmer. In *Dialogue and Deconstruction: The Gadamer-Derrida Encounter.* Edited by Diane Michelfelder and Richard Palmer. Albany: SUNY Press, 1989.

Dodds, Eric Robertson, ed. *Gorgias,* by Plato. Oxford: Clarendon-Oxford University Press, 1959.

Duckworth, Alistair. *The Improvement of the Estate.* Baltimore: Johns Hopkins University Press, 1974.

Eagleton, Terry. *Ideology: An Introduction.* London: Verso, 1991.

———. *Literary Theory: An Introduction.* Minneapolis: University of Minnesota Press, 1983.

———. *Walter Benjamin or Towards a Revolutionary Criticism.* London: Verso, 1981.

Euben, J. Peter. *The Tragedy of Political Theory: The Road Not Taken.* Princeton: Princeton University Press, 1990.

Euripides. *Andromache.* Translated by John Frederick Nims. In *Euripides.* 5 vols. Edited by David Grene and Richmond Lattimore. Chicago: University of Chicago Press, 1958.

———. *The Bacchae.* Translated by William Arrowsmith. In Grene and Lattimore, *Euripides.*

———. *Hecuba.* Translated by William Arrowsmith. In Grene and Lattimore, *Euripides.*

———. *Heracles.* Translated by William Arrowsmith. In Grene and Lattimore, *Euripides.*

———. *The Medea.* Translated by Rex Warner. In Grene and Lattimore, *Euripides.*

———. *The Phoenician Women.* Translated by Elizabeth Wyckoff. In Grene and Lattimore, *Euripides.*

———. *The Suppliant Women.* Translated by Frank William Jones. In Grene and Lattimore, *Euripides.*

Finley, J. H., Jr. *Three Essays on Thucydides.* Cambridge: Harvard University Press, 1967.

Fish, Stanley. *Is There a Text in This Class? The Authority of Interpretive Communities.* Cambridge: Harvard University Press, 1980.

———. *Self-Consuming Artifacts: The Experience of Seventeenth-Century Literature.* Los Angeles: University of California Press, 1972.

Foucault, Michel. *Discipline and Punish: The Birth of the Prison.* Translated by Alan Sheridan. New York: Pantheon, 1977.

Friedlander, Paul. *The Dialogues: First Period.* Translated by Hans Meyerhoff. Vol. 2 of *Plato.* 3 vols. Bollingen Series 59. Princeton: Princeton University Press, 1964.

Gallie, W. B. *Philosophy and the Historical Understanding.* New York: Schoken, 1964.

Gasché, Rodolphe. "Deconstruction as Criticism." *Glyph* 6 (1979): 177–215.

———. " 'Setzung' and 'Ubersetzung': Notes on Paul de Man." *Diacritics* 11 (1981): 36–57.

Gearhart, Suzanne. "Philosophy Before Literature: Deconstruction, Historicity, and the Work of Paul de Man." *Diacritics* 13 (1983): 63–81.

Geertz, Clifford. *The Interpretation of Cultures.* New York: Basic, 1973.

Goldhill, Simon. "The Great Dionysia and Civic Ideology." In *Nothing to Do with Dionysos? Athenian Drama in Its Social Context.* Edited by John J. Winkler and Froma I. Zeitlin. Princeton: Princeton University Press, 1990.

———. *Reading Greek Tragedy.* Cambridge: Cambridge University Press, 1986.

Grube, G. M. A. *The Drama of Euripides.* London: Methuen, 1941.

Guthrie, W. K. C. *The Sophists.* Cambridge: Cambridge University Press, 1971. Originally published as Part I of *A History of Greek Philosophy,* Vol. III. (Cambridge University Press, 1969).

Habermas, Jurgen. "An Alternative Way out of the Philosophy of the Subject: Communicative Versus Subject-Centered Reason." In *The Philosophical Discourses of Modernity: Twelve Lectures.* Translated by Frederick G. Lawrence. Cambridge: MIT Press, 1987.

———. *Legitimation Crisis.* Translated by Thomas McCarthy. Boston: Beacon, 1973.

———. "Remarks on the Concept of Communicative Action." In *Social Action.* Edited by Gottfried Seebas and Raimo Tuomela. Dordrecht, Netherlands: D. Reidel, 1985.

———. "A Reply to my Critics." Translated by Thomas McCarthy. In *Habermas: Critical Debates.* Edited by John B. Thompson and David Held. Cambridge: MIT Press, 1982.

———. "What Is Universal Pragmatics?" In *Communication and the Evolution of Society.* Translated and introduced by Thomas McCarthy. Boston: Beacon, 1976.

Harding, W. D. "The Dexterity of a Practised Writer." In *Jane Austen: Northanger Abbey and Persuasion, A Casebook.* Edited by B. C. Southam. London: Macmillan, 1976.

Havelock, Eric A. *The Liberal Temper in Greek Politics.* London: Cape, 1957.

Hopkins, Robert. "Moral Luck and Judgment in Jane Austen's *Persuasion.*" *Nineteenth-Century Literature* 41 (1987): 143–58.

Hunt, Everett Lee. "Plato and Aristotle on Rhetoric and Rhetoricians." In *Studies in Rhetoric and Public Speaking, In Honor of James Albert Winans.* New York: Russell, 1962.

Irwin, Terence. *Plato's Moral Theory: The Early and Middle Dialogues.* Oxford: Clarendon-Oxford University Press, 1977.

Jameson, Fredric R. "Ideology and Symbolic Action." *Critical Inquiry* 5 (1978): 417–22.

———. "The Symbolic Inference; or, Kenneth Burke and Ideological Analysis." In *Representing Kenneth Burke.* Edited by Hayden White and Margaret Brose. Selected Papers from the English Institute, New Series 6. Baltimore: Johns Hopkins University Press, 1982. Originally published in *Critical Inquiry* 4 (1978): 507–24.

———. "Three Methods in Sartre's Literary Criticism." In *Critical Essays on Jean-Paul Sartre.* Edited by Robert Wilcocks. Boston: G.K. Hall. Originally published in *Modern French Literary Criticism,* edited by John K. Simon (Chicago: University of Chicago Press, 1972).

Jarratt, Susan C. *Rereading the Sophists: Classical Rhetoric Refigured.* Carbondale: Southern Illinois University Press, 1991.

Johnson, Claudia L. *Jane Austen: Women, Politics and the Novel.* Chicago: University of Chicago Press, 1988.

Kahn, Charles H. "Drama and Dialectic in Plato's *Gorgias.*" *Oxford Studies in Ancient Philosophy* 1 (1983): 75–121.

Kaufer, David S. "The Influence of Plato's Developing Psychology on His Views of Rhetoric." *Quarterly Journal of Speech* 64 (1978): 63–78.

Kennedy, George. *The Art of Persuasion in Greece.* Princeton: Princeton University Press, 1963.

Kerferd, G. B. *The Sophistic Movement.* Cambridge: Cambridge University Press, 1981.

Kierkegaard, Søren. *The Concept of Irony, with Continual Reference to Socrates.* Edited and translated by Howard V. Hong and Edna H. Hong. Princeton: Princeton University Press, 1989.

Kirkwood, G. M. "Hecuba and Nomos." *Transactions of the American Philological Association* 78 (1947): 61–68.

———. *A Study of Sophoclean Drama.* Cornell Studies in Classical Philology 31. Ithaca: Cornell University Press, 1958.

Kitto, D. H. F. *Greek Tragedy: A Literary Study.* 3d ed. New York: Barnes and Noble, 1961.

Knoblauch, C. H., and Lil Brannon. *Rhetorical Traditions and the Teaching of Writing.* Upper Montclair, N.J.: Boynton, 1984.

Knox, Bernard M. W. *The Heroic Temper: Studies in Sophoclean Tragedy.* Berkeley: University of California Press, 1964.

Kraut, Richard. "Comments on Gregory Vlastos, 'The Socratic Elenchus.'" *Oxford Studies in Ancient Philosophy* 1 (1983): 59–69.

Laufer, Romain. "Rhetoric and Politics." In *From Metaphysics to Rhetoric.* Edited by Michel Meyer. Studies in Epistemology, Logic, Methodology, and Philosophy of Science 202. Dordrecht, Netherlands: Kluwer Academe, 1984.

Lentricchia, Frank. *Criticism and Social Change.* Chicago: University of Chicago Press, 1983.

Lesky, Albin. *Greek Tragedy.* 3d ed. Translated by H. A. Frankford. London: Ernest Benn, 1978.

Lloyd-Jones, Hugh. *The Justice of Zeus.* Sather Classical Lectures 41. Berkeley: University of California Press, 1971.

Longo, Oddone. "The Theater of the *Polis.*" In *Nothing to Do with Dionysos? Athenian Drama in Its Social Context.* Edited by John J. Winkler and Froma I. Zeitlin. Princeton: Princeton University Press, 1990.

Lusching, A. E. "Euripides' *Hecabe:* The Time Is Out of Joint." *Classical Journal* 71 (1975–76): 227–34.

MacCannell, Juliet Flower. "Portrait: de Man." In *Rhetoric and Form: Deconstruction at Yale.* Edited by Robert Con Davis and Ronald Schliefer. Norman: University of Oklahoma Press, 1985.

MacIntyre, Alasdair C. *After Virtue: A Study in Moral Theory.* 2d ed. Notre Dame: University of Notre Dame Press, 1984.

McKeon, Richard. "The Uses of Rhetoric in a Technological Age: Architectonic Productive Arts." In *Rhetoric: Essays in Invention and Discovery.* Edited and introduced by Mark Bachman. Woodbridge: Oxbow, 1987. Originally published in *The Prospect of Rhetoric: Report of the National Development Project,* edited by Lloyd F. Bitzer and Edwin Black (Englewood Cliffs, N.J.: Prentice Hall, 1971).

McKim, Richard. "Shame and Truth in Plato's *Gorgias.*" In *Platonic Writing, Platonic Reading.* Edited by Charles L. Griswold, Jr. New York: Routledge, 1988.

Meridor, Ra'anana. "Hecuba's Revenge: Some Observations on Euripides' *Hecuba.*" *American Journal of Philology* 99 (1978): 28–35.

Meyer, Michel. *Meaning and Reading: A Philosophical Essay on Language and Literature.* Pragmatics and Beyond: An Interdisciplinary Series of Language Studies. No. 3. Amsterdam: John Benjamins, 1983.

———. "The Modernity of Rhetoric." Foreword to *From Metaphysics to Rhetoric.* Edited by Michel Meyer. Studies in Epistemology, Logic, Methodology, and Philosophy of Science 202. Dordrecht, Netherlands: Kluwer Academe, 1989.

———. *Rhetoric, Language, and Reason.* University Park: Pennsylvania State University Press, 1994.

———. "Toward an Anthropology of Rhetoric." In *From Metaphysics To Rhetoric.* Edited by Michel Meyer. Studies in Epistemology, Logic, Methodology, and Philosophy of Science 202. Dordrecht, Netherlands: Kluwer Academe, 1989.

Mill, John Stuart. "Grote's Plato." *Essays on Philosophy and the Classics.* Vol. 11 of *Collected Works.* 29 vols. Toronto: University of Toronto Press, 1978.

Murray, Gilbert. *Euripides and His Age.* London: Oxford University Press, 1965.

Murray, R. L. "Persuasion in Euripides." Ph.D. diss. Cornell University, 1964.

Nietzsche, Friedrich. *On the Genealogy of Morals.* Translated by Walter Kaufmann and R. J. Hollingdale. In *On the Genealogy of Morals and Ecce Homo.* Edited by Walter Kaufmann. New York: Vintage-Random, 1967.

Nussbaum, Martha C. "Consequences and Character in Sophocles' *Philoctetes.*" *Philosophy and Literature* 1 (1976): 25–51.

——. *The Fragility of Goodness: Luck and Ethics in Greek Tragedy and Philosophy.* Cambridge: Cambridge University Press, 1986.

Ober, Josiah. *Mass and Elite in Democratic Athens: Rhetoric, Ideology, and the Power of the People.* Princeton: Princeton University Press, 1989.

Ostwald, Martin. *Nomos and the Beginnings of the Athenian Democracy.* Oxford: Clarendon Press, 1969.

Pangle, Thomas L. *The Ennobling of Democracy: The Challenge of the Postmodern Age.* Baltimore: Johns Hopkins University Press, 1992.

Plato. *Socrates' Defense (Apology).* Translated by Hugh Tredennick. In *Plato: The Collected Dialogues.* Edited by Edith Hamilton and Huntington Cairns. Bollingen Series 71. Princeton: Princeton University Press, 1961.

——. *Gorgias.* Translated by Terence Irwin. Oxford: Clarendon-Oxford University Press, 1979.

——. *Meno.* Translated by Benjamin Jowett. Introduced by Fulton H. Anderson. New York: Bobbs-Merrill, 1949.

——. *Phaedrus.* Translated by R. Hackforth. In Hamilton and Cairns, *Plato.*

——. *Republic.* Translated by Paul Shorey. In Hamilton and Cairns, *Plato.*

——. *Symposium.* Translated by Michael Joyce. In Hamilton and Cairns, *Plato.*

Plochmann, George Kimball, and Franklin E. Robinson. *A Friendly Companion to Plato's Gorgias.* Carbondale: Southern Illinois University Press, 1988.

Podlecki, Anthony J. "The Power of the Word in Sophocles' *Philoctetes.*" *Greek, Roman, and Byzantine Studies* 7 (1966): 233–50.

Polansky, Ronald M. "Professor Vlastos's Analysis of Socratic Elenchus." *Oxford Studies in Ancient Philosophy* 3 (1985): 247–60.

Poovey, Mary. *The Proper Lady and the Woman Writer: Ideology as Style in the Works of Mary Wollstonecraft, Mary Shelley, and Jane Austen.* Chicago: University of Chicago Press, 1984.

Popper, Karl Raimund. *The Spell of Plato.* Vol. 1 of *The Open Society and Its Enemies.* 2 vols. London: Routledge, 1945.

Poster, Mark. *Critical Theory and Poststructuralism: In Search of a Context.* Ithaca: Cornell University Press, 1989.

——. *Essential Marxism in Postwar France: From Sartre to Althusser.* Princeton: Princeton University Press, 1975.

Potkay, Adam. *The Fate of Eloquence in the Age of Hume.* Ithaca: Cornell University Press, 1994.

Poulakos, Takis. *Rethinking the History of Rhetoric: Multidisciplinary Essays on the Rhetorical Tradition*. Boulder: Westview Press, 1993.

Pucci, Pietro. *The Violence of Pity in Euripides' Medea*. Ithaca: Cornell University Press, 1980.

Robinson, Richard. *Plato's Earlier Dialectic*. 2d ed. Oxford: Clarendon Press, 1953.

Roochnik, David. *The Tragedy of Reason: Toward a Platonic Conception of Logos*. New York: Routledge, 1990.

Rorty, Richard. *Contingency, Irony, and Solidarity*. Cambridge: Cambridge University Press, 1989.

———. *Philosophy and the Mirror of Nature*. Princeton: Princeton University Press, 1979.

———. "Pragmatism, Relativism, and Irrationalism: Presidential Address." *Proceedings and Addresses of the American Philosophical Association* 53 (1980): 719–38.

Rose, Peter W. *Sons of the Gods, Children of Earth: Ideology and Literary Form in Ancient Greece*. Ithaca: Cornell University Press, 1992.

Rosen, Stanley. *Hermeneutics as Politics*. New York: Oxford University Press, 1987.

———. *Plato's Sophist*. New Haven: Yale University Press, 1983.

———. *The Quarrel Between Philosophy and Literature: Studies in Ancient Thought*. New York: Routledge, 1993.

Rosenmeyer, Thomas G. "Gorgias, Aeschylus, and *Apate*." *American Journal of Philology* 76 (1955): 225–260.

Ruechert, William. "Some of the Many Kenneth Burkes." In *Representing Kenneth Burke*. Edited by Hayden White and Margaret Brose. Selected Papers from the English Institute. New Series 6. Baltimore, Johns Hopkins University Press, 1982.

Ryan, Michael. *Politics and Culture: Working Hypotheses for a Post-Revolutionary Society*. Baltimore: Johns Hopkins University Press, 1989.

Sartre, Jean Paul. *What Is Literature?* Translated by Bernard Frechtman. New York: Philosophical Library, 1949.

Seeskin, Kenneth. *Dialogue and Discovery: A Study in Socratic Method*. Albany: SUNY Press, 1987.

Segal, Charles. *Tragedy and Civilization: An Interpretation of Sophocles*. Cambridge: Harvard University Press, 1981.

Smith, Barbara Herrnstein. *Contingencies of Value: Alternative Perspectives for Critical Theory*. Cambridge: Harvard University Press, 1988.

Solmsen, Friedrich. *Intellectual Experiments of the Greek Enlightenment*. Princeton: Princeton University Press, 1975.

Sophocles. *Antigone*. Translated by David Grene. In *Sophocles*. Edited by David Grene and Richmond Lattimore. 2 vols. Chicago: University of Chicago Press, 1991.

———. *Philoctetes*. Translated by David Grene. In *Sophocles*. Edited by David Grene and Richmond Lattimore. 2 vols. Chicago: University of Chicago Press, 1991.

Sternfeld, Robert, and Harold Zyskind. *Plato's Meno: A Philosophy of Man as Acquisitive*. Carbondale: Southern Illinois University Press, 1978.

Swearingen, C. Jan. *Rhetoric and Irony: Western Literacy and Western Lies*. New York: Oxford University Press, 1991.

Tanner, Tony. *Jane Austen*. Houndmills, England: Macmillan, 1986.

Tave, Stuart M. *Some Words of Jane Austen.* Chicago: University of Chicago Press, 1973.

Thomson, D. *Euripides and the Attic Orators.* London: Macmillan, 1898.

Valesio, Paolo. *Novantiqua: Rhetorics as a Contemporary Theory.* Bloomington: Indiana University Press, 1980.

Vernant, Jean-Pierre, and Vidal-Naquet, Pierre. *Myth and Tragedy in Ancient Greece.* Translated by Janet Lloyd. New York: Zone, 1988.

Vickers, Brian. *In Defence of Rhetoric.* Oxford: Clarendon-Oxford University Press, 1988.

Vlastos, Gregory. "Afterthoughts on the Socratic Elenchus." *Oxford Studies in Ancient Philosophy* 1 (1983): 71–74.

——. *Socrates: Ironist and Moral Philosopher.* Ithaca: Cornell University Press, 1991.

——. "The Socratic Elenchus." *Oxford Studies in Ancient Philosophy* 1 (1983): 27–57.

Volosinov, V. N. *Marxism and the Philosophy of Language.* Translated by Ladislav Matejka and I. R. Titunik. Cambridge: Harvard University Press, 1986.

Waithe, Mary Ellen. "Aspasia of Miletus." Vol. 1 of *A History of Women Philosophers.* Edited by Mary Ellen Waithe. 4 vols. Dordrecht, Netherlands: Nijhoff, 1987.

Warminski, Andrzej. "Ending Up/Taking Back (with Two Postscripts on Paul de Man's Historical Materialism." In *Critical Encounters: Reference and Responsibility in Deconstructive Writing.* Edited by Cathy Caruth and Deborah Esch. New Brunswick: Rutgers University Press, 1995.

Weil, Simone. "The *Iliad,* or the Poem of Force." Translated by Mary McCarthy. *Politics* 2 (1945): 321–31.

Wess, Robert. "Notes Toward a Marxist Rhetoric." *Bucknell Review* 28 (1983): 126–48.

White, James Boyd. *Herakles' Bow: Essays on the Rhetoric and Poetics of the Law.* Madison: University of Wisconsin Press, 1985.

——. *When Words Lose Their Meaning: Constitutions and Reconstitutions of Language, Character, and Community.* Chicago: University of Chicago Press, 1984.

Whitman, Cedric H. *Sophocles: A Study of Heroic Humanism.* Cambridge: Harvard University Press, 1971.

Wilson, Edmund. *The Wound and the Bow: Seven Studies in Literature.* New York: Oxford University Press, 1970.

Winkler, John J. "The Ephebe's Song: *Tragoidia* and *Polis.*" In *Nothing to Do with Dionysos? Athenian Drama in Its Social Context.* Edited by John J. Winkler and Froma I. Zeitlin. Princeton: Princeton University Press, 1990.

Winnington-Ingram, R. P. *Sophocles: An Interpretation.* Cambridge: Cambridge University Press, 1980.

Young, Iris Marion. *Justice and the Politics of Difference.* Princeton: Princeton University Press, 1990.

Zuntz, G. *The Political Plays of Euripides.* Manchester: Manchester University Press, 1955.

Index

Abrahamson, Ernst L., 116, 127

Abuse of rhetoric, 10–11, 33, 41, 108, 261*n*4

Action: in Burke, 246–47; communicative, 6, 260*n*10, 267*n*9; and discourse, 222; and justice, 213; and knowledge, 21, 196–97, 200, 201–2; political, 179; and rhetoric, 4, 200, 213, 220; and the subject, 207; symbolic, 227, 250; writing as, 140, 143–44, 175–76

Adkins, Arthur W. H., 31, 32, 37, 116, 265*n*21

Adorno, Theodor, 180, 184

Aeschylus, 98, 260*n*9, 265*n*24

Aesthetic: vs. the political, 245–48, 249; and rhetoric, 248

Agamemnon, 119–30, 127–29

Agency, 179–80, 232

Alienation, 168–69

Allegory, 196, 197, 199, 206, 208, 212, 214, 268*n*6

Althusser, Louis, 222–24, 225, 242, 255

Anderson, Benedict, 265*n*2

Antithesis, 224

Arendt, Hannah, 264*n*4, 264*n*14

Aretē, 117

Aristophanes, 263*n*1

Aristotle: on appearance, 9–10, 158; on language as assertion, 6; on the law of contradiction, 201; Plato compared to, 259*n*6; his practical notion of persuasion, 51, 86, 177, 268*n*2; his reform of rhetoric, 8–12; and refutation, 53; on theoretical vs. practical science, 210; on tropes, 198; and virtue, 70

Arrowsmith, William, 118, 264*n*6

Audience: as a control on rhetoric, 11–12, 33; and politics, 233; as positioned, 214, 236; reconstitution of, through rhetoric, 14, 52, 59, 76, 78, 216; responsibility of, 4; unavailability of, 16, 20, 114, 168–69

Auerbach, Nina, 266*n*1(1)

Augustine, 171–73, 176, 178